Richard

THE
YOUNG
KING
TO BE

About the Author

Josephine Wilkinson is an author and historian. She received a First from the University of Newcastle where she also read for her PhD. She has received British Academy funding for her research in to Richard III's early life and has been scholar-in-residence at St Deiniol's Library, Britain's only residential library founded by the great Victorian statesman, William Gladstone. Her other books include *Mary Boleyn: Henry VIII's Favourite Mistress* and *The Early Loves of Anne Boleyn* both published by Amberley. The second volume *Richard III, From Lord of the North to King of England* will be published in 2010. She lives in York.

Also by Josephine Wilkinson

Richard

THE
YOUNG
KING
TO BE

JOSEPHINE
WILKINSON

AMBERLEY

Front cover: This portrait of Richard III was painted in around 1516, and is a copy of a lost original which it is believed Richard sat for. It shows no sign of Richard's supposed deformity, this may be explained by the fact that it was privately owned by the famous Paston family and was not part of the Royal Collection altered to show the alleged deformity attributed to Richard by the Tudors. *Courtesy of the Society of Antiquaries.*
Back cover: Misericord carving of Richard showing his supposed hunchback. *Courtesy of Jonathan Reeve.*

This edition first published 2009

Amberley Publishing Plc
Cirencester Road, Chalford,
Stroud, Gloucestershire, GL6 8PE

www.amberley-books.com

© Josephine Wilkinson, 2008, 2009

The right of Josephine Wilkinson to be identified as the Author
of this work has been asserted in accordance with the
Copyrights, Designs and Patents Act 1988.

British Library Cataloguing in Publication Data.
A catalogue record for this book is available from the British Library.

ISBN 978-1-84868-513-0

Typesetting and Origination by Diagraf (www.diagraf.net)
Printed in Great Britain

Contents

PREFACE

I have long been fascinated by King Richard III. It probably began when I first found out that he had a society dedicated to him: the Richard III Society. Their mission is, simply, to reclaim Richard's battered reputation. Of course, Richard is not the only king to have such a dedicated following. There exists a White Hart Society for Richard II, a Henry VI Society, a Society of King Charles the Martyr and a Charles II Society. No doubt there are others. Yet, there is something fascinating about Richard III. He is arguably the most intriguing character in English history. Few others have possessed the ability to polarise opinion in the way he does. Few have engendered so much hatred – or so much devotion – as Richard has.

Richard was a deeply pious man and, indeed, this work, and my commission to write it, grew out of a study of Richard's spiritual beliefs and religious activities. Richard was also passionate about military affairs; he loved books, clothes, jewellery, colour, pomp and music, and he maintained high moral standards. He was also the father of at least two illegitimate children; he was belligerent, defiant and capable of cold blooded murder. Richard III is a paradox and an enigma. He and his history have long been hidden beneath a cloud of hostility. Such hostility derives from two sources: southern anger at his 'tyranny' and Tudor enmity. Moreover, it is not confined to the era in which it originated, but persists into the present day.

Modern scholarship continues to divide itself between the traditionalist view of Richard and that of the revisionists. It is inevitable that, at some point, the Ricardian scholar will be asked which 'side' he or she is on. Their answers are often met with derision or surprise, as though they ought to 'know better'. It does not have to be that way. Richard's story is as complex as the man himself, too complex to be seen in terms of simply good or bad. His actions were dictated by the situation in which he found himself, but more than that, much of it was directed by the circumstances of the house into which he was born. Its history and its perceived place in the succession to the throne of England and France and the Lordship of Ireland were enormously influential, as were the activities of his father; especially the activities of his father. Then there is Richard the man. He had thoughts of his own. Echoes of them can be discerned in his actions, the faith he held, the things he owned, the saints to whom he appealed, the charities he supported, the chantries he founded. We hear them expressed most clearly in the statutes he drew up for his collegiate church at Middleham and in his Act of Settlement.

To hear Richard, and to understand him, it is necessary to return to the beginning, for before Richard was a king he was a man and before that a boy, born into a family whose thoughts and ideals, background and outlook he engaged with, embraced or rejected. His family influenced him as he did it, and it is here, with his parents, his sisters and his brothers, cocooned within the history and the heritage of the House of York that we must first encounter Richard Plantagenet, future King of England. Only when all these factors are brought to the fore will we be able, perhaps, to see Richard through a glass less darkly.

While writing is a solitary activity, nothing can be accomplished without the assistance of others. There are many people to whom thanks are due for the help they have so generously provided. Initial thanks must go to the British Academy, who provided the funding for the preliminary research for this project. Thank you to the Rev. Peter Francis, warden, and to Patsy Williams, head librarian at St Deiniol's Library, Hawarden, for allowing me unlimited access to their wonderful collection during my time as a resident scholar at the library. Also to the staff of the National Archives at Kew, especially the chef who was inspired to add vegetarian curry to the lunch menu one rainy Friday. I am very grateful to Don Spaeth, Head of the Department of History at Glasgow University for my appointment as an Honorary Research Fellow. It was a pleasure and a privilege to work in your magnificent library. Thanks also go to Dr Andrew Roach for all his help and encouragement, and to his family, Helena, Imogen and Alexander Roach for giving me a lovely home during this time.

Thanks are also due to Judith Ridley and Rebekah Beale, librarians at the Richard III Society, who supplied me with articles from back issues of *The Ricardian*. Thank you to the staff of the library at York University and

York City Archives. Much of this work was undertaken at York Minster Library; it is certainly an inspiration to write about Richard in a place that was known to him and which he visited at least once.

Finally, thanks must go to my mother, Mrs Hazel Wilkinson, whose support and unfailing faith in me went beyond anything that can be expressed. To her, I dedicate this work, et aussi à mon cher N. parce que l'âme ne meurt jamais ...

York
May 2008

Dramatis Personae

Richard III (1452-1485): Youngest son of Richard, third Duke of York and youngest brother to Edward IV. Richard is referred to successively as Richard Plantagenet; Lord Richard; Richard, Duke of Gloucester. He always signed himself as Richard Gloucester and this is how he is referred to here. He ascended the throne as King Richard III.

Richard, third Duke of York (1411-1460): The father of Richard III.

Cecily Nevil, Duchess of York (1415-1495): Mother of Richard III

Edward IV (1442-1483): Earl of March and, briefly, Duke of York following the death of his father. Edward is the eldest brother of Richard III.

George, Duke of Clarence (1449-1478): Elder brother to Richard III.

Anne Mortimer (c.1388-c.1414): The daughter of Roger (VII), Earl of March and mother to Richard, third Duke of York. Her descent from Lionel, Duke of Clarence provided one of the bases for the Yorkist claim the throne through their Mortimer connection.

Anne Nevill (1452-1485): daughter of Richard, Earl of Warwick. Anne was wife and queen to Richard III.

Edmund Beaufort, first Duke of Somerset (c1406-1455): A grandson of John of Gaunt, he rivalled Richard, Duke of York in his claim to the throne.

Edmund Beaufort, styled third Duke of Somerset (c1438-1471): Son of the first Duke of Somerset.

Edmund (III), Earl of March (1352-1381): Son of Lionel, Duke of Clarence.

Edmund, Earl of Rutland (1443-1460): Elder brother to Richard III, he was killed at the battle of Wakefield.

Edmund of Langley, first Duke of York (1341-1402): Fourth surviving son of Edward III; founder of the House of York.

Edmund Tudor, first Earl of Richmond (c.1430-1456): Father of Henry Tudor. He was the half-brother of Henry VI.

Edward, second Duke of York (c.1373-1415): Uncle to Richard, third Duke of York.

Edward, Earl of Lancaster (1453-1471): Only son and heir to Henry VI and Marguerite d'Anjou.

Edward of Middleham (c.1476-1484): Only son of Richard III and Anne Nevill.

George Nevill (1432-1476): Younger brother to Richard, Earl of Warwick.

Henry VI (1421-1471): Lancastrian king; great-grandson of John of Gaunt. His grandfather, Henry IV, deposed and murdered Richard II.

Henry Tudor (1457-1509): Future Henry VII. He was the son of Edmund Tudor and Lady Margaret Beaufort.

Joan Beaufort (1379-1440): Youngest child of John of Gaunt by his mistress, Katherine Swynford. Their children were later legitimised by Richard II. Henry IV upheld this, but debarred them and their heirs from the succession.

John of Gaunt, first Duke of Lancaster (1340-1399): Third surviving son of Edward III; founder of the House of Lancaster, rival claimants to the throne.

Lionel, first Duke of Clarence (1338-1368): Second surviving son of Edward III. He was uncle to Richard II, whose nomination of his Mortimer cousins provided one of the bases for the Yorkist claim to the throne.

Richard II (1367-1400): Grandson of Edward III. Although married twice, he had no children. He nominated his Mortimer cousin Roger (VII) as his heir to the throne, thus ignoring the claims of John of Gaunt and his heirs. Richard was overthrown and murdered by Gaunt's son, Henry, who took the throne as Henry IV.

Richard, Earl of Cambridge (1385-1415): He and his wife, Anne Mortimer are the parents of Richard, third Duke of York and grandparents to Richard III.

Richard, Earl of Warwick (1428-1471): Called the 'Kingmaker', Warwick was the cousin of Richard III and the father of Richard's wife, Anne Nevill.

Richard Nevill, Earl of Salisbury (1400-1460): Eldest son of Joan Beaufort and Ralph Nevill.

CHAPTER 1

'RICHARD LIVES YET', 1452

Richard Plantagenet, the future King Richard III, came into the world during the autumn of 1452. A note written into his book of hours at a much later period of his life records his date of birth as 2 October. The Warwickshire antiquary, John Rous, offers more details, stating that Richard:

> was born on the Feast of the Eleven Thousand Virgins. At his birth Scorpio was in the ascendant, whose sign is the house of Mars. And as Scorpio was smooth in countenance but deadly in his tail, so Richard showed himself. [1]

Rous, in presenting Richard's astrological data, expresses his belief in a discipline that was taken much more seriously in the time in which he lived than it generally is now. In the fifteenth century astrology was regarded as a science, one that was used to make certain assessments of people and their condition. For instance, it was used in medicine in order to diagnose illness and devise suitable treatments. It could also be used, as Rous does here, to make certain judgements regarding character. As such, it would be worthwhile to take a few moments to see what could be said about Richard astrologically.

Rous notes that Richard was born on the Feast of the Eleven Thousand Virgins. Since this feast took place on 21 October, the antiquary is clearly mistaken. Richard's true date of birth, as established by the entry in his book of hours, was 2 October. Rous also states that Scorpio was in the ascendant at the time of Richard's birth. This is interesting, but it is not much help to anyone wishing to draw up a birth chart for Richard.

The birth chart is essentially a map of the sky as it appears at the point of birth. It shows the placements of the sun, moon and the planets as they appear to make their way through the zodiac. Each planet (in astrology the sun and the moon are referred to as planets) and house of the zodiac is said to influence certain aspects of a person's life, outlook, future and even appearance.

As a younger son who was expected to make little or no impression on the world stage it is probable that no attempt was be made to record Richard's exact birth data. It is known that his place of birth was Fotheringhay Castle in Northamptonshire, which was owned by his father as part of his Mortimer inheritance, and which was his mother's favourite residence. Cecily gave birth to several of her children here. The castle is situated at 52N31'59" latitude and 0W26'14" longitude. Since the exact time of Richard's birth is unknown, it is impossible to draw up a detailed chart. All that can be said about Richard Plantagenet astrologically is that he was born on 2 October 1452 and that, if Rous is correct in his assertion that Scorpio was on the ascendant at the time, he was born between 7.45am and 10.29am.[2]

Richard, then, was born while the sun was passing through the zodiac sign of Libra. People born under Libra are generally cultured, diplomatic and have a good sense of justice. Negatively, they can be indifferent and inconsistent.

The ascendant or rising sign is that which appears on the eastern horizon at the moment of birth. Astrologers believe that it influences the outward appearance of a person, the facial characteristics as well as the personality as it is seen by others. When asked to guess a person's 'star sign', very often it is the ascendant sign that is given because it is the characteristics of that sign that provide the persona that people present to the world. Scorpio is ruled by Mars, which in turn is characterised by activity and competitiveness, guardedness and paranoia. It influences power, sexual energy, courage, self-assertion, strength and initiative. Many of these characteristics sit well with what we know of Richard, and which will reveal themselves as this study unfolds. Mars is also the god of war, which ties in with Richard's career as a soldier. Physically, the classic features of Scorpio rising are a square jaw, penetrating eyes and a quiet manner.

One interesting aspect of Richard's Martian ascendant is that it influences physical strength. It is sometimes claimed that Richard was a sickly child who was not expected to survive. Gairdner, for instance, states: 'Thus of this family of twelve five had been lost when Richard was a child; and it would seem that Richard himself was slender and sickly.'[3] Sharon Turner adds that:

As the person of Richard was unquestionably short, tho his face was handsome, and as his figure was small and had been much weakened by illness, and
his left arm seems to have been a shrunk or defective limb; it is rather singular
that he should have been so fond of personal exhibitions in public state, where
almost every surrounding courtier must have excelled him in that appearance
and deportment which strike or fascinate the eye.[4]

Turner supports his account by appealing to Rous. He then explains that
he had it on good authority that Richard had suffered serious illness as a
child before he laments having lost his note of the authority from which he
took 'the facts of Richard's previous illness'; thus he is able only to speak of
it from memory, 'without being able to specify the reference.'[5]

It is not impossible that Richard had some illness as a child; indeed, it
would have been highly unusual if he had not. Certainly, contemporary
records hint that there might have been problems surrounding his birth.
Perhaps part of this could be explained by his mother's age which, by the
standards of the day at least, was fairly advanced as far as the bearing of
children was concerned. At the time of Richard's birth, Cecily of York was
thirty-seven years old. She had already produced ten children, four of whom
had died in infancy or soon afterwards.

According to John Rous[6], Richard was 'retained within his mother's
womb for two years and emerging with teeth and hair down to his shoulders'. Although it is not unusual for babies to be born with hair and teeth, a
gestation period of two years is clearly fanciful. Nevertheless, the chronicler
could have been elaborating upon information that Cecily's labour had been
a worryingly long one and that all had not gone well. As a matter of fact,
Cecily alludes to this herself in a letter she wrote to the Queen, telling her of
'th'ecomerous labour, to me full painfull and unesy...'[7]

Cecily's difficult labour progressed from being mere historical fact to
become the stuff of legend; it was apparently known to Thomas More, who
includes in his *History of King Richard III* the suggestion that Richard's had
been a difficult birth:

> The Duches his mother had so muche a doe in her trauaile, that shee coulde
> not bee deliuered of hym vncutte: and that hee came into the worlde with the
> feete forwarde, as menne bee borne outwarde, and (as the fame runneth) also
> not vntothed.[8]

On More's evidence, then, Richard's was a breech birth following a long
labour and the well-being of both the mother and the baby were a cause for

concern at the time. Moreover, More's assertion that Richard was born 'not vntothed' reflects Rous's own testimony which asserts that the future king was born with a complete set of teeth.

More's account of King Richard III was a major source for Shakespeare, whose young Richard, Duke of York, Gloucester's nephew, announces:

Marry, they say my uncle grew so fast
That he could gnaw a crust at two hours old.[9]

Shakespeare, of course, is exaggerating, as is Rous when he states that Richard had a full set of teeth. Natal teeth tend to come in ones or twos. Nevertheless, had Richard indeed been born with teeth he would have been considered fairly unusual; the phenomenon occurs in about one in one thousand newborn infants. Because of their rarity, natal teeth have some interesting and varied superstitions attached to them.

Natal teeth were viewed in France and Italy as portents of future good fortune for the child. King Louis XIV, Cardinal Richelieu and Cardinal Mazarin were all born with teeth and all went on to enjoy the privileged life that power, wealth and success can bring. Sir William Cornwallis the Younger, a contemporary of George Buck, whose work takes the style of the paradox, also states that to be born with teeth was fortuitous, at least he believed it to be so for Richard:

His beinge toothed as soone as borne, me seemes rather a blessinge, then anie imputation, as beinge a prognostication of his future worth, since it was an extraordinarie and noe vnproffitable marke, for nurses houlde the cominge out of Childrens teeth to be verie painefull.[10]

Mostly, however, natal teeth are thought to be unlucky. This belief goes at least as far back as Pliny the Elder, although, here, it applies only to female children. As time went on, the bad luck associated with natal teeth was extended to boys.

Quite why a child born with teeth should be considered unlucky is not now known, although it might have had something to do with various practical problems that can arise as a result of them. One such difficulty is associated with the discomfort often caused to the mother while breast-feeding. This might be severe enough to make the experience a deeply unpleasant one for the mother, which could in extreme cases affect the mother-child bonding process. In Cecily's case her elevated status would suggest that she employed the services of a wet nurse to feed Richard, although she might have chosen to suckle him herself in emulation of the great ladies of the Old Testament, Sarah and Hannah.[11]

Physical difficulties can arise that would affect the baby more directly. Natal teeth typically occur in the position of the mandibular central incisors and can be problematic for the child if they rub against the tongue. If the teeth are loose there is a small chance that they may be inhaled should they become dislodged.

Natal teeth have been associated with abnormalities such as cleft palate and Pierre Robin syndrome. This last is a very rare condition characterised by a small lower jaw and a cleft palate or a high arched palate. While the jaw bone will continue to grow during childhood, so that it will usually have corrected itself by adulthood, the cleft palate cannot be outgrown. Had Richard suffered any of these conditions, his ability to eat would have been impaired. His hearing would probably also have been affected, as would his facial development. In short, the resultant deficiencies would have been obvious to anyone observing him eating or who spoke to him. Richard, as king, frequently ate in public. One of those invited to watch him eat was the Silesian diplomatist and knight errant Niclas von Popplau, who left a physical description of the King:

> King Richard is ... three fingers taller than I, but a bit slimmer and not as thickset as I am, and much more lightly built; he has quite slender arms and thighs, and also a great heart.[12]

That Popplau makes no mention of any facial disfigurement might be due to discretion on his part, or perhaps he desired to flatter a king who had shown him kindness and courtesy. However, no other contemporary writer notes a hearing impediment in Richard, while none of his portraits suggest that he had a cleft palate. This is significant because Richard's enemies had a particular interest in presenting him as deformed wherever possible and they wasted no opportunity to do so.

Had Richard been born with teeth, they clearly caused him few, if any, problems; they certainly did not lead to any facial disfigurement. Moreover, there is no evidence to suggest that Richard was an undersized, sickly baby who was not expected to live. His alleged frailty is the product of the misreading of a contemporary verse, which includes the line, 'Richard liveth yet'. This phrase simply notes that Richard was still living at the time at which the rhyme was written, while four of his siblings had not survived.

The verse, entitled *A Dialogue between a Secular and a Friar*, came into the possession of Augustine Vincent, Windsor Herald, clerk in the Tower

Record Office and genealogist, who died in 1626. The text is presented in two columns, one in Latin, the other in English, on a vellum roll, illustrated by a representation of the friar and the secular man of the title, and eleven coats of arms.

As the rubric explains, the verse is presented as a dialogue between 'a secular asking and a friar answering at the grave of Dame Johanna of Acres'. Dame Johanna, or Joan of Acres, was the second daughter of King Edward I and the consort of Gilbert de Clare, Earl of Gloucester. She died in 1305 and was buried in the church of the Augustine friars at Clare in Suffolk, of which she was the founder. The verse shows the lineal descent of the lords of the honour of Clare, from the time of the foundation of the Augustine friars in 1248 until 1 May 1460.

Why Richard should be included in this verse is made clear by the family tree it then goes on to describe. Joan of Acres's marriage to Gilbert de Clare produced a daughter who married Sir John de Burgh, Lord of Ulster. Their only child married Lionel, Duke of Clarence, who was the second surviving son of Edward III. The title of Clarence, which Richard's brother George would eventually hold, is taken from the honour of Clare. The daughter of Lionel, Duke of Clarence, Philippa, married Edmund Mortimer, Earl of March. By means of the Clare Scroll, Richard could trace his lineage through Ralph de Mortimer, Llewelyn the Great and Cadwallader and all the way back to Brut and the Trojans. It linked him to the maternal branch of the family of his father, Richard, the third Duke of York.

Richard, Duke of York was of royal blood, being the great-grandson of King Edward III. His grandfather was Edmund Langley, Earl of Cambridge and first Duke of York, who had married Isabel, the daughter of Peteri, King of Castile and Leon. The couple had two sons and one daughter who survived. Their eldest son, Edward, inherited his father's title of Duke of York; the second son, Richard, surnamed Coningsburgh from the place of his birth, would become earl of Cambridge. Richard of Coningsburgh married Anne Mortimer, the daughter of Roger Mortimer, fourth earl of March and sixth earl of Ulster. Roger was descended from Edward III through his mother, Philippa, who was the daughter of Lionel, Duke of Clarence. It is Duke Lionel's family that is featured in the rhyme *A Dialogue between a Secular and a Friar*.

Richard of York was only four years old when his father, the earl of Cambridge, was executed for conspiring against King Henry V in October 1415 on the very eve of that king's great victory at Agincourt. In his generosity, Henry did not extend the father's attainder to the son. When the boy's uncle was killed at Agincourt, Henry recognised York as his heir; moreover, when another uncle, Edmund Mortimer, died, York inherited the patrimony of the earls of March and Ulster as well. A royal ward, he was initially placed into the custody of the chief gaoler of the Lancastrians, Sir Robert Waterton. Following the death of Henry V and the accession of the infant Henry VI, York's wardship and marriage were sold to Ralph Nevill, Earl of Westmorland for 3,000 marks. Perhaps it was felt that the boy, through whose veins coursed the blood of Clarence, York and Mortimer, would disown the ambitions of his rebellious father and embrace the cause of the House of Lancaster. For Westmorland was the husband of Joan Beaufort, a descendant of John of Gaunt, Duke of Lancaster through his mistress, Katharine Swynford. It was into Joan's hands that the wardship and marriage of York fell following the death of Westmorland two years later. At some point prior to 18 October 1424, Joan betrothed the thirteen-year-old Richard to her youngest daughter, Cecily.

Cecily Nevill, who was born on 3 May 1415, was only nine at the time of her betrothal to Richard of York. She was descended on her father's side from Robert Fitzmaldred, Lord of Raby, who lived during the reign of King John (1199-1216). Robert married Isabelle Nevill, the daughter of Geoffrey Nevill of Brancepeth. Their son, also called Geoffrey, united the Fitzmaldred lands in Teesdale with the extensive Nevill estates of Raby, Barnard, Durham, Sheriff Hutton and Middleham. Geoffrey also adopted his mother's surname of Nevill, causing the Fitzmaldred name to fall into disuse.

In time, the Nevills would acquire lands in the south and midlands of England as well as in Wales. However, their power base was to remain primarily in the north of England, where they would become involved in the occasional dispute with the Bishop of Durham, their feudal lord, and from which they would emerge to serve their king in campaigns against the Scots or the French as the need arose. Through good service and prudent marriages, the Nevill family would eventually become more powerful even than the mighty Percy family of Northumberland.

Fourteen children were born of this love-match between Ralph Nevill and Joan Beaufort, augmenting the brood that the earl had already fathered by his first wife, the daughter of Hugh, Earl of Stafford.[13] Of the sons, the eldest was Richard, the future earl of Salisbury, ally of the Duke of York and father of Richard, Earl of Warwick. William, the future Lord Fauconberg, would become the father of the man known to history as the Bastard of Fauconberg. George Lord Latimer, whose family would eventually include the future queen of England, Katherine Parr. He was followed by Robert, who would become Bishop of Durham, and Edward, the future Lord Abergavenny. Four sons, Cuthbert, Henry, John and Thomas were to die without leaving their mark on the pages of history. Of the daughters, the eldest was Catherine, who would marry, firstly, John Mowbray, second Duke of Norfolk and then Sir John Woodville, the son of Richard Earl Rivers. Eleanor would become the wife of Richard Lord Spencer, upon whose death she would marry Henry Percy, Earl of Northumberland. Anne would become the Duchess of Buckingham upon her marriage to Duke Humphrey; her second husband would be Walter Blount Lord Mountjoy. Jane would become a nun. Finally, there is Cecily, the youngest child of the family.

Cecily Nevill has long been considered a woman of great piety. However, much of the religious feeling for which she is best known became prominent mainly during the last decade of her life. By that time she would have seen two of her sons fall in battle, and one whose blood was shed at the hands of another who would die peacefully in his bed. Certainly, it was as the twilight began to settle on her tumultuous life that Cecily's devotions became more regimented and austere. Nevertheless, her thoughts had not always been turned primarily towards God. A beauty of some renown, men were naturally attracted to her, and this inspired the romantic soubriquet by which she was sometimes known: the 'Rose of Raby'.

Cecily Nevill would know seven queens in her lifetime. The first was Joan, the widow of King Henry IV. After Joan was Catherine, the dowager of Henry V, followed by Marguerite d'Anjou, who would be in turn Cecily's great friend and then her enemy. Queen Elizabeth was the consort of her son, Edward, while another son, Richard, would make a queen of his wife, Anne. Lastly, Cecily's granddaughter, Elizabeth of York, would become the wife of her youngest son's conqueror and the mother of a new dynasty, that of the Tudors. Similarly, there were five kings in Cecily's life, Henry V, Henry VI, Edward IV, Richard III and Henry VII. Had fate turned out differently, Cecily's husband would have ascended the throne as King Richard III, and she would have been his queen. Cecily was acutely aware of this fact, and she would emphasise it at every opportunity. All that, however, was still in the future.

Cecily's husband, at the age of eleven, was knighted at Leicester by John, Duke of Bedford. Three years later, on 6 November 1429, he attended the coronation of Henry VI. Richard of York also acted as a constable at a duel in the presence of the King before he accompanied him to Paris for his French coronation in 1430. In 1433 he was admitted into the Order of the Garter, but it was not until May 1436 that Richard of York finally had his chance to prove his worth as a member of that great order of knighthood. The occasion arose with the death of the king's lieutenant in France, the

Duke of Bedford. In the power vacuum that followed, rebellion had broken out which rendered English interests in France vulnerable. Paris was threatened, Dieppe was lost and major uprisings in the Pays de Caux had left only Caudebec and Arques secure. Henry was keen that 'some great prince of our blood' should rule in France, and so York, who was the best candidate after the King's uncle, Humphrey, Duke of Gloucester, was appointed to go.

His eagerness to serve his king notwithstanding, York's departure for France was delayed. The reasons for this are unclear but might have had to do with finance, problems with administration or mustering. Whatever the case, York and his entourage arrived at Harfleur in June; unfortunately, as a result of their belatedness, they were unable to save Paris. However, they did manage to re-establish the English military position in Normandy and regain control of the Pays de Caux.

York's role in France was more political than military. He appears to have acted as a negotiator and administrator, almost as a viceroy, leaving military matters to his retainer, John Talbot, Earl of Shrewsbury and Waterford, a veteran of warfare in France whose campaign during the autumn of 1436 saw the return of the Norman city of Rouen to English hands.

York's indentures were due to expire in the spring of the following year. He requested, and was granted, permission to return to England. His successor as lieutenant was to be Richard Beauchamp, Earl of Warwick. However, like York before him, Warwick's departure for France was also delayed, so York was forced to continue in his post and did not leave for England until November.

The Duke and Duchess of York continued in England for three years, until, in 1439, the Earl of Warwick died, once again leaving a power vacuum in France. Arrangements were set in train for York to take up his post of lieutenant of France once again. However, this time, his appointment was not a foregone conclusion. He faced competition from Cardinal Beaufort, Bishop of Winchester. The cardinal was the second son of John of Gaunt and Katharine Swynford and, in this instance, he appeared to have been acting at the behest of his nephew, John Beaufort, Earl of Somerset. Another rival for the post was Humphrey, Duke of Gloucester, the King's uncle. In the event, York's suitability for the appointment and, no doubt, his previous experience, ensured that he was chosen, and so York prepared once again for life in France.

The Duke received sealed indentures for his appointment of lieutenant, in which capacity he was to serve for five years with an annual income of £20,000 to be paid by the English exchequer. This was to be paid for as long as Normandy was in danger. He was also to receive suitable ordinance, maintenance, agreed councillors and provision for shipping. Once more, however, York's departure was delayed. The reason, once again, is not entirely clear. As with the previous occasion, it could have been related to trouble over financing or recruitment.

It has been suggested that it was during Duke Richard's tenure of the lieutenancy of France that his wife showed her true colours as a 'spendthrift'.[14] Cecily's extravagance was said to be a drain on her husband's resources. Certainly, her love of opulence and grandeur had already been established by the time she returned home to Fotheringhay. Here, she had a throne room where she would give receptions 'with the state of a queen', sheltered behind securely defended walls far away from the talk of the villagers who nicknamed her 'Proud Cis'.[15] John Wigmore, who handled the Duke's finances, spent almost £608 in London on clothes for Duchess Cecily. These included an open surcote with mantle and cope hood made by John Legge, a tailor of the king's wardrobe; almost sixty yards of crimson velvet lined with ermine were used to create this ensemble. It was decorated with 325 pearls, thirty of which cost £6 each, and 8½ oz gold. The Duchess also had a privy re-upholstered for her when she and the Duke visited Caen in 1445, while a gold cup purchased for her use by John Paddyshale, a London goldsmith, cost a staggering £54.

Yet, Cecily was not the only one with expensive tastes; her husband owned a collar, called 'white rose', which was studded with precious stones and valued at £2,666. This would later come into the possession of Sir John Fastolf, at whose house the Yorks' youngest son, Richard, would one day stay.

In time, the Duke and Duchess of York would have twelve children, although not all would survive childhood. They are named in the aforementioned rhyme, *A Dialogue between a Secular and a Friar*:

Sir, after the tyme of long bareynesse,
God first sent Anne, which signyfieth grace;
In token that all her hertis heavynesse
He (as for bareynesse) wold fro hem chase.
Harry, Edward, and Edmonde, eche in his place
Succeeded; and after tweyn daughters came,
Elizabeth and Margarete; and afterwards William
John after William nexte borne was,
Which both be passed to God's grace.
George was nexte: and after Thomas
Borne was; which sone after did pace
By the path of death to the heavenly place;
Richard liveth yet. But last of alle
Was Ursula, to hym whom God list calle[16]

Of these children, John, William, Thomas and Ursula, went 'by the path of death to the heavenly place'. The fate of Harry is not recorded. Ursula, the youngest daughter of York, was born in 1455 but died while still a baby. In the case of young Richard, the phrase 'Richard liveth yet' makes no comment upon the state of his health, nor is it intended to. It merely shows that, at the time of writing, Richard was still living.

If Cecily had decided to engage a wet nurse to suckle Richard, and this would be usual for a lady of her status, such as woman would have been chosen for her physical characteristics, which would resemble those of the child's mother as far as possible.[17] Apart from feeding the baby, the wet nurse would also bathe him frequently and anoint him with oil, such as myrtle or rose. She would then wrap him tightly in swaddling clothes so that he would resemble a tiny mummy, his legs stiffened by the cloth and stretched out to prevent deformity. Unfortunately, the same process of bandaging also had the effect of weakening the limbs for a time.

Richard, as a soul newly born into the world, was understood to be tainted with Original Sin; the sin that descended upon Adam and Eve as they partook of the forbidden fruit which led to their expulsion from Paradise. The soul must turn back to God and find salvation by acknowledging the sacrifice made on its behalf by Christ on the cross. Thus the road to becoming a Christian must begin with the first step, baptism.

The most poignant sign of salvation is water. Noah and his family, eight people in total, had been saved from the flood by the grace of God. Later, the waters of the sea parted to allow the Israelites to cross to safety before closing upon their Egyptian pursuers. John the Baptist sealed his message of salvation by immersing the penitent in living waters. This ritual was taken up by the Christian Church and modified slightly to become the sacrament of baptism. Living water, that which springs up naturally from the earth, is seen as a sign of life. The water of the sea is symbolic of death and the mystery of the cross. Baptism, therefore, signified communion with the death of Christ.

It was considered most desirable to baptise babies on the day upon which they were born. To delay would result in their going to dwell in limbo should they die without the benefit of this sacrament. If the actual day of birth was not practicable, then the baby should be baptised before it was one week old.

The castle in which Richard was born had its own chapel and it could have been here that the first stage of his initiation into the Church took place. On the other hand, the small village beyond the castle walls, in tiny, ancient Fotheringhay, stood the church that already held much significance for the House of York. Richard's baptism could have been held there.

The baby Richard lay in the arms of the midwife as the priest came to the church door to meet them. Having asked the sex of the child, the priest made the sign of the cross on the baby's forehead, breast and right hand. He placed salt into his mouth and a candle, lit from the Easter candle, was held in the child's right hand. In this way, Richard carried into the church the light that signified his enlightenment and salvation. His white garment symbolised that he had risen with Christ.

The name given to the baby as the sacrament of baptism was conferred upon him was Richard. The name derives into two words: the Germanic 'rich', coming ultimately from the Celtic meaning king, and 'ard' via Old French, meaning hardy or bold. The name given to Richard, therefore, carries the meaning 'bold ruler', or 'ruler of power'. It is mentioned in the Domesday Book and was probably brought to England with the Anglo-Saxons.

It is possible that the name of Richard was chosen because of its strong presence within the family. His father was Richard, Duke of York, whom the baby would grow up to resemble. His grandfather was the executed Richard, Earl of Cambridge. There was a Richard in his mother's family too. Cecily Nevill's cousin was Richard, Earl of Warwick, and it is possible that this man, who would become known to history as the Kingmaker, stood as godfather to the new-born boy. If so, it is possible that Richard was named after him.

Conversely, Richard might have been named after a saint. After all, each of his brothers and sisters bore the names of saints. His eldest sister was named after Anne, the mother of the Virgin Mary. Edward might have been named after Edward the Martyr, a tenth-century King of England whose cult had begun in 1001. However, this saint's sphere of influence was quite small and is centred primarily in the West-Country. A more feasible choice is Edward the Confessor, the patron saint of England and of English kings. It is a most suitable name for the son of a man who descended from kings and who was very much aware of his position in the line of succession.

Edmund was probably named after St Edmund of East Anglia, over whose shrine King Cnut ordered the abbey of Bury St Edmunds to be built in 1020. The next child, a daughter, was named Elizabeth. While not a saint, Elizabeth is the mother of John the Baptist, who was one of Cecily's favourite saints.

In Margaret's case, there are several saints after whom she could have been named. One such St Margaret is the great niece of Edward the Confessor who, after the defeat of Harold at the Battle of Hastings, fled to Scotland where she married King Malcolm III. Margaret helped reform ecclesiastical life in Scotland, removed Celtic customs and founded Dunfermline Abbey. She was a great benefactress to the poor and one of the patron saints of Scotland. Her connections with Edward the Confessor favour her as the namesake of Margaret Plantagenet, although her strong Scottish connections make it less probable. More plausible is Saint Margaret of Antioch, also known as Marina. She was widely known throughout Europe and, like Mary, was a virgin. St Margaret is frequently invoked against infertility and is the patron of, among others, wet-nurses and pregnant women. It is tempting to speculate that Cecily invoked this saint while carrying the daughter who was to bear her name, perhaps indicating that this, as with her younger brother, was a difficult pregnancy.

For George there could be only one saint. St George, most significantly is the patron of the military nobility and the English royal house. It is appropriate that his name should be represented in a house that was headed by a military man who was of royal blood.

Turning to Richard, it is possible that he was named after the eighth-century saint, pilgrim and confessor of Wessex. However, nothing appears to connect this saint with the House of York, even allowing for the legend that he was 'King of the English'. Of course, Richard was the youngest of four surviving sons and would realistically have had no hope of reaching the throne. It is more probable, therefore, that his name-saint was Richard of Wyche, sometimes known as St Richard of Chichester. If so, it was an inspired choice and one that was appropriate to Richard's own interests as a boy and to the ideals he would hold when he grew to manhood: the crusader spirit. Richard of Wyche was named as one of the collectors of the subsidy for the crusades and was later appointed to preach the crusade in London. [18]

Richard of Wyche is depicted above the image of King Richard and his son in the Richard III Window in the Collegiate Church of St Mary and St Alkelda at Middleham. This was given in the king's memory by the Richard III Society in 1934. Here, the saint is shown in his bishop's robes and mitre, with the bishop's staff in his left hand and a bible in his right. He was elected Bishop of Chichester in 1244, taking over from Ralph Nevill. The parentage and other family connections of Ralph Nevill are unknown. That Geoffrey de Nevill, an ancestor of Richard's mother, claimed kinship with Ralph allows the possibility that he was a distant relative of the Nevills of Raby, thus providing a link between St Richard and Richard Plantagenet. St Richard was canonised in 1262.

In giving the new baby the name of Richard, however, his family might have been tempting fate. Richard was an inauspicious name for a child of the

English royal house to bear. The ill-luck attached to it dated back as far as Richard I, who was killed by an assassin's arrow during the siege of Chalon. Richard II was deposed by his cousin, Henry of Bolingbroke, and either murdered or was allowed to starve to death in Pontefract Castle. Richard, Earl of Cambridge, cousin to Richard II and grandfather to Richard Plantagenet, was executed as a traitor for his part in the Southampton Plot. Richard, Duke of York, father to Richard Plantagenet, would be slain and beheaded in the snows of Wakefield. Subsequent Richards in the family, including Richard Plantagenet himself and his young nephew, Richard, fourth Duke of York, would not escape the ill-starred influence of this name.[19]

There are several interpretations of Richard's surname of Plantagenet. One suggestion is that it originated with Geoffrey of Anjou who, as a young man, delighted in the sport of hunting and is believed to have planted the bright yellow broom, or *genesta*, as cover for his game. On the other hand, Geoffrey is said to have worn a sprig of broom in his helm as a means of being recognised on the field of battle in the days before the use of heraldry. A similar story has Geoffrey wearing broom, a symbol of humility, while on crusade in Jerusalem, and that he adopted the name at the same time. The crusades also provide the backdrop for a fourth interpretation, that Geoffrey was scourged with broom twigs at Jerusalem.

Whatever the origins, however, the name of Plantagenet was not used in Richard's family until 1448, when the Duke of York adopted it as a surname in order to emphasise his royal status and his right to the power that it should have brought him. However, even as he delighted in the arrival of his youngest son, little did York know that events were conspiring to bring him the opportunity to press this right further than even he could have imagined.

CHAPTER 2

THE WHITE ROSE, THE RED ROSE, 1453

Ten months after the birth of Richard Plantagenet, three events occurred that would have a significant impact upon his father's bid for recognition and a position of power within the government of the kingdom. The first of these was the defeat of the English army as it attempted to win back Gascony from the French. This catastrophe also witnessed the death of the heroic John Talbot, Earl of Shrewsbury and Waterford, nicknamed the 'Terror of the French'. The second event was the outbreak of hostilities in the north of England between the Nevills and their powerful rivals, the Percy family. Lastly and perhaps most directly was the sudden and complete collapse of King Henry VI.

Henry VI was a king more suited to wear the mitre than the crown. His character has been sketched by John Blakman, who describes him as

A man of pure simplicity of mind, truthful almost to a fault. He never made a promise he did not keep, never knowingly did an injury to any one. Rectitude and justice ruled his conduct in all public affairs. Devout himself, he sought to cherish a love for religion in others. He would exhort his visitors, particularly the young to pursue virtue and eschew evil. He considered sports and the pleasures of the world as frivolous, and devoted his leisure to reading the Scriptures and the old Chronicles. Most decorous himself when attending public worship, he obliged his courtiers to enter the sacred edifice without swords or spears, and to refrain from interrupting the devotion of others by conversing within it's [sic] precincts. He exhorted his clergy in frequent letters, and charged them to consider their trust as emanating from the authority of the most high.

He delighted in female society, and blamed that immodest dress, which left exposed the maternal parts of the neck. "Fie, fie, for shame!' he exclaimed, 'forsooth ye be to blame'. Fond of encouraging youth in the path of virtue he would frequently converse familiarly with the scholars from his college of Eton, when they visited his servants at Windsor Castle. He generally concluded with this address, adding a present of money: 'Be good lads, meek and docile, and attend to your religion.'

He was liberal to the poor, and lived among his dependants as a father among his children. He readily forgave those who had offended him. When one of his servants had been robbed, he sent him a present of twenty nobles, desiring him to be more careful of his property in future, and requesting him to forgive the thief. Passing one day from St Albans to Cripplegate, he saw a quarter of a man impaled there for treason. Greatly shocked he exclaimed: 'Take it away, take it away, I will have no man so cruelly treated on my account.' Hearing that four men of noble birth were about to suffer for treason to him, he sent them his pardon with all expedition to the place of execution.

In his dress he was plain, and would not wear the shoes, with the upturned points, then so much in fashion, and considered the distinguishing mark of a man of quality.

He was careful to select proper persons in the distribution of Church preferment; and anxious to promote the real Happiness of his two half brothers, the Earls of Richmond and Pembroke he had them carefully brought up under the most upright and virtuous Ecclesiastics.[1]

This account presents a man of the utmost honesty and integrity, someone who is sincere in his religious beliefs and seeks to encourage a similar devotion in others. Henry is shown to prefer modesty in women and at once a dislike of and a fascination for the 'charms' of womanhood. He is a man who finds the rather revealing fashions of the time to be a source of temptation and, as a result, the source of inner guilt as his repressed but very active sexuality makes its presence felt.

The trappings of the world held no interest for King Henry. He dismissed fashion as frivolous and disliked physical games, preferring instead the intellectual pursuits of scholarly discourse and the satisfaction of seeing others gain from such exercise. He was generous and anxious to help those who were less fortunate than himself, and his compassion extended even to those who had committed treason against him. His family were important to him, and he dedicated himself to their advancement.

A man of peace, Henry had opened a dialogue with King Charles VII of France for a truce between their two countries. Part of the negotiations involved the return to Charles of Maine and Anjou, which were currently being held by the English. Henry thought that this was the best way to establish peace because the surrender of these two holdings would enable the English to hold on to Normandy. Furthermore, the truce would be sealed by a marriage between Henry and Marguerite d'Anjou.

Marguerite d'Anjou was the daughter of René, Duke of Lorraine and Anjou, and the niece of King Charles VII. Polydore Vergil writes of Marguerite as a:

> Woman of sufficient forecast, very desirous of renowne, full of policie, councell, comely behaviour, and all manly qualities, in whom appeared great witt, great diligence, great heede and carefulnes: but she was of the kinde of other women, who commonly are much geven and very readie to mutabilitie and chaunge.[2]

Agnes Strickland, on the other hand, notes that the new queen's 'precocious charms and talents created the most lively sensation at the court of her aunt, the queen of France'. To be sure, Strickland continues, 'there was no princess in Christendom more accomplished than my lady Marguerite of Anjou. She was already renowned in France for her beauty and wit, and all the misfortunes of her father had only given her an opportunity of displaying her lofty spirit and courage.'[3]

Lady Marguerite's precocious charms and talents had also caused a sensation at the court of Henry VI in England and the King eagerly listened to flattering reports of the renowned beauty. He asked for a portrait to be painted of her. Preferring truth to flattery or propaganda, Henry pointed out that young women 'should be painted in their kirtles simple, and their visages like as ye see, and their stature, and their beauty, the colour of their skin, and their countenances.'[4]

Still, for all Henry's romantic notions, his marriage to the beautiful Marguerite was, in the end, decided by diplomatic negotiation and treaty. As she made her way to her new life in England, amid all the ceremonies, gaiety and tournaments that accompany such occasions, Marguerite met Richard, Duke of York at Mantes where she supped with him a meal which cost of £5 5s 1d. The next day she dined with the Duke, the expenses incurred this time being a mere £4 7s 5½d. The day after that, she departed Mantes for Vernon where she spent one night before moving on to Rouen. Her arrival at that city was almost certainly the occasion at which the Duchess Cecily wore her magnificent and costly dress.

Now, eight years after these happy events, the sainted king had suffered a seizure that left him unable to speak or even to move. The cause of it was a mystery. Shock over the events in France could have been a factor. However, it was probably no coincidence that the first attack of the illness that was to incapacitate the King occurred while his wife was pregnant with their only child. It could be that Henry's natural, though repressed, sexuality spilled over to the point where he could no longer cope, with the result that his entire system shut down. Another possibility, or perhaps a contributing factor, might have had physical origins. It is possible that King Henry had inherited the malady from his maternal grandfather, King Charles VI of France. Charles, whose epithet, 'the Mad' sometimes gave way to another, 'the Glass King'. One of the ways in which the French king's illness manifested itself was in the deluded belief that he was made of glass. Charles thought that he would shatter if he were touched. As with Henry, Charles' illness appears to have been triggered by emotional trauma. The first recorded instance of it occurred in 1392 when an attempt was made on the life of his friend and advisor, Olivier de Clisson.

In Henry's case, it took the form of complete physical and mental collapse that has been likened to catatonic schizophrenia. According to *Whathamstede's Register*, the King lost his wits and his memory, he was unco-ordinated and unable to walk or hold his head upright, and it was difficult for him even to move.[5]

Henry was staying at his hunting lodge at Clarendon at the moment of his descent into darkness. He was kept there for two months, out of sight, while the government pretended that all was well and continued to rule in his name. By October, however, it had become obvious that such a state of affairs could not be maintained. A meeting was called to discuss the situation. Conspicuously absent from this meeting was Richard of York, whose peers had not seen fit to summon him.

Why York, who ought to have been present at the meeting, was overlooked was due to the escalating rivalry between him and Edmund Beaufort, Duke of Somerset. In some ways the rivalry between York and Somerset can be seen as a duel, a personal quarrel between the two Dukes. However, they were vying for the highest of stakes. The object over which they fought was not the love of a woman nor was it a matter of honour, strictly speaking, but the still more valuable prize of recognition within the court and the power that came with it. More precisely, their duel was over who should exercise the most influence over King Henry VI.

Somerset felt himself to be in a particularly strong position and, since the King appeared to favour him, he was probably correct in his assumption. However, York felt that, whatever the King's personal preferences, he, York, was the more appropriate choice, due to his birthright, certainly, but also because of his ability. In this York was probably correct.

The ensuing argument would inspire Shakespeare to write a scene in which the competition between the two Dukes is symbolised by the selection of the roses:

Richard Plantagenet:
Let him that is a true-born gentleman
And stands upon the honour of his birth,
If he suppose that I have pleaded truth,
From off this briar pluck a white rose with me

Somerset:
Let him that is no coward nor no flatterer,
But dare maintain the party of the truth,
Pluck a red rose from off this thorn with me [6]

As a consequence of this colourful exchange, the image of the two roses would become the stuff of legend and romance. On the other hand, although the roses were immortalised by Shakespeare, the symbolism of the white rose and the red rose dates from a much earlier time. The first mention of them in the context of the civil wars between the houses of York and Lancaster occurs as early as 1486. The Croyland Continuator, speaking of the Battle of Bosworth Field, notes that:

The year one thousand, hundreds four, and five
To eighty added, when of August came
The twice eleventh day, the Boar's tusks quail'd
And, to avenge the White, the Red Rose bloom'd. [7]

Alas for both romance and heraldry, it has been argued that the red rose was not formally adopted as a badge by the Lancastrians until the Tudor period. [8] Indeed, evidence suggests that it was introduced by Henry Tudor himself after his accession as King Henry VII. Of course, roses had been used by members of the House of Lancaster as decoration, particularly on tombs, prior to this. The most obvious example is that of Henry IV in Canterbury Cathedral, whose effigy is adorned by a mantle decorated with five roses. Similarly, the tomb of the Black Prince, also in the cathedral at Canterbury, features double six-petalled roses on the edge of the tester.

As to the House of York, however, the image of the rose is much more prolific. The rose emblem is found on the seals of Richard, Duke of York as well as that of his uncle, Edward, the second Duke of York. Roses also

feature on the coinage of Edward IV and Richard III. By their nature, coins
and seals are not able to convey the colour of the roses depicted upon them.
However, where it was possible to use colour, the roses of the House of
York were always white. Therefore, enamelled white roses feature among
the jewels of Margaret of York's bridal crown; Edward IV kneels against
a background powdered with white roses-en-soleil in the royal window
at Canterbury; white roses appear in the window of the church at Sheriff
Hutton in Yorkshire; white roses feature on their standards of both Edward
IV and Richard III. In each of these examples the presence of a white rose is
a good indication that this was indeed the colour of the rose of the House
of York.

It is often believed that the House of York took the white rose badge
from the heraldry of the Mortimer family, whose arms are depicted suspended from a rose bush. However, the rose badge goes back even further
than this. Eleanor of Provence, queen to Henry III, was associated with a
rose, the colour of which was reputed to have been white. Eleanor's sons,
Edward I and Edmund Crouchback, carried on the tradition which was to
pass through the House of Plantagenet to become most famously associated
with the Yorkist branch.

To return to the scene in the Temple garden, Shakespeare highlights the
dispute between the Dukes of York and Somerset. As they pluck their respective roses, their supporters select blooms whose colours match those selected
by the two Dukes. However, Shakespeare, as so often in his writings, reflects
history not as it actually happened but as it came to be interpreted.

The dispute of which the Bard writes is commonly said to have erupted
when Somerset was given an office coveted by York, that of lieutenant and
governor-general of France and the duchies of Normandy and Guyenne.
Contemporary chroniclers, Whathamstede, Waurin and Thomas Basin,
attribute York's enmity with Somerset to the latter's appointment to a post
that York wished to regain. York, who had previously held this commission,
was anxious to extend his tenure to a third term. Unfortunately for York,
and for English interests in France as it turned out, Somerset won the day.

York might have been resentful at being overlooked in favour of Somerset
but to attribute the rivalry between him and Somerset to it is to make a very
simplistic assessment of the situation. By far the largest part of the problem
was Somerset's French policy. This, in turn, was influenced by his attitude to
Maine, where he had held office as captain-general and governor since 1438
and from which he had received lands rights four years later. If Maine were
to be ceded to France as part of King Henry's policy Somerset wanted compensation. He spent a year negotiating with the government and finally won

a grant of 10,000 *livres tournois* from the *quatrième*, a tax on certain beverages such as wine and cider. This was, in fact, paid in full until war broke out in 1449. Only after he had secured this compensation would Somerset allow the cession of Maine. It was at this point also that he agreed to take up the post of lieutenant and governor-general of Normandy.

Somerset then made a grave mistake. He took it upon himself to carry out a plan that had been concocted between himself and the Duke of Suffolk as long ago as 1447: the capture of the Breton town of Fougères. His implementation of this plan had two serious consequences. First, it caused France to declare war on England on 17 July 1449. Second, it pushed Brittany, with whom England was seeking an alliance, into an alliance with France instead. Moreover, there was a delay of several months before reinforcements could be sent to Somerset, which opened a window of opportunity to the French. They took advantage of this to invade Normandy.

The duchy of Normandy had been in English hands since the time of King Henry V. However, when France invaded in 1449, Somerset's grip proved to be decidedly insecure. His inadequate arrangements for the duchy's defence soon became clear. Normandy was overrun within a year. Town after town fell with barely a fight, while Somerset personally surrendered the capital, Rouen, as well as several important fortresses. He then negotiated safe passage for his family and a few retainers, leaving at once for Caen. This town he also surrendered before embarking for England, where he arrived in August 1450.

The fall of Normandy had exposed the fact that King Henry was bankrupt. It was generally considered, by those in power as well as among the lower orders, that Henry had been betrayed by certain men at court who had their own best interests at heart rather than those of the King, whose English possession they had plundered at the same time as they handed over those in France. Chief among these was William de la Pole, Duke of Suffolk.

Suffolk had been arrested and imprisoned in the Tower in January 1450 accused of treason in his dealings with France as well as various acts of corruption and violence in local and general administration. He was saved from trial by the intervention of King Henry, but his reprieve was short-lived. Liberated from the Tower, he wound up his affairs and prepared to leave the kingdom. However, as he left Dover, his ships were intercepted by a small fleet. He was taken aboard the flagship of this fleet and transferred to a small boat where he was beheaded upon the orders of the unidentified commander. Yet, whatever his faults, Suffolk was not solely responsible for the disaster that had befallen England; he was but one man and, while his removal had been advantageous from the point of view of the welfare of the country, there were others who remained in power who were just as corrupt and self-serving as Suffolk had been.

As to Somerset, it was his sheer lack of competence, greed and maladministration that so enraged Richard of York, not least because York had a personal stake in the duchy that encompassed both his political and dynastic ambitions. For, with the backing of the court, if not at its behest, he had begun marriage negotiations during his last lieutenancy between his son Edward, now titled Edward of Rouen, and one of King Charles' daughters. York thought that the King's daughter, Joanne, would make a suitable bride, but Charles suggested Princess Madeleine instead. York continued to press for his choice, but the French king proved stubborn. As more and more letters were exchanged,[9] the Duke's lieutenancy in France expired and he was obliged to return to England. York was not entirely honest with the King; he stated instead that his impending departure was in response to his being summoned to a parliament. However, he assured Charles of his continued interest in the marriage, which he expected to discuss with Henry VI when he reached England.

As far as the French were concerned, the proposed marriage between one of their princesses and Edward of Rouen would be of no consequence for some years to come because the prospective bride and groom were so young. As such, the continuing dialogue was probably little more than a show of goodwill on the part of the French. For the English, however, it was much more significant than that. Marguerite d'Anjou, although of childbearing age, was Charles VII's niece, not his daughter. A child born to Edward and a daughter of Charles VII would take precedence over any child that Marguerite might produce. As the grandchild of the King of France, it would take its place in the line of succession to the throne of France. In the end, however, it was all academic. Charles VII continued to dig in his heels over which daughter to negotiate away and so the matter was eventually dropped.

All the while, the Duke of York had continued to show an interest in his titles, such as that to the crown of Castile, about which he began to make enquiries in 1445. This title came from his grandmother, Isabel, the daughter of Peteri, King of Castile. When it came to England, however, the Duke found that his relations with King Henry's ministers had turned decidedly chilly. He was apparently accused of mishandling funds that had been intended for the defence of Normandy and a rumour began to spread in which it was claimed that his conduct in the duchy had been less than exemplary. York was vindicated on both counts.

On the other hand, York had received very little of the promised annual income of £20,000 during his tenure as lieutenant of France. The result was that he was owed some £38,666 in unpaid wages. Add to this a further £10,000 in arrears from his hereditary pension, as well as bad tallies in return for loans amounting to some £26,000 by the year 1446, and the Duke's difficult financial position becomes clear. He was unable to finance his garrisons or pay his soldiers and servants.

It is sometimes thought that the Duke of York opposed Henry's policy of peace with France. On the contrary, he had complied with Henry's requests to offer aid to the dauphin, who was campaigning in Alsace, and the proposed marriage between Edward of Rouen and a princess of France formed part of the peace negotiations. Still, there was a strained atmosphere at the court, and this was intensified following the death of Humphrey, Duke of Gloucester.

Duke Humphrey was the youngest son of King Henry IV by his first wife, Mary of Bohun. He had been protector of England during Henry VI's minority, and held the offices of constable of Dover, Warden of the Cinque Ports and chief justice of the forests south of the Trent. He was also King Henry's most fervent opponent as he negotiated away English interests in France. On 18 February 1447, Gloucester was arrested after a dinner held at St Saviour's Hospital and arrangements were set in train for him to be tried for treason in parliament. Five days later he was dead. While the cause of death was probably a stroke, and the fact that he lay unconscious for three days would support such a theory, the circumstances surrounding his death, and especially the timing of it, soon gave rise to rumours that he had been murdered. One chronicle, the *Vitellius A XVI*, offers the following report:

> Some seid he died for sorowe, some seid he was murdred bitwene ij ffedirbeddes; And some seid he was throst into the bowel with an hote brennyng spitte. And when he was founded deed he was laide opyn, that all men myght behold hym ... but no wounde nor tokyn of wounde cowed be persaived upon hym.[10]

Whatever the truth surrounding his death, the removal of the Duke of Gloucester meant that Richard of York now became the nearest male heir to the English throne. Whether this position aroused the jealously of certain members of the court is a matter for speculation. What is certain is that Duke Richard, who had entertained every confidence of being returned to France once again, waited for over a year for his commission that, in the end, he realised was never to come. Instead, the post was given to Edmund Beaufort, Duke of Somerset. York, on the other hand, would take up the lieutenancy of Ireland.

York's appointment to Ireland is sometimes interpreted as a snub to a man who had fallen out of favour with the ruling elite, that it was really a form of exile. On the contrary, while he might have been disappointed not to return to Rouen, his posting to Ireland was perfectly reasonable considering his position there. He had extensive land holdings, inherited long ago from the de Burgh family when Elizabeth de Burgh married Lionel, Duke of Clarence, as well as lands held from his Mortimer ancestors. It gave him the opportunity to provide military service in combination with taking care of his own interests as a great landowner. The appointment brought the Duke near sovereign powers and, since it contained provision for him to appoint a deputy whenever he wished to return to England, it could hardly have been a form of exile.[11]

Still, notwithstanding this incentive to take up his post in Ireland, York, somewhat characteristically, did not leave England straight away but set out for Ireland in July 1449. Four months later, on 21 October 1449, Duchess Cecily gave birth to their third surviving son, George, who would grow up to be the fascinating Duke of Clarence. Cecily, then, was pregnant as she made the crossing over the Irish Sea. The Duke of York used the occasion of his new son's baptism to bring together the two rival Anglo-Irish houses of Butler and FitzGerald. These families were represented respectively by the Earls of Ormond and Desmond. The baptism took place in the church of St Saviour.

Less than a year after this happy event, the family of York returned to England. It was a sudden and unexpected turn of events; the Duke had not even sought the King's position to leave his post. The reasons for the usually unhurried Duke's behaviour in this instance are several and varied. The most immediate cause, however, was almost certainly the return from France of Edmund Beaufort, Duke of Somerset following the loss of Normandy. York was furious with Somerset's conduct and he expressed his anger in no uncertain terms. He thought that Somerset had surrendered Rouen prematurely after showing the minimum of resistance. This went against all the military manuals and chivalric treatises of the period. What was worse, York had retained his captaincy of Rouen and it had been his own officers who were on duty at the time of Somerset's surrender. As captain, York was indentured to hold the town for the King. Somerset's failure to preserve Rouen was, therefore, a matter of personal dishonour for York. This is highly significant in view of the fate of York's own father, Richard, Earl of Cambridge, who had been tried and executed as a traitor for his part in the Southampton Plot against Henry V in 1415. York's anger and utter disgust at Somerset's behaviour compelled him to a confrontation. As he wrote in June 1450, having learnt of the loss of Rouen:

My power cannot stretch to keepe it in the king's obeisance, and verie necessitie will compell me to come into England ... For I have leaver be dead than anie inconvenience should fall therunto by my defaule, for it shall never be chronicled ... that Ireland was lost through my negligence ... For I have example in other places (more pitie it is) for to drede shame.[12]

York left Ireland with every intention of holding Somerset accountable for his actions.

The situation between the Dukes was not improved by the fact that Somerset, as a member of the Beaufort family, could be seen as a rival to York's claims as heir presumptive to the English throne. The usurpation of Henry IV had led to dynastic uncertainty and had disrupted the line of succession as it had been declared by the childless Richard II, who had nominated, in turn, his Mortimer cousin and then his uncle, the first Duke of York, as his heirs, from both of whom Richard of York descended.

It should nevertheless be emphasised that, at this moment in time, York's concern was simply to be recognised as heir presumptive to the throne; it would be another ten years before he would feel compelled to press his right to wear the crown. In spite of this, it appears that there were those who would seek to hasten such a development. Already there were rumours that attempts would be made to depose King Henry and replace him with Richard of York. In March 1450 treasonable discussions were said to have taken place in Ipswich to that effect. Later that summer, the rebel Jack Cade had adopted the name John Mortimer in order to suggest a blood relationship with the Duke. The implications were obvious. One of Cade's demands was that King Henry should 'take abowte hym a nobill persone, the trewe blode of the Reame, that is to say the hye and myghty prince the Duke of Yorke'. Such activity did a disservice to the Duke, not least because the King, with his uncertain hold on both government and reality, believed them. It could have led to York's attainder for treason.

Somerset's claim as heir presumptive also came through his descent from Edward III; in his case, from John of Gaunt, but he was of illegitimate lineage. Gaunt had fathered four children with his mistress, Katharine de Röet, more usually referred to as Katharine Swynford due to her status as the widow of Sir Hugh Swynford. The couple later married and their children were legitimised by Richard II in 1397. Henry IV upheld the legitimacy of the Beauforts, but added the stipulation that they were to be debarred from the succession.

The Beaufort line, their legitimacy notwithstanding, was never intended to inherit the throne of England, but they were too influential to ignore.

The family, currently represented by Edmund, Duke of Somerset, included Richard of York's own wife. Moreover, Edmund of Somerset's niece was Margaret Beaufort. Margaret would become the mother of Henry Tudor, the future King Henry VII.

Interestingly, in this connection, Edmund Beaufort was known to have enjoyed a romantic liaison with Queen Catherine of Valois, the widow of the hero of Agincourt, King Henry V. Naturally the affair was shrouded in obscurity at the time and it remains so today. However, it was about that time, 1427–28, that parliament passed legislation to control the remarriage of dowager queens, and it is highly probable that the romance between Edmund and Catherine was a significant factor behind the drawing up of this Act. In addition, it is believed by some that another result of this liaison was the birth of Edmund Tudor.[13] It is not known when the boy was born, and much rests upon the date of the marriage between Queen Catherine and Owen Tudor. This took place under conditions of absolute secrecy, possibly in order to evade the consequences of violating the Act of 1427-28. If Somerset was the father of Edmund Tudor, it would make him also the grandfather of Henry Tudor and the Tudor dynasty would have descended from Beauforts on both sides.

A man so well connected as Somerset would have every reason to hope that that which had been decreed could just as easily be reversed. In fact, there was no guarantee that Henry VI would continue to uphold the injunction imposed by his grandfather; the restoration of the Beaufort family was by no means impossible. As such, he too had an interest in seeking to establish recognition as heir presumptive to Henry VI.

All this, then, was at stake as Richard of York made his way across the Irish Sea to England. He was anxious for the English possessions in France, for the loss of which he held Somerset personally responsible; he was angry about the personal dishonour that had befallen him as a result of Somerset's actions; he questioned both the motives and the integrity of those who placed themselves closest to the throne and who exerted such a controlling influence over the King; he was afraid of attainder; he was fretful about the debts he had incurred while serving the King; finally, he was concerned that he should be recognised as heir presumptive to the throne, for which position he saw Somerset as his greatest rival. While Somerset was still in France, York could relax somewhat and concentrate on his duties in Ireland. However, the return of Somerset to England left him with no choice but to take action. He left Ireland without seeking royal permission; his need to be close to the King was now a matter of urgency.

Having landed at Beaumaris in Anglesey with a large retinue, York made his way towards his marcher estates, through which he entered England.

He then proceeded to cross the country, advancing towards Westminster. As soon as King Henry was alerted to his movements he sent out a party to seize the Duke. It had already been acknowledged among the courtiers that York was not only in a position to exact retribution on the corrupt but that he was more than willing to do so. They were happy to obey the King's command and a party led by Sir Thomas Stanley was detailed to secure York. Despite such efforts to intercept him, the Duke managed to evade capture.

York presented himself at Westminster a bitter man, complaining that he had been treated like a traitor. However, when he was received by the King he was greeted with grace and good humour, while the Duke showed the appropriate deference and respect to his sovereign. He informed Henry that all he wanted to do was to uphold law and order, to offer his services to the crown and to ensure that those who served themselves rather than the King should be exposed and punished. Government propaganda that claimed the contrary belongs to a later time.

York presented his grievances in two bills, as they were referred to by King Henry, which were then rapidly circulated. In the first, York is on the defensive:

> Please it your highnesse to conceive, that sith my departing out of this your Realm, by your commandement, and being in your service in your land of Ireland, I have bin informed that diverse language, hath bene sayde of me to your moste excellente estate whiche shoulde sounde to my dishonour and reproch, and charge of my person: howe be it that, I aye have bene, and ever will be, your true liegeman and servaunt: and if there be any man that wyll or dare say the contrarie, or charge me otherwise, I beseech your rightwisenesse to call him before your high presence, and I wyll declare me for my discharge as a true Knighte ought to do, and if I doe not, as I doubt not but I shall, I beseech you to punishe me as the poorest man of your lande: And if hee bee founde untrue in his suggestion and information, I beeseech you of your highnesse that he be punished after his desert, in example of all other.[14]

York protests his loyalty to the King in the face of accusations, written and spoken, against his honour. He then goes on to speak of the attempts that were made to prevent his entering England. Men had been placed at Chester, Shrewsbury and at other places with the intent that York should not pass into the kingdom. He then mentions the various acts of treason that had taken place supposedly on his behalf and at his behest, but which had no other purpose than to 'have undone me and myne issue, and corrupted my bloude'. He begs the King to look into these matters and to serve justice on those who were behind them, 'for mine intent is fully to pursue to your high-nesse for conclusion of these maters.' We see, therefore, one of York's main concerns, which is the fear of being branded a traitor and attainted.

In his reply, the King assured York that he recognised his humble obedi-ence 'that yee in your selfe shewe unto us as well in worde as in deede'. He set about explaining that the rumours he had heard concerning the Duke and his supposed intentions to displace him had led the King to send men to restrain the Duke as he attempted to enter England. Moreover, the manner of the Duke's departure from Ireland – suddenly and without permission – seemed to confirm the rumours. As to the traitors, York would be given his chance to prove their guilt, upon which they would be dealt with as the case required. Having calmed the Duke's fears, Henry then declared, 'upon thys for the eating of your hearte in all such matters, we declare, repute, and admitte you as our true faythful subiecte, and as your faythfull cosyn'.

In the second bill, York shifts his stance from personal concerns to draw-ing the King's attention to the 'greate murmer & grudging, is universally in this your realm, in that justice is not duely ministred to such as trespasse & offende against your lawes'. In other words, York speaks of the need to transform justice in such a way that those who had broken the laws of the realm but who had not yet been brought to justice would no longer get away with their crimes. To this end he offers the King his own services in dispens-ing justice. He urges Henry to arrest without bail those indicted of treason 'of what estate, degree or condition soever they be, and them to committe to the Tower of London and to other of your prisons, there to abyde without Bayle' where they should await trial and receive due punishment in accord-ance with the law.

King Henry accepted York's assessment of the justice system and agreed to his request with regard to the punishment of the guilty. He added, how-ever, that custom and expedience dictated that he should continue to be advised by a council, whose members should be all with equal voice, rather than just one man. In view of this, the King sent for his chancellor and other lords who would reply to these great matters. Among other measures taken, York's chamberlain was elected speaker and Somerset was imprisoned in the Tower, but the Duke failed to consolidate his gains. Within a few weeks Somerset was released and life gradually returned to the way it had been before. Those who surrounded the King saw no reason for radical change such as York was proposing. There was to be no 'night of the long knives' at Westminster.

It was just as York's diplomacy was proving unsuccessful that the situ-ation in France began to worsen. Bordeaux, the birthplace of Richard II, had been lost, bringing to an end three hundred years of English presence in Gascony. French troops were advancing to the siege of Calais. York, whose hatred for Somerset increased with each disaster, decided to try a different approach. As the year 1452 dawned, the Duke saw that only way to release the King from Somerset's influence and to ensure that the much needed reforms to the justice system would be carried out would be to resort to armed rebellion. He issued a declaration against Somerset and appealed to his kinsmen and friends for assistance.

Unfortunately for York, neither his kinfolk nor his followers would rally to his cry. An attack on Somerset, so they thought, appeared too much like an attack on the King, and that they could not support. Only the Earl of Devon and Lord Cobham stood with the Duke as he made a stand at Dartford on 1 March 1452. The Duke looked on with dismay as his brother-in-law, the Earl of Salisbury, and the Earl Warwick, his wife's cousin, stood on the opposing side. There was to be no fighting that day. Instead, the King's council proposed negotiations. York agreed and heralds were sent from each side. York responded by demanding the arrest and trial of Somerset for his incompetence in France. This was agreed and the two sides went their separate ways. It was too easy. Later, as York entered the King's tent, he was shocked to find Somerset standing in his usual place by the side of the King.

York had been betrayed. Shamefully, he was forced to ride before the King in the manner of a prisoner as the party made its way back to London. The Duke escaped trial for treason only because such a trial would have exposed the activities of Somerset, thus leading to the condemnation of the King's favourite. The Duchess of York interceded with Queen Marguerite d'Anjou on her husband's behalf, with the two women meeting at the shrine of Our Lady at Walsingham. In a letter written some time afterwards, Cecily thanks the Queen for allowing her to come:

> unto youre moost worthi and moost high presence, where un to than [you pleased] full benignely to receyve my supplicacon to the same, made for your humble, true man and servaunt, my lord my husband, whose infinite sorow, unrest of hert and of wordly comfort, causid of that that he herith him to be estrangied from the grace and benevolent favour of that most christen, most gracious and most mercifull prince, the kyng our soverayn lord, whos maieste roiall my said lord and husbond now and ever, God knoweth, during his lif hath be as true, and as humble, and as obeisant liegeman ... [15]

Cecily's pleas had found a sympathetic response for York was accepted back into favour, but only after being forced to take a humiliating public oath of loyalty to the King. He was made to understand, moreover, that any further misconduct would lead him to a traitor's death. The memory of his own father's fate had taught York the lesson he needed to save himself; he had the good sense to heed this warning and as a consequence he kept out of politics for the next eighteen months. Going back to his estates, he spent time with his family, which had just welcomed another son, Richard. He also became involved in family disputes, the reopening of old wounds. As such, at the onset of King Henry's illness, York was occupied elsewhere. His Nevill kinsmen were once again warring with their age-old enemy, the powerful Percy family of Northumberland. No one could remember when the feud had begun or what had initiated it. The driving force behind it, however, was a continual dispute over property. The holdings over which these great families fought formed a tangled web that covered Cumberland and Yorkshire. Although it had never actually fully abated, there had been uneasy truces. One such 'truce' had been broken when Sir Henry Percy, known as Hotspur, the son of the first Earl of Northumberland, was killed at the battle of Shrewsbury in 1403 as he fought on his father's side in the rebellion against King Henry IV. The rebellion was defeated and the lands of the rebels were forfeited. The Percy honours and several of their holdings passed out of their possession.

Fifty years later the Percies were still bitter about their loses. These included two magnificent manors, Wressle in Yorkshire and Burwell in Lincolnshire. They had eventually been granted to Ralph, Lord Cromwell, an experienced minister with a long record of loyal service to Henry VI. In August 1453, Cromwell's niece and co-heiress, Maude Stanhope married Sir Thomas Nevill. The bride would, in due course, inherit the former Percy manors which, as a result of her marriage to Sir Thomas, would fall into Nevill hands. This was too much for the Percies to tolerate. They attacked the bridal party at Heworth Moor just outside York as it made its way to one of the Nevill's Yorkshire estates. Fortunately for the Nevills, they were attended by a strong force of retainers and the Percies were successfully subdued. The incident, however, led to a reawakening of hostilities.

The two sides faced each other. The Percies: Northumberland and his sons, Poynings and Egremont, and their cousin Lord Clifford, took their stand at Topcliffe in the North Riding of Yorkshire. The Nevills: Salisbury, Warwick, Sir Thomas and Sir John, and their allies, Lord FitzHugh and Lord Scrope of Bolton, assembled four miles away at Sandhutton. Nothing came of the standoff on this particular occasion, but it would not be long before blood was spilled.

Salisbury and Warwick rode south and arrived in London only four days after the confrontation. A meeting was called and it was agreed that the only man who could deal with the crises was Richard, Duke of York. Not unnaturally, York vividly recalled the day some eighteen months previously when Salisbury and Warwick had stood against him at Dartford. He would take some convincing if he were to yield to their requests for assistance. As it happened, circumstances were developing that would allow him to bargain with the Nevills in such a way that would satisfy each side. York's greatest enemy, Edmund Beaufort, Duke of Somerset, had recently been awarded estates in Glamorgan which had previously been held by the Nevills. York would help the Nevills against the Percies if they in turn would assist York in removing Somerset from Glamorgan and also help him to reform the government. With his new-found backing, led by the Earls of Salisbury and Warwick, in place, York once more attempted to claim his position as a senior member of the council.

At some stage, probably at about this time, when he was concerned simply with reforming the government, the Duke of York was presented with a translation of Claudian's the *Consulship of Stilicho*. Here, the people of Rome and other nations urge the celebrated Roman general, Stilicho, to take on the responsibilities of consulship and restore good government to the empire that had been ruined by the corrupt and self-serving advisors of its immature emperor. The parallels between York and Stilicho are all too obvious, not least to the translator, who urged York to 'marke stilicoes life'. For, in a curious foreshadowing of the situation his youngest son would face not too many years hence, York's primary concern, and his main argument in support of his bid for power, was that the weak King was being influenced by those who had their own interests at heart rather than those of the King or the State.

Perhaps inspired by the *Consulship of Stilicho* and heartened by its message, York was at last able to realise his ambition. He and his Nevill allies arrived at the council meeting, where John Mowbray, Duke of Norfolk spoke of the loss of Normandy and Gascony and called for Somerset's impeachment. Two days later Somerset was sent to the Tower, where he would remain for over a year. Significantly, however, he was not formally accused of anything and he would face no trial.

For his part, York might have rid himself of his main rival, but he now had a new and formidable enemy with whom he was forced to contend. Somerset's removal and the king's incapacity had propelled the redoubtable Queen Marguerite d'Anjou to the head of the court party. As with Queen Catherine of Aragon at a later time, Marguerite came from a culture in which women were expected to play a major part in the ruling of the country should circumstances dictate it. In Catherine's case, she was raised and educated with this prospect in mind under the auspices of her mother, Isabella of Castile, a queen in her own right. For Marguerite, the situation was slightly different, but she would still be expected to exercise authority in the event that her husband should be incapacitated or absent. That event had now occurred. Furthermore, Marguerite's position was particularly strong since she had given birth to a son, Edward of Lancaster. The baby prince was only one year younger than the Duke of York's youngest boy, Richard, and he had displaced York in the line of succession. However, the Queen was not entirely secure. The prince might die. Should this happen, York would regain his place as the heir to the throne. Faced with this dilemma, the lords looked to King Henry for signs of recovery:

> the seid Lieutenant [York], and the seid Lordes Spirituelx and Temporelx, were at the Kynges high presence, and in the place where he dyned; and anoon aftir his dyner was doon, the seid matiers were opened and declared by the mouth of the Bishop of Chestre, right conyngly, saddely and wurshipfully, nothyng in substaunce chaunged from the seid instruction, added ne dyminished... And thereupon the seid Bishop of Chestre shewed and decared, howe that the openyng and declaryng of the seid matiers, by th'avis of the Lordes that were sent to Wyndesore, was put uppon hym, howe be it he thought hym self right unable therto; and that he furst opened and shewed to the Kynges Highnesse the 111 first Articles, as it was advised by the Lordes or they went ...[16]

The attempts of the lords to continue government in the face of the King's illness certainly exposes their sense of desperation; but it also reflects their faith that the King would recover his wits and put an end to the dispute that was looming over the leadership of the Council and the government of the country, but their efforts were in vain. As 1453 drew to a close, there was every possibility that the situation would develop into civil war. It was suggested that York should be made protector, but Queen Marguerite did all in her power to prevent it. At the parliament summoned in February 1454, she 'made a bille of five articles, desiryng those articles to be graunted; wherof the first is that she desireth to have the hole reule of this land'[17] in other words, she demanded to be made regent in preference to offering the protectorship to Richard, Duke of York. The potentially explosive state of affairs was defused when York acknowledged the claims of the young prince, who was made Prince of Wales on 15 March 1454. York's willingness and ability to see reason won all but the most radical lords over to his side. They accepted the prospect of a reformed régime led by the Duke. At the same time, Chancellor John Kemp, who had been hostile to the promotion of York, died. As a result, one month later York was made protector and defender or the realm:

> As to this Article, it is advised by the seid Lordes, that the seid Duke shall be chief of the Kinges Councill, and devysed therfor to the seid Duke a name different from other Counsaillours, nought the name of Tutour, Lieutenant, Governour, nor of Regent, nor noo name that shall emporte auctorite of goveraunce of the lande; but the seid name of Protectour and Defensour, the whiche emporteth a personell duete of entendaunce to the actuell defence of this land, aswell ayenst th'enemyes, if eny happe to be, that God forbede, duryng the Kynges pleaser, and so that it be not prejudice to my Lord Prince; and thereupon an Acte to be made by auctorite of this present Parlement.[18]

For his part, the Duke of York:

> reherced unto the seid lordes that he as the kinges true liegman and subgit was by commaundement directed unto him undre the kinges prive seal come hidre to the kinges greet counsail, and wolde with all diligence to his power entende to the same and to all that that sholde or might be to the welfare of the king and of his subgetes, but for asmoche as it soo was that divers persones suche as of longe tyme have been of his counsail have be commaunded afore this tyme by what meanes he watte never to entende upon him but to withdrawe thaim of any counsail to be yeven unto him, the which is to his greet hurte and causeth that he can not procede with suche matiers as he hath to doo in the kinges courtes and ellus where, desired the lordes of the counsail abovesaid that they wolde soo assente and agree that suche as have been of his counsail afore this tyme might frely w'oute any impediment resort unto him and withoute any charge to be leide unto thaim yeve him counsail from tyme to tyme in suche matiers as he hath or shal have to doo. To the which desire alle the lordes abovesaide condescended and agreed as to that thing that was thought unto theim juste and resounable, and fully licenced alle suche persones as he wolde calle to his counsail frely withoute any impediment to entende unto him, and commaunded this to be enacted a monge thactes of the counsaill.[19]

The office of protector is perhaps best defined as that of a chief councillor who was responsible for the defence of the realm against internal rebels and foreign enemies. York used his position to forbid wardens of the Scottish Marches from illegally extending their powers into Yorkshire. Since the Percies were wardens of the East Marches towards Scotland, this act might be seen as a deliberate manoeuvre against that family. It could be construed that York was using his official powers to exact personal revenge in a family feud. On the other hand, by encroaching beyond their territory, the Percies were showing a blatant disregard for royal authority, the very authority that it was York's responsibility, and his long-held wish, to uphold. York was simply doing the job he had been appointed to do.

The Percy family chose to see things differently. Angered by York's pronouncement, they joined forces with Henry Holland, Duke of Exeter. Holland, a former ward of the Duke of York, was, like his former guardian, one of King Henry's closest living relatives. He was descended from Elizabeth, daughter of John of Gaunt, Duke of Lancaster. Such a close blood relationship to the King might have led Exeter to believe that he should have been made protector of England instead of York. Moreover, he, too, was involved in a property dispute with Cromwell. As a result, he was only too pleased to pool his resources with Thomas Percy, Lord Egremont against Duke Richard and Lord Cromwell. However, York's zeal in fulfilling the terms of his protectorship, which included the suppression of rebellion, ensured that Exeter was swiftly dispatched to Pontefract Castle. Egremont came into conflict with Sir Thomas and Sir John Nevill at Stamford Bridge, the scene of the last great victory of Anglo-Saxon England. The Nevills were victorious, capturing Lord Egremont and his brother, Richard Percy. The Nevill family sued Egremont for damages. Having won their case, they were awarded the sum of £11,200, which Egremont, with an annual income of a mere £100, could not pay. In this way, Egremont and his brother were kept out of harm's way in debtor's prison. They would spend the next two years in Newgate. York continued to work for the State with the same assiduity as he had in France and Ireland. He showed himself to be a capable statesman, ensuring also that the lords were consulted and represented as he sought to govern to the best of his ability in what were, after all, the most difficult circumstances.

CHAPTER 3

On the Banks of the Nene, 1454-1455

Richard was only nineteen months old when his father became protector of the realm. The demands of office and the dispute between the Percies and the Nevills meant that the Duke of York could have seen very little of his tiny son. Also at this stage in Richard's life, his elder brothers, Edward and Edmund, were living in their own separate household at their father's castle at Ludlow on the Welsh marches. A letter[1] written to the Duke and signed by both of them, offers some insight into how they passed their time and what things were of interest to them at this stage in their lives. It begins very formally and very respectfully as the brothers praise their father and ask for his blessing. The letter is also interesting for its use of the term 'natural' to mean legitimate; it was only in the next century that the term came to be applied exclusively for illegitimate children:

> Right hiegh and ryght myghty Prince, oure ful redouted and ryght noble lorde and ffadur; as lowely with all oure herts, as we youre trewe and naturell sonnes can or may, we recomaunde us un to your noble grace, humbly besechyng your nobley [noblesse] & worthy ffaderhode daily to geve us your hertely blessyng: thrugh whiche we trust muche the rather to encrees and growe to vertu, and to spede the bettur in all matiers and things that we schall use, occupie, and exercise.

The brothers go on to acknowledge news they have received concerning their father's affairs, wishing him well in matters of business and protection against his enemies:

Ryght high and ryght myghty Prince, our ful redouted lorde and ffadur, we thanke our blessed Lorde not oonly of your honourable conduite, and good spede in all your matiers and besynesse, and of your gracious preuaile ayenst thentent & malice of your evilwillers, but also of the knowledge that hit pleased your nobley to lete us nowe late have of the same by relacion of Syr Watier Duereux knyght, and John Milewatier, squire, and John at Nokes, yoman of your honourable chambur.

They come now to thanking their father for the green gowns he had sent to them, while politely asking for certain other items to be sent:

Also we thonke your noblesse and good ffadurhod of our grene gownes, nowe late sende unto us to our grete comfort; beseching your good lordeschip to remembre our porteux, and that we myght have summe fyne bonetts sende un to us by the next seure messig' [messenger], for necessite so requireth.

The two young men ask their father for bonnets, which they deem necessary to have. Since the letter was written during Easter week, it can be guessed that Ludlow Castle, perched as it is upon a promontory overlooking the Teme was somewhat cold and that the mists that arose from the river permeated into their rooms and added to the general chill. The 'porteux' requested by the two Earls was a breviary containing all the services except marriage.

Edward and Edmund next turn to what was probably the main reason for their writing, the ill-treatment they felt they were receiving from others in their society:

Overe this, ryght noble lord and ffadur, please hit your highnesse to witte that we have charged your servant William Smyth, berer of thees for to declare un to your nobley certayne things on our behalf, namely, concernyng and touching the odieux reule, and demenyng of Richard Crofte and of his brother. Wherefore we beseche your gracious lordschip and full noble ffadurhood to here him in exposicion of the same, and to his relacion to yeve ful feith and credence.

The Richard Crofte and his brother mentioned here are probably the sons of minor gentry who had been placed in the household at Ludlow to be educated alongside the two Earls. The ungrateful pair appear to have been bullying the sons of their benefactor, who were now asking their father to intervene. The letter ends:

Ryght hiegh and ryght myghty Prince, our ful redouted and ryght noble lorde and ffadur, we besche almyghty Jhu [Jesus] yeve yowe a good lyfe and long, with asmuch contenual perfite prosperite, as your princely hert con best desire. Writen at your Castill of Lodelowe on Setursday in the Aster Woke [Easter Week].

The letter is signed, 'your humble sonnes, E. March, and E. Rutland.'

That Edward and Edmund feel that they can write to their father about such apparently trivial matters as gowns and bonnets and the bullying behaviour of their companions shows that the House of York was a close family and that there was much concern for the welfare and happiness of each of its members. The letter is very deferential and its tone formal in parts, but it demonstrates a genuine interest on the part of the two young Earls in their father's affairs and well being and allows us to believe that the family were bound together by mutual ties of affection as much as dynastic interests.

In spite of the absence of his elder brothers, Richard's life was far from empty. He, along with his nearest siblings, George and Margaret, remained with his mother and a large entourage of servants and retainers. Although his father owned several castles, including Ludlow where Edward and Edmund lived, his main home at this time was probably Fotheringhay Castle where he was born.

Fodringeia, as it is given in the Domesday Book, was originally one of the clearings, or 'hays' in the extensive forest of Rockingham. The King's deer were brought here to graze in the lush and fertile meadows that lay along the banks of the river Nene.

The property had been the freehold of Turchill during the time of Edward the Confessor, when it extended some five hundred acres and was valued at £8. In 1086 William the Conqueror granted it to his niece, Judith. Her daughter, Maud, married Simon de St Liz, who built the castle in about 1100. The castle was presented to Edmund of Langley, the first Duke of York by his father, Edward III. He rebuilt the castle, the keep now taking the form of the fetterlock, which Edmund had adopted as his badge, and which subsequently became one of the devices of the House of York.

Duke Edmund's son, Edward, the second Duke of York, founded and endowed the collegiate church at Fotheringhay, and he had been obliged to mortgage a substantial part of his estate to do so. Following his death at Agincourt, his body was brought back to England for burial in the church. The castle formed part of the inheritance of his nephew, Richard, the third Duke of York, in which several of whose children, including the future Richard III, were born.

An account dating from the time of Maria de Valentia describes Fotheringhay as:

> A castle with a certain tower, is built of stone, walled in, embattled, and encompassed with a good moat. Within are one large hall, two chambers, two chapels, a kitchen, a bakehouse, built all of stone; with a porter's lodge and chambers over it, and a drawbridge beneath. Within the castle walls is another place, called the manor; in which are houses and offices, and an outer gate with a room over it. The site of the whole contains ten acres.[2]

Much later in its history, King Henry VIII gave the castle in dowry to Catherine of Aragon. Shortly afterwards it was visited by John Leland, who described it as 'a castle fair, and meatly strong, with very good lodgings in it, defended by double ditches, with a very ancient and strong Keep'.[3]

Sadly, nothing now exists of this once magnificent castle except a large mound, fosses and a large block of stonework. Visitors to the site today will see this block enclosed within a black railing featuring thistles at each corner. Plaques commemorate the two monarchs who are most associated with the castle: Richard III and Mary Queen of Scots. The presence of thistles and the positioning of the plaques, Mary's in the centre, make it clear that this simple monument was erected in honour of the Queen, rather than the King. Richard's plaque is off to one side and the information printed on it shows that it was put in place at the behest of the Richard III Society.

Even nature seems to have set aside Richard at Fotheringhay. The site by which the River Nene idly flows is scattered with clumps of thistles. Their grey-green foliage and purple flowers make an impressive show each year. Tradition has it that they were originally planted in the area of the castle by the ill-fated Queen Mary herself; certainly thistles are not commonly known in this part of the Northamptonshire landscape.

Richard's parents held very strong religious beliefs and their piety marked every aspect of their lives. His father involved himself in several religious causes. He took very seriously his role as patron of the friary of Our Lady of Little Walsingham, an important place of pilgrimage. In 1441 he had alienated a close to the friars, consisting of three acres of land, a garden and a cottage, which lay to the south of the adjoining priory.

Perhaps the most important of Duke Richard's religious projects was the augmentation and re-organisation of the chantry at Fotheringhay. The work had begun under his predecessor, Edward, the second Duke of York, but Edward's death in 1415 led to its suspension. York had secured a yearly pension of 100s in 1432, and this should have ensured the completion of the chantry, which he had intended to be his final resting-place. As it happened, the work would be unfinished at the time of his death and responsibility for it would pass to his son, Edward. The services at Fotheringhay followed the Sarum rite, and two of the saints whose feasts were to be celebrated as doubles were Edmund and Katherine, both of whom would be listed among the favourite saints of York's wife, Cecily, as well as those of his youngest son, Richard.

The Duke of York's religious projects were not confined to Fotheringhay. He granted the chapel of St Mary Magdalen to the hospital of the Holy Trinity, The Virgin Mary and St John the Baptist at Ludlow. The hospital had originally been established as a place of refuge for the poor and infirm. Due to its situation at the entrance to the town, it came to be used as a resting-place for travellers also. The chapel had adopted the Augustinian rule by the late fourteenth century and, with the dawning of the fifteenth, it was in the process of evolving into a small college for priests. Their primary function was to serve as chantry priests performing obits in the hospital church and the chapels of Ludlow. The Duke of York had intended services to be said there for his own soul and that of his Duchess.

Duke Richard was also involved with the Palmers' Guild in partnership with Duchess Cecily. The Palmers' Guild is believed to have been founded in 1284 by Ludlow burgesses who financed it through rent-charges on their property. Their purpose was to endow three chaplains to say prayers for the living and the dead in general and for the honour of the Cross of Christ. By 1393, the prayers were not so generalised and they came to be applied to individual members of the guild. This led to a need for an increased number of chaplains and the extra buildings necessary to accommodate them. The Duke and Duchess of York were listed among those for whom prayers were to be said. The couple were admitted as members of the Palmers' Guild for a fee of £16 13s 4d.

Duchess Cecily, whose piety would in time become almost legendary, shared her husband's interest in the Yorkist collegiate church at Fotheringhay. Aside from the window dedicated to her beloved St Bridget, Cecily's major contribution was the naming of several windows in the nave after the name saints of five of her children, Edmund, Margaret, John, George and Ursula. The window dedicated to a royal Richard might be Richard I, who is known to have been depicted in English glass such as that in the window at St Mary's Hall, Coventry. An alternative suggestion might be Richard II, who was included in the College statutes for daily prayers and masses and who was, of course, an important figure to the Yorkists. Lastly, it might depict Richard, Duke of York, father of Richard Plantagenet. Considering his connection with the church, Duke Richard is the strongest candidate. He, too, has been portrayed elsewhere in glass; a head survives in Cirencester and a stained glass window in Trinity College, Cambridge, shows him full-length, wearing armour and a coronet. Sadly, the windows at Fotheringhay are no longer extant, so no comparisons can be made.

It was on the banks of the Nene, in the great castle that belonged to his father, in the shadow of the beautiful church of Fotheringhay, that Richard took his first, tentative steps into the world. Once weaned, he was fed with solid food softened in the nurse's mouth. A rocker, perhaps two, would help lull him into quiet slumber. One of these might have been his former wet nurse retained to perform other duties for the baby. It is possible that this was Anne of Caux, who was later given a grant for life 'in consideration of her poverty' of 2*ol* per year.[4] Richard would sleep in the dark, since it was feared that light would dazzle his eyes, and he would be left to cry because it was understood to strengthen the body. As soon as he began to crawl he would be followed about to ensure that he came to no harm. It is possible that a child, perhaps the son or daughter of a servant, would perform this service. As he grew, Richard's diet would be based on milky foods. Later he would be given bread, eggs from which the shells and whites had been removed, and apples served cored and peeled.

Richard had a servant to launder his clothes, while a male physician would accompany his nurse at meal times in order to supervise his diet. While it seems that Richard was pampered, and to a large extent he was, he would also be made to become acclimatised to the cold from an early age to harden him for war. As occasion demanded, Richard, George and Margaret would leave Fotheringhay for one of their father's other castles. Richard probably spent a significant amount his time in transit between Fotheringhay, Baynard's Castle, Berkhampstead and Ludlow.

Baynard's Castle was the Duke of York's London town house on the banks of the Thames. Situated just to the south of Old St Paul's, it was built in the thirteenth-century by Robert Fitzwalter, who gave it to the Blackfriars of Chancery Lane in 1278. Having later become a royal property, the castle was rebuilt by Humphrey, Duke of Gloucester, brother to King Henry V.

Berkhampstead had come to the House of York as a gift to Edmund of Langley from his nephew, Richard II. Langley's name was taken from the royal manor in which he was born, King's Langley. This manor lay adjacent to Berkhamptead. The castle would remain in the hands of the House of York until its extinction, at which point it would be returned to the crown. Richard's mother, Cecily, would spend most of her life here following her widowhood; it was at Berkhampstead, therefore, that she made the strict observances of a semi-monastic life. The castle was described by Leland as:

A large, old castle, occupying a rather low position at the foot of a hill. It is surrounded by a moat, into which, as I could see, part of the flow of the nearby river is channelled. I notice several towers and the motte of the keep in the middle ward of the castle, but my impression was that it was largely ruinous.[5]

Ludlow Castle[6] was built by Walter I de Lacy on a natural ridge and defended on three sides by the river Teme. Its function was to act as a military outpost, a stronghold on the Welsh border and a power base for the conquest of Ireland. When de Lacy died in 1085, he left his estates to his son, Roger. Ludlow remained in de Lacy hands until the last male heir died in about 1240 at which point the patrimony was shared between his two daughters. Through marriage it came into the possession of Geoffrey de Geneville, a baron from the Champagne region of France and a distant relation of Eleanor, queen to King Henry III. Since Geoffrey spent much of his time in Ireland, he gave the castle and the surrounding estates to his son, Peter.

It is to Peter that the magnificent range of domestic buildings, the ruins of which are still to be seen within the castle's inner bailey, are attributed. Following the conquest of Wales by Edward I, Ludlow Castle lost its function as a military stronghold and it began a new life as a luxurious palace. When one of Peter's daughters, Joan de Geneville, married Roger Mortimer of Wigmore, the castle became the property of the Mortimer family. Roger Mortimer was one of those who overthrew King Edward II, and he was later created Earl of March, a title that would be bestowed on Richard III's father, his elder brother, Edward, and, briefly, held by himself. However, Roger's ambition was to prove his downfall. He was executed by his rivals in 1330.

The Mortimer family were eventually restored to royal favour and they found themselves once more in a position of power; as had been noted, they were nominated heirs to the crown of Richard II. The last male Mortimer, Edmund, fifth Earl of March, died in 1425 and Ludlow Castle and estates became the property of his sister, Anne Mortimer. Lady Anne passed the possessions on to her son, Richard, Duke of York. Upon the accession of his son, Edward of March as King Edward IV, the castle became crown property.

In whichever of his father's castles he might find himself, Richard would be surrounded by people, for the family employed a large household staff, each assigned their own tasks and some even having servants of their own. Castles were generally safe places to be, especially during outbreaks of plague or other devastating illnesses because the microcosm of castle life provided a sort of quarantine, cocooning those within its walls against the diseases ravaging without.[7]

Richard had access to a regular supply of water, which was provided on each floor, either in 'lavers' or hand basins, or drawn from a well, or supplied by an elaborate series of reservoirs or cisterns. Castles were also well provided with latrines, commonly referred to as garderobes. Their name came from the fact that clothes were often hung in them because the smell was believed to destroy lice and fleas. The garderobes jutted out from the wall allowing both waste and the hay used as toilet paper to drop into the castle moat or directly into the river. Waste water from the kitchens was used to flush out the shafts.

Such precautions went some way to reducing the level of disease within the castle, but could not prevent it altogether. Moreover, as a child, Richard would be susceptible to the childhood ailments that were considered a normal and unavoidable part of growing up. Fevers were 'cured' using a number of methods, one of which was to wrap a spider inside a raison before swallowing it. Freshly baked bread pressed to the lips while still warm was thought to be beneficial against plague, as was a mixture of mustard and garlic. Vinegar mixed with herbs was another favourite. Such a concoction was often used by thieves or looters as they went into the homes of plague victims. It is still known and sold today under the name of 'Four Thieves Vinegar'. The misery of the common cold was eased by a mixture of honey and liquorice.

If Richard cut himself while playing the wound could easily become infected. The danger to life was lessened by the use of various herbs. Boiled hawthorn leaves applied as a poultice would remove small foreign bodies and so reduce the risk of infection. The wound itself might be treated with plants such as mouse-ear, daisies or Solomon's seal.

More scientific approaches to medicine followed the work of Galen, the second-century Greek anatomist and physician. He maintained the ancient teaching that the body contained four humours, blood, yellow bile (or choler), black bile (or melancholy) and phlegm, which had to be kept in balance in order to maintain good health. Very often, the balance was upset leading to illness and bloodletting was the trusted method used to restore it.

Richard's position as the youngest member of his family meant that he was spared the anguish of seeing siblings he had come to know and love die. Only Ursula, who was born when Richard was three years old, would be lost to him. On the whole, Richard's early childhood was probably quite idyllic. The presence of George and Margaret would have ensured that he would never be lonely. On the other hand, he probably knew very little of his two elder brothers, Edward and Edmund at this stage, although Cecily almost certainly told her youngest children about the exploits of their elder brothers, and perhaps even read their letters out to them. The young Richard lived in a small sheltered environment into which the outside world probably rarely penetrated, where he was watched over by nurses, assisted by servants and nurtured by the love of his mother, his sister and his brother. On those rare occasions when events beyond the castle walls did encroach on the life of the youngest Plantagenet, they usually involved his father. One such occasion took place in early 1455, when Richard was only two-and-a half years old. King Henry VI had recovered from his illness as suddenly and completely as he had succumbed eighteen months previously.

CHAPTER 4

A LA GUERRE, 1455-1459

Blessed be God, the Kyng is wel amended, and hath ben syn Crisemesday, and on Seint Jones day comaunded his awmener to rise to Caunterbury with his offryng, and comaunded the secreterie to offer at Seint Edwards.[1]

The recovery of King Henry VI had a profound effect on the daily life of the court and the government. The first thing he did was to surround himself once again with his old favourites. Somerset was released from the Tower; a move that was of great concern to the Duke of York, while the presence of the Percies on the council further threatened his position. The lords of the realm were spilt into two sides. On the one side was the court party augmented by the presence of Somerset and the Percy family; on the other stood York and the Nevills. The Yorkists were by far the weaker side and their power and influence rapidly waned.

Then York, Salisbury and Warwick suddenly left London, apparently without taking formal leave of the King. Their reasons for doing so are unclear, even the chroniclers are divided on the subject. The pro-Yorkist *Benet's Chronicle* states that the Duke of Somerset became involved in a conspiracy to destroy York and his allies, telling the King that York had intended to remove him and rule in his place.[2] The fairly neutral *Chronicon Angliae*, on the other hand, claims that York found the changes made in the council, that is, the restoration of the Duke of Somerset and the creation of Thomas Bourchier Archbishop of Canterbury, unacceptable. It was this that had prompted his departure, with his allies, without permission and without taking formal leave of the King.[3] It is possible, given the climate of hostility that prevailed at court, that they might have decided, even at this early stage, to raise an army to protect their interests militarily. What is certain is that the Yorkists were summoned to a council meeting, which was due to be held at Leicester on 21 May 1455. It is possible that the court intended to put York on trial. On their side, the Yorkists appear to have been firm in their belief that they would be assassinated if they attended the meeting. Instead they gathered together an army and as they began their march south, messengers were sent to the court.

Somerset seems to have been unaware of York's activities at this point. When he found out that York was advancing towards London with a large force, it was already too late for him to begin mustering an army. Ironically, it had always been Somerset's boast that he had a spy in the household of every noble; if that were the case, he had been badly let down. The royal party, with Somerset, Humphrey Stafford, Duke of Buckingham, the Percies and Lord Clifford, set off for St Albans, believing it to be a safer haven than the capital. But for the absence of the Queen, the party resembled a court progress.

Travelling northwards, the royalist faction received a succession of messages from the Yorkists, each of which said roughly the same thing. They affirmed their loyalty to the King. They declared their willingness to set aside all personal quarrels in exchange for being allowed to appoint a council of their own choosing. Ominously, they disclaimed all responsibility for whatever inconveniences that might occur should their requests not be met. As the royal party continued on, another message made it clear just how close the Yorkist forces now were; York's abilities as a general were now becoming obvious. Somerset, on the other hand, had not yet completed the process of mobilisation. The royal army was greatly outnumbered.

In view of the situation that was becoming more threatening by the hour, Somerset advised the King that they should advance no further, but to stand their ground and face the enemy in the open fields instead. The Duke of Buckingham took a more moderate view. He suggested that they advance to St Albans as planned and invite the Duke of York to peaceful negotiations in the convivial setting of the dining room. He pointed out that York was not an unreasonable man and that he had drawn back once before, at Dartford. King Henry weighed up the conflicting advice; fundamentally a man of peace, he opted to follow Buckingham's proposal. The royal party made their way towards the town of St Albans, arriving at about nine o'clock in the morning of 22 May 1455.

The proximity of the Yorkist army was made all too clear when they were found to be encamped in Key Field on the eastern side of the town behind the houses of Holywell Street and St Peter's Street. The royalists set up their headquarters in the market-place. As always before any battle, heralds passed between the two camps as attempts were made to bring the two sides to negotiation rather than to arms. As Buckingham had pointed out, this had worked at Dartford, when York had drawn back. This time, however, the Duke was in no mood for compromise. This time, there would be no betrayal and no humiliation. In a move that revealed the wisdom of Somerset's advice to King Henry, York indicated that unless Somerset was handed over, battle would ensue. The King, supported by Somerset, the Percies, Buckingham and Clifford, refused to give in to these demands. As a consequence, the opening shots of the sporadic struggle that would come to be known as the Wars of the Roses were fired.

The town of St Albans was surrounded by the remains of a Roman wall, but this was no longer of use for defence. Instead, the town relied on a series of well-maintained barricades. These were now manned by Lord Clifford's men. In the event, the barricades proved very effective in keeping the Yorkist army at bay. York was forced to attack in the narrow lanes of the town, exposing his men to Clifford's arrows. After a skirmish lasting an hour, neither side had gained the upper hand. Then the court party was outwitted by a tactical manoeuvre executed by Richard, Earl of Warwick, who led the Yorkist troops through the back gardens of the town and onto the market square. Among the casualties of the assault was the Duke of Somerset, for whom a prophecy that he would die under a castle was fulfilled when he was hacked to death before the Castle Inn. Henry Percy, Earl of Northumberland and Thomas, Lord Clifford were also killed. Posterity must judge whether or not these deaths, which served York's purpose so well, were coincidental. King Henry, who also took part in the fighting, received an arrow wound to the neck and took refuge in a tanner's cottage. York, once he had secured the victory, issued orders that the King should be taken to the more appropriate setting of the nearby abbey.

As soon as the fighting was over, York went to the King and knelt before him. He begged his forgiveness and assured him that he had not intended any harm to come to him; it was his enemies at the court alone whom he had wished to remove. It could be said that Henry showed himself to be gracious in defeat. In fact, he had little choice. He told York that he readily forgave him and then allowed himself to be escorted back to London. Riding in procession, King Henry VI was surrounded by the flower of the Yorkist nobility: York rode at his right hand, Salisbury to his left, while Warwick rode on in front, bearing the sword. The Yorkists had won a decisive victory; the uneasy peace it brought would last four years.

The man whose strategy had paved the way for the Yorkist victory was Richard, sixteenth Earl of Warwick and sixth Earl of Salisbury. Born on 22 November 1428, Warwick had only recently become actively involved in politics. Much of his early adult life had been spent attempting to settle a dispute with his elder half-sisters over the Warwick inheritance. Although he had been made a councillor in 1449, he rarely, if ever, came to court. At Dartford he had rallied to King Henry's side against the Duke of York, in spite of the fact that York was married to Warwick's aunt, Cecily Nevill. However, Warwick preferred to keep away from the court, which continued to be dominated at the time by the Duke of Somerset.

In June 1453 Warwick was spurred into action against Somerset when the Duke seized the lordships of Glamorgan and Mogannwg, which were in the custody of Warwick's brother, George. Warwick occupied the castles of Cardiff and Cowbridge; when the King's commissioners ordered him to surrender them, he refused. The collapse of King Henry in August 1453 provided the perfect opportunity to remove Somerset from his grip over the council and the court. Warwick, anxious to see the back of this enemy, became an early ally of the Duke of York by default. His change of allegiance eventually led him to fight on the Yorkist side in the encounter at St Albans.

Following the victory at St Albans, York once again held the reigns of power. He redistributed offices previously held by Somerset and his friends: York became constable and he bestowed the office of captain of Calais on the Earl of Warwick. A bill passed through parliament asserting that Somerset and two of his friends, Thomas Thorp and William Joseph, were to be held responsible for St Albans. They were accused of having concealed the letters the Yorkists had sent to the King just prior to the outbreak of hostilities, and these were produced and circulated in order to prove that every attempt had been made to secure a peaceful outcome. When the bill became law it granted immunity to those who had fought on the Yorkist side.

As the parliamentary session for 1455 came to a close, Richard of York issued a proclamation that stated that Humphrey, Duke of Gloucester had lived and died a loyal subject. In doing so, he exonerated Gloucester from the 'crime' of becoming involved in a feud with his uncle, Henry Beaufort, bishop of Winchester over French policy. As we have seen, Gloucester had been arrested for treason only to die under mysterious circumstances before he could be brought to trial. York's later support of Duke Humphrey was probably influenced by his own altercation with the Duke of Somerset, which was also partly over French policy. Therefore, the Yorkist faction associated itself with a man who, in the public eye at least, had acted to preserve English interests in France, thus contrasting him markedly with the incompetent Somerset.

When parliament reopened in November 1455, York's primary concern was to secure a second term as protector and defender of the realm. His appointment last time was aided when the long-standing feud between the Nevills and the Percies took on a more aggressive turn in the North Country. This time his nomination was smoothed by rioting in the West Country. The unrest was caused once again by a private conflict, but the fact it had broken out at all was enough to convince parliament that the Duke of York was, as before, the man to suppress such activity.

York's second protectorate would last only three months or so. Henry, who had been too ill even to attend the parliament that saw his power transferred into the hands of the Duke, soon recovered, but this time he retained York and the Nevills on his council. His decision must have been due, at least in part, to York's successful handling of a crisis in Calais. The town was the only English territory in France not to have fallen into the hands of Charles VII.

Notwithstanding his new-found popularity with the King, York found himself once again in conflict with the redoubtable Queen Marguerite. Having found little support for her cause in London, she had taken Prince Edward on a tour of the castles and estates belonging to the duchy of Lancaster and the Earldom of Chester. The pro-Yorkist *English Chronicle* offers a picture of the situation:

> The quene with such as were of her affynyte rewled the reame as her lyked, gaderyng ryches innumerable. The offices of the reme, and specially the erle of Wylshyre tresorere of Engelond for to enryche hymself, peled [fleeced] the pore peple, and disheryted ryghtefulle eyres, and dede meny wronges. The quene was defamed and desclaundered [denounced], that he that was called Prince, was nat hir sone, but a bastard goten in avoutry [adultery]; wherefore she dreding that he shulde nat succede hys fadre in the crowne of Englond, allyed vn to her alle the knyghtes and squyers of Chestreshyre for to haue thyre benyuolence, and helde open householde among theym; and made her sone called Prince yeue a luery of Swannys to alle the gentilmenne of the contre, and to many other thorought the lande; trustyng thorough thayre streynghte to make her sone kyng; makyng pryue menys to some of the lordes of Englond for to styre the kyng that he shulde resygne the croune to hyre sone: but she coude nat bryng her purpose aboute.[4]

John Bocking, writing to John Paston, notes that 'my Lord York is at Sendall [Sandal] stille, and waytith on the Quene and she up on hym'.[5] Queen Marguerite was joined in September by the King over whom she exerted her influence in the creation of new appointments.

Naturally these nominations elevated the queen's friends and supporters to positions of influence and power. Gradually, the court party began to look very much as it had before St Albans. Lord Egremont had escaped from prison and the son of the late Duke of Somerset had succeeded to his father's title. The tide had begun to turn against the House of York, but it was to be a slow process yet. Certain events showed that the power of York and Warwick were still very much needed. One instance of this was when a party of French raiders attacked the Kent coast and sacked Sandwich. The threat of action by York and Warwick was enough to prevent a full invasion. In recognition of this, Warwick was made admiral and keeper of the seas, an appointment that had previously been held by the Duke of Exeter.

The general desire for peace led to some interesting events at this point. York, Salisbury and Warwick promised to endow a chantry at St Albans. Masses were to be said for the souls of those who had fallen in the vicious battle in which blood literally did run in the streets. They also agreed to pay compensation to the Percies and the Cliffords. Most amazing of all, however, was an event that took place at St Paul's on 24 March 1458, and which is generally known as Loveday. The rival parties came together and marched arm-in-arm into the cathedral; Salisbury with Somerset, Warwick with Northumberland, Richard of York with Queen Margeurite. Still, no matter how peaceable the two factions appeared to be, each had come with thousands of men-at-arms who remained not so inconspicuously in the background.

Gradually the uneasy peace began to fragment and, by autumn, the sense of hostility that filled the air was as tangible as the early morning mists. The first to feel the effects of it was the Earl of Warwick, who had returned to his post at Calais. Acting under orders from the Queen, the English exchequer had begun to reduce the amount of money sent to the Earl. In consequence, Warwick found it increasingly difficult to pay the men of the garrison. It was a situation that had once been all too familiar to the Duke of York a few years previously. Still, Warwick decided to take matters into his own hands. He replenished his funds by taking up acts of piracy. Using his own personal fleet of some ten ships, he launched his new career by attacking a Spanish fleet. Six ships were captured and Warwick became emboldened. His next target was the famous Hanseatic Bay fleet, which carried salt from France to the Hansa towns of Northern Germany and the Baltic.

While the English people celebrated the Earl's exploits, the court found them an embarrassment. Queen Margeurite called for Warwick's resignation. If his piracy was not bad enough, his diplomatic activities with the Duke of Burgundy suggested that he was following some Yorkist agenda.

Warwick was summoned to London in October in order to explain himself regarding the Hanseatic fleet incident. While he was in the capital he was attacked by the royal guard. He managed to escape and make his way back to Calais, but his exploits at sea had proved the catalyst for renewed hostilities between the royal party and the House of York.

The Queen ordered a meeting to be held at Coventry. Conspicuously absent from the list of those summoned were the Duke of York, the Earls of Salisbury and Warwick and their allies. No matter. York organised his own meeting, which was to be held at his castle at Ludlow. As the time of the meetings drew near, men from each side began to make their way to the respective venues. Warwick left Calais in the hands of Lord Fauconberg, while Salisbury moved south from his home at Middleham accompanied by his sons, Sir Thomas and Sir John Nevill. Also in his entourage were his retainers, Sir Thomas Harrington, Sir Thomas Parr and Sir John Conyers. As the Yorkists approached the Welsh Marches, the royalists set up patrols to try to intercept them. Warwick managed to reach Ludlow, but his father, Salisbury, was compromised. He managed to evade the royalists but it was due only to the Queen's hesitation that he managed to escape altogether. The two Stanley brothers, Lord Thomas and Sir William, uncertain as to which side they should support, ended up on opposite sides. Lord Thomas hesitatingly offered his support to the Queen, while Sir William, with greater determination, went over to the Yorkist side. When the two parties finally met, at Blore Heath, battle was joined between Salisbury, now backed by Sir William Stanley, and a division of the royal army, the Cheshire forces commanded by Lords Audley and Dudley.

What happened next is shrouded in mystery. The battle that took place at Blore Heath is one of the least documented events in English history. Accounts of it occur in Gregory's Chronicle and in Waurin's *Recueil des croniques*, but neither account is trustworthy in that they are late, in the case of Gregory, or a later interpolation in the case of Waurin. What is known is that both Audley and Dudley were killed and the victory went to Salisbury. Still, it was a hollow victory. Royalist forces, who were continuing to make their way to meet the enemy, captured Sir Thomas and Sir John Nevill. These two men and their ally, Sir Thomas Harrington, spent the next nine months as guests of King Henry behind the walls of Chester Castle.

CHAPTER 5

AN ATTEMPT ON THE
THRONE, 1459-1460

Whatever might be said of the Duke of York's political manoeuvres, he did not allow them to interfere with the education of his youngest son. In the early years Richard's schooling had been the province of his mother who had engaged a governess to supervise her son's learning. The lady chosen for the task was probably the daughter of Sir Edward Cornwall, Baron of Burford, and the widow of Sir Hugh Mortimer, a collateral branch of the House of York.[1] Once he reached the age of reason, Richard was considered ready for the next step in his intellectual development.

It was at about the age of six or seven that a boy would be taken away from his nurses and placed into the care of men, and it is at this time also that his formal education would begin. For some children, especially royal children, this process might begin at an even younger age. Edward V was given a male governor at the age of three, with the hope that 'he may be brought up in virtue and cunning' while his grammar master, John Giles, was engaged three years later.[2]

Richard's elder brothers, Edward and Edmund, probably followed the more conventional path. Whatever their father's pretensions and ambitions, they were not royal princes; at least, they were not legally recognised as such. Even so, it was a very different matter again for Richard, whose position in the family meant that, unlike his two elder brothers, he would not be expected to play a major part in its destiny.

It was not impossible that Richard's father, who was heir presumptive to the throne until the birth of Prince Edward, could have become King of England. In the event, he was still one of the most powerful and significant magnates in the land. That meant that he had properties and titles to preserve and to leave to his heir apparent, Edward. His second son, Edmund, was heir presumptive. As they grew to manhood, with the responsibilities and obligations of marriage and fatherhood, Richard could expect to be passed over in favour of any children Edward, and then Edmund, might have. Too far down in the family line of succession to be of much use, the best the youngest son might expect was marriage to the daughter of a prominent family or a life in the church.

Such a politically ambitious family as the House of York might have been expected to choose the former course, but it was difficult to find a family who were equal to or above them in terms of status or wealth; to marry their son into a family of lower station would be to diminish the House of York and insult their son. However, some evidence exists to allow the speculation that Richard's formal education had initially been directed with his entry into the church as its ultimate goal.

The first indication that young Richard Plantagenet might have been destined for the church, although it is certainly not conclusive, lies in his handwriting. It is rather beautiful and is generally neat and easy to read, in contrast to the almost illegible jottings of many of his peers. Such handwriting reveals a high level of learning and implies that Richard was someone who felt comfortable with scholarship, books and writing. A second indication is that Richard had acquired a good grounding in grammar, such as would be required of a churchman. Third, his ability to read Latin extended beyond that which would be necessary in order merely to follow litany; it exceeds the knowledge of the language that would have been considered sufficient for a layman. Moreover, a recent study of what remains of Richard's library[3] has revealed that many of the books in his collection were in Latin even where editions in English were easily available.

Whatever path he was intended to take, Richard's education was suddenly and violently disrupted. The peace and tranquillity, security and happiness he had known thus far in his boyhood all came to an end as his father's quest for power and influence became more forceful; life took a sudden and frightening turn.

The battle of Blore Heath, Salisbury's victory notwithstanding, had been indecisive; what was worse, it had put the Yorkist faction into an awkward position. From their place of safety at Ludlow, York's primary seat in the Welsh Marches, the leaders composed a letter to King Henry, a manifesto in which they tried to explain their actions. The King was not impressed. The court's reaction was to offer a pardon to all who would lay down their arms. Clearly the Yorkists had no intention of obeying. They set up their artillery on Ludford Bridge and awaited the royal army, who were now approaching

Ludlow. That it was headed by the King in person was significant. The idea of waging war against the King was too much for many to contemplate. York could only watch as, one by one, those peers who had pledged their support to him abandoned his camp for that of the King. This could only have revived the anxious memories of Dartford in the Duke's mind.

York, his sons Edward, Earl of March and Edmund, Earl of Rutland, along with the Earls of Salisbury and Warwick and Lord Clinton, now stood alone. Even the troops the Earl of Warwick had brought over from Calais had abandoned them. Their cause was hopeless. With nothing more to lose, they attempted to bombard the royal party into submission. As night fell, the reality of their situation became all too clear. There was nothing for it but to flee. York and Rutland took refuge in Ireland. Edward and the Nevills fled in a different direction, ending up at Newton Abbot, where they sought shelter in the home of John Dinham, a Devonshire squire. In the morning they used the squire's money to buy a boat to take them to Calais. At Ludlow, Duchess Cecily, her daughter, Margaret, and her two sons, George and Richard, were left to the mercy of the King's forces. What feelings overwhelmed the seven-year-old Richard as he watched his father's enemies advance on the family home can only be imagined. He, his brother and sister and their mother were left to face the royal army as best they could. As one chronicler put it:

> King Harry rode into Ludlow, and spoiled the Town and Castle, where-at he found the Duchess of York with her two young sons [then] children, the one of thirteen years old, the other of ten years old.[4]

In fact, George was ten years old and Richard, as noted, had just turned seven. Another account suggests that the situation was more desperate than this:

> The toune of Ludlow longyng thane to the duk of York, was robbed to the bare walles, and the noble duches of York vnmanly and cruelly was entreted and spoyled.[5]

Entreted can mean entreated with, dealt with or persuaded. Spoyled can mean anything from robbery to rape. Richard had witnessed appalling violence against his mother and, all too aware that his father and elder brothers had left him, he must have feared for his life. As it was, he was made a prisoner of war. Cecily and her three youngest children were taken to Coventry where a parliament was being held. It declared the Duke of York and the other leading Yorkists:

For their traitorous reryng of were [war] ayenst youre seid moost noble persone, at Ludeford afore specified, in the Feldes of the same, in form afore
reherced, be reputed, taken, declared, adjugged, demed and ateynted of High
Treson, as fals traitours and enemyes ayenst youre moost noble persoon.

As a result, they:

And everich of theym, forfaite from theym and their heires...all their Estates,
Honoures and Dignitees, which they or eny of theym hath within this youre
Realme of Englond, and within Wales and Ireland.[6]

Richard of York was attainted. He was no longer in a position to help himself or his family. His property was now in the hands of the King. Once
again, Duchess Cecily went to King Henry and asked him to allow her husband to 'come to hys answere and to be reassayvyd unto hys grace; and the
kynge humbley graunted hyr grace, and to alle hyrs that wold come with
hyr'. Cecily's appeal to the King earned her a royal pardon and an allow-
ance of 1,000 marks (£666 13s 4d) out of the Duke of York's estates to
support herself and her children. The Duchess, her sons and daughter were
then placed into the custody of Cecily's sister, Anne, Duchess of Buckingham
at Tunbridge Castle in Kent, 'and there she was tylle the fylde was done at
Northehampton, and she was kept fulle strayte and many a grete rebuke'.[7]

Tunbridge was one of the hereditary homes of the de Clare Earls of
Gloucester; Edward I had been entertained there by Gilbert de Clare.
Through de Clare's sisters and co-heiresses the patrimony of the House
of Clare had descended to the Beauchamp Earls of Warwick, the Stafford
Dukes of Buckingham, and the Mortimer Earls of March. It was, then, a safe
house and life might even have become sufficiently settled to allow Richard
to resume his education.

In Ireland, York had been busy gathering support. In return for conces-
sions to the Anglo-Irish community, he secured personal protection and the
resources he needed for an armed assault on England. At a conference held
in Waterford, which was attended by the Earl of Warwick, plans for the
invasion were finalised. In June, the Earls of Warwick, Salisbury and March
together with William Nevill, Lord Fauconberg, landed in Kent. They immediately professed their loyalty to King Henry and reiterated York's concerns
over mismanagement within the government and the need for juridicial
reform. They very quickly managed to win support in the South-East and
London before moving on to Northampton, where they engaged the royal
army. This time the Yorkist forces were triumphant. Queen Marguerite

managed to escape, fleeing to the safety of Harlech with her son, Edward, Prince of Wales. The Yorkists submitted to King Henry before taking him back to the capital, where they established a government in his name.

Meanwhile, young Richard had moved on to London, where he continued to live with his mother, his brother, George and his sister, Margaret. The small family probably did not remain at one address for very long, and it seems that they shifted between at least three. It is easy to believe that Baynard's Castle on the Thames was out of bounds to them due to its being an obvious place of refuge for the family and thus a prime target for Lancastrian aggression. Evidence suggests that they stopped for a time at Paston's law-chambers at Temple.[8] A letter written by Christopher Hausson, one of the servants of Sir John Paston, betrays the itinerant nature of the young boy's life at his point. It shows that the family had moved on to Sir John Fastolf's mansion at Southwark, near Tooley Street, opposite the Tower of London.[9]

To the Right Worshipful Sir and Master John Paston at Norwich, be this letter delivered in haste.

Right worschipfull Sir and Maister, I recomaund me un to you. Please you, to wete, the Monday after oure Lady-Day [15 September 1460], there come hider to my maister ys place my Maister Bowser, Sir Harry Ratford, John Clay, and the Harbyger of my Lord of Marche, desyryng that my Lady of York myght lye here untylle the comyng of my Lord of York and hir tw sonnys, my Lorde George and my Lorde Richard, and my Lady Margarete hir dawztyr, whiche y graunt hem, in youre name, to ly here untylle Mychelmas. And she had not ley here but ij. dayes but sche had tydyng of the londyng of my Lord at Chestre. The Tewesday after my Lord sent for hir, that sche shuld come to hym to Harford [Hereford]; and theder sche is gone. And sythe y left here both the sunys and the dowztyr, and the Lord of Marche comyth every day to se them... Wreten at London the xij. day of Octobre. Your owne Servaunt, Christopher Hausson.[10]

Hausson's letter allows a tantalising glimpse into the private life of the House of York at that time. The dating suggests that Richard celebrated his eight birthday at Sir John Falstolf's Southwark mansion. It speaks of the concern shown by Edward of March for the safety and welfare of his younger siblings, and is further testimony to the closeness and affection that existed within the family. Even though his military and political activities kept him occupied, he still made time to visit his brothers and sister. Perhaps he wanted to reassure them with regard to the future. He may have wanted to allow himself to shed, at least for a time, the burden of command. On the other hand, if events were to go the Yorkist way, these children would become princes and princess of the blood. They would become very important people with significant parts to play in any future Yorkist régime, hence their vulnerability to hostility from the Lancastrian army.

For Richard, Edward now became a hero, someone to whom he could look for security, to provide him with a role model, to fill the emptiness left in his life by the absence of his father. His very presence made the eight-year-old feel safe; the kindly Edward, with his sweet smile and his calm, self-assured demeanour, became an idol to his youngest brother; he could do no wrong, he would make the world alright again, a new father-figure until the actual father came back.

That Richard and his family were staying at Sir John Fastolf's house is significant. Fastolf, who is believed by some to have provided the model, with much artistic licence, for Shakespeare's character, Falstaff, was a great friend and ally to the House of York. Born in 1380, he served under Lionel, Duke of Clarence in Ireland and Aquitaine. He saw service at the battle of Agincourt after which he was appointed captain of the Bastille de St Antoine, which he defended during the disturbance following the battle of Baugé in 1421. He held the post of lieutenant of Normandy during 1422 and distinguished himself in the Duke of Bedford's defeat of the Dauphinist-Scottish forces at Verneuil in August 1422. Fastolf was created knight-banneret in 1424 and was admitted into the Order of the Garter two years later. He held the governorship of Le Mans until the autumn of 1427. February 1429 saw him victorious at the Battle of the Herrings, so called because he held back enemy forces by setting up barrels of herrings as a stockade at Rouvrey.

The glory with which Fastolf had covered himself was seriously tainted in the summer of 1429. Lords Talbot and Scales were forced to retreat from Beaugency, at which point the van, captained by Fastolf, managed to evade seizure by means of prudent withdrawal. Talbot, who was captured, later accused Fastolf of cowardice and demanded he step down as a Knight of the Garter. The case carried on until the 1440s and, notwithstanding Fastolf's vindication, his golden reputation was tarnished. Nevertheless, John, Duke of Bedford continued to show confidence in Fastolf, and he gave him several more captaincies.

At some point prior to 1445, John Fastolf came into the service of the Duke of York. However, his association with the House of York ensured that he was denied the respect and recognition that a man of his status and experience should have expected. Yet this did not prevent Fastolf becoming a great landowner. His extensive estates were primarily in the Pays de Caux, although he returned to England occasionally, buying land in Norfolk, especially at Caister, and at Southwark on the Thames. It is at the mansion at Southwark that Richard stayed in 1460 according to Hausson's letter to Sir John Paston.

Here, Richard found himself surrounded by opulence because Fastolf spared no expense in the furnishing of his houses. His standards were high indeed, as was his taste in luxury, but he had the wealth to accommodate them both. One of his most treasured possessions was the 'white rose' collar given to him by the Duke of York as a pledge against a loan. This transaction took place at Fotheringhay Castle in December 1452, two months after York's son, Richard was born. It can only be guessed whether or not this piece was shown to Richard during his time in Fastolf's home. The magnificence of the collar would certainly have enraptured Richard, but that would have been nothing compared to the history of the piece. Richard III is known to have loved gems and jewellery and it might have been the beauty, glamour and associations of this piece that awakened his interest.

Another item belonging to Sir John was a beautifully illustrated book containing the principles of knighthood and chivalry. This book, the *Boke of Noblesse,* had been written by William Worcester in about 1451. Worcester was the secretary, personal attendant and agent of Sir John Fastolf. Its message is clear and precise: Fastolf, who had experienced first-hand the miserable state of the people of Normandy following the expulsion of the English, used Worcester's work as an invitation to his princely acquaintances to emulate their ancestors by seeking to reclaim English territories in France in the interests of the common weal. The recovery of Normandy was, he firmly believed, something that both could and would be achieved. Of course, Richard was certainly not in a position to declare war on France. On the other hand, the implications of Worcester's book were not to be lost on him. Little did he suspect that, at some point in the future, he would have an opportunity to act upon Fastolf's urging – and to experience for himself the bitter disappointment when such ambition was thwarted.

As Richard took his first tentative steps into the world of chivalry and knighthood, the new Yorkist government was in the process of summoning a parliament. Richard's father remained in Ireland until just prior to its meeting, although the reasons for his delay in returning to England remain obscure. As Hausson's letter shows, York had been in contact with Duchess Cecily, whom he had arranged to meet on his return. The Duke landed in North Wales and travelled to Ludlow where he met his Duchess and, together, they made their way towards the capital to arrive at London in early October 1460. Shortly afterwards, at Baynard's Castle by the Thames, the members of the House of York were reunited for the first time for almost a year. It was a wonderful eighth birthday present for Richard.

The parliament had been scheduled for 10 October. York marched into the parliament and pointedly placed his hand on the empty throne. The company stood in stunned silence. Then the Archbishop of Canterbury, Thomas Bourchier, moved forward and asked the Duke if he had come to see the King. The Duke's answer was shocking: 'I do not recall that I know anyone within the kingdom whom it would not befit to come sooner to me and see me rather than I should go and visit him'. [11] It was a declaration of intent: no longer satisfied with asserting his right to the succession and the reformation of the government, York now claimed his right to wear the crown:

> To the which Richard Duc of York, as sonne to Anne, Doughter of Rogier Mortymer Erle of Marche, son and heire to Phelippe, Doughter and heire to Leonell, third goten son of the seid Kyng Edward the third, the right, title, roiail dignite and estate, of the Corones of the Realmes of Englond and of France, and of the Lordship and Land of Irelond, of right, lawe and custume appertayneth and belongeth, afore any issue of the seid John of Gaunt, fourth goten son of the same Kyng Edward. [12]

York's reasoning is straightforward. His claim was by right of inheritance through his Mortimer descent which, although it followed the female line, was superior to that of the king because it originated with the third son of Edward III, Lionel, Duke of Clarence. The claim of Henry VI stemmed from Edward's fourth son, John of Gaunt, Duke of Lancaster, whose son usurped the throne of Richard II to become Henry IV. Thus, the Lancastrian kings were not the legitimate heirs to the thrones of England and France and the lordship of Ireland. Rather the crown belonged to House of York, at the head of which stood Richard of York. Now he was firmly and formally claiming his right.

Quite when York had decided he would make good his claim to the throne is not known. The question might have been discussed and agreed at the meeting in Waterford. This, however, is improbable, given the reaction of York's own supporters. It was not a popular move, not least because they had entered England and had managed to attract popular support precisely because they had asserted their loyalty to King Henry. The matter was discussed by the lords who sent the Earl of March to urge his father to accept a resolution. A compromise was eventually reached, which was then enshrined in an Act of Accord. By the terms of this Act, King Henry VI was to be allowed to remain king for the rest of his life, with York, rather than Edward, Prince of Wales as his heir. At the same time, York swore an oath that he would not:

> Suffre to bee doo, consented, procured or stirred, any thing that may be or sowne to the abriggement of the naturall lyf of Kyng Herry the sixt, or to the hurt or amenusyng of his Reigne or dignite Roiall, by violence or eny other wise, ayenst his fredome and libertee: But that yf any persone or persones, wold doo, presume any thyng to the contrary, I shall with all my power and myght withstande it, and make it to bee withstoude as ferre as my power wull strecche yerunto.[13]

This oath was also taken by York's sons, Edward and Edmund, who were to follow their father in the line of succession. In years to come, Edward, if he remembered it at all, would break this oath in one of the most tragic scenes ever to be played out in the history of medieval monarchy when his victim would be none other than the helpless King Henry VI. For the moment, their father was:

> Entitled, called and reputed from hens forth, verrey and rightfull heire to the Corones, Roiall Estate, Dignite and Lordship abovesaid; and after the decesse of the said Kyng Herry, or when he wull ley from hym the said Corones, Estate, Dignite and Lordship, the said Duc and his heires, shall ymmediatly succede to the said Corones, Roiall Estate, Dignitee and Lordship.[14]

There was more. It now became high treason to speculate upon the death of the Duke of York. His rights as Prince of Wales, Duke of Cornwall and Earl of Chester were established and an annual income of 5,000 marks was granted to him. A further 3,000 marks was awarded to Edward of March, while Edmund of Rutland received 2,000 marks. This arrangement was highly acceptable to York but not to Queen Marguerite, who quickly moved to press her own family's interests.

Marguerite's resistance paved the way for further military action. The ensuing battle took place on 30 December 1460:

> The said Duke of York, incautiously engaged the northern army at Wakefield which was fighting for the king, without waiting to bring up the whole of his own forces; upon which, a charge was made by the enemy on his men, and he was without any mercy or respect mercilessly slain.[15]

The Duke's severed head was adorned with a paper crown in mockery of his claim to the throne and spiked on Micklegate Bar in York, through which kings have, by long tradition, made their triumphal entrance into the city. The seventeen-year-old Edmund, Earl of Rutland was murdered in cold blood as he retreated across the bridge at Wakefield at the battle's end. The Duke's struggle for the throne had come to a terrible, bloody end.

For Richard of York's family the manner of his death, perhaps even more than the fact of it, plunged them into despair. Indeed, it was a tragedy that ought not to have happened. The *Short English Chronicle* notes that:

> The Duke of Yorke, the Erle of Rotland, and the Erle of Salysbury, with mych other pepull, rode northwarde to kepe her Crystmas. And there lay at Wakefelde to stope hem the Duke of Excester, the Duke of Somersett, the Erle of Wildeshire, the Lord Roose, with other lordys and myche other pepull, and so fell upon hem and slowe the Duke of Yorke, the Erle of Rotland, the Erle of Saylsbury ... [16]

The *Short English Chronicle* describes an ambush, in which York, his son and his brother-in-law fall victim to the Lancastrian forces as they make their way to the north in order to celebrate the festive season. However, this is almost certainly not the whole story. Rather, having arrived at York's castle of Sandal, the Duke, Earl Edmund and the Nevills held tight to await reinforcements. Meanwhile, the Lancastrians had garrisoned Pontefract and were amassing a large army in the surrounding area. York was effectively besieged and his supplies, not substantial to begin with, rapidly depleted. The situation was worsened by the fact that it was now Christmas-tide and an armistice had been agreed for the duration of the festive season. The already meagre supplies had to go still further so that York was eventually obliged to send out foraging parties.

It is at this point, when York was at his most vulnerable, that the Lancastrians decided to act. According to Jean de Waurin, the Burgundian chronicler, York was tricked into leaving the security of his castle only to be set upon by the enemy. In another version, related by the *English Chronicle*, York was betrayed by Lord Nevill, brother to the Duke of Westmoreland, who at first offered support to York only to attack him as soon as he had won his trust. The *Register of the Abbot Whathamstede* suggests that the Lancastrians attacked suddenly on the day before the Christmas armistice was due to expire. Whatever the truth of it, and no one knows for certain, the consequences were disastrous for the Yorkists. Richard of York was among those who fell, having been 'slain out of hatred for having claimed the kingdom than anything else'. [17]

York's head was severed from his body and spiked on the Micklegate Bar in York. Shakespeare certainly enjoyed the irony:

> Off with his head and set it on York gates,
> So York may overlook the town of York.[18]

The Duke's ignominious end was shared by Salisbury and several devoted adherents. Edmund, Earl of Rutland was also killed:

> The Earl of Rutland, a youth of seventeen years of age, flying from the sanguinary scene, was overtaken by lord Clifford, who plunged his dagger into his breast, notwithstanding the earnest entreaties of his tutor to spare his life.[19]

Hall's account of Rutland's death emphasises the human tragedy of this horrific incident:

> While this battaill was in fightyng, a prieste called sir Robert Aspall, chappelain and schole master to the yong Earl of Rutland ii. sonne to the above named Duke of Yorke, scace of the age of xii. yeres [in fact, he was seventeen years of age], a fayre gentleman and a maydenlike person, perceivyng the flight was more savegard, than tariyng, bothe for him and his master, secretly conveyed therle out of the felde, by the lord Cliffordes bande, toward the towne, but or he coulde enter into a house, he was by the sayd lord Clifford espied, folowed, and taken, and by reson of his apparell, demaunded what he was. The yong gentelman dismaied, had not a word to speake, but kneled on his knees imploryng mercy, and desiryng grace, both with holding up his handes and making dolorous countenance, for his speache was gone for feare. Save him sayde his Chappelein, for he is a princes sonne, and peradventure may do you good hereafter. With that word, the lord Clifford marked him and sayde: by Gods blode, thy father slew myne, and so wil I do the[e] and all thy kyn, and with that woord, stake the earle to the hart with his dagger, and bad the Chappeleyn bere the erles mother & brother worde what he had done, and sayde.[20]

The young Earl of Rutland, shown in this narrative to be even younger than his true age in order to highlight the horror and pathos of the scene, is so afraid that he is unable to speak. His chaplain urges Clifford to spare the life of the boy, to whom he refers as the son of a prince. That young Rutland was being led to safety as he was cut down makes his death all the more heart-rending; had Sir Robert managed to get the boy away sooner, his life would have been spared. As it was, the vengeful Lord Clifford murdered the young Earl in retaliation for his own father's death.

Yet, if the chroniclers are to be believed, this was not all the horror of which they were capable. Their bloody deeds would affect the House of York in a still more profound manner. Most of the chronicles agree that Richard of York was slain during the fighting. However, a story that arose very soon after the battle of Wakefield offers an alternative and still more harrowing version of events. The account occurs, once again, in the *Register of the Abbot Whethamstede*. This document, which is contemporary to the events it describes, is pro-Yorkist, although it is not uncritical of Richard of York at times. According to this account, York survived the battle only to be captured, at which point:

> They stood him on a little anthill and placed on his head, as if a crown, a vile garland made of reeds, just as the Jews did to the Lord, and bent the knee to him, saying in jest, 'Hail King, without rule. Hail King, without ancestry. Hail leader and prince, with almost no subjects or possessions'. And having said this and various other shameful and dishonourable things to him, at last they cut off his head.[21]

The author is correct to point out the correspondences between the treatment of Duke Richard at the hands of his enemies and that meted out to Christ prior to the crucifixion. Many of the elements are there: the hill, the mocking references to kingship, the crown, here made of reeds rather than thorns, the derision and, finally, the execution itself. In the case of the Duke of York, however, this is almost certainly not what had happened.

As Hall relates the tale, Lord Clifford, having murdered the young Earl of Rutland, then went on to vent his anger on the dead body of the Duke of York. He struck off the corpse's head, 'and set on it a croune of paper, & so fixed it on a pole, & presented it to the Quene.'

A crown had indeed been placed upon York's head but, as Hall notes, it was made of paper, not reeds,[22] and it is difficult to known why, if Whethamstede's account had been accurate, anyone would bother to fashion a paper crown as a replacement for the one made of reeds it already bore. Still, whatever the materials, the crown had served its purpose.

In this particular instance, it is not the historical accuracy of the account that is important. Rather, its significance lies in the fact that it represents the origin of a family mythology that would affect the way in which the then eight-year-old Richard Plantagenet would come to see his father and how he would interpret the nature of kingship. In particular, that mocking crown would haunt him like a half-remembered nightmare, casting its dark shadow over his waking thoughts and troubling his deepest dreams.

It is possible that the deeply mourning Richard, whose own personal faith was at least equal to that of his parents, sat alone with his father's book of hours and contemplated the intensely personal dimension to the Duke's piety. Had he done so, he would have seen that, in addition to the expected prayers to the guardian angel, there were also references to several saints, each of whom appeared to have been selected by the Duke for a specific purpose.

Richard of York's choice of favourite saints is worthy of comment. The first, Edward the Confessor, is an appropriate patron for a man who was descended from kings and who had come to believe himself to be the rightful King of England. St Edward is central to the coronation rite, which takes place within his own abbey of Westminster. The new monarch receives Edward's crown while sitting in Edward's chair. He is given Edward's ruby ring, which was first used by Richard II who then donated it to the shrine for use in future coronations. Newly anointed kings and queens go to Edward's shrine and place the coronation crown upon the altar in offering and homage before changing into the new crown and the robes they will wear to leave the abbey. Edward, of course, was the name given to York's second son. The fascinating and meaningful traditions surrounding the coronation were to be especially significant to the fourth surviving son of York who would become King Richard III.

George is another appropriate saint for a would-be King of England owing to his patronage of England. He is also the patron of soldiers, and as such would appeal to a man of war like Richard. The Duke, as we have seen, named one of his sons, the future Duke of Clarence, after this saint.

St Christopher is traditionally the patron saint of travellers and symbols of his cult were strongly evident along the medieval pilgrim routes. Confraternities dating as far back as the first century invoke Christopher against sudden and unrepentant death, thus the sight of Christopher's icon is said to afford protection against sudden death for the rest of that day. As such, Christopher is an appropriate saint for those who, like Richard of York, were exposed to the danger of sudden death as they go into battle.

This is probably also the reasoning behind York's choice of Barbara as one of his special saints. As the patron saint of armies, Barbara is an obvious patron for a soldier. Like St Christopher, she guards against sudden and unrepentant death.

The presence of St Anthony in the Duke's book of hours is more difficult to explain. Perhaps the reason Richard chose to include a memorial to this saint was simply because he was a popular saint and York was merely following convention. On the other hand, York was involved with several religious houses and Anthony is considered to be the founder of Christian monasticism.

Another Christian founder is Saint Anne, the mother of the Virgin Mary. Her cult, as matriarch of the holy dynasty, was gaining in popularity during the medieval period, as was that of the Three Kings. Like Christopher, the Three Kings were invoked by travellers, and so would have appealed to one who had been obliged to cross water several times in his career. However, their significance for Richard of York probably lay in their association with kingship and the baptism of Christ. The traditional dating of Christ's baptism is 6 January. The Three Kings worshipped Christ and gave him the presents that reflected his status as king (gold), God (frankincense) and doctor (myrrh represents the Kings as doctors of souls, as expressed in the doctrine of resurrection). Later, they were baptised by the Apostle Thomas and later still, consecrated as bishops. The ceremonies of the consecration of a king and that of a bishop are very close. The 6 January was also the date of birth of Richard II, whose nomination of his Mortimer cousins as heirs to his throne provided one of the grounds for Richard of York's claim to the throne. The feast of the Three Kings was, therefore, a special day of commemoration for Richard of York.

York's book of hours contained standard prayers for protection, such as those said at the Elevation of the Host and a devotion to the Seven Words of Christ on the cross. It also featured the Fifteen Oes of St Bridget, so called because each prayer begins with the vocative 'O'. Bridget would play a significant part in the lives of more than one member of the York family, but would be especially important to York's wife, Duchess Cecily.

That many of the saints to whom the Duke of York had appealed were associated with the English royal house in general, and Richard II in particular, suggests that the Duke harboured some feeling that his destiny was divinely driven. Politically, he had come to consider himself the rightful heir to Richard II. As such, the House of Lancaster were mere usurpers, upstarts who must and would be removed from the throne that they had no right to occupy. Perhaps the Duke's youngest boy, Richard, was instilled with the belief, however deeply buried or undeveloped at this point, that his own family, the House of York, were the rightful kings of England. In a child whose piety was as-yet just awakening, this was profound indeed; and at the very least, it gave the young Richard a sense of place in the world.

In the hushed, numbed days following the death of his father, as the winter snows buried the dead and the icy winds whispered to the living, did

Richard silently contemplate the beautiful Yorkist badges with which he was surrounded? For everywhere he looked, during those dark and lonely days, Richard's eyes fell on the badges of the House of York.[23] There was the white rose, a badge of the Mortimers. The white hart had been one of the badges of Richard II, which he had taken from his mother, the Fair Maid of Kent. The ostrich, also associated with Richard II, this time through his first queen, Anne of Bohemia, was thought to have been brought to England from the East by the Crusaders. It was regarded as a symbol of endurance and martial ardour. This resonated with the Yorkist characteristics of pluck and fortitude as they sought to stand up for all that was right. The falcon had been the badge of Edmund of Langley, the first Duke of York, as had the fetter-lock, which had embraced the new-born Richard in the castle keep of Fotheringhay. The falcon encircling a maiden's head came from Conisbrough, the place of birth of the father of the Duke of York; while the white lion was a herald of the Earldom of March. The Earldom of Ulster entitled the family to wear the badge of the black dragon. The right to the badge of a blue boar with tusks and cleis and gold members came to them through their descent from King Edward III, while the honour of Clare entitled the family to the black bull, a badge that would be adopted by George, Duke of Clarence. Each badge anchored Richard with the past and brought his royal lineage to the fore in his youthful mind. For now though, just for a while, they stood simply for forlorn hope and the aching emptiness of loss.

CHAPTER 6

THE SUN IN SPLENDOUR, 1460-1461

In December 1460, Edward, Earl of March was in the Welsh Marches where he had been sent by his father. The Duke had detailed him to raise troops and restrain the activities of the Welsh Lancastrian forces. This was Edward's whereabouts, then, when news of his father's death reached him, probably at Gloucester, where he had spent Christmas, or perhaps at Shrewsbury, as one contemporary historian has it.

The loss of the Duke of York was absolutely devastating, but Edward had no time to grieve. The Queen's army was making its way south towards London, sacking and pillaging as it went. The Croyland Continuator paints a vivid picture of the horror, bloodshed and sacrilege that was committed in the aftermath of the battle of Wakefield. The royalist troops, not satisfied with unlimited murder, rampaged through town and countryside alike as they made their way to London:

> The victors, in their elation, ran amok and 'swept on wards like a whirlwind from the north, and in the impulse of their fury attempted to overrun the whole of England ... Besides the vast quantities of property which they collected outside, they also irreverently rushed, in their unbridled and frantic rage, into churches and the other sanctuaries of God, and most nefariously plundered them of their chalices, books, and vestments, and the unutterable crime! broke open the pixes in which were kept the body of Christ and shook out the sacred elements therefrom. When the priests and the other faithful of Christ in any way offered to make resistance, like so many abandoned wretches they were, they cruelly slaughtered them in the very churches or churchyards.[1]

The Croyland Continuator's aversion to the people of the north is obvious here, as is his shock at the sacrilege committed by the undisciplined army as it made its way south. The people in the path of this devastation were terrified of the 'malice of the Northernmen'. The towns that were most affected were those that had belonged to the Duke of York, such as Grantham and Stamford. As Edward prepared to meet this army, still drunk with victory, news came in from the west that forced him to alter his course. Jasper Tudor, Earl of Pembroke and James, Earl of Wiltshire were marching on Hereford. Therefore:

> thearl of Marche beyng in Shrewesbury, hering the deth of his fadre, desired Assistance & Ayd of the town for tavenge his fadres deth; & fro thense went to Walys, wher, at Candelmasse after, he had A batail at Mortimess Crosse … '[2]

In this manner Edward was brought to a confrontation at Mortimer's Cross close to his late father's castle of Wigmore. This time the victory went to the Yorkists. Edward 'put to flyght the Erle of Pembroke, the Erle of Wylteschyre. And there he toke and slowe of knyghtys and squyers'.[3] Another, Owen Tudor, the former husband of Catherine de Valois and father to the Earl of Pembroke, was beheaded in the market place at Haverfordwest. His head was spiked on the top of the market cross, where a mad woman came to tenderly comb his hair and wash the blood off his face.

According to the Tudor chronicler, Edward Hall, as the Earl of March went into battle he gazed skyward and saw something quite unusual in the sky:

> on Candelmas day in the morning, at whiche tyme the sunne (as some write) appered to the erle of March like iii sunnes, and sodeinly ioined all together in one, and that vpon the sight thereof, he toke suche courage, yt he fiercely set on his enemies.[4]

The sight that had so struck Edward was a parhelion. This meteorological phenomenon occurs when light from the sun or the moon is refracted and reflected by ice crystals in the atmosphere. In this instance, the effect produced an image of three suns in the sky. As Hall notes, Edward drew inspiration from this vision, which he took as a portent of victory. He afterwards incorporated it into his favourite heraldic badge, the Sun in Splendour: 'for the which cause, men imagined, that he gaue the sunne in his full brightnes for his cognisauce or badge.'

A piece of Yorkist propaganda told of how Edward, here styled 'The Rose of Rouen', saved England from the Lancastrian onslaught:

Be-twixt Cristmas and Candelmas, a litel before the Lent.
Alle the lords of the north they wrought by one assent
For to stroy the sowthe cuntre they did alle hur entent
Had not the Rose of Rone be, al Englond had be shent.[5]

Curiously, Edward now appears to have rested on his laurels. For their part, notwithstanding their defeat at Mortimer's Cross, the Lancastrian army had continued to advance. Queen Marguerite and her northern lords backed by a large force then encountered troops led by the Duke of Norfolk and the Earl of Warwick who still had the hapless King Henry in tow. Battle was joined on 17 February in what came to be known as the Second Battle of St Albans. This time, the Lancastrians won the day. King Henry was rescued and the royal forces, lead by Marguerite d'Anjou, advanced towards London.

The situation had now become very dangerous for the House of York. Had Duke Richard not declared his hand and announced his intention to take the throne, the situation might not have been so perilous. As it was, the Queen had every right to expect that the father's ambition had transferred to the sons. In this she was correct. Edward had taken over his father's struggle and had shown himself to be unrelenting in his quest to press the late Duke's right to wear the crown. Should Edward fail, there were still two other sons behind whom Yorkist forces would rally. This meant that Richard and his brother, George, had now become legitimate targets of the royal forces; they were enemies who must be got out of the way in order to preserve the Lancastrian hold on the throne.

Cecily Nevill, Duchess of York knew this all too well. She saw no option but to send her two youngest sons abroad for their own safety.

The duchesse of York modyr unto the fforenamyd Erle of march , fferyng the fforune of that world set ovyr the See hyr ij yonger Sonys George & Rychard unto a towne In Flaundyrs namyd iteryk, where they Restid a whyle.[6]

At only eight years of age, Richard Plantagenet, who was probably still in shock over the events that had overtaken his family, was now to taste the bitter despair of exile.

The place chosen for the refuge of Richard and George was Burgundy, a virtually independent state blessed with enormous resources and wealth. Its Duke, Philip the Good, had supported the English cause during the Hundred Years War and had been an ally of King Henry V. He is probably best known for being responsible for the capture of Joan of Arc, whom he turned over to the English in 1430. However, when English fortunes began to decline,

Philip changed allegiance and sided with France. He negotiated the Treaty of Arras with the French king, Charles VII in 1435, and with the peace he also acquired most of the province of Picardy. Over the next two decades, Philip conquered more lands until his duchy embraced the area covered by present day Belgium and Luxembourg, as well as most of the Netherlands and large areas of northern and eastern France. Duke Philip's court was magnificent and it enjoyed a reputation for being the most fashionable in Europe. In addition, it was famously associated with chivalry, not surprisingly, since it was Philip himself who had instituted the Order of the Golden Fleece. Philip's court was also strongly associated with intellectual pursuits, especially literature and painting.

In fact, Burgundy was home to three courts at this time.[7] One of these, which was based in Brabant and Flanders, was that of Duke Philip the Good. The second was that of Philip's son and heir, Charles the Bold, Count of Charolais. Charles's court was based at The Hague, although he was more usually to be found camping out in some far-flung field with his army. Lastly, there was that of Louis, the dauphin of France, who was living in exiled at Jemappes.

The three courts, although living in close proximity to each other, held widely differing views towards the Yorkists. The dauphin was their strongest champion, but this was mainly because his father, King Charles VII, with whom he delighted to disagree in everything, was a staunch Lancastrian supporter. The dauphin's enthusiasm was countered by Charles the Bold, who resented the influence Louis exercised over Burgundian policy. Consequently, Charles, like the French king, was on the side of the Lancastrians. Older and wiser, or perhaps just more wily, Duke Philip did not commit himself either way. All the same, the presence in his court of the two Yorkist children was something of an embarrassment to the Duke, who installed them at Utrecht and placed them in the care of one of his illegitimate sons, Bishop David.

Richard and George were able to continue their studies under the good bishop's tutelage and they were given what George Buck describes as 'a liberal and princely' education.[8] The Victorian historian, Alfred Owen Legge, goes as far as to say that:

> Had they been permitted to grow to manhood in the polished Court where constitutional law was respected, literature and the fine arts cultivated, and the expiring customs of chivalry cherished, their characters would have been formed upon a higher model than was possible in war-distracted England, and the name of Richard III handed down as the greatest of mediaeval princes.[9]

Legge certainly makes a good point when he notes that Richard's education had been seriously disrupted by the events that had engulfed his family.
Nevertheless, Richard was far from unlearned. Rather, he appears to have
been possessed of a natural capacity to absorb scholarship and was probably capable of teaching himself should the need call for it. At Utrecht the
opportunity to expand his knowledge coupled with a natural curiosity and
superior intellect ensured that this prince would acquit himself very well in
any academic activity. Moreover, although it cannot be said for certain, it
can nevertheless be speculated that Richard and George received the rudi-
ments of chivalric training while at the court of Philip the Good. Indeed, to
be the 'guests' of such a duke and to be surrounded by knights of the Golden
Fleece it would be curious had they not received some level of instruction,
however informal it might have been.

Meanwhile, news of Warwick's defeat at St Albans was the catalyst
Edward of March needed to stir him into action and he set out for London
at the head of a large army.[10] Happily for Edward, London was all too aware
of the atrocities that had been committed by Queen Marguerite's forces as
they made their way south and the people were unwilling to admit them
into the city. News of Edward's imminent arrival further encouraged them
in their resistance.

Edward joined the Earl of Warwick in the Cotswolds, perhaps at Burford
or Chipping Norton. Together they made for the capital, which they reached
on 26 February. Edward's arrival could only be expressed in messianic
terms:

> Lette us walke in a newe wyne yerde, and lette us make us a gay gardon in
> the monythe of Marche with thys fayre whyte ros and herbe, the Erle of
> Marche.[11]

However, all was not well in the garden of March. The recapture by the
Lancastrians of King Henry VI, who had been a passive spectator at the
Second Battle of St Albans, had destroyed the political capital of the Yorkist
régime at a stroke. No longer in possession of the king's person, they lost
all claim to the obedience of his subjects. It would be much better, surely,
to be able to offer the people a different king. It is probably for this reason,
more than any other, that Edward, Earl of March seized the crown in March
1461.

Events now took up their own momentum; the *Great Chronicle of
London* offers an account of Edwards 'election':

In the halle sett In the kyngys see with Seynt Edward Ceptre In hys hand,
where he soo beyng sett and his lordys spirituell & temporell standyng abowth
hym & the halle being ffull of people, anoon afftyr that silence was com-
maundyd, It was there shewid the Rygthfull enherytaunce of this prynce by ij
maner of wayes, as ffirst by the Ryght & Tytle of the duke of york his ffathyr,
And secundaryly by the fforffeture made by kyng Henry, which he commyt-
tid contrary the ordynancys made & stablisshid In the parliament, holdyn at
westmynstre al alhaluyntide last past, In Concideracion whereof It was then
again axid of the people, If they wold have therle of march to be theyr kyng,
And it was answered ye ye ... [12]

King Edward IV's formal justification for his taking the throne, his *Titulus
Regius*, opens with the tracing of his genealogy beginning with Henry III,
down through Edward I, Edward II and on to Edward III. The crown then
passed to Edward III's son, also called Edward, known as the Black Prince.
The Black Prince predeceased his father, thus the crown was inherited by
his surviving son, Richard II. The document then goes on to describe how
Edward III's second son, William of Hatfield, died without issue, but the
third son, Lionel, Duke of Clarence, left a daughter, Philippa. This daughter married Edmund Mortimer, Earl of March, thus providing one of the
foundations for Edward's claim. This claim, of course, had previously been
pressed by Richard of York, and this is also highlighted. Edward's right to
the throne is also claimed through Edmund and Philippa's daughter, Anne,
who married Richard, Earl of Cambridge, a grandson of Edward III. Also
observed is the childless Richard II's nomination of his Mortimer cousins as
his heirs. Edward IV was a Mortimer through his father.

As he presented it, then, King Edward IV's claim rested upon three heads:
his descent from Edward III through the male line; his decent from Edward
III on the female line; and Richard II's nomination of his Mortimer cousins
as his heirs. Having established Edward's right and title, the *Titulus Regius*
relates the history of Richard II's removal by Henry Bolingbroke, who
usurped the throne as King Henry IV. Henry was the son of Edward III's
fourth son, John of Gaunt, Duke of Lancaster. Henceforth, the crown passed
through the usurping Lancastrian line until it was won back by the rightful
heir to the House of York, Edward, Earl of March, now King Edward IV.[13]

Edward IV, rightful King of England and France and Lord of Ireland,
heard a *Te Deum* at St Paul's on 4 March before he made his way to the
Palace of Westminster. Here he took the oath and was invested with the
King's robes and the cap of estate and the sceptre was placed in his hand.
Then, sitting on the marble chair known as the King's Bench, he expounded

his title to the throne. King Edward was then officially acclaimed by the assembled company. He was now in possession of the realm of England. Edward, Earl of March, still only eighteen years old, was now King Edward IV. What he had just undergone had been a sort of investiture into the office of king. His official coronation would come later.

Naturally, not everyone accepted Edward's elevation to kingship. He continued to face opposition from the as-yet undefeated House of Lancaster and their supporters. Under Queen Marguerite, they had returned to the north of England in order to prepare for the next stage of their campaign, the object of which was now to retake the crown. A letter written by Henry VI at this stage reveals his feelings towards the new king:

> ...for as much as we have very knowledg that our great trator, the late Earle of March hath made great assemblies of riotouse and mischeously disposed people; and to stirr and provoke them to draw unto him he hath cried in his proclamations havoc upon all our trew liege people and subiects, thaire wives, children and goods, and is now coming towards us, we therefore pray you and also straitely charge you that anon upon the sight herof, ye, with all such people as ye may make defensible arraied, come unto us in all hast possible wheresoever we shall bee within this our Realme, for to resist the malitious entent and purpose of our said trator ... [14]

The result was a skirmish at Ferrybridge at which the Earl of Warwick received an arrow wound in the leg. The Lancastrian side lost John, Lord Clifford, assumed to be the murderer of Edmund, Earl of Rutland:

> The Lord Clifford either for heat or paine, putting off his gorget, suddenlie with an arrow (as some saie) without an head, was stricken in the throat, and immediately rendred his spirit ... This end had the lord Clifford, which slue the earle of Rutland kneeling on his knees ... ' [15]

The next day, Palm Sunday, 19 March saw the bloodiest battle of the entire civil war: the Battle of Towton. The findings of the Towton Mass Grave Project, carried out on behalf of the North Yorkshire County Council Heritage Unit reveal some gruesome details about the injuries sustained by the fighting men. It was found that many of the victims had sustained injuries that were far in excess of those necessary to cause death. In particular, cuts, chops, incisions and puncture wounds were found, mainly about the heads and faces of the victims. Some bones were detached and evidence that attempts had been made to severe noses and ears was revealed. In the main, the injuries were inflicted after the victim had been rendered helpless, and so were probably sustained at the point of death.[16]

The battle, bloody as it was, and fought amid the biting frost and driving snow of the Yorkshire winter, finally went to the Yorkist army. God had at last smiled on the House of York. The crown of England rested securely in King Edward's hands.

Following the battle the survivors of the two sides scattered. Queen Marguerite, King Henry and their son fled to Scotland. The Earl of Devonshire was hunted down and beheaded. The Earl of Wiltshire was brought to Edward, who by now had moved on to Newcastle. Edward ordered the Earl's execution and the head was sent to London to be displayed on London Bridge.

Edward remained for a while in the north, where he made enquiries about the events surrounding his father's death. Then, as he journeyed south, he stopped off at York and took down his father's head from Micklegate Bar. The remains of the Duke of York and the Earl of Rutland were interred at Pontefract. Once he reached the capital, the new king began to make plans for his coronation. He also recalled his two brothers from exile.

The triple motif of the parhelion proved prophetic, just as Edward had thought it would. Edward had consolidated his right to wear the crown on the third battle of his campaign. His kingship was justified on three heads, descent on two sides from Edward III and nomination of his Mortimer ancestors as his heirs by Richard II. Lastly, the battle that had brought him to the throne would lead to the reunion of the three surviving Plantagenet brothers: Edward, George and Richard.

At Utrecht, the tolerant treatment of Richard and George turned to near reverence as news of Edward's victory reached the court of Duke Philip the Good. The two boys were now princes of the blood, consequently they were shown due consideration and it is reported that they were 'resceyued, cherysshed and honoured' by Duke Philip. In their turn, the new king's supporters were delighted to learn of Philip's favourable reception of the two young princes. 'This pleases them wonderfully', writes Nicholas O'Flanagan, Bishop of Elphin to Francesco Coppino, Bishop of Terni and Legate of the Apostolic See, 'and they believe that there will be great friendship between the Duke and the English by an indissoluble treaty, and that one of these brothers will marry the daughter of Charles'.[17] The daughter in question was Mary of Burgundy, the only daughter of Duke Philips' heir, Charles the Bold, Count of Charolais. While Philip did not desire any such match, he did hope to consolidate his good relations with England. Seeing the presence of the two princes as an opportunity to demonstrate his friendship, he sent for them.

Richard and George were at Sluys on 17 April, from where Master Antonio, physician to Francesco Coppino, wrote to his master:

> The two brothers of King Edward are at Sluys, and are to come here tomorrow or Saturday after dinner. I have been asked by the English to go and accompany them as a mark of respect, although I have not been told, offering myself in your name to do such things as are honourable and lawful.[18]

The princes travelled on to Bruges the next day and their arrival was remarked in a letter written by Prospero Camulio, the Milanese ambassador, to Francesco Sforza, Duke of Milan. The ambassador noted that Richard and George were eleven and twelve years of age respectively.[19] Another contemporary account, that of chronicler Jean de Waurin,[20] gives George's age at this stage as nine years old and Richard's as eight. While this is true of Richard, who would not celebrate his ninth birthday until October 1461, George, by April of that year, was indeed eleven years old, as stated by Master Antonio.

The boys were lodged in the town of Bruges where they were surrounded by officers. Here, Duke Philip did all in his power to honour them, even visiting them at their lodgings upon their arrival. They were fêted and the city held a banquet in their honour. Philip then sent them on to Calais with an escort of palace guards and courtiers.

Richard and George landed in England about 12 June 1461, well in time for Edward's coronation, which had been set for Sunday 28 June. The two princes were to play a prominent part in it. Two days prior to the coronation, they were created Knights of the Bath along with twenty-six others so honoured.

The Order of the Bath is the second highest order of chivalry in England. The name is taken from the ritual washing that formed part of the ceremony, and which was itself inspired by the rite of baptism. Richard, still only eight years old, was placed in a bath and instructed in the rites of the Order by the presiding Lord or knight. The Lord then dipped his hand into the water and made the sign of the cross on Richard's left shoulder, front and back, which he then kissed. Having been dried and clothed Richard was taken to the chapel of St John at the Tower, where he spent the night in vigil, silently praying before a single lighted taper, accompanied by his fellow knights, the governors and a priest.

As dawn broke, Richard went to confession, attended matins and then heard Mass. Next he was ceremonially put to bed for a short sleep before being dressed in a majestic costume. This consisted of a doublet with black hose, a coat of red tartan, or tartarin, a rich cloth, possibly silk, imported from the Orient. The coat was held by a white leather girdle with no buckle. On his head he wore a white coif, and about his shoulders he wore a red tartan mantle trimmed with white ermine and a blaze at the breast. A pair of white gloves knitted with the same blaze motif finished the costume. Ready now for the final rite, he followed behind a young man who carried his spurs and sword as he rode through the Tower courtyard to the royal lodgings. Here Richard was received by the King, at whose command his spurs were fastened onto his heels. Edward himself girded his brother with the sword, kissed him and urged him, 'Be thou a good knight'.

Richard next returned to the chapel, where he offered up his sword and swore before God to uphold the rites of the church. As he left the church, he was accosted by the King's Master Cook, who demanded Richard's spurs as his fee and threatened that if Richard were to do anything contrary to the Order, he would hack the spurs from Richard's feet. Next he was led to dinner although he was not permitted to eat or drink or even to look about him. When finally he was allowed to return to his chamber, he was invested with a blue robe with ermine trim and a blaze of white with gold tassels pinned to the left shoulder and a hood to match the robe. The following day, Sunday 28 June, Richard and the other new Knights of the Bath, all similarly attired, rode from the Tower to Westminster, where they assisted at the coronation of King Edward IV.

The rituals and trappings surrounding the Order of the Bath are replete with symbolism.[21] The presence of the bath itself showed it to be connected with spiritual purification and initiation, while nudity symbolised casting off the sinfulness of the old and being reborn into a new, spiritual life. This concept is also seen in the sign of the cross that was made on Richard's shoulder. In the medieval period the cross of Christ was believed to have been made from the wood of the Tree of Life, which is deeply associated with the fall of humankind and Original Sin. It was, therefore a symbol of redemption, marking Richard's new life of purity. The kiss on Richard's shoulder is symbolic of his entering into fellowship with his fellow knights and a token of good will and good faith.

Of the vestments worn by Richard, the black of the hose represented the death that awaited him as a result of the blood he would be required to shed in the service of the church and his king. The blood itself was symbolised by the red tartan of his coat. The white of the girdle was another symbol of purity, while the girdle itself might represent sovereignty, wisdom and strength. The fact that it was the girdle of the sword, confirms this suggestion, and adds the symbolism of Richard's going out on a journey or mission, representing a stage in life. The buckle is a symbol of self-defence and protection. That Richard's girdle had no buckle might signify his vulnerability and reliance upon outside forces. This would most certainly mean God, as well as the knowledge that right service to the King and the keeping of the rites and ways of the Order would protect him. His clothes were trimmed with ermine, another sign of purity, but also of chastity and innocence. The blaze decoration on Richard's mantle and gloves rehearses the symbolism of purity and transformation. It also represents defence and protection, and the passing from one state to another. Another meaning of the blaze could be death, since it was understood that the soul, often depicted as a flame, left the body at death. The ritual mantle is still another symbol of transformation, referring to Richard's change from a sinful life to one of purity, while gloves represent purity of heart.

Richard's admittance into the Order of the Bath, therefore, was more than a mere ceremony, however solemn, designed to confer knighthood upon him. It marked a major turning point in his life. The symbols of transformation contained within the rite were not merely figurative. They truly represented the metamorphosis that Richard experienced as he left behind his former existence to face the future as a knight.

On 28 June, Edward's coronation day, George was made Duke of Clarence. George, then, was to remain a layman. He would become a great magnate like his father and, until Edward married and produced a son, he would be heir presumptive to the throne. Richard was also to remain a layman, notwithstanding whatever preparation he might previously have undergone for a life as a churchman. Second in line to the throne, he would lead a military life and he would be raised to the dignity worthy of his status. Therefore, Richard Plantagenet KB was created Duke of Gloucester on 1 November 1461. He was nine years old.

CHAPTER 7

RICHARD GLOUCESTER, 1461-1465

When Richard Plantagenet was created duke of Gloucester, he was only the third man in England to have been so honoured. The title, however, had already shown itself to be an unlucky one for its Plantagenet bearers. The first Duke of Gloucester, Thomas of Woodstock, Earl of Buckingham, was uncle to Richard II. He had died in mysterious circumstances at the time that king was actively purging his kingdom of the Lords Appellant. Richard II had issued orders to the Earl of Nottingham to murder Thomas, who was in prison at Calais. The Earl, unable to bring himself to carry out the King's command, instructed one of his valets to do it in his stead. Thomas, who was apparently already seriously ill, was allowed to make his confession to a chaplain before being told to lie on a bed. A feather bed was then placed on top of him and he was suffocated. During the first parliament of Henry IV, John Hall, Nottingham's valet, was charged with the murder and his confession was read out.[1]

The second Duke of Gloucester was Humphrey of Lancaster, the youngest son of Henry, Earl of Derby, who later became King Henry IV. Duke Humphrey had been arrested following a dinner at St Saviour's Hospital, and his death soon afterwards led to speculation that he had been murdered.

Richard, then, was the third Duke of Gloucester - he would always sign himself Richard Gloucester, not Richard of Gloucester. Very little is known of the young Duke's everyday life at this period, although it is possible to reconstruct it to an extent from the evidence available. The accounts of Robin Cousin, keeper of the great wardrobe, suggest that Richard continued to live with his sister, Margaret, and his brother, George, in a household of their own. Their place of residence, which was supervised by the royal household, was the palace of Greenwich, where one of the towers had been especially prepared for their use.

At the time at which Richard lived there, Greenwich was known as Placentia, 'the pleasant palace'. Placentia, with its moat and battlements, was set within 200 acres of land, which today forms Greenwich Park. It was built in 1427 by that great royal builder, the ill-fated Humphrey, the second Duke of Gloucester. In 1445, Duke Humphrey lent the house to Henry VI and Marguerite d'Anjou to use as their honeymoon retreat. The couple took over the palace following the death of the Duke two years later. Marguerite installed terracotta tiles bearing her monogram, glazed the windows and built the landing stage and treasure house.

Richard and George occasionally accompanied their brother, Edward, as he travelled through his kingdom. It appears that they were active in the service of the new king. As early as 13 November 1461, the two young Dukes are listed among those who were given commissions of array, in this case, for the purpose of raising troops for the King's defence against his enemies in Scotland and Henry VI, his queen, Marguerite and their adherents.[2]

One of Robin Cousin's accounts[3] shows that he conveyed items belonging to Richard and George as well as King Edward by pack horse from London to Leicester. However, most of Cousin's expenses arose from the cost of journeys made between London and Greenwich for the purpose of supplying clothes and other items for the two Dukes as the need arose. On one such occasion he brought two gowns of green cloth for 'the lords of Clarence and Gloucester'. The evidence contained within Cousin's account suggests that, by 30 September 1462, Greenwich had become a settled household. Stores were built up, mainly in the form of soft furnishings, such as pillows, bolsters, hooks for carpets, tenterhooks. Two small chests and a standing coffer were brought to the palace, as well as several hundred nails of various sizes and for various uses. Equipment for horses was supplied making the boys less dependent on Edward for transport. George of Clarence was given henxmen, or pages of honour who would act as companions and who would receive their education alongside him. Clearly George had begun his training as a knight. Richard, although he was now almost ten years of age, had not.

No records exist to allow us to insight into Richard's education at this stage of his life. All the same, some idea of his daily routine can be had by looking at the ordinances later laid down by King Edward IV for his own son, Edward, Prince of Wales.[4] The ordinances were probably based upon the routine set out by the King's own parents, and as such would also have been followed by his siblings, including Richard.

According to these ordinances, then, the young Duke would have been awakened at a time convenient to his age and allowed to dress undisturbed by all except those who were deemed necessary to assist him; these would include one or two servants, a chamberlain and a chaplain. He would then attend matins before going on to hear mass in a chapel or closet. On holy days the appropriate divine service would be said and Richard would make an offering at the altar. Sermons would also be said on the usual days and these would be attended by such servants as could be spared.

Richard would then go to breakfast, at which he was probably accompanied by his brother and sister. Following this he would be 'occupied in such vertuous learning as his adge shall now suffice to receave'. It would then be time for dinner, or 'meate'. At a later date, Richard would issue an ordinance of his own, in which he would stipulate that dinner should be served no later than eleven o'clock. During dinner, stories that were considered suitable for a boy of his station would be read out to him. These stories would teach Richard about virtue and honour, cunning, wisdom and acts of worship; just as importantly, they would teach him nothing that might stir him to vice. After dinner it was time for 'disportes and exercyses as behoveth his estate to have experience in'. Evensong would be attended at a convenient hour, following which the children would be served supper. There now followed a period of recreation before Richard was prepared for bed; the curtains would be drawn at about eight o'clock.

Quite what the 'disportes and exercyses' Edward had in mind are not specified. It is possible that there was some martial element introduced into Richard's education at this point, such as horse riding and hunting. On the other hand Richard, brimming with energy as he was, would expend it playing such games as chyrystone mary bone, which used cherrystones with marrow bones as markers or bats. Cobnutte, which was similar to conkers, was popular, as were quaytyng or quoits and kayles, a type of skittles. As he grew, Richard might have played with bows and arrows, perhaps getting into mischief firing arrows over the castle walls. Football was, of course, a communal game and, then as now, it would take only a handful of young boys or men armed with a ball for a game to break out. Palm, a game brought to England from France in the early part of the fifteenth century was a ball game played, as the name suggests, with the flat of the hand. Tennis, very similar to palm in its early form, was also all the rage. In Richard's time tennis was also played with the hand; the racquet would not appear until the sixteenth century. A particularly cruel game mentioned by

Thomas More and possibly known in Richard's day is cokesteel, in which a cockerel is buried up to its neck in the ground and used as a target for missiles. The value of this game from a military perspective would be enough to justify it in Richard's day. Richard might have built miniature castles of his own using tile shards. As winter fell, he could have skated on the frozen Thames, wearing skates complete with sheep-bones for blades. During summer, the river provided him with the opportunity to learn to swim. As an intellectual pursuit, possibly during the recreational period after supper, it is possible that he enjoyed a game of chess, the educational significance of which had already been recognised by the late thirteenth century.

It is highly probable that Richard and George also spent some time in the household of Thomas Bourchier, Archbishop of Canterbury, who was related to the House of York by marriage. Bourchier's brother, Henry, had married Isabel, the sister of the late Richard, Duke of York. In spite of this, Thomas had at first remained a staunch Lancastrian. He was chancellor of England and acted as a mediator during the quarrel between the Dukes of York and Somerset. When Somerset was confined in the Tower during York's first protectorship, Bourchier paved the way for his release upon the King's recovery. Curiously, he managed to retain the Duke of York's confidence even though his attempts at mediation were not always successful, and despite his acceptance of office in King Henry's re-established court. After the first battle of St Albans Bourchier was retained as chancellor, while his brother, Henry, was appointed treasurer. Bourchier made the opening speech to the Lords and Commons on 9 July and prorogued the parliament at the end of the month. When York was reappointed protector, Bourchier announced the royal assent. Still, the Bourchiers' fortunes changed when the focus of power shifted further towards Queen Marguerite's party, although Bourchier did continue his peacemaking efforts between the two sides.

Following the skirmish at Ludford Bridge, which saw the dispersion of the Yorkist leaders, Bourchier, his brother, Henry and their half-brother, the Duke of Buckingham, took an oath of allegiance to Henry VI. Their loyalty would waver, however, when Henry's two sons, Thomas and John, were attainted. This was an indication of their increasing loss of power in the face of the escalating strength of the Queen's party. When the Yorkists regrouped during the summer of 1460 they found Archbishop Thomas on their side.

Whatever his support of the House of York, Thomas remained loyal to King Henry. This highlights the problem faced by the Duke of York when he tried to win men over to his side. While most interpreted his attack on the government as an attack on the King, Thomas Bourchier could see the difference, and his primary aim was to establish peace between the two factions.

In view of this, he greeted York's open declaration of his intention to take the throne with dismay, although he did agree with the compromise that York should be recognised as Henry's heir. It would take the death of the Duke of York at Wakefield and the sight of the victorious Queen Marguerite at the gates of London to persuade Bourchier fully to embrace the Yorkist cause. He accepted that Edward of March should replace Henry as king, and it was he who placed the crown on Edward's head on 28 June 1461.

How long Richard and George lived with Thomas Bourchier is not known. All that can be said is that Thomas was recompensed much later 'because in time past at the king's request he supported the king's brothers the Dukes of Clarence and Gloucester for a long time and at great charges'.[5]

Wherever they found themselves, Richard and George continued their services to the King. Duke Richard's name is included among the witnesses to a charter granting the annexation of the 'township of Southtoundertemouth to the borough of Cliftondertemouth Hardenasse', dated 23 June 1463.[6] Although the names of both Dukes were included on charters such as this, it soon became clear that George of Clarence was asserting his own importance as the elder of the King's two brothers and heir presumptive. His arrogance and sense of superiority soon became obvious to all. At a mass held at Canterbury Cathedral on 27 August 1463, Clarence ordered the sword to be carried before him with the point uppermost. Similar behaviour was witnessed elsewhere. The chronicler John Stone, writing about the arrival of the Dukes at Canterbury, notes 'the lord George Duke of Clarence with his brother'.[7] So overshadowed was Richard by his brother that he was not even mentioned by name.

During the first years that followed his coronation, Edward began to reward those servants who had remained loyal to the House of York and who had offered their assistance to the family. One of these was John Shelton, esquire, who was rewarded for his good service to the King and his brothers.[8] Edward also began to make provision for his brothers. George, Duke of Clarence, as the elder of the two, was given higher priority than Richard Gloucester. Consequently, the King endowed his heir with extensive estates in the north of England that had been confiscated from the Percy family. George also received the honour of Richmond in Yorkshire. To these were added other confiscated estates south of the Humber, in the West Country and the midlands. In time, he would receive the lordship of the county of Chester, which normally formed part of the appanage of the Prince of Wales. By 1466 George was being appointed to commissions of the peace in eighteen counties, most of which were in the south-west and south-central England. In the following year his lands were valued at 5,000 marks.

In this big giveaway, Richard Gloucester was also granted great estates. The Paston Letters hint that Richard might receive possession of Caister,[9] although nothing seems to have come of this. He was given the manor and lordship of Kingston Lacy in Dorset and the lordships of Richmond in Yorkshire and Pembroke in Wales. Edward awarded him lands forfeited from the De Vere Earls of Oxford in Essex, Suffolk and Cambridge. On 12 August Richard 'and the heirs of his body' were granted the castle of Gloucester and the fee farm of the town of Gloucester, and he was appointed to the office of constable of Corfe Castle.[10] On his tenth birthday, 2 October 1462, Richard was given the post of Admiral of England, Ireland and Aquitaine. In March 1464, Richard and George received life grants 'that they may have all their charters, letters patent and writs in Chancery and all other courts quit of fee or fine'.[11] Two months later, Richard was given a commission of array in the counties of Gloucester, Worcester, Warwick, Wiltshire, Somerset, Dorset, Devon, Cornwall and Salop.[12]

On paper, Richard's endowments appear lucrative and generous. In practice, they were far from it. Moreover, Clarence was jealous of Gloucester's lordship of Richmond, so Edward took it back and awarded it to Clarence instead. The Lordship of Pembroke, although nominally held by Gloucester, remained under the control of William, Lord Herbert. By January 1464 the De Vere estates had been restored to John, thirteenth Earl of Oxford. Edward giveth and Edward taketh away.

Still, Edward compensated his little brother for his loss of Richmond by awarding him, on 9 November 1462, all the forfeited estates of Robert, Lord Hungerford and Moleyns and the lordship of Chirk Castle in the Welsh Marches. However, by the suppression or muddling of certain information, Moleyns's grandmother, Margaret, was able to convince King Edward that her husband had enfeoffed all his lands so that she might pay off his debts. These included debts incurred as a result of his capture at Castillon in 1453; the ransom and other expenses amounted to £9,961. The widow's petition to the King was kindly received and, six months after it had been awarded to Richard, the Hungerford grant was cancelled also. When, in 1468, the Hungerford lands would once again be settled on Richard, he would find that many of them had already been given over to trustees in order to repay the great debts incurred by the ransom of Robert Hungerford from the French. In the end, Richard was given the newly-forfeited estates of Henry Beaufort, Duke of Somerset. Unfortunately, these lands were poorly endowed. Richard had to make do with an income of some £500 per annum, which was considerably below the income enjoyed by his brother, George of Clarence.

Edward had catered for the needs of his brothers, albeit somewhat unfairly. He had yet to confirm his position in the succession and to justify his position as king. Moreover, although George, Duke of Clarence was his heir presumptive, it was more desirable to have an heir apparent, a son to whom Edward could pass on a throne made secure by birthright and lineage.

The first problem was easily overcome by resorting to myth. Edward invoked the *Prophecy of the Eagle*, a work that was influenced by Geoffrey of Monmouth's *Historia regum Britannia*. In it, an angelic prophecy made to Cadwallader spoke of the promise of the defeat of the Saxon enemy and the restoration of the Britons. For Edward, the Yorkists fitted easily into the role of the returning Britons, while the Lancastrians could be cast as the usurping Saxons. Now the Britons, represented by the House of York, the true heirs of Cadwallader, had fulfilled the ancient prophecy and right kingship had been restored.

Still, this did not entirely solve Edward's problem. His claim to the throne came through the female line. According to an edict issed in 1376 by King Edward III, the crown could be passed only through the male line. A woman could inherit the crown, but only so that she could pass it on to her husband. Edward overcame this by appealing to the story of the daughters of Zelophehad, which is related in Numbers 27. Zelophehad died in the wilderness leaving no sons. His possessions should have gone to his daughters who, having discovered that they would not be allowed to inherit, took their case to Moses. They asked why the name of their father should be taken away from his family simply because he had no son. They then asked Moses to give them a possession among their father's brethren. Moses consulted the Lord, who judged in favour of the daughters. They were to be granted their father's inheritance: 'If a man dies, and he has no son, then you shall cause his inheritance to pass to his daughter.' Inspired by this story, King Edward IV used it to consolidate his right to the throne. The line of succession from Edward III through Lionel, Duke of Clarence and his daughter, Philippa, that is, through the female line, was lawful and binding under an edict that came directly from God.

A roll upon which all the events leading up to Edward's accession are illustrated, depicts Reason who stops the Wheel of Fortune by driving a spoke into it. Edward, the 'eternal King of England' sits at the top of the wheel. Another roll contains an image of God's right hand pointing to Edward in an obvious attempt to demonstrate that his accession was achieved by divine will. The accompanying legends give the proof: 'This was done by the Lord' and 'If God is for us who will be against us?'[13] Edward's kingship was the Lord's doing, and it was marvellous in the eyes of the House of York.

For Richard Gloucester, the son of one who should have been king and the brother of an anointed king, there was great comfort in the certainty that destiny was guiding the course of the journey his family was to take. For him, Edward was the realisation of the angelic prophecy that foretold the return of the righteous, sacred king. For Edward, king-by-right and the first sovereign of the House of York, there remained a sense of urgency to found a dynasty and to maintain the hold of the white rose on the throne, and for that he had to marry.

The legality, or otherwise, of King Edward's marriage would become of vital importance in the weeks following his death. A revelation would be made at some point in the early summer of 1483 which would have a profound affect on the course Richard would take. It is not an exaggeration to say that what Richard would learn at that time would change the course of English history. Be that as it may, as the summer of 1466 unfolded, King Edward IV undertook to fulfil one of the most important aspects of royal duty: he took a wife with whom, he hoped, he would produce heirs. The facts of Edward's marriage appear, at least on this instant, quite clear, although far from uncontroversial.

Edward's want of a bride had already been the subject of discussion. *Gregory's Chronicle* reflects this as it remarks that 'men mervelyd that oure soverayne lorde was so longe with owte any wyffe, and were evyr ferde that he had be not chaste in hys levynge.'[14] Edward's marriage, not unnaturally, had become a matter of interest, as had his sex life in general. 'Edward', notes Dominic Mancini, 'on taking possession of the kingdom behaved for a while in all things too dissolutely.'[15] Perhaps this should be of no surprise. The young King Edward IV was a handsome man, tall and blessed with a fine figure. As Thomas More puts it, Edward was 'of visage louelye [lovely], of bodye myghtie, stronge, and clean made'.[16]

More was born in 1477 or 1478 – even his father was unsure of the exact date – and so could have been only five or six years old when Edward died in 1483. It is not impossible that the future chancellor saw the King into whose England he had been born. If he did, he could not fail to have been struck by Edward's magnificent height. Of course, by that time, Edward's life of indulgence and debauchery had taken its toll on his legendary beauty. Nevertheless, More would have spoken to those who remembered the late king in his prime and so was able to offer a fair description of him as he had appeared in his glorious youth.

Nor was More exaggerating in order to heighten the comparison between Edward and his younger brother. Vergil says of the King: 'King Edward was very taule of parsonage, excedinge the stature almost of all others, of coomly vysage, pleasant looke, brode brestyd, the resyduw even to his fete proportionably correspondent ... '[17] Mancini notes that Edward's beauty was the source of great vanity: 'He was wont to show himself to those who wished to watch him, and he seized any opportunity that the occasion offered of revealing his fine stature more protractedly and more evidently to on-lookers.'[18] Edward could have the pick of the ladies of his kingdom, and his subsequent behaviour showed that he indulged his lustful desires. Still, whatever his looks, Edward was in want of a wife, not merely to satisfy his need for companionship, to keep him from sin, or even to flatter his vanity. As a king, his marriage would be expected to serve political ends as well as to provide sons to whom he would leave the kingdom.

The matter of Edward's marriage had first been addressed many years previously, long before he became king. Even while he was still only three years of age, the high aspirations of his father were reflected at every turn as he discussed the matter with King Charles VII of France. The question was next raised in 1452 and again in 1455. On each of these occasions the prospective bride was a daughter of Jean, Duke d'Alençon. Again, nothing was to become of the negotiations.

Upon Edward's accession, the matter of finding a suitable queen became more pressing. An alliance with Burgundy was proposed. This would have united Edward with the beautiful Mademoiselle de Bourbon, one of Duke Philip's nieces and sister-in-law to the Duke's heir, Charles, count of Charolais. The proposal fell through due to Duke Philip's reluctance to form an alliance to so new and, as yet, insecure a dynasty. Other prospective brides included Mary of Guelders, the Scottish regent; then negotiations for Mademoiselle de Bourbon were opened once again; a match with Isabella of Castile offered another possibility. Edward, however, appears to have taken the matter into his own hands. According to Polydore Vergil:

> [Edward IV] sent Richard Earl of Warwick, ambassador into France to demand in marriage a young lady called Bona of Savoy, sister to Charlotte, Queen of France, and daughter of Louis, Duke of Savoy.[19]

The Earl took on his mission wholeheartedly, since he was ardently in favour of Edward forming stronger ties with France. Such ties, which Warwick hoped would secure peace and prosperity between the two nations, would be cemented by the proposed marriage. Still, whatever Edward's political intentions, they were quickly swept aside when his heart was suddenly and hopelessly captured by a young and beautiful widow who had brought a suit to the King concerning lands given to her by her late husband in jointure;

her name was Elizabeth Grey, née Wydeville. As the Croyland Continuator tells it, King Edward:

> Prompted by the ardour of youth and relying entirely on his own choice, without consulting the nobles of the kingdom, privately married the widow of a certain knight, Elizabeth by name; who, though she had only a knight for a father, had a duchess for a mother.[20]

Holinshead offers a pen-portrait of the lady who had 'so kindled the kings affection towards hir, that he not onelie favoured hir suite, but more hir person:

> For she was a woman of a more formall countenance than of escellent beautie; and yet both of such beautie and favour, that with hir sober demeanour, sweet looks, and comelie smiling (neither too wanton, nor too bashfull) besides hir pleasant toong and trim wit, she so alured and made subject unto hir the heart of that great prince, that after she denied him to be his paramour, with so good maner, and words to well set as better could not be disguised; he finallie resolved himself to marrie hir, not asking counsel of anie man, till they might perceive it was no bootie to advise him to the contrarie of that his concluded purpose ... [21]

Elizabeth, like Anne Boleyn nearly seventy years later, refused to give in to the King's advances unless he made her queen. The charming widow's refusal drove Edward wild. No woman had ever refused him before; he was simply confounded.

Edward was not the only one to be confounded. His courtiers were quite dismayed at his choice of bride. Quite simply, there was no political capital to be made out of a marriage with Elizabeth Wydeville. Indeed, she was considered to be a most unsuitable bride for the King. For one thing, she was a commoner, as Croyland points out. A descendant of Simon de Montfort, Elizabeth was some five years older than Edward, an impoverished widow, and the mother of two sons, Thomas and Richard. Furthermore, she had strong Lancastrian links. Her late husband was Lord John Grey, who had died fighting on Henry VI's side at St Albans. Her father was Richard Wydeville, Lord Rivers and her mother Jacquetta of Luxembourg, the widow of John of Lancaster, Duke of Bedford. Both her father and brother, Anthony, Earl Rivers and Lord Scales, had fought against Edward IV at Towton. Lastly, Elizabeth was English; Edward was expected to marry abroad for political and diplomatic purposes and to bring in a large dowry with which he might revive the royal coffers.

The rationale behind Edward's marriage to Elizabeth can be expressed by one work only: lust. Mancini tells of how Edward 'pursued with no discrimination the married and unmarried the noble and the lowly'. Elizabeth, as we have seen, was a widow and, while she could certainly not be considered lowly, she was not Edward's social equal, not being of royal blood.

Mancini goes on to relate the story of how the King was attracted by Elizabeth's 'beauty of person and charm of manner'. Yet, try as he might, Edward 'could not corrupt her virtue by gifts or menaces'. Mancini continues, 'The story runs that when Edward placed a dagger at her throat, to make her submit to his passion, she remained unperturbed and determined to die rather than live unchastely with the king.'[22]

Here, Mancini contradicts himself. In a later passage, he claims that Edward 'took none by force'. With Elizabeth, however, this was apparently not the case. Edward seems to have tried to threaten her into submission, but still, the lady refused. Edward's remedy for such obstinacy, as Mancini asserts, was to overcome the woman 'by money and promises'. Did Edward, then, avail himself of a ruse employed by many a young and handsome man on the rare occasion that he was turned down by a woman and promise Elizabeth marriage if she slept with him? Then, having allowed him to have his way with her, did Elizabeth hold Edward to his promise? Perhaps the marriage was a shotgun affair, with Elizabeth telling Edward that she was carrying his baby, a pregnancy that mysteriously disappeared once the nuptials had been celebrated. This seems improbable if the account by Robert Fabyan is to be believed:

> King Edward espoused Elizabeth, late the wife of Sir John Grey ... which spousals were solemnized early in the morning at a town named Grafton, near Stony Stratford; at which marriage were no persons present but the spouse, the spouses, the Duchess of Bedford her mother, the priest, two gentlewomen, and a young man to help the priest sing. After which spousals ended, he went to bed, and so tarried there three or four hours, and after departed and rode again to Stony Stratford, and came as though he had been hunting, and there went to bed again. And within a day or two, he sent to Grafton to the Lord Rivers, father unto his wife, showing him that he would come and lodge with him a certain season, where he was received with all honour, and so tarried there by the space of four days. In which season, she nightly to his bed was brought in so secret manner that almost none but her mother was of counsel.[23]

It can readily be seen that the unsuitability of his wife was not lost to the King. Knowing that Elizabeth would not be accepted by the court and the

higher nobility, he married her in a clandestine ceremony that was nevertheless conducted by a priest, and was attended by the bride's mother and a few
other witnesses.

Although the wedding took place during the early hours of 1 May
1464, the King's Council was not informed of it until later that autumn.
Contemporary chronicles speak of the shock with which the Wydeville marriage was greeted. According to Jean de Waurin,[24] the King's council told
him outright that Elizabeth was not his match and that, however good and
beautiful she might be, he must be aware that she was not a suitable wife for
so high a prince as himself. Years later, Isabella of Castille would remember
the slight, instructing her ambassador to advise King Richard III:

> That the Quene of Castelle was turned in hure hart fro England in tyme past for
> the unkyndenes the whiche she toke against the king last decessed whom god
> pardone for his refusing of here and taking to his wiff a wedowe of England.[25]

How different things might have been if Edward had married Isabella of
Castile. She would never have married Ferdinand of Aragon, there would
have been no Catherine of Aragon, no Mary Tudor, indeed, there might have
been no Tudor dynasty. England might have remained a Catholic county.

Then there was the reaction of Edward's mother, Duchess Cecily, to the
marriage. Mancini reports of her fury upon hearing the news:

> On that account not only did he alienate the nobles with whom he afterwards
> waged war, but he also offended most bitterly the members of his own house.
> Even his mother fell into such a frenzy, that she offered to submit to a public
> inquiry, and asserted that Edward was not the offspring of her husband the
> Duke of York, but was conceived in adultery, and therefore in no wise worthy
> of the honour of kingship.[26]

Cecily's words are harsh indeed and they are clear evidence that the Duchess
was highly displeased with her son's rashness in marrying such an unsuitable
lady as Elizabeth Wydeville. However, if this report is true, it does not necessarily follow that Cecily was admitting to an adulterous affair and that the
King was illegitimate. They could easily have been words spoken in anger,
with no other purpose than to hurt the King and to seek to explain his behaviour by dissociating him from the honourable Duke of York. Whatever, the
case, the fact that they had been spoken at all would return to haunt Edward.
The Earl of Warwick, the Duke of Clarence, and then even Edward's loyal
and loving brother, Richard, would make good use of them in their turn.

According to Thomas More, writing some fifty years after the event, Cecily confronted Edward directly with her displeasure. After much altercation, he said to her,

> That she is a widow and hath alredy children, by gods blessed Ladye, I am a
> bacheler and haue some too; and so eche of vs hath a profe that neither of vs is
> lyke to be barain [barren].[27]

More's story is apocryphal, but it does highlight the fact of Edward's known promiscuity and that he had fathered several illegitimate children although, More's assertion aside, he does not appear to have acknowledged any of them. Mancini, furthering the story of Edward's marriage, notes that the Duke of Clarence:

> Vented his wrath more conspicuously, by his bitter and public denunciation
> of Elizabeth's obscure family; and by proclaiming that the king, who ought to
> have married a virgin wife, had married a widow in violation of established
> custom.[28]

Of Richard's response, Mancini states that 'the Duke of Gloucester, being better at concealing his thoughts and besides younger and therefore less influential, neither did nor said anything that could be brought against him.'

It is important to bear in mind that Mancini had never met nor even seen Richard, and that any intelligence he had of him came from those who were, in all probability, as unacquainted with the Duke as Mancini was. Furthermore, he is writing with hindsight of an event that would become highly significant in time to come in much the same way as he makes much of a perceived enmity between Richard and the Wydeville family, This, too, would become apparent only after the death of King Edward. Certainly, the late king's marriage to Elizabeth would provide one of the means by which Richard would later justify his accession to the throne. At the time of the marriage, however, Richard was not yet twelve years old. To take Mancini's assessment of his reaction at face value is to read it in consideration of other, much later, events.

On the other hand, although he was young, Richard would not have been unaware of the consequences of Edward's marriage and was perhaps puzzled by his brother's choice of bride. On the other hand, like many young boys, he probably trusted the judgement of his older brother; Edward was an adult, he was king and he must have known what he was doing. There is nothing to say that Richard would not have been pleased. At this point in time, however, his opinion can have been of little consequence. Richard, as Mancini correctly points out, had precious little influence with the King or anyone else at this stage of his life.

There was one who perhaps had more cause than most to be disappointed with Edward's behaviour in the matter of his marriage, however, and that was Richard, Earl of Warwick. The Earl had been in Scotland negotiating an alliance between Edward and 'the relict of the late King of Scotland'. As *Warkworth's Chronicle* notes: ' … when the Earl of Warwick came home and heard this, then was he greatly displeased with the king; and after that rose great dissension ever more and more between the king and him … '[29]

It is acceptable to assert that Edward's marriage, and especially the clandestine manner in which it was contracted, was a major factor in the disillusionment that developed between the King and the Earl. For the moment, however, whatever differences existed between the two men were kept under control. Indeed, Warwick was among those who escorted the new queen into the chapel of Reading abbey, where she was openly honoured. Moreover, whatever animosity was brewing between Edward and his powerful cousin, it was not allowed to interfere with another important matter with which the King was concerned: the much interrupted education of Duke Richard.

King Edward made arrangements with Warwick for Richard to go to the Earl's home at Middleham in North Yorkshire. It would be strange indeed to think that Edward should have entrusted the young Duke to the care of Warwick had he thought that the Earl had become an enemy, or even that any attempt might be made to lead Duke Richard astray. As it was, Richard, who had recently celebrated his thirteenth birthday, left for the north in the autumn of 1465. Here, at the palatial Middleham Castle in the heart of the Yorkshire Dales, under the watchful eye of the Kingmaker himself, Richard Gloucester would learn the ways of a knight.

CHAPTER 8

A PAGE AT MIDDLEHAM, 1465-1466

The term 'chivalry', as it was defined in Richard's time, referred simply to knighthood, horse-soldiery or cavalry. It was the collective term for mounted, fully-armed fighting men. It stood also for the position and character of a knight: bravery, prowess in war, to be warlike, proficient in the military arts, practised in arms and martial achievements. It is only as recently as the late eighteenth century that 'chivalry' came to be applied to honourable and courteous behaviour; still later, in the early nineteenth century, it might be used to refer to a gallant gentleman. As Richard knew and understood the term, therefore, to be chivalrous was to be a man of war.

The definition of chivalry as the 'position and character of a knight' is especially significant in the context of a study of Richard III. The word 'knight' in its earliest usage, c.893, meant simply a boy, lad or youth. Fifty years or so later it denoted a boy or lad employed as an attendant; by extension, it came to mean a male servant of any age. By the twelfth century, it continued to be used in the servile sense for a military servant or the follower of a king or another person of rank. Later, a knight could be the servant of a lady, perhaps her attendant or her champion in war or at the tournament. Used in this specific way, the expression could even be applied to a woman. By now the term might also be used for a common soldier.

However, the way Richard would have understood it, and as it applied to him, a knight was a military servant of the King or another man of superior rank. He would be a feudal tenant holding lands given to him by such a person on condition that he would, when required, serve in the field as a mounted and fully-armed fighting man. Thus, as we shall see, Richard came to hold vast lands in Yorkshire and elsewhere, which were awarded to him by Edward for services already rendered and for others that were expected to be so in the future. The elevation of a knight to military rank was conferred upon him by the King or other qualified person, such as when Edward invested Richard as Knight of the Bath. Such an honour was restricted to those of noble birth who had served a proper apprenticeship, ideally as a page and then a squire, to the profession of arms. This requirement applied even to those of the highest rank, such as Richard.

The Victorian historian, Alfred Owen Legge[1] contrasts the respective dispositions of Richard and his brother George as he explains King Edward's reasons for placing Richard under Warwick's tutelage: Upon the return of the two boys from Utrecht, it was immediately obvious to the King that there was a gulf of difference between their two personalities. George of Clarence was amiable, sunny and light hearted. Richard, on the other hand, was pale of face, with a reserved but courteous manner, whose love of reading commanded respect rather than affection. Clarence had, moreover, a resolute and restless spirit, to which Legge attributes King Edward's distrust of him. Richard, he continues, was 'reserved, cautious, firm of will, endowed with discretion beyond his years. In him we may believe that the sagacious King detected the dawn of a fearless and subtle genius.' It was for this reason that Edward sent Richard to learn the more physical pursuits of knighthood: riding, hunting and the handling of weapons. Legge points to Edward's 'contempt' for learning, which caused him to underestimate Richard's intellectual achievements.

In fact, there is nothing to substantiate Legge's claim that Edward had any contempt for learning. Four of the King's chancellors were the founders of colleges or had promoted scholarship in some way. The Croyland Continuator, who knew him, describes Edward as 'a most loving encourager of wise and learned men.'[2] Secondly, such an assessment takes no account of the fact that intellectual aptitude is not necessarily incompatible with more robust physical activities. Edwards's own brother-in-law, Anthony, Earl Rivers, is the perfect example of someone who excelled in each of these areas of life.

As Richard's life changed from, perhaps, being dedicated to God to being dedicated to his king, he followed correct procedure as dictated by tradition and, conceivably more importantly at this stage, dictated by his brother King Edward IV. Richard was taught the ways of chivalry as a page in the household of his cousin and possible godfather, Richard, Earl of Warwick.

Richard, Earl of Warwick, was his royal cousin's senior by twenty-four years. He was by far the most powerful magnate in the country. His lands

included large parts of North Yorkshire, inherited from his Nevill ancestors, and which he oversaw from his magnificent castles at Middleham
and Sheriff Hutton. He was also warden of the Western Marches towards
Scotland, for which Carlisle was the centre of administration. Through
his mother, the dowager countess of Salisbury, Warwick had inherited the
estates of the Montagu Earldom of Salisbury. This brought him extensive
lands in south-central England. His marriage to Anne Beauchamp, heiress
to Richard Beauchamp, Earl of Warwick, brought him not only his title but
also his estates lying in the south and midlands of England as well as the
lordship of Glamorgan in South Wales. The rewards given him by the grateful Edward IV enabled him to expand his revenues even further and led
to his acquisition of confiscated Lancastrian lands. With the decline of his
greatest rivals, the Percies of Northumberland, Warwick became the most
powerful individual in the country after the King.

Of the countess of Warwick, Anne Beauchamp, John Rous has this to
say:

> This gode lady was born on the manor of Cawersham by redyng in the counte
> of Oxenford and was euer a full devout lady in Goddis seruys fre of her speche
> to euery person familiere accordyng to her and thore degre. Glad to be at and
> with women that traueld of child. full comfortable and plenteus then of all
> thyng that shuld be helpyng to hem. and in hyr tribulacons sho was euer to
> the gret plesure of God full pacient. to the grete meryte of her own sowl and
> ensample of all odre that were vexid with eny aduersyte. Sho was also gladly
> ever companable and liberal and in her own persone semly and bewteus and
> to all that drew to her ladishup as the dede shewid full gode and gracious. her
> reson was and euer shall.[3]

It is during his sojourn with the Earl of Warwick that Richard met his
future wife and queen, Anne Nevill, the daughter of the Earl of Warwick.
Certainly they both attended the lavish festivities laid on at Cawood
Castle to celebrate George Nevill's enthronement as Archbishop of York.
George Nevill, a younger brother to Richard of Warwick, was a humanist
and a noted Greek scholar. His entourage was associated with one of only
three centres in England in which the study of Greek thrived, the other
two being the University and town of Oxford and Canterbury University.[4]
George was Chancellor of Oxford from 1453 until 1456, when he
resigned upon his provision to the bishopric of Exeter. He returned to
the post in 1461, and there he would remain until he was exiled in consequence of his support of Warwick's rebellion in 1472. George encouraged

scholarship and was a collector of books, some of which he donated to the library of his college, Balliol.

During his second Chancellorship George was translated from Exeter to the Archbishopric of York. It was his enthronement to this office, on 22 September 1465, that was attended by Richard, Duke of Gloucester who was but twelve years of age at the time. Richard sat in the main chamber with the Duchess of Suffolk on his right hand and the countesses of Westmorland and Northumberland to his left. Also present were the Earl of Warwick's two daughters, Isabel and Anne.

The banquet following the enthronement was a most sumptuous affair that demonstrated to Richard, not only what money could buy, but also the power and munificence of the church. Richard helped his Nevill relatives, their allies and their retainers to eat their way through a menu that included dishes of venison, mutton, swan and signets, peacock, coney, partridges, woodcock, capon and geese. Fish dishes included herrings, salmon, codling, pike, turbot, sturgeon, mackerel, tench, crabs and ling. There were hot custards and date compotes as well as many other 'suttleties', such as 'a suttletie of Saint George', 'dolphin in foil' and 'a dragon'. The meal was accompanied by malmsey, Hippocras, wine and ale, and damask water was provided for the washing of hands after each course.[5] Such lavishness gave Richard a taste of what his future held as he made his way to the home of his powerful cousin, the Kingmaker.

As he took up residence at Middleham, Richard exchanged the formal gardens of Greenwich, the lush forests of Ludlow and the beautiful Nene valley at Fotheringhay for the verdant, gentle landscape of hills and dales. The Earl of Warwick's castle at Middleham is surrounded by the unparalleled beauty of the Yorkshire Dales; Wensleydale, through which flows the meandering Ure, which would eventually join the Swale as it moved southwards to become the Ouse just prior to its entering York. This river, then, watered two places that would come to mean so much to Richard Gloucester.

Silence reigns in this country, broken only by the cry of a lone peregrine falcon as it gently glides on the breeze in search of prey. The heathers, purple and white, were just coming into flower as Richard arrived and saw Middleham for the first time. There was the unmistakable scent of autumn in the air. Although the days would remain golden for some time yet, the nights were already cold and the mornings dusted with the frosts that would inevitably give way to snow. Richard was used to the outdoor life, yet he would not fail to notice that, here, the air was crisper, the winds harsher, the water colder, but the fires warmer.

The township of Middleham was much more significant in the late fifteenth century than it is today, having since exchanged its status with nearby

Leyburn. In the centre of it all was the magnificent and luxurious castle, which was to be Richard's home for the next four years or so. By the time Richard lived there, Middleham Castle had already enjoyed a long history. Its story began some 400 years previously with a motte and bailey castle set high on a ridge to the south west of the present castle. It was about twelve metres high and enclosed within a six-metre wide ditch. The bailey, which was kidney-shaped, stood to the east of the motte surrounded by its own ditch. The site, today called William's Hill and which affords a marvellous view of the surrounding countryside, is grassy and strewn with fallen trees. Visitors who make their way over its undulating surface are usually watched by inquisitive sheep or cows from the farm in whose land it now is, and by the magnificent and equally enquiring race horses, whose stud backs onto the grounds of the present castle. The old castle was probably made of timber, and so has succumbed to time and the elements. No evidence allows us to assume that there were any stone buildings, although it is possible that any stone used was transferred to the new castle.

Prior to the Norman Conquest, Middleham and the lands round about were the property of Gilpatric. In 1069, they were granted to Alan the Red, whose father was Count Eudo of Penthièvre in Brittany. The count was one of the chief supporters of King William and so it is safe to guess that the estate was an expression of the Conqueror's recognition and gratitude.

Alan's principal castle was at Richmond. This jewel on the banks of the Swale provided protection from Scottish invasion at a time when the Scottish border extended as far south as the Rey Cross on Stainmore in Westmorland. Since Norman rule was resented in the area, it is possible that Alan built the castle at Middleham to control the road that led through Wensleydale as far as Skipton.

Sometime prior to 1086 Alan granted Middleham Castle to his brother Ribald, whose descendants were to hold the property until 1270. However, the old castle of Middleham was abandoned during the twelfth century. At this point the keep of the new building had been built, probably by Ribald's grandson, Robert FitzRanulph.

The last of the FitzRanulf line was Ralph FitzRanulph, who died without an heir male. In 1270, his daughter, Mary, married Robert de Nevill. Their son was Ralph, first Lord Nevill of Raby. Ralph Nevill also inherited his grandfather's estates of Raby, Brancepeth and Sheriff Hutton. Meanwhile, he added to the structure of Middleham Castle, building a stone curtain wall, corner towers and the chapel off the eastern wall of the keep.

Ralph left his estates to his son, also named Ralph, who distinguished himself during the reign of King Edward III. The King rewarded him by making him Warden of the Western Marches. Upon his death the estates passed to his son, John, third Lord Nevill, whose prowess as a soldier and administrator earned him the gratitude of Edward III. He saw much action in the French campaigns of John of Gaunt, Duke of Lancaster, who retained him for life and made him one of his lieutenants. Later, he served Richard II in Gascony and on the Scottish Marches. He employed his immense wealth, gained in service as well as two well-judged marriages, to renovating his castles, mainly at Raby and Sheriff Hutton.

John's son, Ralph, the fourth Lord Nevill, saw service in France in his youth but was primary responsible for the care of the West March and the town and castle of Carlisle. Already one of the most powerful men in the north, his marriage to Joan Beaufort as his second wife, increased his assets still further. Richard II made him first Earl of Westmorland in 1397, to which was added the Honour of Penrith two years later. However, Ralph, Richard Gloucester's grandfather on his mother's side, turned his back on Richard II and became a supporter of Henry Bolingbroke as he made his bid for the throne. Bolingbroke, now Henry IV, repaid Ralph by granting him the Honour of Richmond and making him Marshal of England. Ralph remained loyal to Henry IV throughout the Percy rebellions and the Southampton Plot. Such loyalty was rewarded with more honours and grants of lands.

When it came to the disposal of Middleham Castle, Ralph chose to overlook his eldest son by his first marriage to Margaret, daughter of the Earl of Stafford. Instead, he appointed as his heir Richard, his eldest son by Joan Beaufort. Richard Nevill, Earl of Salisbury, who supported his brother-in-law, Richard, Duke of York, was beheaded with the Duke at Wakefield. His estates passed to his eldest son, also Richard Nevill, whose power and exploits would earn him the epithet, the Kingmaker. It was, therefore, to the Kingmaker's household that Richard Gloucester was sent to learn the courtly and chivalrous ways of knighthood.

As stunning as the countryside in which it was set, Richard's new home was the very essence of luxury.[6] Each of its many owners had added to it so that now it was indeed palatial. The many windows allowed light to flood in. This was then reflected against the plastered and whitewashed walls; the decor and the size and situation of the windows lent a sunny and airy feel to the spacious chambers. Tapestries and painted features broke up the plain whiteness of the walls, adding colour and warmth. Comfort and hygiene were catered for; all the chambers were provided with hearths or open fires. There were many drains and the private chambers had their own latrines. A separate block, accessed by a covered bridge, contained a further eight latrines.

The castle complex was massive; the twelfth-century keep alone measured 32 by 24 metres; a second floor was added to it at some point during the fifteenth century, probably prior to Richard's time there. A well-guarded, unroofed staircase with a porter's lodge placed half-way up, led to the living area on the first floor. This comprised an impressive Great Hall to the eastern side, which was approached through a small ante-room at the head of the external staircase. Servants bringing food and drink from the kitchen used a spiral staircase built into a tower at the south-east corner of the keep. A small chapel nestled just off the Great Hall in the north-east tower. To the west of the Great Hall, accessed by a small passageway, was the Great Chamber. With its large fireplace, latrine, cupboards and drains, this was a comfortable and functional room. Separated from it by a partition wall was another, smaller inner chamber, the privy chamber. This also had its own latrine, cupboards and large fireplace, and it was here that the lord of Middleham would pass his private moments.

The ground floor of the keep was taken up by a kitchen on the west side and a cellar to the east. The windows of the kitchen were small and set high into the walls. Four large recesses provided cupboard space, wells sunk into the floor provided water and drains took away waste. There were also circular containers built into the floor, which might have served as fish tanks. Food was cooked on the hearth, which was set into the wall that divided the kitchen from the cellar.

To the east of the keep, attached to the wall against the outside staircase, was another chapel. This one was much larger than the one off the Great Hall, and it was probably used for masses held for the household and servants. It comprised three storeys, the lower two probably serving as basement, vestries and, perhaps, priest's lodgings. The third floor, the chapel itself, was reached from the stairhead, but this is so badly ruined that all that can be said of it is that it had tall traceried windows on the north and south sides and a stone vaulted roof. The rooms below were also vaulted and had small, round-headed windows.

It was within these luxurious surroundings, amid such beauty, that the thirteen-year-old Richard learned the ways of a knight by performing the duties of a page. His guardian, the Earl of Warwick, was granted £1,000 for the maintenance of the boy who waited on the ladies of the household to learn courteous behaviour. Richard was given music lessons by one of the Earl's minstrels; probably, he would have learned to sing romances, perhaps even accompanying himself on an instrument such as the harp. Although the chaplain encouraged Richard's reading, he would have been delighted to see that his pupil's skills in this area were already quite advanced.

An entry in *Liber Niger*, the book of Edward IV's household accounts, gives an insight into Richard's activities at Middleham. The henxmen (squires or page boys) were placed under the supervision of a master, who would:

> Lern them to ride clenly and surely, to drawe them also to justes [joustes], to
> learn hem to were theyre harneys [harness - armour], to haue all curtesy in
> wordez dedes and degrees, dilygently to kepe them in all rules of goynges and
> sittinges, after they be of honour. Moreouer to teche them sondry langages and
> othyr lernynges vertuous, to herping, to pype, sing, daunce, and with other
> honest and temperate behauing and pacience; and to kepe dayly and wykely
> with thees children dew conuenitz, with correcions in theyre chambres accord-
> ing suche gentylmen; and eche of them to be vsed to that thinges of vertue
> that he shalbe most apt to lerne, with remembraunce dayly of Goddes seruyce
> accustumed.[7]

Although no records of Richard's activities as a page at Middleham survive, it is possible to construct at least some of his training and daily routine from the *Liber Niger* as well as the Ordinance of King Edward IV. Richard would sit together with the other henxmen in the hall at mealtimes, where they would all be served at one sitting. His meals would be served in two or three portions of prepared food, according to the master's orders. This would vary according to the meal. For breakfast Richard would have two loaves, one serving of meat, probably boiled, and one gallon of ale. On fasting days supper was one loaf and a gallon of ale, according to his age. In winter Richard would share two wax candles, four Paris, or large wax, candles and three bundles of wood with his fellows. They were also allowed rushes and litter. Their clothes and bedding were supervised by a controller, and each page was assigned at least one servant according to their rank who would look after their clothes and chambers. Anything else Richard might need was to come from the royal wardrobe upon application to the King's chamberlain. The master of the pages would watch over him and report on his progress to the King.

Part of young Richard's knightly training was to acquire skills in horsemanship, which, according to the *Liber Niger* would have included jousting. In his *Chronicle*, John Hardyng also mentions jousting as part of the knightly curriculum:

> At fourteen yere they shalle to felde I sure,
> At hunte the dere, and catch an hardynesse ...

At sixtene yere to werray and to wage,
To juste and ryde, and castels to assayle.[8]

Since no records exist of Richard ever having taking part in the joust or
the tourney, it has been construed that he did not approve of or enjoy such
sport. However, this activity formed so important a part of the training of a
knight that it is difficult to see how he could have avoided it. In fact, one of
Richard's books, *Ipomedon*, which he acquired as a youth, tells the story of
a young man whose ambition was to become 'the best knight in the world'.
This knight was a skilful hunter who, when he saw that this failed to win
him recognition, status and the heart of the woman he loved, went on to
take part in the tournament. In the character of Ipomedon, Richard had the
perfect role model and example of how an idealistic young knight should
behave. An annotation in Richard's handwriting in his copy of *Ipomedon* is
revealing: *tant le desieree*, 'I have longed for it so much'.

Certainly Richard enjoyed the hunt, which was regarded as semi-mili-
tary training. Then, as now, Middleham days begin early, with horses being
exercised from daybreak. Middleham, so famous today for its equine connections, did not have such a reputation in the fifteenth century. Today
horses are bred at one of several studs within the township, but in the fifteenth century those that Richard cared for and learned to ride came from
nearby Jervaulx Abbey. The land round about provided good hunting and,
just as they are today, the horses were probably exercised on Middleham
Moor which flanks the somewhat winding road to nearby Coverham.
Richard became an accomplished rider, adept at handling weapons while
on horseback. In connection with such training was the ability to wear the
harness, the armour of a soldier.

To put on armour required the assistance of a squire. Even so, Richard
had to know about the various pieces of armour, whereabouts on the body
they were worn, how they were tied and what their function was by helping
other knights to don theirs. At first, Richard probably felt uncomfortable
wearing such awkward and cumbersome pieces, but very quickly his harness
would become as natural to him as his every day clothes. In any case, tech-
niques in metalworking, and the greater distribution of the various pieces
on the knight's body had made the harness relatively light when compared
to that of earlier times. A good suit of plate armour could cost somewhere
in the region of £33.

In putting on his harness,[9] then, Richard was first dressed in his arming doublet, which was made of fustian, a coarse cloth made of cotton and
flax, and which he worn against his skin. The doublet was lined with satin,

which was pierced with several holes for ventilation. It was fitted with gussets of mail to protect vulnerable and exposed parts of the body and to aid movement. Strong waxed cords attached to the doublet allowed the various pieces to be tied onto it, such as a standard, or standing collar, and padded hose. The hose was not fitted with mail gussets because they would have chaffed Richard's skin.

Next, Richard was given leather shoes which were then fastened on and over which he wore mail sabatons. The articulated sabatons were attached to his feet before the greaves, or jambs, were buckled in place. Greaves were made in two vertical pieces hinged together and were worn over the shins and calves. Cuisses were used to protect the upper legs; since these extended only to the top of the thigh, again for ease of movement, Richard wore mail shorts, or perhaps a mail skirt, to protect the pelvic area. Polynes, or knee pieces with shaped wings, protected the area between the greaves and the cuisses.

Over the doublet Richard wore body armour that protected his chest and back. Like the greaves and the cuisses, this was hinged vertically on one side and held in place with buckles on the other side and over the shoulders. His lower arms were covered with the vambrace, which was buckled and tied to the arming doublet with laces. The rerebrace protected the upper arm and was attached in the same manner as the vambrace. The cowter, or elbow-cop, came next, and it protected the area between the arm harness in the same way as the polynes did on the legs. Pauldrons, or shoulder guards, covered the tops of Richard's arms and his shoulders, front and back. Richard was then handed his gauntlets. These, together with mail mittens, protected his hands, wrists and cuffs.

The last piece of harness to be put on was the helm or helmet. There were several styles in use during the Wars of the Roses, the most common being the sallet and bevor or mentonnièrre. The sallet encased Richard's head in protective metal. It was always worn over an arming cap, which not only preventing chaffing, but also helped absorb the impact of blows to the head. Richard might have used a visored sallet, which was introduced during the latter half of the fifteenth century. These had either single or double eye slits. The bevor consisted of two or three plates that were shaped to wear over the face. A lower plate was contoured to fit over the chin, while a V-shaped extension at the front was attached to the breastplate to protect the throat. Alternatively, Richard might have opted for an armet. This consisted of a skull, a visor, cheek pieces, similar to those of the bevor although larger, and a rondel, which gave further protection to the back of the head. The throat and upper chest was protected by the gorget plate, mail standard or a metal wrapper. Whichever helm Richard chose to wear, it might have had a key-hole at the top to allow insignia to be inserted. This enabled recognition at a time when not all knights wore heraldry on tabards or jackets.

Although apparently well covered in protective harness, there were still parts of the knight's body that were exposed and vulnerable to a skilfully wielded weapon. In particular the joints were left unprotected, as were the groin, the lower abdomen and the under the arms. The right weapon skil-fully aimed could pierce these vulnerable areas and, at the very least, render the knight incapable of defending himself. An upward thrust into the lower abdomen could penetrate into the chest cavity causing injury to the lungs or the heart. Moreover, Richard, like any man-at-arms, would have to be able to fight, mount his horse unaided, spend a penny, run, bend, swing at the waist and generally live in his armour for a time should his proximity to the enemy make it prudent to do so.

Richard, with his slim figure and youthful good looks, would have cut quite a spectacular figure in harness, especially if he wore over it a tabard in his heraldic colours of murrey and blue. He might not have felt especially uncomfortable; certainly, by the time he was old enough to wear it harness had become lighter and easier to wear, and movement was aided by the mail between the pieces at the elbows, knees and loins. However, the eye slits of the helmet, of whatever type, were narrow and restricted the vision, thus making them very claustrophobic to wear. Also, full harness had little in the way of ventilation and, once the helmet was put on, the fighting man would soon find himself soaked with perspiration. This led to dehydration and thirst; many men were killed simply because they removed their helm in order to drink. One can only imagine Richard's relief at arriving back at the castle after a hard day's practice with weapons and riding in harness; the prospect of a hot bath, the water heated by his servant on one of the many fires, must have been very inviting indeed. What a shame, though, that he could not afterwards put on the exaggeratedly piked shoes that had for so long been the fashion for gentlemen; Edward had proclaimed 'that the beakes or pikes of shooes and boots should not passe two inches, upon paine of cursing by the cleargie, and forfeiting twentie shillings.'[10]

Richard's training included handling various forms of weaponry.[11] There were several swords in the fifteenth-century armoury. To begin with, there was the very broad, short sword of some twenty-eight inches in length. Another sword was somewhat longer, being forty inches in length, with a narrower long hilt which could be used with one or two hands. There was also the thrusting sword, with its long narrow blade and long hilt; this also had a blunt edge close to the crossguard so that the knight could grip it in his left hand for close-quarter fighting. The thrusting sword was kept in a scabbard slung from the hip. The scabbard might also hold an eating knife and a steel to sharpen the blade. This sword was also used on ceremonial occasions, such as coronations.

On the other hip the knight would wear a dagger. This might be the rondel, a triangular-shaped dagger, which could be a long as fifteen inches. Used to exploit vulnerable areas of the opponent's armour, the rondel was a deadly weapon indeed. Daggers, like swords, could be highly decorated to reflect the status of the owner.

A particularly formidable weapon was the poll-axe, mounted at the head of a shaft of some four to six feet in length. It consisted of a long spike at either side of which was an axe-head and a hammer, or a crow's beak and a hammer. The man wielding such a weapon could stab, crush or cut his enemy, even if the enemy wore full harness, while the shaft could be used to parry blows. A man on horseback could be hooked out of the saddle and pulled to the ground by the poll-axe, while the blows rained on him from the hammer would kill him, or at the very least, render him unable to defend himself.

The battle-axe was shorter but no less deadly, while the war hammer was a hand weapon similar to the head of the poll-axe in design but with no spike and with a serrated hammer and crow's beak instead of the axe. Lastly was the mace, which was similar in size to the war hammer; its head was equipped with six interlocking metal plates with spikes, perhaps forming a multifaceted diamond-shape.

Still, knightly training was not all physical exercise and hard work. Richard engaged in intellectual activities as well. During his time in the Kingmaker's household, he might have been introduced to a knight by the name of Sir Thomas Malory of Newbold Revell. Malory had led a colourful life that ranged from the highest forms of chivalry to the depths of imprisonment for crimes of which he may or may not have been guilty. He saw active service in Gascony, and it is easy to imagine him beguiling the young page with his exciting tales of derring-do. Malory is generally believed to have been the author of *Le Morte d'Arthur*, a tale of chivalry, romance and adultery. The time had not yet come, however, when the legend of the King of the Britons would have a deeper resonance for Richard.

It was most important that Richard should understand just what it meant to be a knight, what it was that separated the knight from the ordinary man. In time to come, William Caxton would translate and print Ramon Lull's *The Book of the Ordre of Chyuarly*, and he would present a copy of it to Richard, who by then had become king. Richard would recognise much of what was contained within this book because he had learned it during his youth at Middleham.

Lull presents an idealistic picture of knighthood in a text that takes the form of a conversation between an old knight, now retired and living as a hermit, and a young king who is seeking ordination into an order of knighthood. The young king is eager, wise and virtuous, but he is unaware of what knighthood really means. The old hermit takes it upon himself to instruct him. For Lull, and so for Richard, knighthood was a semi-mythical institution ordained by God:

> Whan Charyte / Loyaulty / Trouthe Iustyce and veryte fayllen in the world / thenne begynneth cruelte / Iniurye / desloyalte and falsenes / And therfore was erroure and trouble in the world / In whiche god hath created man in jntencion that of the man he be knowen and loued / doubted / serued and honoured At the begynnyng whan to the world was comen mesprysion justyce retorned by drede in to honour / in whiche she was wonte to be / And therfore alle the peple was deuyded by thousandes / And of eche thousand was chosen a man moost loyal / most stronge / and of most noble courage / & better enseygned and manerd than al the other.[12]

The knight, singled out by divine providence, was to be provided with a horse, the most noble of beasts, and he was to be equipped with the finest armour. He must not compound with evil. The knight learned that a man was superior to a woman.

> Of as moche as a man hath more of wytte and of vnderstandyng / and is of more stronger nature than a woman / Of soo moche may he [be] better than a woman / For yf he were not more puyssaunt and dyfferent to be better than the woman / it shold ensiewe that bounte and strengthe of nature were contrary to bounte of courage / and to good werkes / Thenne al thus as a man by his nature is more apparaylled to haue noble courage / and to be better than the woman / In lyke wyse moche more enclyned to be vycious than a woman / For yf it were not thus / he shold not be worthy that he had gretter meryte to be good / more than the woman.[13]

The knight's intellect and strength made him capable of both virtue and vice. He was lord over many men and was served by a squire as well as by the common people who would till his land while he took to sport.

Much of this philosophy is symbolised in the equipment of a knight.[14] His sword, being shaped like a cross, symbolises the vanquishing of God's enemies.

Its two edges represent Chivalry and Justice, two qualities of the knight, and signify that the knight should defend temporality and spirituality. The spear represents truth; its iron tip signifies strength to overcome falsehood. The pennon shows that truth is not afraid to be seen. The helm symbolises dread of shame. The haubergeon, or chain mail shirt, when tightly closed, is like a fortress against vice. The fortress metaphor stems from the haubergeon being made up of many pieces of mail in the same way that a fortress is made up of many stones. The fortress represents the Order of Chivalry because it too consists of many members. A fortress defends the knight against his foe, while the Order defends him against vice. The leg harness represents a knight's duty to defend the highways and to punish wrongdoers, and to look to his own safety. Spurs symbolise swiftness and diligence in providing necessary equipments. They also represent expedition in helping king and country in times of need. The gorget signifies obedience and that the knight should speak no evil nor be gluttonous. The whip also represents obedience. The mace or pole-axe is a symbol of courage and the knight's authority and duty to punish those who disobey the King. It also represents his duty to put down all vices and enforce virtue. The dagger is symbolic of trust in God. The shield is the symbol of the office of knighthood and signifies the knight's duty to mediate between princes and the people; it also represents his loyalty to his lord, whom he will defend with his body in time of peril. The gauntlets symbolise that a knight should raise his hands to thank God, but also that he should not make a false oath or touch evil. The saddle has two main areas of significance. In its firmness it symbolises sure courage, in its size, the great charge and burden of chivalry. That a knight is mounted so high on his horse represents that he should have higher ideals than ordinary men; just as the knight is a heavy burden to the horse, so is chivalry to the knight. The bridle and reins signify restraint. The testier (horse's head-stall) means reason. The harness signifies the need for worldly goods, while the coat represents the knight's function as the protector of the weak and helpless.

A knight was required to study the theoretical as well as practical aspects of knighthood prior to his admittance into the Order. It was his duty to instruct his own son, who would follow in his footsteps. He was expected to defend the faith, to protect his lord and to maintain justice, to hunt and exercise himself, but he must not neglect his soul, for courage is superior to physical strength because of its spiritual quality. The knight must defend the weak and helpless and use his castle and his horse to protect the people. He must not commit unsocial acts, but set up courts and establish trading communities. It is his duty to punish wrongdoers and to challenge traitors to armed combat. To fail in any duty was to incur dishonour.

Richard would have found much in Lull's book to stir his soul and inspire his imagination, but, unlike Lull's young king, Richard did not live within the pages of a book. His idea of chivalry was tempered by the limits and practicalities of everyday life. For him, then, the practical side of knightly instruction came under the Earl of Warwick, while the idealism was born of literature. Yet, Richard had another instructor in addition to the one to whom Edward has entrusted his education, one who remained quietly in the shadows of Richard's life, a mentor so secret that perhaps even King Edward could guess neither his identity nor the strength of his influence over his younger brother: the shadow of their father, Richard, Duke of York.

The message of chivalry, with its emphasis upon the common weal, and the association with honour and loyalty, must have resonated strongly with Richard's perception, as it began to develop, of his father. The seeds of his father's legend were indelibly planted in the young Richard's mind while he was staying in John Fastolf's home, which was strewn with reminders of the late Duke of York. Family histories, stories of the Duke's exploits embellished to hagiographic proportions, tales of his battles, his bravery and his honour, all added to the grandeur of his memory and raised him to almost God-like status in the mind of his youngest child.

The efforts of Richard's mother to keep the legend alive: her description of herself as 'Cecily, the king's mother and late wife unto Richard in right king of England and of France and lord of Ireland' might have been prompted by her need to redefine her role as a result of Edward's marriage to the unsuitable Elizabeth, but it also emphasised her husband's claim to kingship. Richard of York, who had been closely identified with the betrayed eponymous Roman general of the *Consulship of Stilicho*, came to be viewed by his son even more as the wronged king-by-right. His kingship, based as it was upon his descent through the Mortimer line and back through the mists of time to the Welsh kings Llewelyn the Great and Cadwallader, had finally been vindicated in his son, Edward, but he had been betrayed by those who should have recognised him as king, yet did not. They thus failed in their duty to their liege lord and were unworthy of the name of knight. Chivalry did not apply to them.

Much of Richard's perception of his father and his rightful kingship, and his deep attachment to his memory found expression in his loyalty to King Edward. For Richard, Edward was the worthy, divinely appointed successor to Richard of York; it was he who fulfilled his father's destiny, he who carried the House of York to the throne where God had always intended it to be. Edward's reign had even been inaugurated by a star, the glorious sun in splendour, just like the birth of Caesar or the coming of Christ. Edward deserved Richard's love, devotion and loyalty, and Richard was happy to give in great measure. What better way to prove it than to become the best knight, Ipomedon in the flesh, ready to serve his king, his beloved brother?

Richard's qualities as a knight were formed by the instruction he received under Warwick at Middleham, refined by chivalric literature and driven by his desire to live up to and emulate the example of his father. The legend upon which young Richard had been weaned would become more and more the guiding principle in his life.

Still, Richard did not spend his entire time with Warwick at Middleham Castle. Warwick, like many another important man with a number of offices and estates to attend to, did a fair amount of travelling. It is certain that Richard accompanied his cousin on at least some of these journeys, such as the one he made to the city of Warwick. Here Richard was among those who gave offerings at the Collegiate Church of St Mary's; he probably also visited the tomb of Richard Beauchamp, the former Earl of Warwick. However, there was one journey that Richard did not take with the Earl of Warwick, since its object concerned only Richard and not his cousin. Early in 1466 Richard was summoned to his brother's court where he was to be created a Knight of the Garter.

CHAPTER 9

HONI SOIT QUI MAL Y PENSE, 1466

The first Knights of the Garter were Edward III's son, Edward the Black Prince and his companions of the 1346 Crécy campaign. In all, twenty-six knights were admitted into the Garter including the King, and their number has remained fixed to the present day. Moreover, simply being of royal blood appears to have been no guarantee of such an honour. As Halsted observes, King Edward III, who founded the order, did not grant membership to his son, Thomas, Duke of Gloucester. The Duke had to wait until the honour was conferred upon him by his nephew, Richard II.

Outside the intimate circle of the Order of the Garter, a squire would be examined to see if he were worthy of the honour of being made a knight. According to Lull, the examination would be carried out by a knight of great integrity. The squire must demonstrate that he both loves and fears God. He must not have an evil disposition. He must not be too young when he is knighted. He must be nobly born. The examiner must enquire into the squire's habits of life. He must be assured that the candidate is not seeking knighthood for his own advantage. The knight must have wealth enough to maintain his household. He must never have done a treacherous deed nor have any gross vices. He must not be maimed or over fat.[1]

This last stipulation, which calls for physical wellbeing is particularly interesting in the context of a study of Richard III. One of the many things that people 'know' about King Richard is that he was deformed. He was a hunchback with a withered arm, and his mind and character was just as deformed as his body. This view has persisted for centuries. For most people, it was instilled in them by Shakespeare. In the play *The Tragedy of King*

Richard III, Richard is a 'hunch-backed toad'[2] or a 'lump of foul deformity'. He is even made to say of himself:

> ...I that am not shaped for sportive tricks
> Nor made to court an amorous looking-glass[3]

Richard's historians have tended to accept as fact that the King was mis-shapen. Agnes Strickland, somewhat gleefully, proves her point by printing a poem entitled *The Honour of Cheshire*:

> The king's own brother, he, I mean,
> Who was deformed by nature,
> Crook-backed and ill conditioned,
> Worse faced - an ugly creature;
> Yet a great peer, for princes peers
> Are not always beauteous.[4]

Vergil's description of Richard is no more complimentary:

> He was lyttle of stature, deformyd of body, thone showlder being higher than thother, a short and sowre cowtenance, which semyd to savor of mischief, and utter evydently craft and deceyt. The whyle he was thinking of any matter, he dyd contynually byte his nether lyppe, as thowgh that crewell nature of his did so rage agaynst yt self in that lyttle carkase.[5]

For James Gairdner, '[Richard's] bodily deformity, though, perceptible, was probably not conspicuous'.[6] Desmond Seward offers: 'Probably the irregularity of his shoulders and deformed arm were barely apparent, no doubt disguised by the tailor's art'.[7] Michael Hicks states: 'We know him [Richard] to have been short, slight and perhaps even a hunchback'.[8] Alison Weir, after a short discussion of Richard's alleged physical imperfections, concludes:

> It would appear that he did have some slight deformity which eyewitnesses either did not notice or were too tactful to refer to overtly ... There must, after all, have been some grain of truth in what the early Tudor chroniclers wrote, for there were many people still alive who could have pointed out any gross anomalies in their works, people who remembered Richard well.[9]

Weir raises a good point as she speaks of early Tudor chroniclers. However, it is not only chroniclers who have contributed to the layers of uncertainty about Richard's appearance. In his *History of King Richard III*, Thomas More, himself a knight, makes the following comment upon Richard's appearance as he relates how the Queen and Shore's wife:

> Haue by their sorcery and witchcraft wasted my [Richard's] body. And therwith he plucked vp hys doublet sleve to his elbow vpon his left arme, where he shewed a werish withered arme and small, as it was neuer other [...] And also no man was there present but wel knew that his harme was euer such since his birth.[10]

This passage is loaded with significance for several reasons. Firstly, More asserts that Mistress Shore is a good friend to Queen Elizabeth Wydeville despite her having been the favourite mistress of the late King Edward. Second, it suggests the Queen's knowledge and use of witchcraft. Next, and more importantly, More alleges that it was a well-known fact that Richard's arm was 'werish', or shrivelled, withered, and, moreover, that it had been that way from birth. A last but not unconnected point is that, however well known it might have been that Richard had a withered arm, More failed to reveal it in an earlier description he gave of Richard.

When More first introduces him to his readers, Richard is still Duke of Gloucester.[11] In comparison to his brothers he is 'in bodye and prowesse farre vnder them bothe', being 'little of stature, ill-fetured of limmes, croke backed, his left shoulder much higher than his right'. The withered arm that Richard was supposed to have had since birth is strangely absent from this register of imperfection, unless it is included in the 'ill-fetured of limmes' comment. Still, More corrected this apparent oversight when the opportunity later presented itself. Richard, now has a werish, withered arm, with which he had been afflicted his whole life.

Thomas More observes that Richard was crook-backed with his left shoulder much higher than the right. His description is, in fact, borrowed from the description of Richard given by the antiquary and chantry priest, John Rous, although he asserts that Richard's hunchback affected his right shoulder, rather than his left.

Richard's hunchback is also testified to in a document held in the York City Records. Here it is reported that a certain Master Burton said that 'Kyng Richard was an ypocryte, a crochebake, and beried in a dike like a dogge'.[12] Another tradition is connected to the cenotaph in the church at Sheriff Hutton, where local custom, still current as recently as a century ago, refers to the child whose effigy lies atop the monument as 'Little Crumplin'. This rustic epithet is believed to allude to his father's alleged hunchback.

That Richard had unequal shoulders is accepted on the authority of John Rous, Polydore Virgil and Thomas More. However, they cannot agree upon which shoulder was the higher. Thomas More is the only authority for Richard's withered left arm.

To this catalogue of deformity must be added John Rous's account of Richard's unusual birth, which was, of course, taken up by Thomas More. According to these accounts, Richard was born with a full set of teeth, it was a breach birth during which it was necessary for his mother to be cut, and he had hair down to his shoulders. Unfortunately, it is not specified whether the hair touched the 'normal' shoulder or the higher one.

The unlucky Richard, then, displayed a catalogue of physical deficiencies, defects and deformities involving a protracted labour and difficult birth, with the child emerging complete with teeth and hair. He was hunchbacked, or at the very least had unequal shoulders, as well as a withered left arm.

Before making an analysis of the King's alleged misshapenness, it is worth mentioning the case of Edmund of Lancaster, the second surviving son of King Henry III. Edmund's epithet was 'Crouchback', and in a recent study it has been said of him that:

> It is likely that the deformity is described first by Tudor propagandists, but infact [sic] referred to the Crusader's Cross that Edmund would have borne on the shoulder of his cloak, probably as a brother of The Hospitallers or of The Templars.'[13]

Unfortunately for Richard, he is nowhere depicted as having worn such a cross on his shoulder or anywhere else. That a cross was traced on his shoulder as part of the ceremony to confer upon him the status of a Knight of the Bath could hardly count in this instance. Nevertheless, the connection between the crusader Edmund and the would-be crusader Richard, though tenuous, is certainly interesting. Perhaps the term 'crouch' had been used for Richard in reference to his interest in the crusades. Given the context of the remark recorded in the York Records, this seems improbable. Burton did disparage Richard, for which he was duly rebuked. It must be said, however, that Burton was not reproached for having called Richard a 'crochebake' but for saying that he had been buried in a dike like a dog. It was immediately pointed out to him that 'the King's good grace [Henry VII] hath beried hym like a noble gentilman'. The material point here, therefore, is the affront to King Henry rather than to Richard III.

According to documentary evidence, then, Richard did have some sort of physical deformity, although respective authors are unable to agree on the details. At this point it would be useful to consult portraits of Richard to see how he was observed by artists.

Of all the extant portraits of Richard, only two can be accepted as reliable representations of the sitter. The earliest is now in the possession of the Society of Antiquities. This beautiful work had almost certainly formed part of the collection of the Paston family of Oxnead in Norfolk. It has been dendrochronologally dated to 1516, give or take four years. It is not, therefore, contemporary to Richard. However, the style, colour and pattern of the costume as well as the jewellery worn by Richard strongly suggest that it is a copy of a lost original for which Richard did sit, and as such, it can be considered a faithful likeness.[14]

The second portrait is that which belongs to the Royal Collection. This one, as with the one held by the Society of Antiquaries, was probably painted prior to the second decade of the reign of King Henry VIII. Once again, it is almost certainly a copy of a lost original and like the portrait held by the Society of Antiquaries it probably represents a faithful study of the King. That is to say it did so in its original state. At some point after its completion the Royal Collection portrait was defaced. An X-ray examination shows that it had been altered to make the right shoulder higher, the right eye narrower and, perhaps, the nose slightly larger. Indeed, the X-ray was not really needed because the over-painting has faded to the point that the original line of Richard's shoulder, complete with jewelled collar, and the lower edge of the eye can be quite clearly discerned. Richard was turned into a hunchback with a mean expression and a grotesque appearance. These alterations were probably made during the Tudor period in order to depict Richard in a way that better represented their image of him as a monster. Interestingly, it is the right shoulder that is shown to be higher, in contradiction to Thomas More's description of Richard, but in agreement with that of Rous. This would be explained by the fact that More's work was not then known publicly, nor was it ever meant to be.

The Royal Collection portrait has been copied many times. With each subsequent portrait Richard becomes more deformed and more grotesque. In some, he is a decrepit, stooping monster, whose careworn face betrays the weariness of an age the King would never attain in life.

Portraits of Richard have attracted the attention of psychiatrists, who have found that Richard's expression betrays someone in the grip of acute or chronic anxiety.[15] Perhaps, but more noticeable still is Richard's obvious intelligence. A representation of Richard known as the 'Broken Sword' portrait shows a benign, charming face, the youthfulness of which reflects more accurately Richard's true age at the time of his death. This portrait, which was probably painted during the final decade of the life of Henry VIII, was later altered to remove some of Richard's deformities. The left shoulder was originally much more raised, bringing it into agreement with More but in contrast to the supposed deformities emphasised earlier in the Tudor period. The left arm, which originally ended in a stump, now has a hand, albeit slightly misshapen. The broken sword itself, held by Richard in the ceremonial position, symbolises his lack of power and the failure of his reign.

The descriptions of Richard by writers such as Rous, More and Vergil, and the altered and grotesque portraits of the King, gave rise to a concept of physical deformity that found its fullest flowering in Shakespeare's representation of Richard in *The Tragedy of King Richard III*. Various performers have offered what are often ingenious interpretations of the Bard's Richard. Alan Howard played him with a deformed leg, walking awkwardly with the aid of chain attached to a heavy iron boot. His hand is permanently encased in a glove complete with inbuilt dagger in reference to Vergil's assertion that Richard was 'ever with his right hand pulling out of the sheath to the myddest and putting in agane, the dagger which he did alway were'.[16] Anthony Sher gave his Richard III crutches, thus lending him a sinister spider-like quality as he thrashes about the stage. Henry Goodman's Richard was the victim of polio. His deformity, which was as much mental as physical, stemmed from his antipathy towards his malformation. As portrayed by Kenneth Branagh, Richard delivers the famous opening soliloquy dressed only in his underpants as his malformed body is being straightened out on a rack. However, the most celebrated representation of Richard III is that of Sir Laurence Olivier. This knight of the theatre portrayed a Richard complete with humped back – the hump being on the left side – a limp caused by uneven legs and a claw-like left hand, two fingers of which are permanently bent inwards over the palm.

Each of these actors seeks in some way to represent the 'bottled spider' of Act I, scene iii. Here, 'bottled' means swollen or protuberant, signifying Richard's hunchback. The spider reference implies his poisonous nature. The theatrical Richard, like many of the actors who portray him, is legendary, and that is the realm in which this character belongs. However, legend is the pearl that encloses a grain of hard fact. What, then, are the 'facts' about Richard appearance?

Modern medicine has pronounced its own opinion on the type and causes of Richard's deformities.[17] His hunchback might have been the result of a condition known as Kyphoscoliosis, which results in a backward and sideways curvature of the spine. Alternatively, Richard might have suffered from a rare congenital condition called Sprengel's Deformity. This causes the scapula on one side, or occasionally both sides, to be smaller than normal and fixed higher up. When looked at from behind, the shoulder on the affected side might appear to be higher than the other, and the neck would appear shorter; as a result, the victim could well be described as a crookback. The muscles surrounding the scapula are deficient and may be composed partly of bone, cartilage and fibrous tissue. This leads to a restriction of movement in which the victim is unable to raise the arm straight out from the side to a greater or lesser degree. Importantly for Richard, however, this condition need not necessarily interfere with a person's ability to fight because other movements are not always restricted.

There are several conditions or circumstances that might lead to a withered arm, as attributed to Richard by Thomas More. One such circumstance relates to the birth of the child and his position in the family. Richard was Cecily's eleventh child and as such might have been a large baby. He could also have lain abnormally *in utero*. This is an interesting point since it would be consistent with More's suggestion that Richard's might have been a breech birth. That his mother could not give birth to him uncut does not necessarily mean that she underwent a caesarean section; any such procedure in the fifteenth century would almost certainly have resulted in her death. When this is added to Rous' statement that Richard was two years in the womb - clearly impossible, but suggestive of a long labour - an awkward delivery might have caused some over-stretching or tearing of the nerves of the baby's arm. Depending on how high or low on the arm the injury occurred, Richard could have been left with Klumpke's Paralysis. Even if the injury did not occur at birth, either of these conditions could have developed later in life. For Richard, this could easily have been caused by a bad fall from a horse or an injury sustained during weapons practice. An attempt to overcome such a difficulty might lead to overdevelopment of the muscles in the unaffected arm, leading to visible unevenness. This was accepted by Paul Murray Kendall, who attributes Richard's unevenness to the rigorous training he underwent as a page in the Earl of Warwick's household.[18]

Klumpke's Paralysis would also affect the hand, giving it a claw-like appearance, although this is not reproduced in any portrait of Richard. Not even the 'Broken Sword' portrait, which nevertheless does seem to show some abnormality of the left hand, represents the hand as being claw-like. Perhaps more telling is that no contemporary source, hostile or otherwise, has seen fit to comment upon such a malformation. Silence speaks volumes in this regard.

An alternative suggestion is that Richard might have had Erb-Duchenne Palsy; which is caused by an injury to the Brachial Plexus. This condition affects movement and feeling in the arm, but it probably would not have caused withering of the arm, although it might have made the arm limp. If the sternomastoid muscle was also involved, some movement of the head would be affected. This muscle controls the level and poise of the shoulder when the arm is used. Any damage to it would cause the affected side to become depressed or lowered making the unaffected shoulder appear higher.

Another condition that might have caused injury to Richard's arm is acute urticaria, or hives.[19] Urticaria is a rash consisting of white or red weals on the skin. The weals, which are often circular, look like the mild blistering caused by nettle stings, they are itchy and are usually accompanied by flaring of the surrounding skin. The rash typically appears suddenly and disappears within twenty-four hours. It is triggered in susceptible persons by various causes, one of which is an allergy to certain food-stuffs such as strawberries.

In a curious passage in his *History of King Richard III*, Thomas More[20] gives a rather detailed account of Richard entering the council chamber at the Tower of London. It is about nine o'clock in the morning. The Duke is smiling and apologetic for having slept in. He then turns to the Bishop of Ely, John Morton, in whose household More would later live as a page, and says, 'My lord, you haue very good strawberies at your gardayne in Holberne, I require you let vs have a messe of them'. The Bishop is happy to oblige and the strawberries are duly sent for. Richard then leaves the lords to talk while he slips away, presumably to eat the strawberries. More than an hour goes by before Richard returns; when he does, his mood has changed. More describes him as 'knitting the browes, frowning and froting and knawing on hys lippes'. Richard now enters into an increasingly heated diatribe that leads to his accusation of the Queen and Mistress Shore of witchcraft and that will end with the impromptu execution of Lord Hastings. During the course of this, Richard bears his arm to show it werish and withered.

Clearly, Richard is in some distress and the reader is led to conclude that it is as a result of his brooding upon his fancy that he is the victim of witchcraft. On the other hand, More is careful to mention Richard's change of mood and his withered arm in connection with his having eaten strawberries. The hypothesis is that Richard was aware that he was allergic to strawberries and that, if he eats them, they will produce an urticarial rash on his arm. He eats them, therefore, in order to produce precisely this affect. Once achieved, and it would not take long, he can then accuse Hastings of being in league with the Queen and Mistress Shore. The significance of the latter of these two ladies is that she became the mistress of Lord Hastings following the death of King Edward. Richard can confront Hastings with the physical 'evidence' of the women's witchcraft and, by extension, Hastings's own guilt. As Hastings is dragged from the Tower, Richard swears by St Paul, 'I wil not to dinner til I se thy hed of'. In other words, the sudden appearance of the rash on Richard's arm is proof of the guilt of Hastings, Queen Elizabeth and Mistress Shore. Its fading, which would coincide with the death of Hastings, is further proof of their supernatural-aided conspiracy against him. Another effect of Urticaria, in a more severe form, concerns the tongue and throat, both of which can become swollen. This might explain Richard's frothing and gnawing at his lips, which perhaps indicates some oral discomfort.

Unfortunately for this theory, Richard did not complain of a rash, that is to say, More did not speak of one. More's narrative distinctly notes a werish, withered arm; in the Latin version of the *History* the term used is *macilentum*, from *macilentus*, meaning thin or lean. Richard's arm, then, was shrivelled, not itchy, flared or covered with weals.

Amid all this medical speculation, one fundamental factor has been overlooked, which is to establish whether or not Richard was indeed deformed and if so, to what extent. Any deformity in Richard would have been of crucial importance because people were, as they continue to be, judged to a large extent upon their outward appearance. Moreover, had Richard indeed been destined for a church career, it would have been necessary to take into account the interdiction in Leviticus 21.16-23:

> And the Lord said unto Moses, 'Say unto Aaron, None of your descendants throughout their generations who has a blemish may approach to offer the bread of his God. For no one who has a blemish shall draw near, a man blind or lame, or one who has a mutilated face or a limb too long, or a man who has an injured foot or an injured hand, or a hunchback, or a dwarf, or a man with a defect in his sight or an itching disease or scabs or crushed testicles; no man of the descendants of Aaron the priest who has a blemish shall come near to offer the Lord's offerings by fire; since he has a blemish he shall not come near to offer the bread of his God, both of the most holy and of the holy things, but he shall not come near the veil or approach the altar, because he has a blemish, that he may not profane my sanctuaries; for I am the Lord who sanctify them.

Any physical deformity, such as an injured hand or a hunchback, or certain types of illness, such as leprosy, would preclude entry into the church. Such a priest would be forbidden to approach the holy altar for he would profane the holy sanctuary. His very presence would be a blasphemy.

Had Richard been deformed or ill, any ecclesiastic ambition would have been thwarted. He would have been ineligible for ordination and forbidden to officiate at services. Moreover, if the interdiction were to be extended to those who were *persona mixta*, that is to say, kings, it would also preclude Richard's ascension to the throne.

This interdiction is, of course, concerned with purity. One could not come into the presence of God if one were impure. This is because physical deformity and illness were the outward expressions of impurity and sin. What, then, are the facts of Richard's alleged deformities?

The claims of Thomas More, John Rous and Master Burton are contradicted by John Stow, who maintains that he had spoken to men who had known and seen Richard, and who had said that he 'was of bodily shape comely enough, onely of low stature, which is all the deformity they proportion so monstrously'.[21] Similarly, Catherine, countess of Desmond claims to have danced with Richard and had declared him to be the 'handsomest man in the room except his brother Edward, and was very well made'.[22] Sharon Turner[23] relates a similar story, in which the extremely long-lived countess asserted that Richard was 'in no way personally deformed of crooked'.

The evidence of these witnesses might reasonably be dismissed as hearsay, although they do introduce a tantalising element of doubt. On somewhat firmer ground is the contemporary chronicler Jehan de Waurin,[24] who gives an account of the exile of George and Richard at Utrecht following the deaths of their father and brother at Wakefield. Waurin describes George as being nine years old and Richard eight. While this is true of Richard, who would not celebrate his ninth birthday until October 1461, George, by April of that year, was eleven years old. Perhaps it was George who was undeveloped for his age and not Richard, as is usually supposed.

Better than a chronicle, however, is the fact that there were times in Richard's life when his naked or partially clothed body was seen by other people. Many of these were public occasions when any deformity would have been obvious and noted. One instance was during the ritual washing and signing with a cross that Richard underwent prior to his investiture as a Knight of the Bath. That no mention of any deformity was made on this occasion, however, is an argument from silence. No written record of the event exists, so it cannot be said for certain that no deformity was noted. Vergil, speaking of Richard's death at Bosworth, states that:

> The body of king Rycherd nakyd of all clothing, and layd uppon an horse bake with the armes and legges hanginge downe on both sides, was browght to thabbay of monks Franciscanes at Leycester, a miserable spectacle in good sooth...[25]

Although Vergil goes on to say that Richard was 'deformyd of body', he notes only uneven shoulders. He makes no mention of a hunchback or a withered arm.

Could it be, then, that Richard's only 'deformity' was a slight unevenness of the shoulders? If so, it might be interesting to note that he shares this condition with Thomas More himself.[26] Clearly, there was no real defect in the King's figure other than that which existed in the eyes, or rather the minds, of those who would disparage him. Why they should do so is every bit as interesting as the methods they used.

It had long been believed that the outer form of a person reflects the nature of the soul within. This is the philosophy behind the 'ugly sisters' of the Cinderella tales. Interestingly, not every version of the story depicts the step-sisters as ugly in appearance, occasionally they are outwardly beautiful, but their charming countenances conceal their wicked hearts. In other versions, the sisters are ugly and they are cruel to Cinderella. Their wicked natures are reflected in their outward appearance. This is the approach that is perhaps the most familiar, having been used in the version of the fairy tale as told by Disney.

Similarly, in Oscar Wilde's *The Picture of Dorian Gray*, the portrait represents Dorian's wicked soul. As he embraces evil and depravity, the picture bears the consequences, growing old and ugly while Dorian himself remains young and beautiful.

However, nowhere is this concept more obvious than in the medieval period, where outward appearance was all-important because it was considered both to reflect the inner soul and to display ones status. It finds its most enchanting treatment in Dante's *Il Paradiso*, the third cantica of the *Commedia Divina*. As she gazes upon the infinitesimal point that is God, the beloved Beatrice becomes transformed:

> Beauty past all knowledge was displayed to me -
> Not only ours: the joy of it complete
> Her Maker knows, I think, and only He (Canto XXX, 19).

In this canto, Dante is left alone with Beatrice after the light of God and the angels has vanished from his view. Her closeness to the Divine has endowed Beatrice with such beauty that even an artist such as Dante is unable to find the words to describe it.

However, it is usually ugliness and deformity that attracts the most attention. In the version of *The Secret of Secrets* known as *The Gouernaunce of Prynces*, it is shown how the soul follows the condition of the body:

[C]ertayne thynge hit is that the Sowle whyche Is the fourme of the body, sueth the kynde and the complexcion and the properteys of the body... More-over the Sow[l]e is the begynnynge and cause of al the natural mevynges of the body.

One sign of a coward or a weakling was 'a man stowpynge and nought vpryght,' while the tokens of a shameless man are 'ryst opyn eighyn [eyes] and glysinynge, and the eighliddes full of blode and grete and shorte; Hey vprerid shuldres; the body Somewhate Stowpynge.' A small-hearted man is 'lytill visage, lytill eighen, and lytill all othyr lymes of the body, and lene y-flesshide.' 'Han the shuldres bene moche vprerid, thei tokenyth orribill kynde and vntrouthe.' A man who has his 'lymes dyfformyd out of kynde', is best avoided because 'to wickidnesse thay bene enclynet.'[27]

Such thinking is ultimately influenced by the biblical concept of the correlation between sickness and sin. Sickness represented the power of Satan and was seen as a punishment for sin, whether it be in the form of some transgression of God's laws or of apostasy. Thus, Psalm 38, which speaks of illness, sin and divine punishment, tells of the psalmist's friends abandoning him because of his sin. Luke 13.10-12 relates the experience of a woman whose spinal curvature had been caused by a demon. The woman is the victim of an agent of the Devil, who has left her with a crooked back. Her efforts to attend the synagogue are a testament to her faith. Jesus sees and understands her plight and, conferring his grace upon her, cures her. In giving Richard a crooked back, his detractors are implying that he not only had no faith, but also that he was in the grip of the Evil One. Hell's black intelligencer indeed!

Mark 2.1-12 recounts the story of the cripple whose friends lower him into the room where Jesus is sitting. Jesus tells the man that his sins are forgiven, for which he is rebuked. Jesus then tells the man to pick up his mat and walk, which he does. The point of the story is to encourage the readers' understanding of Jesus as God. The implication is that sin and illness are linked; forgive the sin and the illness is cured. Richard's malformation is physical proof of his corrupt nature. What is more, on a much deeper level, Richard's sins are unforgivable, even by God.

Such biblical concepts correlate with cognitive bias. Whether or not they were aware of it, Richard's detractors were drawing upon a powerful psychological phenomenon which connects with symmetry, beauty and what is known as the 'halo effect'. Richard's deformities, as described by historians and chroniclers, make him asymmetrical. One shoulder, whether the left or the right, is conspicuously higher than the other. More shows him to have one withered arm. As such, Richard appears lop-sided, crooked. Human beings are inherently attracted by symmetry.[28] Unevenness, whether in a face or body, repels, while evenness is seen as attractive. The Greeks understood this well as they applied the concept of cosmos, 'order' (from which 'cosmetic') to their perception of beauty. Greek statues are not asymmetrical. They represent the highest ideals of human beauty, the perfection that reflects goodness and divinity.

This concept is, in turn, allied to what psychologists call the 'halo effect'. Here, the general impression, or sometimes one particular feature of someone, is extended to influence judgement of that person. In practice, if a person is good looking, they are considered more likely to be successful, kind, intelligent, well-adjusted and popular. Conversely, there is the 'devil effect' which, naturally, works the opposite way. Depicting Richard as a hunchback or with a withered arm More, Rous, Vergil and perhaps even Burton unknowingly exploited cognitive psychology, which is itself based upon the use of cultural stereotypes. In their case, such stereotypes were strongly influenced by the biblical model regarding sin and infirmity. People would augment a perceived fault in Richard so that it would come to represent the nature of his personality and his soul.

To describe someone as deformed in Richard's day could be to represent their moral disfigurement, ugliness or crookedness. Indeed, one of the submeanings of the word 'ugliness' was moral offensiveness. It was only a short step, therefore, to extend the metaphor to include the physical appearance of a person, thus implying that their inner abnormality was reflected in the outward appearance.

This transformation had in fact begun to occur during Richard's time, although it would not fully develop until the Tudor period. A parallel case to that of Richard is found in the accusation of deformity that was levelled at Anne Boleyn. In this instance, her detractors spoke of 'a sallowish complexion, as if troubled with jaundice. She had a long projecting tooth under her lip, and on her right hand six fingers. There was a large wen under her chin'.[29] A less hostile source noted merely 'upon the side of her nail upon one of her fingers some little show of a nail'.[30] Significantly, because Anne was a woman, her supposed deformities are such that would spoil her beauty. At the period in which Anne lived a woman's appearance was a vital asset as she made her career in the world. To describe her thus is to mock and denigrate her over one of the sources of her feminine power. This was in turn linked to vague accusations of witchery and of charming the helpless King Henry VIII into marring her.

The greater the crime, therefore, the stronger was the need for vilification and the more ferocious the attack. Richard's 'crime' was to be a good man who accepted a throne that he had come to believe to be rightfully his. It is important to note that those who rebelled against his reign did not do so with the noble motive of rescuing or avenging the two princes, supposed victims of Richard's 'tyranny', but rather to secure the throne for themselves.

Even before Richard acceded to the throne, he was vulnerable to attack. When More included the detail of the withered arm in his narrative of Hasting's arrest he did so in order to deflect attention from the very real charge made by the protector against the Wydevilles. More's motives are not difficult to find. Dr John Morton was working in league with the Wydevilles, who were planning to depose Richard from his post as protector. The Wydeville faction was aware that King Edward V had no rightful claim to the throne because he was the illegitimate son of a man whose own legitimacy had, by that time, been called into question, and as such should never become king. They were equally aware that Richard was now the only legitimate and legal claimant to the crown. This accounts for their haste to intercept the young Edward as he made his way from Ludlow, and to bring him to London and crown him before, as they thought, Richard could find out the truth and take steps to prevent it.

Thomas More had spent part of his childhood at the home of John Morton in much the same way that Richard had at the home of the Earl of Warwick. As he worked on his history of King Richard III, More could not have been unaware of Morton's complicity in a plot to place an illegitimate king on the throne. Since he claimed to be writing a history, and as Morton's involvement with the Wydevilles was too well known for him to omit it, he invented the story of Richard's werish, withered arm to deflect attention and, perhaps, to inject a little humour. After all, what better wheeze than to depict a man whose military skills and proficiency as a soldier were renowned even among his enemies as a cripple?

The literary device employed by More was ingenious. Aware that the Tower meeting took place on a Friday, he brought in the strawberries because Friday is sacred to the Goddess Frigga, who concealed young children in a strawberry patch before smuggling them into heaven.[31] The correlation between this legend and the supposed fate of the Princes in the Tower is obvious.

However, More might also have been influenced by the Corpus Christi plays[32] in which the soul of the sinner is depicted as a hog; this is particularly clever because the bore was Richard's cognisance. In the plays the cursed are herded to the left side of God and are forced to carry their wicked deeds on their backs, thus giving the impression of having hunchbacks. Note also, that the left side corresponds with More's assertion that Richard's left shoulder was raised and that it was his left arm that was werish.

The Tudor attack upon Richard, achieved by means of accusations of deformity with all the inherent connotations of immorality and spiritual bankruptcy, was designed purely to make him detestable from the outset. They felt their campaign to be justified because they knew that they would have to defend their overthrow of Richard. With this in mind, they began to prepare the people to believe the stories about the atrocities that they would attribute to Richard. On a subconscious level, the human mind responds more readily, at least in the first instance, to images rather than to intellectual thought or reason. It was easier to make people accept Richard as an evil man if he could be seen as ugly and deformed.

Their motive for this was simple. It was essential for them to draw attention away from the fact that the Tudor dynasty was itself illegitimate. During the medieval period and beyond, it was believed that deformity in children resulted from God's judgment upon both parents. It was associated with illicit conception and, especially, incest.[33] Although Richard was not the fruit of an illicit, incestuous relationship, the validity of Edward IV's marriage was extremely doubtful. Edward was, of course, the father of Elizabeth of York, Henry Tudor's queen. Her legitimacy had to be beyond question because the security of Tudor dynasty rested upon pure and legal lineage. This was the reason why Henry VII ordered the destruction of all copies of Richard III's Act of Settlement. It in, Richard had declared Edward's children illegitimate.

In addition to this, Henry Tudor's own legitimacy was highly problematic, a fact that was carefully guarded. Margaret Beaufort, Henry's mother, was the grand-daughter of John Beaufort, who died in 1410. John was the eldest of the illegitimate sons of John of Gaunt, Duke of Lancaster and his mistress Katherine Swynford. The Lancastrian kings of England descended from John of Gaunt, but his illegitimate children by Katherine, from whom Henry Tudor descended, were never meant to inherit the crown. There were, then, two sound reasons why King Henry VII was unsuited to wear the crown of England.

Henry Tudor was compelled to justify his taking of the throne just as Richard before him had been obliged to do. Richard's justification was that he was the only legitimate male heir to the House of York, and so the only person eligible to accede to the crown. This was enshrined in a legal document, the Act of Settlement, published in January 1484. However, the only legitimate claim to the throne Henry Tudor and his heirs had was that of conquest. This, in the end, is how Henry Tudor validated his right to rule. Of course, he was quite correct to do so; conquest does justify the taking of a throne. If one were to deny Henry's kingship on this ground, one must also deny it to William I, with all that that would entail.

However, there is more, Isaiah 35.4-6 speaks of the removal of physical defects and ailments during the Messianic era:

> Behold, your God
> will come with a vengeance,
> with the recompense of God.
> He will come and save you
> Then the eyes of the blind shall be opened,
> and the ears of the deaf unstopped;
> then shall the lame man leap up like a hart,
> and the tongue of the dumb sing for joy

King Richard III established his reign in messianic/millenarian terms. This resonates throughout the Act of Settlement. The Tudors' depiction of Richard as physically deformed was their way of indicating the 'failure' of Richard's own 'messianic' reign. The sword, signifying authority, power and royalty,[34] was well and truly broken. Post-Bosworth descriptions of Richard's physical appearance are biased, yet they are based upon religious principles that firmly resonate with medieval thought.

Richard's ordination into the Order of the Garter on 4 February 1466 was recognition on the part of King Edward that his youngest brother had achieved the military standards required of him. The intellectual and chivalric virtues aside, the Order of the Garter also represented for Richard the high spiritual values that resonated with his view of kingship. Richard, like his brother, Edward, was devoted to St George in whose honour the Order was established. This and its connection with King Arthur appealed strongly to the young knight.

Richard owned a copy of Geoffrey of Monmouth's *Historia regum Britanniae*. This is a chronicle of the Kings of Britain from Brutus to Cadwallader. Its magical pages transported the adolescent Duke to the romantic realm of the semi-legendary figures of Arthur and Merlin. Lear and Cymbeline were also there, as was the angelic prophecy of the return of the Britons. Richard had acquired this particular copy after he became king, and he signed it to indicate his proud ownership: *Ricardus Rex*.

Another book in Richard's library was the Fitzhugh Chronicle. Sometimes known as Brompton's Chronicle or the Anonymous Chronicle, this work seeks to continue, and occasionally correct, Geoffrey of Monmouth's history. The signature in Richard's copy is given as *Richard Gloucestr*, which means that he obtained this book prior to his acquisition of the Monmouth. Although the date of his acquisition of this volume is unknown, his interest in such legends is clearly indicated as being a sustained, rather than a passing, one.

Perhaps Arthur's story, which resonated so strongly with the fate of his own father, gave Richard a sense of being part of something much greater than himself. Richard, the son of one who should have been king and the brother of an anointed king, might have taken comfort in the conviction that destiny was righting the course of the path his family was meant to follow. He saw in Edward the fulfilment of the angelic prophecy of the return of the righteous, sacred king. When Edward made Richard a Knight of the Garter, he confirmed Richard's philosophy and enhanced his sense that providence was guiding the way of the House of York: to Richard, King Arthur, the once and future king had returned to life in the form of his brother, Edward.

The link between the Order of the Garter and the Arthurian legends was no accident. When King Edward III established the Order, he based it upon the theme of the Round Table. Sandford, in Book Three of his *Genealogical History of the Kings of England*, states that:

> Many solemn tournaments, and other Exercises of Warr are performed at Dunstable and Smithfield, but more especially at Windsor, where King Edward [that is, Edward III] designed the Restoration of King Arthur's Round Table, in imitation of which He caused to be erected a table of 200 Foot Diameter, where the Knights should have their entertainment of Dyet at His Expence, amounting to 100*l* per Week. In emulation of these Martial Associations at Windsor, King Philip of Valois practised the like at his court in France, to invite the Knights and valiant Men of Armes out of Italy, and Almain [Germany] thither, least they should repair to King Edward, which, meeting with success, proved a Countermine to King Edward's main Design, who thereby finding that His Entertainment of Stranger Knights was too general, and did not sufficiently oblige them His in the following Wars, at length resolved on one more particular, and such as might tie those whom he thought fit to make His Associates, in a firm bond of friendship and honour.[35]

Edward III, therefore, restricted the numbers admitted to the order to 'five-and-twenty besides the sovereign'. The members of this fraternity are styled Equites Periscelides, or, Knights of the Garter.

As a Knight of the Garter, or a Knight of the Order of St George, as they were also called, Richard wore a surcoat of crimson velvet with a hood of the same colour and material. A mantle of purple velvet lined with white sarcenet was worn over the left shoulder. The mantle was decorated with the arms of St George, argent a cross gules embroidered with a garter and the motto of the knighthood, *Honi soit qui mal y pense*. Richard also wore a collar of gold, which featured alternatively enamelled red roses within the garter and knots, and from which was suspended the figure of St George on horseback killing the dragon. This pendant was also enamelled and decorated with precious stones. On his left leg Richard wore the garter, the buckle and pendant of which were gold enamelled and set with diamonds, the garter itself being enriched with gold, pearls and precious stones, and featuring the motto.[36]

The knights would meet each year at Whitsuntide to talk of their exploits of the previous year, to joust and tourney. The Round Table came to represent comradeship and fraternity, and it gave knights the context within which to expend their energies in the cause of good and honour. For King Edward III, engaged in wars with France, the creation of the Order of the Garter attracted to his cause the flower of European knighthood.

The symbolism of the Garter is illustrative of this. One legend has it that it was inspired by gallant assistance to a lady, whose garter had slipped from her leg as she danced. The gentleman involved silenced the laughter by proclaiming *honi soit qui mal y pense*: 'shame on him who thinks ill of it'. Other accounts suggest that the garter was used as a device by the crusading King Richard I. Still another explanation is that the garter is simply an emblem of union, both in the sense of a brotherhood of soldiers and of warlike qualities.[37] It is possible that each of these legends has some basis in truth, but they ignore the most profoundly spiritual meaning of the garter, which is that it is a symbol of the Virgin Mary. The shape of the garter represents the feminine creative principle, depicting as it does the female reproductive organ. Such symbolism is strengthened by the fact that the knights wore roses and pearls, both of which are associated with the Virgin. In the Christian tradition, pearls signify purity and spiritual grace and as such represent the virgin birth, while the rose is one of the icons of the Virgin Mary; the five petals symbolise the five letters of her name in Latin: Maria.

In this, then, lies the significance of the Order of the Garter for Duke Richard, much more so than for his brother, Edward. For Richard, knighthood, soldiery and war would become inseparable from chivalry, and chivalry was the quintessence of the knightly ideal. On the other hand, the symbolism of the order with its deep associations with the Virgin Mary resonated with Richard's maturing theological outlook. As he grew to manhood, Richard's devotion to the Virgin would become more marked and more profound.

CHAPTER 10

THE KING, THE EARL AND A MARRIAGE, 1467-1468

From his unique standpoint as a member of Earl of Warwick's household, Richard Gloucester was able to witness the gradual breakdown of relations between his brother, the King, and their powerful cousin, the Kingmaker. Almost from the time Edward ascended the throne, Warwick had been in favour of an alliance between England and France. During this time the French King, Louis XI, had held Richard of Warwick in high regard. When John of Calabria spoke of Warwick as a traitor and the instrument of the fall of Henry VI and Marguerite d'Anjou, Louis is said to have replied that he 'had more reason to speak well of the Earl of Warwick than of many others, not excepting his own relations, as the Earl had always been a friend to his crown'.[1]

King Edward, on the other hand, was more enthusiastic about an Anglo-Burgundian partnership. Edward's attitude is understandable when it is considered that King Charles VII of France had adopted the Lancastrian cause during the 1450s, when Edward's own father had begun his quest for greater recognition and power. Moreover, Charles had encouraged Scotland to do the same. The concord between France and Scotland had allowed Queen Marguerite d'Anjou to find safe exile in Scotland, while many of her entourage found refuge in France or Burgundy. Warwick felt that any attempt to gain Scottish support for the Yorkist cause was more than welcome.

In 1461 Charles VII was succeeded by his son, Louis XI who, for his duplicity and talent for playing one side off against the other, was given the nickname, 'the Spider King'. Louis XI made advances to both the

Lancastrians and the Yorkists, but he refused to commit himself to either side. He was interested in forcing Duke Philip the Good of Burgundy to give up his independence and make Burgundy part of France. So far, Philip had managed to defend himself against Louis and to keep his duchy intact.

The situation took a new turn when illness forced Philip temporarily to cede power to his son, Charles, count of Charolais. Charles was hostile towards the House of York, but he was even more so towards France. On the basis that 'my enemy's enemy is my friend', Charles eventually began to respond to Edward's overtures; had it not been for commercial rivalry between the two countries, compounded by Warwick's efforts to secure an alliance with France, Edward and Charles would probably have established cordial relations much sooner than they eventually did.

Edward's marriage to Elizabeth Wydeville had brought matters to a crisis. Such divisions in foreign policy led to tensions between Edward and his cousin of Warwick. The Earl was angered, not least because he had been seeking to unite the King with a princess of France; in this respect, Warwick was merely continuing a plan that had been initiated by the late Duke of York. Edward's impetuosity in marrying Elizabeth both undermined the Earl's self-esteem and made him appear ridiculous in the eyes of the French. However, since Edward had presented his marriage as a *fait accompli*, there was little anyone could do but to accept the situation with the best possible grace.

The ill feeling between Edward and Warwick was played out on a stage much closer to home as well. Richard of Warwick could only watch with increasing annoyance as his influence over Edward diminished and his family ambitions became ever more frustrated. The cause of this was, of course, Edward's marriage to Elizabeth Wydeville. As Luchino Dallaghiexia writes to the Duke of Milan:

> Since her coronation she [Elizabeth] has always exerted herself to aggrandise her relations, to wit, her father, mother, brothers and sisters. She had five brothers and as many sisters, and had brought things to such a pass that they had the entire government of this realm, to such as extent that the rest of the lords about the government were one, the Earl of Warwick, who has always been great and deservedly so.[2]

It is, perhaps, not unnatural that the King should seek to advance the Queen's relatives, although, here, it is Elizabeth who is portrayed to be the driving force behind it all. However, it was how Edward did it, in what Warwick perceived to be an underhand way, that made it all the more unacceptable.

One of the consequences of Edward's favour towards his Wydeville relatives was that he provided good marriages for the Queen's family. This deprived Warwick of the chance to find suitable husbands for his own daughters, Isabel Nevill, who was born in 1451, and Anne, her junior by five years. In reality, the only fitting husbands for the two young women were Edward's own brothers, Richard and George. Edward showed no enthusiasm for such alliances, and Warwick would have to live with that; for now.

Despite his growing frustration with Edward's behaviour, Warwick was still able to work in support of the King when Edward initiated diplomatic discussions between England, Burgundy and France. Burgundy had placed severe restrictions on English trade; the aim was to push Edward into a corner, the only escape from which was to treat with either Burgundy or the French. As the situation worsened, with England having taken up a policy of retaliating in kind, Edward was eventually forced to meet representatives of both nations over the negotiating table. Although the discussions were primarily concerned with trade, the new accord between England and Burgundy was to be sealed with the marriage of Edward's sister, Margaret of York. For Charles of Burgundy had recently become a widower.

Margaret was nineteen years old when Isabel of Bourbon, the wife of Charles of Burgundy, died. At that point, Margaret was betrothed to Don Pedro of Aragon, the nephew of the late Duchess Isabel. However, even before Don Pedro's demise, which occurred within a year of his aunt's death in June 1466, renegotiations had begun for Margaret's hand. These had been initiated by Charles himself, who had sent one of his closest advisors, Guillaume de Clugny, to treat with Edward. The English king promptly appointed a negotiating team, led by the Earl of Warwick and including William, Lord Hastings and Sir John Wenlock. They were quickly despatched to Boulogne with instructions to negotiate two marriages: that of Margaret to Charles; the second between George of Clarence and Charles' daughter, Mary of Burgundy. However, the duchy of Burgundy, which was still facing threats from France, was anxious to obtain a defensive alliance with England. They were interested only in Margaret and so, to his disappointment, Clarence's prospective match with Mary came to nothing.

This development came as a major blow to Warwick, who still harboured hopes of strengthening Anglo-French relations. This was clearly also the wish of the French King Louis, who confided his affairs to the Milanese ambassador, Emanuele de Jocopo. The ambassador related the news to his master:

They are already agreed for the most part, in this manner, that King Edward and the King of France henceforth and for ever become brothers in arms, and will live as brothers together, making perpetual peace between the realms of England and France. King Edward will yield, quit and renounce all rights, actions and claims which belong to him, and which pertain or may pertain upon the kingdom of France. His majesty will give his second daughter to the second brother of King Edward, to wife, because the first is married to the daughter of the Earl of Warwick, giving them as dowry part of the territory of the Duke of Burgundy and of Charolais, upon whom they have agreed to wage a war of extermination, dividing the state between them. Thus, King Edward is to have the lordship of Holland, Zeeland and Brabant for his brother aforesaid, and his Majesty the Verno, the County of Flanders and the rest of their dominions.[3]

That is to say, instead of entering into a defensive agreement with England, Burgundy will be attacked by the joint forces of England and France and Duke Charles's lands will be taken and divided between King Louis of France and King Edward, with Edward's half going to his second brother as part of a marriage settlement between him and the French princess, Jeanne. Meanwhile, Margaret of York would be married to Philip of Savoy, the brother of Queen Charlotte of France. For his part, King Edward would give up all rights to the crown of France.

Unfortunately for de Jacopo's account, the idea of Edward renouncing his right to the French throne is probably no more than wishful thinking on the part of King Louis XI. The same would apply to the plan to invade Burgundy and the subsequent division of the lands. There is also confusion concerning Edward's brothers, their marital status and the object of the negotiations between Louis and Warwick. At this point the Duke of Clarence was not married to the Earl of Warwick's daughter, or to anyone else for that matter. Edward's 'second brother' can only refer to Richard. At fifteen years of age, Richard was not too young to be married according to the standards of the day, and it would appear that an attractive dowry was being made available for him; but King Louis had never shown an interest in Richard, rather, the focus of his attention and his intrigues was George of Clarence.[4]

Nevertheless, de Jacopo's communication does reflect the somewhat convoluted nature of the negotiations and diplomacy that were being carried on behind the scenes at this point. In addition, it supports the conjecture, first noted in diplomatic correspondence two months previously, that King Louis XI of France was being solicited to assist England to conquer lands held by Charles, Duke of Burgundy. This, then, reopened the old wounds between Edward and Warwick concerning the Earl's desire for an alliance with France.

The talks with France, now taking place on English soil, continued and agreements were reached regarding a peace treaty. On the other hand, King Louis's offer of a French sponsored marriage for Margaret of York and a generous pension for Edward failed to come to fruition. Edward had left Warwick in charge of the discussions with the French, partly because he wanted to remain on good terms with the Earl and partly because he wanted to use the talks as leverage in his negotiations with Burgundy.

It was during the negotiations with the ambassadors sent by Duke Charles that a long-planned tournament between Queen Elizabeth's brother, Anthony, Lord Scales, and Anthony, Bastard of Burgundy, was finally to take place. This was set to occur in London in the early summer of 1467. Because of the heavy Burgundian presence and the lavish ceremonies that were planned to accompany the joust, Edward felt it prudent to have Warwick out of the way. As such, the Earl and Sir John Wenlock were despatched to France at the head of an embassy detailed to further discuss Louis' proposal. They left England on 28 May accompanied by French ambassadors who were making their way home.

As the negotiations led by Warwick continued, France offered generous deals and lucrative contracts with England, such as free fairs, a reduction in the tolls that had restricted the trade of cloth and wine, and the offer of as much free velvet, silk and damask as the English wanted. Once more, the Milanese ambassador considers himself sufficiently privy to King Louis' private thoughts to be able to write to his master:

> There is a fresh report that M. Charolais has again opened secret negotiations to take King Edward's sister to wife, confirming once more the old league with the English. If this takes place, they have talked of treating with the Earl of Warwick to restore King Henry in England, and the ambassador of the old queen of England is already here.[5]

This report, dated 19 May 1467, is the first hint of the *rapprochement* between Richard of Warwick, King Louis of France and Marguerite d'Anjou that would eventually lead to the Readeption of King Henry VI. As though to underline its menace, such talk of the removal of King Edward coincided with supernatural omens. These had not escaped the notice of the monks at Croyland. The Continuator of the *Croyland Chronicle* writes of them:

In the same year also, there were certain wondrous signs in England; and in divers places there appeared unto many persons, terrible prognostics, replete with no better auspices. For, one day, there were seen in the heavens three suns, and a shower of blood; as the grass and the linen clothes stained therewith, abundantly testified to all beholders. This latter came down in manner just like a gentle shower. Beside this, horsemen and men in armour were seen rushing through the air; so much so, that Saint George himself, conspicuous with the red cross, his usual ensign, and attended by a vast body of armed men, appeared visibly to great numbers [...] A certain woman too, in the country of Huntingdon, who was with child and near the time of her delivery, to her extreme horror, felt the embryo in her womb weeping as it were and uttering a kind of sobbing noise. The same was also heard by some other women, who were surprised in no slight degree thereat. This we know to have happened but seldom indeed, although we read that the most holy forerunner of our Lord, through joy at our approaching salvation, leaped in the womb of his mother. We may, however, not without very fair reason, suppose, that now possibly, under circumstances directly the reverse, even the children unborn deplored our impending calamities, upon the approach of the scourge of Divine vengeance, our sins requiring the same.[6]

The ominous signs reported by the Croyland Continuator feature three suns, which could be interpreted as King Edward's badge, the sun in splendour. The rather sinister shower of blood might be seen to suggest the decline of the House of York amid much bloodshed. Only time would tell.

Richard's whereabouts at the time these portents were witnessed are not known. It is possible, though not probable, that he had accompanied Warwick to France. What is more reasonable is that he remained in England, either at Middleham or, perhaps, at his brother's court. If the latter were the case, he would have witnessed and taken part in the ceremonies surrounding the joust, although he appears not to have been present at the joust itself.

The young Duke could not have been unaware of the difficult atmosphere that had soured relations between his brother and his tutor. His thoughts concerning Warwick's very conspicuous absence during the Burgundian celebrations are his own, and how aware he was of the seriousness of the rift is open to speculation. He could not fail to have noticed the prominent presence of the Wydevilles at the festivities. He must also have noted the absence of his cousin and Warwick's brother, George Nevill, chancellor and archbishop of York. Nevill had been acting in Warwick's stead during the Earl's absence. However, not long after the joust, on 8 June 1467, Edward

Above: 1. The tomb of Edward, second duke of York at Fotheringhay. Duke Edward founded the Collegiate Church of St Mary and All Saints. He is Richard III's great uncle.

Right: 2. Richard, duke of York, father to Richard III; stained glass window at the St Laurence's Church, Ludlow.

3. Fotheringhay; the birthplace of Richard III. To the right is the mound that marks the site of the castle keep, in the background rises the steeple of the Church of St Mary and All Saints.

4. Fotheringhay Castle – all that remains.

5. The Church of St Mary and All Saints, Fotheringhay: The Yorkist badge of the falcon and the fetterlock on a field of blue and murrey.

Above: 6. The Church of St Laurence, Ludlow, a misericord showing the Yorkist badge of the falcon and the fetterlock.

Left: 7. Stained glass at the Church of St Mary and St Alkelda, Middleham, showing Richard of Wyche, Richard III's name saint.

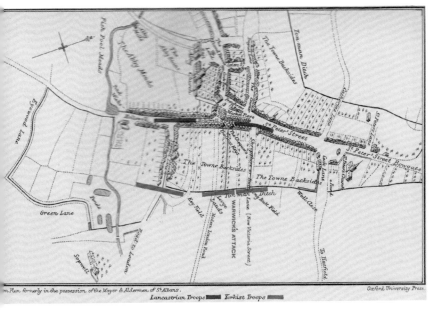

Lancastrian Troops ▬▬ Yorkist Troops ▬▬

8. First Battle of St Albans, the scene of the first Yorkist victory in the Wars of the Roses.

9. Ludlow on the Welsh Marches; one of Richard III's boyhood homes.

Opposite above: 10. Ludlow Castle, situated strategically on a promontory overlooking the Teme.

Opposite: 11. Ludlow Castle showing the range of domestic buildings and the Chapel of St Mary Magdalene, a Norman Round Chapel, where Richard would have worshipped as a boy.

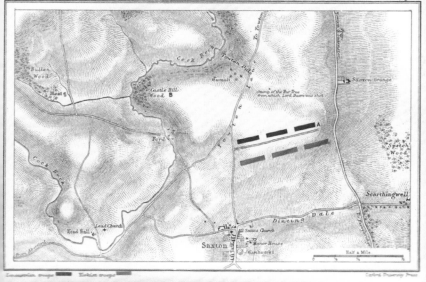

Opposite above: 12. Ludlow Castle showing Mortimer's Tower. As a seven-year-old, Richard watched as his father and two elder brothers escaped through this tower, leaving him, his brother, sister and mother to the mercy of the Lancastrian forces.

Opposite below: 13. Following the Yorkist defeat at the Battle of Wakefield, the duke of York's head was spiked on the Micklegate Bar, York.

Above: 14. The battle of Towton, which secured the victorious Edward of March's place on the throne.

15. Middleham Castle, Wensleydale, North Yorkshire. The home of the earl of Warwick and the setting for Richard's training as a knight.

Opposite above: 16. Middleham Castle, Richard's luxurious, palatial home, where he lived as a page and studied under the tutelage of the earl of Warwick.

Opposite below: 17. Middleham Castle; the western side of the keep held the great chamber on the upper level and the kitchen beneath. The kitchen contained tanks in the floor in which fish were believed to be kept alive until needed.

18. Middleham Castle; a chapel was attached to the eastern side of the Keep. It was entered through an ante-room at the top of the staircase. Although now much ruined, the remainder of the tracery window can still be seen.

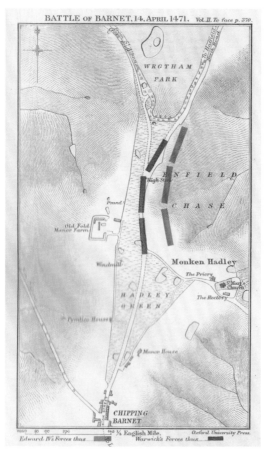

WROTHAM
PARK

E N F I E L D
High St.

C H A S E

Pound

Old Fold
Manor Farm

Windmill

Monken Hadley

The Priory
St Mary's
Church

H A D L E Y
G R E E N

The Rectory

Fynches House

Manor House

CHIPPING
BARNET

¼ English Mile.   *Oxford University Press.*
Edward IV's Forces thus   Warwick's Forces thus

19. The battle of Barnet, 14 April 1471 was the first battle in King Edward's campaign to take back his throne. It was Richard's first opportunity to use the fighting skills he had acquired under the earl of Warwick. He was slightly wounded but acquitted himself well in the field.

20. The 'broken sword' portrait. In this sixteenth-century portrait Richard was originally shown to be more deformed than he appears now: the left arm once ended in a stump and the left shoulder was much higher. These deformities match the description of the King by Sir Thomas More, who said that Richard's left shoulder was raised and the left arm was 'werish'.

21. The Church of St Mary and All Saints, Fotheringhay, features the royal arms in the centre, with Richard's white boar on the right and the black bull of the duke of Clarence on the left.

22. The Wakefield Tower in the Tower of London. Henry VI was held here following his capture by Edward IV and murdered shortly afterwards.

Above: 23. The chapel in the Wakefield Tower. Tradition holds that the saintly King Henry VI was murdered here while at prayer.

Right: 24. King Edward IV is restored following his victories at Barnet and Tewkesbury. The brutal removal of his Lancastrian enemies ensured that he would reign in peace at last.

25. Sheriff Hutton Castle, North Yorkshire. Richard acquired this castle and estates as part of his inheritance in right of his wife from the earl of Warwick.

pointedly removed the archbishop from the chancellorship. Edward personally ensured that Nevill gave up the Great Seal. The King, accompanied by the Duke of Clarence and several others, rode to the archbishop's inn at Charing Cross, where:

> the archbishop did deliver the said seal sealed up in a white leather bag under his signet to the king's own hands, and the king took it, and did so deliver it to John de Audeley to carry with the king to Westminster palace; and on the morrow in an inner chamber within Westminster palace, in the presence of divers lords, judges and masters of chancery, with his own hand, the king delivered the said seal, sealed up as aforesaid, to Master Robert Kirkeham.[7]

Edward, then, oversaw in person the public downfall of his cousin the chancellor and he made the handing over of the Great Seal almost into a ceremony. There could be no more clear evidence of the fall from grace that was now affecting the Nevill family.

Free now from what he almost certainly considered to be interference from an annoyingly meddlesome and imperious subject, Edward next concluded a thirty-year truce with Duke Francis of Brittany. Since hostilities between Brittany and France were something of a tradition, this treaty, which was based upon commerce and by which Edward undertook to protect Breton interests, was intended as a snub to Louis of France. By extension, it was also a snub to Richard of Warwick. Nevill power had clearly faded at the court of the Rose of Rouen, and it had been replaced by that of the Wydevilles.

For his part, the Earl of Warwick must also have been aware that his influence over the King was now a thing of the past. He had worked hard for an alliance with France, but now it was obvious that Edward would not brook such an idea. His brother had been cast aside and it looked as though Warwick would follow him into the wilderness. The not unexpected death of Philip of Burgundy brought to an end the negotiations between England, Burgundy and France. Anthony the Bastard was sent home and Warwick was escorted to the French coast by a number of ambassadors. Having arrived in Sandwich, the Earl was obliged to kick his heels in London, Windsor and then Canterbury as he followed on behind the King's train. Eventually he saw no option but to return to their homes the French ambassadors he had brought with him. They left in August 1467 with nothing to show for their journey or their efforts. Shortly after that Warwick, all but ignored by his king, returned to his estates at Middleham.

According to Jean de Waurin,[8] while Warwick was still in the south, he took George of Clarence and Richard Gloucester with him on a visit to

Cambridge. Here, it is suggested, he proposed that Clarence should marry his elder daughter, Isabel. Were he to do so, Warwick pointed out, he would become heir to half the Earl's vast estates. This was a tempting proposition indeed. We are left to wonder whether or not he also offered the hand of his youngest daughter, Anne, to Richard on equally attractive terms. Hall, without authority but with much imagination, elaborates on this story, placing it immediately after the King's marriage. In this version of the event, Clarence, angry that Edward had married off so many ladies who would otherwise have made more suitable partners for the two Dukes and others of the blood royal, exclaims:

> By the swete saincte George I sweare, if my brother of Gloucester would joine with me, we would make hym knowe that we were all three mannes sonnes, of one mother and one lignage discended, whiche should be more referred and promoted, then strangers of his wifes bloud.[9]

Waurin, as he continues his narrative, states that when King Edward heard of what had taken place, he summoned his brothers into his presence. Edward, a majestic six foot three-and-a half inches tall and proportionately broad, with as yet none of the excess fat that resulted from his life of debauchery and gluttony that would mar his impressive looks later in his life, towered over his younger siblings: the eighteen-year-old George and the fifteen-year-old Richard. He took on that fierce expression that Mancini describes: 'should he assume an angry countenance he could appear very terrible to beholders',[10] and, as Waurin asserts, mercilessly reprimanded his brothers before having them arrested and placed under guard.

The story related by Waurin is certainly compelling and it represents a frightening example of royal power as exercised by King Edward, who not only intimidates his two younger brothers, he also deprives them of their liberty, albeit for a short time; but is it true? It is found in only one chronicle, that of Jean de Waurin. A prominent man of affairs who is contemporary to the events about which he writes, Waurin had been attached to the court of Philip the Good of Burgundy and then to that of his successor, Charles de Charolais. He took an interest in English affairs, and was present at the joust hosted by King Edward at Smithfield. He drew some of his information for his *Chronicle* from the Yorkist *Chronicle of the Rebellion in Lincolnshire* and the *Historie of the Arrivall of Edward IV*, although neither source comments upon this incident. His other sources remain unknown. On the other hand, Waurin uses his imagination almost as freely as More would later accuse Polydore Vergil of doing, and so is not always to be trusted. It is possible that there is a grain of truth in Waurin's account, and that this was later augmented to become a more elaborate story.

The effect of such an experience on George of Clarence and Richard Gloucester can only be imagined. The duke of Clarence was still Edward's heir as he would continue to be until the birth of Edward's first child. Aged eighteen, he must have felt quite indignant at the treatment he had received from his brother. He was possibly defiant; if not openly, then at least in his own heart, although he knew he was too precious to his brother to be allowed to come to any serious harm; at least for the moment.

For Richard, the situation was very different. Not only was he physically much smaller than Edward, and also probably much smaller than Clarence by this point, he was also of much less significance politically. It is possible that Richard knew, even if only on a subconscious level, that he now stood at a turning point in his life. He was a page at the household of his cousin, Richard of Warwick. The Earl was supervising his education, both intellectually and as a knight, and initiating him into the world on a social level as well. Edward, on the other hand, was Richard's brother and his king, for, despite their blood relationship, Richard was still a subject. The young duke seems to have been in awe of his elder brother, at least to a degree. Edward was, for Richard, the fulfilment of certain prophecies; God had guided Edward and placed him on the throne. Edward's reign had been inaugurated under the symbol of triple-suns, a flaming star, surely a sign from God. Edward, then, was not only the highest authority in the land, but he was also supported by the highest endorsement. To defy him could be construed as an act of treason certainly, but it was also to go against the will of the Almighty, and that would surely bring consequences that were too awful to contemplate. Duke Richard had to decide to whom he would give his loyalty, tutor or king. He chose the King, and he chose well. Richard had taken heed of his brother's reaction to Warwick's audacious proposal, whether he had been directly involved or not, and he learned the lesson of obedience.

What is certain is that there was much resentment between King Edward and the Earl of Warwick. It is also reasonable to assume that Warwick's obvious exclusion from the reception and festivities that were laid on for the Burgundian party led to his seeking to take his revenge on the King by attempting to lead the royal brothers astray. It is true that Warwick would later manage to corrupt Clarence and turn him against the King; it is not impossible that the process was begun at this stage. Certainly, by St Valentine's Day 1468, the Milanese ambassador, writing from Tours, was spreading the gossip once again:

> In England the country is in arms. The Earl of Warwick has drawn a brother of
> the king against the king himself. They have not yet come to open hostilities,
> but are treating for an accommodation. The Earl has sent word here.[11]

According to this interpretation, then, while there was as yet no open aggression between Edward and Warwick, the Earl was believed to have won over one
of the King's brothers. We know, of course, that this was Clarence. The rumour
that Warwick wanted to marry one of his daughters to one of the King's brothers was still current, and now it seemed that one brother had been seduced by
the power, wealth and position that such a marriage would bring. This lends
credence to Jean de Waurin's account that Warwick endeavoured to bring the
Duke of Clarence over to his side. Although he appears to have failed, with
Edward taking the harsh measure of arresting both his brothers and placing
them under guard, Warwick had never given up hope that such an eventually
would come about and that Clarence would marry Isabel. Indeed, he had continued to work behind the scenes to obtain the necessary dispensation from the
pope, since any such marriage between Clarence and a daughter of the Earl of
Warwick would be within the prohibited degrees of consanguinity.[12]

For all that, Warwick had not yet fallen entirely out of favour with Edward.
He continued to receive grants and rewards, such as several forfeited lands
in the north as well as the office of justice of the royal forests north of the
Trent, which brought him an annual income of 100 marks. He was to share
with his brother, John, the profits of the royal gold, silver and lead mines
north of the Trent. He also received the lucrative wardship and marriage of
Francis Lovell, whom he promptly married off to his niece, Anne FitzHugh;
such haste probably inspired by the fear that Edward would recommend
a marriage between Lovell and one of Warwick's daughters. Moreover,
Warwick was given an important place in Edward's council, which it did the
Earl no dishonour to accept.

The problem was that Warwick felt that any office was beneath him if it
prevented his dominating the King. As far as he was concerned, that Edward
wore the crown was entirely due to his, Warwick's, efforts and support. He
felt aggrieved that the King did not seem to appreciate this. Nevertheless, a
truce was reached and an apparently harmonious relationship between king
and Earl was resumed. More importantly, any animosity between the two
most powerful men in England was not allowed to taint relations between
Richard Gloucester and his cousin. Indeed, the two travelled together to
York at some point in 1468, where they were both well received.[13]

Still, the marriage between Margaret of York and Duke Charles of
Burgundy was not universally accepted. Waurin notes that it would take

place in spite of the best efforts of Louis XI, Warwick and nearly all the people of England. On his side, the French king had tried to prevent the issue of the papal dispensation. He applied pressure to his financial contacts in Milan to prevent Edward from borrowing enough money to cover his sister's dowry. The flurry of correspondence generated by the Milanese ambassadors attests to King Louis's opposition to the alliance.

As the diplomatic letters had earlier hinted, Louis was becoming increasingly supportive of Henry VI's cause; the proposed marriage did nothing to convince him otherwise. Most ungallantly, the Spider King took advantage of King Edward's standing as *homme à femmes*, as well as the less than pure reputation of the bride's elder sister, Anne, to spread rumours about Margaret, whom he tarred with the same brush. The Milanese ambassador makes it clear that the Duke of Burgundy was anxious to consummate his marriage as soon as may be. He added that the Duke had issued a public edict that no mention was to be made of 'what more and more people know, to wit that his future consort in the past has been somewhat devoted to love affairs, indeed, in the opinion of many she has even had a son.'[14] To refer in any way to this rumour was to incur the punishment of being tied into a sack and 'thrown into the river forthwith.' Notwithstanding the Duke's efforts to quell them, such rumours would persist; even after two years of marriage, Peitro Aliprando was able to write to his master that 'all is not well between the Duke of Burgundy and the King of England, on account of the Duchess, who did not go to her husband a virgin, and they are certainly trying to play a trick upon my master.'[15]

Had there been any substance to these stories, they would have been exploited by Edward Hall, who was always eager to peddle anything detrimental to the Yorkist family; yet all he had to say of Margaret was that she was:

> A fayre virgin, a lady of excellent beautie, and yet more of womanhode than beautie, and more vertue than womanhode, whose innumerable good qualities, beside the giftes of nature, grace and fortune, were so seriously setfurth to Duke Philip, and the earle of Charoloys hys sonne, that bothe the father & the child judged that marriage to be the moste metest matrimony in Christendom, not onely for the excellent qualities and manifold virtues emprinted in the person of the noble virgin, but also for the great profite, alleyance and continuall friendship that should growe and ryse betweene the realme of Englande, and the Dukes landes.[16]

The gentleman, it seems, saved all his venom for Margaret's brother, Richard.

For his part, Warwick was less than satisfied with the alliance. He absented himself from the council which convened at Kingston, and so did not witness Margaret's acceptance of the marriage and its terms. The Duke of Clarence also showed himself to be discontented with the way things had turned out. He had expected a good marriage out of the various treaties between France and Burgundy, but his hopes had been thwarted by the refusal on the part of Burgundy to countenance any such eventuality. If the Earl of Warwick's previous attempts to seduce the young Duke into an alliance with his family had failed, he would now find that any future efforts would not be so readily discouraged.

The people of England, whom King Louis said were displeased at the union, showed their anger by rioting and attacking those Flemish immigrants who had crossed the seas some two decades earlier and had made England their home. The main cause of the violence was not so much the marriage itself, although they thought that was bad enough, but rather the harsh restrictions and increased exchange rate that had been agreed as part of the negotiations. Prices were also raised in Bruges, so that those courtiers who were required to attend the wedding ceremonies were obliged to increase their already considerable outlay.

As to Richard, his thoughts concerning the marriage of his sister, as with so much else at this stage of his life, cannot be known. It can be imagined that there was some degree of sadness at the thought of losing a sister with whom he had experienced so much in their younger days. They had shared many of the highs and lows of life; they had been schooled together, played together, experienced the horror of seeing their father and elder brothers retreat in the face of the enemy, had been taken prisoner of war together and, more happily, had lived in the comfort and opulence of grand and beautiful palaces and castles. Richard assisted with the arrangements for his sister's journey and might have looked with approval at her trousseau, which consisted of silks valued at £1,000, dishes in gold, silver and gilt worth £160, soft furnishings costing £100, as well as £900 in cash and a further £200 paid to her steward to cover her expenses between London and Bruges.

Richard took a great deal of interest in jewellery, and as such, his imagination would have been captured by his sister's wedding coronet.[17] This magnificent piece is quite small, being only 12 cm in diameter and 12 cm high. The coronet, cast in gold, is decorated with pearls, since the name Margaret means 'pearl', and other precious stones. These set off the enamelled white roses of the House of York, which alternate with the red, green and white enamelled lettering that spell out the name, 'Margaret of York'. The coronet supports a diadem with alternating large and small jewelled roses. The lower edge of the diadem features the initials 'C' and 'M' entwined with lovers' knots.

This coronet might have been made for Margaret at the time of Edward's coronation, in which case, it would certainly have been known to Richard. On the other hand, it is possible that it was presented to her by her husband. Richard would have known it in either case because, as we shall see, he would visit his sister whenever it was practicable to do so.

As the spring warmed into summer, Margaret left the Royal Wardrobe to begin her lengthy journey at the dawning of her new life as the Duchess of Burgundy. *Hearne's Fragment* states that:

> Margaret Sister unto King Edward beforesaid, departed from the King, and rode through London behind the Earl of Warwick, and rode that night to Stratford Abbey, and from thence to the sea-side, and went to Flanders to Bruges, where she was married with great solemnity.[18]

This account, while capturing the essentials, very much abbreviates the ceremonial surrounding Margaret's departure. As the preparations got underway, King Edward wrote to Sir John Paston about the forthcoming event, adding:

> We therefore, wele understanding and remembering the good affection ye bere towards us all, our pleasure is, and our said sister, whereupon we greatly trust, desire and pray yow right effectuously that, every excuse or delaye laide aparte, ye will dispose yourselfe to the saide intent and purpose against the first day of June next cominge, according to your honour and degree, and that ye faile not to do us justys, pleas.[19]

Margaret had ridden pillion behind the Earl of Warwick as she left London. This demonstrated to everyone watching that Warwick accepted and approved of the marriage. However, there were those who noticed that Warwick's smile masked his true inner feelings; it was said that the Earl, 'still kept up a show of friendly relations with Edward - twirling between his fingers the white rose which he had taken from his bosom, ere he threw it in the dust and trampled on it.'[20]

The bridal party, which included Duke Richard, stopped at St Paul's, where the bride-to-be made an offering before resuming her journey along Cheapside. Here, she was greeted by the Lord Mayor and the Aldermen, from whom she received a gift of two silver-gilt bowls valued at £100 in gold. Crossing London Bridge, the party stopped for the night at Stratford

Abbey where the court was in residence. This abbey had been the scene of Henry III's reception of the papal legate in 1267 and had witnessed the establishment of peace between the King and the barons. Later, it was one of the religious houses targeted by insurgents during the Peasants Revolt of 1381, when many of its goods were taken and its charters burned. Also during Richard II's reign the abbey experienced more damage, this time by floods. The King, seeing the devastation, personally saw to the restoration of the abbey buildings.

The next morning, Margaret bade farewell to the court and, accompanied by Richard Gloucester and George of Clarence and an impressive retinue, embarked on a pilgrimage to the shrine of St Thomas Becket at Canterbury. This was a poignant moment for Richard, who knew of the archbishop's silent involvement in English coronations. Legend had it that the Virgin Mary presented Thomas with sacred oil, and it was this with which the kings of England were anointed. The oil had been discovered by the Black Prince before being lost and then rediscovered in the Tower by his son, Richard II. Richard, whose piety was on a par with that of Richard Gloucester, wanted to be re-anointed with the oil; unhappily, the request was refused.

Soon after leaving Canterbury, the bridal party were rejoined by King Edward who had ridden on to catch up with them; the King, it seemed, was not yet ready to let go of his little sister. They journeyed on, stopping at Dartford, Rochester and Sittingbourne, before finally arriving at Margate. Richard stood on the quay and watched as the ship bearing his beloved sister to the court with which he was once so familiar faded from sight. The world must have seemed just a little bit lonely as he slowly turned away and prepared for the long journey back to Middleham.

The quiet and stillness that settled upon the House of York following the excitement of the ceremonies surrounding the departure of one of its daughters was not the happy omen it might have seemed. For it is to the marriage of Margaret and Charles that, according to the Crowland Continuator, we must look for the seeds of the unrest that was to disrupt the kingdom not too many months hence:

> This, in my opinion, was really the cause of the dissentions between the king and the Earl, and not the one which has been previously mentioned - the marriage of the king with the Queen Elizabeth. For this marriage of the king and queen [...] had long before this been solemnly sanctioned and approved of at Reading, by the Earl himself, and all the prelates and great lords of the kingdom. Indeed, it is the fact, that the Earl continued to show favour to all the queen's kindred, until he found that her relatives and connexions, contrary to

his wishes, were using their utmost endeavours to promote the other marriage, which in conformity with the king's wishes, eventually took place between Charles and the Lady Margaret.[21]

Quite how far the dissentions between the King and the Earl were to take them could not have been envisaged by either party.

CHAPTER 11

THE WARWICK REBELLION, 1469-1471

Richard Gloucester turned sixteen years of age in October 1468. He was now no longer a minor but considered old enough to play an active part in public affairs. In view of this, in January 1469, King Edward recalled his youngest brother to court. Richard left Middleham far behind as he steadily made his way through countryside whitened by the snows of deepest winter. The silvered trees, the cold blue skies, the cordial welcome in the taverns and inns, their fires warm and inviting, the food hot and comforting, the beds soft and cosy in the tranquil darkness of the winter nights; the beauty of an England that stood on the brink of bloody civil war.

Edward IV's reign, like many another, experienced uprisings and rebellions. Most of them were rapidly quashed. Edward had faced a serious resurgence of Lancastrian activity in 1466 when the Isle of Wight had been taken. At about the same time, a rebellion in the marches of North Wales troubled the captains of the castles of Beaumaris, Caernarvon and Montgomery to the point that they requested assurance that the necessary reinforcements would be available to them. Two years later one of the Kent estates belonging to Earl Rivers was attacked and pillaged by a mob. Now, just as Richard had settled into his life at court in the spring of 1469, a new sequence of rebellions broke out, beginning with those of Robin of Redesdale and Robin of Holderness.

In fact, Robin of Redesdale, or Robin Mend-All as he was sometimes known, may have been involved with two rebellions that spring, although there is very little evidence for the alleged first uprising. According to the very confused primary sources, the first rebellion, if there had indeed been a first, was probably simply a protest against excessive taxes, the beneficiaries of which were perceived to have been the King's favourites. It was a short-lived affair and was quickly dispersed by John Nevill, Earl of Northumberland. The undaunted Robin of Redesdale crossed over to Lancashire, where he began to regroup.

Shortly afterwards John Nevill was confronted by another uprising. This one, led by Robin of Holderness, appears to have been in support of Henry Percy, who had recently been deprived of his earldom in favour of John Nevill. Robin was captured by Nevill and beheaded. It appeared that peace had been restored, but the undercurrent of discontent had not been suppressed.

Robin of Redesdale began to move south towards the end of June gathering yet more supporters as he went. According to some historians, the Redesdale rebellion had been instigated by disaffected members of the Nevill family with the Earl of Warwick at the centre. It is true that there was a heavy Nevill influence behind it all. Robin of Redesdale himself might be identified with John Conyers, a cousin by marriage to the Kingmaker and the son of his steward at Middleham. On the other hand, according to Warkworth, 'Sere William Conyars knyghte was there capteyne, which callede hym self Robyne of Riddesdale'.[1] This refers to John Conyer's younger brother, William. However, the name of Robin of Redesdale most probably concealed a collective which was composed of members of the Nevill affinity of North Yorkshire.[2] Certainly, the Kingmaker's nephew, Sir Henry FitzHugh was involved, as was a cousin, Sir Henry Nevill and a son of Lord Dudley who had married a daughter of George Nevill, Lord Latimer, the Kingmaker's uncle.

It is possibly due to this connection with Warwick that Edward did not take the rebellion seriously. In this he was misguided because the new disturbance was probably fuelled by disaffection that spread across a wider sphere than that of Warwick. The Croyland Continuator notes that 'a whirlwind again came from the north, in form of a mighty insurrection of the commons of that part of the country'.[3] Warkworth describes it as 'a grete insurreccyon in Yorkeschire, of dyvers knyghtes, squyers, and comeners'.[4]

Had the uprising been connected with Warwick in any concerted way, the Earl was playing his cards very close to his chest. As late as May 1469, he was apparently still in favour with Edward. He had been at Windsor to attend the investiture of Duke Charles of Burgundy as a Knight of the Garter. Edward continued to appoint Warwick to important commissions, including one for an oyer and terminer issued on 22 May.[5] This commission, which also included Gloucester and Clarence, covered the northern counties of York, Westmorland and Cumberland. Possibly, it was Edward's reaction to the rebellious activity in those areas.

For all the cordiality that apparently existed between the two cousins, it was only a matter of time before Warwick's frustration with the King spilled over into open rebellion. In fact, he appears to have hardened his heart against Edward finally in 1468 while Duke Richard was still in his care. However, it was not the youngest of Edward's brothers who would form an alliance with the disgruntled Earl, but the middle brother, George.

In spite of the generous grants George had received from him, it is not difficult to see why he should have become disillusioned with his brother. Since the birth of the King's first child, Elizabeth of York in 1466, George was no longer heir presumptive. True, Elizabeth was a girl, but with a man as vigorous and sexy as King Edward, it would surely be only a matter of time before a male heir was born to the royal couple.

Nevertheless, as the King's nearest brother, George had looked forward to a special place at court, but this did not materialise. He could have expected an advantageous marriage, but this was not forthcoming either. Had they succeeded, the negotiations between Warwick and Louis XI for an Anglo-French attack on the Duchy of Burgundy would have been of benefit to Clarence. He would have made a good marriage and enjoyed the lordship of Holland, Zeeland and Brabant. All this the Spider King had dangled before the young Duke's dazzled eyes, and the Duke had not looked away. However, his hopes were dashed by Edward's negative response, influenced by Burgundian lack of interest, to the proposition of a French alliance. With the prospect of a marriage with Isabel Nevill, Warwick's daughter, thwarted by Edward's refusal even to consider the idea, coupled with Edward's preference for the interests of his Wydeville relations over those of Clarence, the Duke saw both his material worth and his self-esteem plummet.

It is no surprise, then, that George of Clarence should have been attracted by an offer of marriage to Isabel when the Kingmaker himself once more broached the subject. To follow this route was, of course, to go against the express wishes of the King. This was certainly serious, but George was easily led. His insolent, arrogant and jealous nature allowed him to overcome any qualms he might have felt about defying his brother. Moreover, it is possible that George was aware that Warwick was proposing to declare Edward a bastard and to replace him on the throne with Clarence.[6]

The illegitimacy or otherwise of King Edward IV is an interesting point and deserves to be examined in full. Edward was born at Rouen, the capital of Normandy, not long into his father's second tenure as lieutenant of France. York had arrived in Normandy at the end of June 1441. Within a fortnight he had set off on campaign to Pontoise, which had kept him away for several weeks. The timing and duration of this campaign is confirmed by the recent discovery of a record in the archives of Rouen Cathedral. It has been claimed that this same record raises interesting questions about the legitimacy of York's second son, Edward.[7] Since Edward was born on 28 April 1442, he was probably conceived in late July or early August 1441. The record in the cathedral at Rouen states clearly that the Duke left the city in mid-July and did not return until 20 August 1441. As such, it is possible that he returned home to his wife to discover that she was pregnant.

Clearly it cannot be stated with absolute certainty that York was not the father of the future King Edward IV merely on the evidence of a single record in the cathedral at Rouen. After all, Cecily might have managed to join her husband for a time. Indeed, it was Cecily's duty, as the ideal medieval wife, the ideal military wife, to accompany her husband wherever he might be posted despite the difficulties of travel, the loneliness of life away from her family and the comforts of home.[8] It is also possible that York managed to return to Rouen on a brief visit.

In calculating the date at which a baby might have been conceived, one has to assume that the mother's menstrual cycle is of average length, that all had gone well with the pregnancy and that the baby was born on time. For a child born on 28 April, the approximate date for conception would be 5 August. Given this set of circumstances it is almost certain that the Duke of York was not present at Rouen at the critical moment. However, this dating relies on factors that can never be trusted to be precise. Babies come in their own time. It is possible that Edward was born late, and that he was conceived prior to his father's departure for Pontoise. Alternatively, and more probably, he had been premature, and so was conceived after his father's return to Rouen.

It is true, however, that as the son of so important an aristocratic family, Edward's epiphany should have been celebrated with all magnificence. As it was, his baptism was an understated affair that took place in a small private chapel in Rouen Castle. No records exist to explain why this should have been so; there is nothing to suggest that the city was under siege or that it was in the grip of plague at the time.

Yet, once again, the situation is not necessarily as suspicious as it may seem. It should be remembered that Edward was not the first son born to Richard and Cecily. The Duchess had already produced the heir to the House of York: Henry. The boy had been born on 10 February 1441 at Hatfield. King Henry VI had marked the event by presenting York with a gift of £100 for his demonstration of dynastic loyalty. He also stood godfather to the child, who was named after him. The heir to the House of York had brought the blessings of the King upon his house, and the fortunes of his family were set upon a more secure course. Unfortunately, Henry appears to have died young, although it is not known for certain when he died.[9] Had he died shortly after his birth it is probable that, given the tragic loss of their first heir, the Duke and Duchess were simply being cautious when it came to Edward who was, after all, the precious new heir to the family. Perhaps they did not want to tempt fate by giving their new son a splendid and ostentatious welcome into the world only to see their hopes dashed once again.[10] On the other hand, it is entirely possible that Henry survived long enough to accompany his parents to France and was still alive when his brother was born. As such, perhaps the Duke and Duchess saw no need to celebrate the spare. We simply cannot know. If, on the other hand, Edward was premature, his survival might have been doubtful. His parents would have been reluctant to subject the baby to such a rigorous and elaborate a ceremony as a baptism with all the trappings. Of course, in this case, there would have been some recording of it and prayers would have been said for the baby.

Whatever the explanation, Edward's minimalist and very private baptism was in marked contrast to the celebrations laid on for his brother, Edmund, who was born a year later. For this second son of York no expense was spared and no honour neglected. His very public baptism took place within the majestic thirteenth-century Cathedral of Notre Dame at Rouen. The Cathedral chapter even allowed the family to use the font at which the Norman Duke, Rollo, an ancestor of William the Conqueror, had been baptised into Christianity. This was an important relic; the House of York was indeed highly honoured.

The contrast between the two baptisms can be explained by taking into account the family's concern about the well-being, or even the survival, of its sons. There is also a political explanation for the lavish celebrations laid on for the new baby. Richard of York appears to have been planning to establish Edmund as a great Norman landowner. As a matter of fact, the preparations for this had already begun, even at this early stage. The arrangement would allow the Duke's inherited assets to pass intact to his eldest son, while Edmund would become the master of such estates as Orbec, Beaumont-le-Roger, Arques, Breteuil, Évreux, Conches and St-Sauveur-Lendelin. Indeed, by the following October a receiver-general, Nicholas Molyneux, had been appointed and a council established to administer the estates in York's absence. Edmund's sumptuous baptism might have been used as part of this plan, designed to ensure that the boy would be accepted in Normandy.[11]

In the end, there is no reason to accept the hypothesis that Edward was illegitimate. The dates given in the register at the cathedral of Rouen and the birth date of the baby can be reconciled by natural means. His cautious baptism can be explained by a natural reluctance of the baby's parents to tempt fate in view of the premature death of the first heir. On the other hand, there are good reasons for lavishly celebrating the birth of the next son, Edmund. He was to be an important landowner in his native Normandy. As such, his extravagant baptism, graced by the important Norman relic of Duke Rollo's baptismal font, made perfect sense.

The case for declaring King Edward a bastard is, therefore, without foundation. Nevertheless, in adopting this strategy, Warwick was making good use of an old and fairly worn practice of manipulating allegations of illegitimacy for political propaganda. A similar approach was to accuse powerful women of adultery. Warwick had apparently accused Marguerite d'Anjou of this very offence in 1460. He later claimed that her son, Edward of Lancaster, was the fruit of a liaison between the Queen and a wandering player.[12] In the case of King Edward, the alleged father was a very tall and rather fetching archer of the Rouen garrison by the name of Blaybourne.

Sources from mainland Europe were already reporting the particularly juicy news of Warwick's attack on Edward as early as the summer of 1469. A letter, dated 8 September 1469, by Sforza di Bettinis, Milanese ambassador in France to the Duke of Milan, states that:

> From England there is news how the Duke of Clarence and the Earl of Warwick persevere more every day in prosecuting the King of England and keep making a great gathering of troops to constrain him and deprive him of the crown. The king, on his side, makes every provision possible to defend himself. The Earl of Warwick has recently sent his ambassador to the Most Christian king [Louis XI] to make an understanding with his Majesty. They left very satisfied from what I could gather. We have not yet heard, however, what arrangements they may have made together, and his majesty is not making any sign of sending them help or subsidy.[13]

It is a testament both to Richard's strength of character and his loyalty to the King that he did not join his former guardian in rebellion. Certainly, of the two, Richard had the least cause to be so devoted. Edward had awarded him certain estates and livelihoods, of course, but many of them were relatively worthless. Others had been removed from Richard by the King in an attempt to calm the indignant feelings of the petulant and resentful Clarence. Yet loyal he remained. Perhaps there was a degree of trepidation guiding Richard's attitude towards the King. The young Duke had already witnessed the violent temper of his brother over the affair with Warwick at Cambridge, where the Earl had offered his daughter to Clarence. Even if a similar offer had not been extended to Richard, the ferocity of Edward's response had been enough to bring Richard to the point where he was forced to make a choice between his king and his cousin and tutor. That he opted for obedience to Edward was wise, especially when it is considered that there would be nowhere to hide and no one to shelter a rebel brother of the King. However, there was more to it than that. As has already been shown, Richard saw the hand of God in Edward's kingship. Edward fulfilled God's plan as revealed by prophecy. Richard's loyalty stemmed from his profoundly sincere piety and his deep-seated devotion to God.

Since returning from Middleham, Duke Richard had accompanied Edward at the trial, held at Salisbury in February 1469, of two alleged traitors Henry Courtney and Thomas Hungerford. The record of the hearings shows that Richard had served as the leading member of the oyer and terminer that had condemned the men to death.[14] Also included in this commission were the Earl of Warwick and the Duke of Clarence. Both conspicuously failed to attend on this occasion.

Courtney and Hungerford were charged with conspiring, on 21 May 1468 and at other times, with having plotted, in league with Marguerite d'Anjou, the 'final death and final destruction...of the Most Christian Prince, Edward IV.'[15] Thomas Hungerford pleaded not guilty and placed himself upon the country. Henry Courtney pleaded a pardon, dated 21 July 1469, of all treasons committed prior to the previous 15 April of that year. He added that he was not guilty of the charges levelled against him and that he, too, put himself upon the country. William Sotehill, the King's attorney then announced that the two men were guilty. After some deliberation, the sixteen-strong jury agreed, noting as they passed their verdict that the convicted men had no goods. As such, it was judged that they should:

> be taken to the prison where they are detained and be drawn thence through the city of New Salisbury to the gallows of Bymerton and there hanged and thrown to the ground alive and that their internals be drawn out of their bellies and burnt while they are alive, that their heads be cut off and their bodies quartered and their heads and quarters placed where the king shall appoint.

The executions took place on 18 January 1469 in the presence of the King; such was Edward's interest in the case.

Richard's detractors have seen in this yet another instance of the Duke's deviousness and guile.[16] Their reasoning is simple. Following the rebellions of 1468-69, most of the Lancastrian plotters were fined; only Sir Thomas Hungerford and Henry Courtney faced forfeiture and execution. Warkworth, as he reports the incident in his chronicle, points out that 'menne seyde the Lorde Stafforde of Southwyke was cause of the seyde Herry Curtenayes dethe, for he wolde be the Eale of Devynschyre, and so the Kynge made hym afterwarde.'[17] In other words, Sir Humphrey Stafford, who was one of the judges, is credited by Warkworth of having influenced justice to the extent that he could persuade the King to convince the judges that Courtney and Hungerford were guilty simply so that he could get his hands on a title that would be rendered extinct by Courtney's death. By extension, the fact that Richard Gloucester was granted the Hungerford inheritance must mean that he, also, had influenced the King, who then dutifully obeyed his loyal subjects and granted them the death penalty they apparently coveted.

This theory, so convenient for those who seek to disparage Richard's name at every opportunity, ignores the fact that Richard had previously been granted the Hungerford estates, although they had later been taken away. It was, therefore, a case of Edward showing himself to be fair and lenient towards a family who later betrayed him and the trust he placed in them. This had happened before to the King; it would happen again. The most obvious example would be that of his own brother, George of Clarence. Moreover, Edward made a point of coming to Salisbury in person to 'do justice on Henry Courtney and Thomas Hungerford, Knights, attaint'.[18] This shows how important it was to the King to see those who had conspired with Queen Marguerite d'Anjou to deprive him of his throne receive due punishment. Certainly both Humphrey Stafford and Richard Gloucester did benefit from the execution of these men, but it does not follow that they were the driving force behind the events at Salisbury. Edward was a most resolute man who was perfectly capable of choosing when to be lenient and when to be unforgiving. There is no question of justice having been overridden or of two men being condemned for anything other than that for which they were found guilty. The most that can be said is that they were possibly scapegoats, nothing more.

Richard was granted the Hungerford inheritance on 23 October 1468, that is, three months prior to the execution of Sir Thomas. There is nothing sinister about this; Hungerford's attainder forfeited the estates to the King, who could then dispose of them as he saw fit. As we have seen, he chose to restore them to Richard, who had been granted them previously.

Richard, then, and his male heirs were granted the lordships and manors of Farleigh, Heytesbury and Teffont, as well as other manors, lordships, rents, reversions, services and possessions in Somerset, Wiltshire, Dorset,

Devon, Gloucester and elsewhere. If Sir Thomas's grandmother, Margaret, Lady Hungerford, had considered resorting to devious tactics once more in an attempt to hang on to the entire inheritance, she thought better of it. She and Richard came to an agreement under the terms of which Richard was to have and enjoy the castle and manor of Farleigh Hungerford as well as a toft in Hungerford called Hungerford Court. These he would hold without interruption by her or the feoffees of Walter, Lord Hungerford. Margaret would have a total of nineteen manors, while the feoffees of the late Robert Hungerford would have ten manors, the profits of which would go to Margaret. Furthermore, there were six manors that had been enfeoffed by Walter, Lord Hungerford and Robert, Lord Hungerford for the establishment of a chantry of two priests at Salisbury Cathedral and, at Heytesbury, an almshouse of St Katherine for twelve poor men with two women to attend them. Also at Heytesbury arrangements were to be made for a schoolmaster. The feoffees were to continue to hold these two premises. Richard agreed and promised:

> To be a mediator and meanes to the kinges highnes and his effectual labour and diligence to get the kynges licence thereof in due fourme to be made within the space of xij monthes next folowyng or rather if he godely can or may at the costes of the said Margaret.

The licence was duly applied for and was granted by Edward.[19]

Richard might have been present at the ceremony at Windsor at which the Order of the Garter was conferred on Duke Charles of Burgundy. He would certainly have been aware of the uprisings that had taken place in the North Country, beginning with rebellion of Robin of Redesdale. It is at this point that Richard's whereabouts, often somewhat obscure during the late 1460s, become more certain. In early June 1469, he accompanied King Edward, Anthony, Earl Rivers and Sir John Wydeville on a pilgrimage to the shrines of St Edmund and Our Lady of Walsingham.

That Edward and Richard had lost a brother who was probably named after the saint made St Edmund's shrine an obvious and poignant choice for the royal brothers to visit. However, St Edmund also had a deeper significance, although more for King Edward than for Richard at this stage. As we have seen, although Edward's rule had been threatened by an insurrection that had originated in the north under Robin of Redesdale, Edward did not appear to have taken the threat particularly seriously. His leisurely pace northwards, making a detour to visit sacred shrines as he went is further testament to his complaisance. Yet, even in this apparently imprudent decision lay sound reasoning, if from a spiritual point of view. When, in 1173, King Henry II learned that his crown was threatened by his own sons, he gathered his troops in Bury and, under the standard of St Edmund, achieved a resounding victory over his enemies. Henry's triumph was ascribed to the holy influence of the saint. It is not impossible that Edward was appealing to the same agency to secure a victory of his own. It was a demonstration of faith of which his more pious brother, Richard, must have wholeheartedly approved.

Having worshipped at the shrine of the sainted king, the reigning king of England and his entourage continued on to the shrine of Our Lady of Walsingham, or Little Walsingham as it was properly known. The party's passage was carefully watched by John Paston, who wrote to his father:

> The Kyng rod thorow Heylysdon Waren towads Walsyngham, and Thomas Wyngfeld promysyd me that he wold fynd the menys that my Lord of Glowsestyr and hym sylf bothe shold shew the Kyng the loge that was breke down and also that they wold tell hym of the breking down of the plase.[20]

The place referred to here is a lodge belonging to Sir John Paston, and which had been ruined by the Duke of Suffolk. It had been the intention of the Pastons to solicit King Edward's assistance in a quarrel between the Pastons and Suffolk, the latest victim of which had been the lodge. The lodge was duly brought to the King's notice but, unfortunately for all concerned, Edward refused to be pulled into the quarrels of his subjects. The lodge, he said 'myght fall downe by the self as be plukyd downe, for if it had be plukyd down, he seyd that we myght have put in our byllys of it, wehn [sic] hys jugys sat on the *oyeer determyner* in Norwyche, he being ther.'[21]

The party arrived at the shrine at Little Walsingham on Wednesday 21 June. The origins of the shrine date back to 1061 when, according to tradition, Lady Richeldis de Favarches was blessed with a vision of the Virgin. During her reverie she was commanded to build a replica of the house in which Gabriel had announced to Mary that she would bear the Christ child.

The identity of Lady Richeldis is not known for certain. She could have been related to the de Clares, who succeeded her son as patrons of the shrine. The de Clares eventually married into the Despenser family, ancestors of the earls of Warwick. The male line having died out 1314, the patronage of Little Walsingham passed to the female line. Through Elizabeth de Burgh, the wife of Lionel, Duke of Clarence, the shrine became the care of the Mortimer family and through them the House of York.[22] Richard, Duke of York took

his patronage of Little Walsingham very seriously, endowing it with donations of land and property, but also making pilgrimages there.

Once again, then, this is an entirely appropriate shrine for both Edward
and Richard to visit. Its strong family connections made it so. Moreover,
that the shrine was dedicated to the Virgin Mary gave it added significance
for Richard. He had a particular devotion to Mary, which would see its fullest flowering during his royal progress to York in the autumn of 1483.

It was during this pilgrimage, that Edward received news that the Earl of
Warwick had, at last, shown his hand. The dispensation for the marriage
between his daughter, Isabel, and the Duke of Clarence had been received
and Warwick had formulated his plans. The marriage was entirely appo-
site to Warwick's foreign policy; as has been seen, when Louis XI entered
negotiations with Warwick, he tempted Clarence with the promise of a pres-
tigious marriage and lucrative lordships. This appealed to the fickle Duke's
vanity which was, in turn, taken advantage of by the Earl.

On the other hand, it is unclear whether or not Clarence had ever seriously intended to usurp his brother. What can be assumed is that Warwick
thought that such an eventuality was not impossible. He made arrangements
for George to sail to Calais. The marriage would take place in the castle of
that town, which was Warwick's headquarters as captain. Somewhat awkwardly for their plans, Edward had considered visiting Calais at the same
time, but had later changed his mind.[23]

Clarence set out for Canterbury, the first leg of his journey, on 7 June. This
roughly coincides with the point in time at which his brothers were embarking on their pilgrimage to East Anglia. At Canterbury Clarence was received
as an honoured guest by the prior and convent of Christ Church and he
spent two days at the prior's lodgings. Next he moved on to Sandwich,
where he was met by the Earl of Warwick and Thomas Kemp, the Bishop
of London; his cousin, George Nevill, archbishop of York, and the prior of
Christ Church joined them soon afterwards. Warwick's ship, the *Trinity*,
was fitted out and ready to sail, thanks to the unsuspecting King Edward,
and it was blessed by Archbishop Nevill on 12 June. Two days later, Cecily,
Duchess of York arrived at Sandwich to see her son.[24] She spent a few days
in the town before the small party went on its way.

It has been suggested that Cecily's presence at Sandwich was deliberately
planned to show her support for the rebellion led by Warwick and Clarence
against Edward. However, this is not necessarily the case. It cannot be said
for certain that she was aware of the extent of the plans being drawn up
by Warwick and Clarence; she might simply have thought that they merely
entailed the marriage between her son and Isabel of Warwick. Furthermore,

Edward's complaisance could have done nothing to persuade her that anything more sinister was taking place. Perhaps she even thought the marriage to be a good idea. After all, Edward had so far managed to father only daughters. Should he die, the throne of England would have been vulnerable indeed without a Prince of Wales. It made sense for Clarence, who would effectively remain heir presumptive until Edward fathered a son, to take a wife and have sons who might one day continue the Yorkist dynasty. If such an interpretation seems naive, Cecily can hardly be blamed. Were there anything more sinister behind the marriage and the Earl's activities, Edward would have initiated an appropriate response, but he did not.

Clarence, accompanied by the Earl of Warwick, made his way to his castle of Queenborough. Warwick then returned to London, where he wrote a letter to the city of Coventry informing the authorities of the forthcoming marriage:

> Ryght trusty and wele-bylouyd, I grete you wele. Forasmiche as hyt hath pleasyd the kinges gode grace to sende at this tyme for hys lordis & other his subgettis to atende a-pon hys hyghnes northward, & that bothe the ryhgt hye & mihgty prince, my lord the Duke of Clarens, & I ben fully purposed in short tyme to be hadde bitwene my sayd lord and my dohgter, to awayte on the same & to drawe vnto oure sayd soueren lord highness, I therefore desire & pray yow that ye woll in the meenetyme yeve knowlache to all suche felissypp as ye nowe make [toward theym] to arredy theym in the best wyse they can, & that bothe ye & they defensibly arrayd be redy apon a day's warning to acompany my sayd lord & me towardes the sayd highnes, as my speciall trust ys in yow, yevyng credens to this berer in that he shall open vnto you on my bihalue...[25]

It was war, then. Considering the way events were unfolding, it can only be guessed what the focus of Richard's prayers might have been as he made his devotions at the sacred shrine of the Virgin Mary. All too aware of the impending danger to his brother, he decided not to trust his luck entirely to the celestial realm. The earliest surviving letter from Richard dates from this time. In his letter, dictated to a secretary at Castle Rising on 24 June 1469, Richard asks for a loan of £100 to help him meet the costs of King Edward's forthcoming campaign:

> Right trusty and wellbeloved we greet you wele. And for as much as the king's good grace has appointed me to attend upon his highness into the north parts of his land, which will be to my great cost and charge, whereunto I am so suddenly called that I am not so well purveyed of money therefore as behoves

me to be. And therefore pray you, as my special trust is in you, to lend me one
hundred pounds of money until Easter next coming at which time I promise
you shall be truly thereof content and paid again as the bearer thereof shall
inform you. To whom I pray you to give credence therein and show me such
friendliness in the same as I may do for you hereafter, whereunto ye shall find
me ready.[26]

A postscript written in the Duke's own hand begs, 'Sir J Say I pray that you
will fail me not at this time of my great need as you will that I show my good
lordship in that matter that you labour me for.' This plea is addressed to Sir
John Say of Broxburn, the chancellor of the duchy of Lancaster, seneschal of
Standon and Anstey, and a close associate of King Edward IV.

Richard, then, at the age of sixteen, was already beginning to form his
own network of personal loyalty such as existed between master and servant and which formed the basis of late medieval aristocratic life. Similar to
the *clientèle* system of seventeenth-century France, it relied upon mutual
and reciprocal support, which took the form of loans, as in this case, or
perhaps the performance of specific duties. Mostly, it was based upon the
expectation that servants would attend to the interests, rights and demands
of their lord.

The system is demonstrated again in Richard's ability to muster troops
where others failed simply on the strength of who he was: 'As for Bernard,
Barney, Broom, and W. Calthorp, ar sworn my Lord of Glowsetyrs men'.[27]
Of these, only Calthorp was an associate of the Duke.[28] Richard had successfully attracted four men to his side. They, in turn, would bring others.

Following a short delay, the archbishop of York arrived at Calais. A week
later, on Tuesday 12 July 1469, George, Duke of Clarence:

took in marriage Isabelle, one of the daughters and heirs of the said Richard
Earl of Warwick, which at that time was present there; and five other knights
of the Garter, and many other lords and ladies and worshipful knights, well
accompanied with wise and discreet esquires, in right great number, to the laud
praysing of God, and to the honour and worship of the world...[29]

The couple stayed together for five days then, leaving the new Duchess at
Calais, Clarence, the archbishop and Warwick returned to London, where
they issued a manifesto under their seals. Dated 16 July, the manifesto highlights the evils of the present reign and declares the intention to remedy
them. Edward was censured for advancing the interests of his Wydeville
relatives as well as men such as Humphrey Stafford, Earl of Devon, and

William Herbert, Earl of Pembroke, who had infiltrated the Yorkist régime and afflicted such evils: 'wheche have caused oure seid sovereyn Lord and his seid realme to falle in grete poverte of myserie, disturbynge the mynystracion of lawes, only entendyng to thaire owen pomocion and enrichyng.'[30]

Then, citing the cases of Edward II, Richard II and Henry VI as examples, the causes and effects of the current troubles were explained. Where the King was estranged from his own blood and took counsel only from those who were not of his blood, this would lead to poverty, 'by wheche the seid princes were so enpoverysshed that they hadde not sufficient of lyvelode ne of goodis, wherby they myght kepe and mayntene theire honorable estate and ordinarie charges withynne this realme.'

That the said seditious persons refused to leave their possessions led to crippling taxes. Lawlessness, rape, 'gret murdres, roberyes, rapes, oppressions and extorcions' broke out where they would not allow laws to be enacted. The coin and household of the King were diminished because they would not leave their goods and possessions to the King. The King was obliged to introduce enforced loans which he would be unable to pay back. He was forced also to spend the goods of the Pope, the wheche were yevyn hym for defence of Christen feyth of many goodely disposyd people of this lond.'

Clarence, Warwick and the archbishop saw it as their responsibility to right these wrongs. They called upon the true subjects of the King to array for war. What was more sinister, in naming Edward II, Richard II and Henry VI in their manifesto, three kings who had been deposed in consequence of the actions of their councillors, Clarence, Warwick and Archbishop Nevill were effectively issuing a thinly veiled threat to Edward. He too would be deposed if he continued to listen to evil-minded councillors.

The more immediate threat to Edward, however, was the rebellion that had revived under Robin of Redesdale. In fact, this new uprising had been arranged by Warwick prior to Clarence's marriage; Robin of Redesdale, although undoubtedly involved, was only the nominal leader. The pilgrimage over, the King moved north to Nottingham, where he hoped to meet up with Devon and Pembroke. What happened next is uncertain; what is known is that neither Edward nor Richard was involved in the battle that ensued. Devon and Pembroke appear to have quarrelled and Pembroke, pressing ahead without his ally, alone encountered the northern rebels. Battle was joined at Edgecote, near Banbury on 26 July 1469. Redesdale claimed the victory after heavy fighting. Pembroke and his brother, Sir Richard Herbert, were taken prisoner and summarily executed by Warwick at Northampton. The father of Queen Elizabeth, Richard, Earl Rivers and one of his younger sons, John Wydeville, met the same fate. The executions were carried out on Warwick's orders, the men being condemned without trail. Warwick had acted illegally and his conduct was prompted by nothing more than his desire for revenge. The Earl of Devon had managed to escape the scene of battle only to be seized by a mob and beheaded at Bridgwater a few days later. From his former guardian Richard learned still another lesson: how to handle sedition. In not too many years hence he would put what he had learned to good use.

In the meantime, one of those who had witnessed the battle from the sidelines was a little boy of twelve years of age by the name of Henry Tudor. He, too, learned valuable lessons that day. The split in the Yorkist ranks provided a wonderful opportunity to the Lancastrians exiled in France, among whom was the boy's uncle, Jasper Tudor, to exploit the French king's dislike of the House of York. Jasper Tudor would soon be in the company and the pay of King Louis, from whom he would receive a nice pension of one hundred *louis tournois*. Tudor would use his influence with Louis, who would come to turn a favourable eye upon Warwick and Clarence.

It is almost certain that Richard was not with King Edward when the latter was taken captive by Warwick a few days after Edgecote. As Warkworth tells it:

> the Archebysschoppe of Yorke had understondynge that Kynge Edwarde was in a vilage beside Northamptone, and all his people he reysyd were fledde fro hym; by the avyse of the Duke of Clarence and the earle of Warwyke he rode with certayne horsemenne harneysed withe hym, and toke Kynge Edwarde, and had hym unto Warwyke castelle a lytelle whyle, and afterwarde to Yorke cite.[31]

Edward was moved from York to Middleham, where he was imprisoned in the very castle that had been home to his younger brother not so long before. There now occurred a repeat of the situation that had taken place some nine years earlier, when he who had deposed the king began to rule in his name. Then, it had been Richard of York who had ruled in the name of King Henry VI; now it was Richard of Warwick who ruled in the name of King Edward IV.

Richard Gloucester had not yet been appointed a place on Warwick's council, nor was he involved in any way with the new government. Still he would not be allowed to distance himself from it for long because the first parliament was set for 22 September 1469, the summonses for which were issued on 7 September. Richard, as Duke of Gloucester, was one of those called upon to attend.[32] It was an awkward situation; he would be required to attend a parliament held by a man who was not king, yet who was acting in the King's place. The real king, Richard's own brother, was deposed in all but name. If he were to attend, he would be fulfilling his duty, but his actions in doing so could be construed as support for the new régime. It might be held that Richard had turned his back on the King in favour of his former guardian and tutor.

In the event, Richard's dilemma was solved when the country was subject to yet more serious disturbances. The Duke of Norfolk was blockading Caister Castle in Norfolk, which was being occupied by Sir John Paston. This dispute had rumbled on for several weeks, but King Edward had been reluctant to intervene even when the Wydevilles had drawn his attention to it. Wales and the north were also experiencing disruption, and the widespread disorder was used as the excuse to cancel the parliament scheduled for September. It has been speculated that the parliament might have been used to grant the Duke of Clarence and the Earl of Warwick permanent control of the government and to reduce the power of the Wydevilles and the Herberts and other opponents by resuming their lands.[33] Whatever the case, when Humphrey Nevill of Brancepeth and his brother, Charles, instigated a Lancastrian rebellion, it proved to be the final straw for Warwick. He failed to raise the necessary troops to counter the rebellion because of suspicions surrounding Warwick's treatment Edward.

Then the unexpected happened. As Warkworth puts it, 'the Kynge scaped oute of the Bisshoppys handes'.[34] A despatch from Milan asserts that Edward was 'going freely to amuse himself by hunting wherever he chose. One day, being in the country, he took the road towards London, and entered the city, where he was very gladly and cordially received.'[35] According to Commines, the Duke of Burgundy had become extremely concerned at what had happened, and privately contrived a way for King Edward's escape …'[36]. Vergil's version of the story states that Edward had corrupted the guards Warwick had placed at the castle to watch him: 'Edward…began to speak fayre unto the constable and speakers thereof, to make requests of them and to put them in great hopes of rewards, that, he corruptyd with his plentyfull and large promises, they let him go'[37]. Such a variety of stories attest to the uncertain nature of Edward's return to freedom; given the circumstances, it seems probable that Edward was simply allowed to escape. This, at least is the opinion of the Croyland Continuator, who states that, 'in a manner almost miraculous, and beyond all expectation, he did not so much make his escape, as find himself released by the express consent of the Earl of Warwick himself'[38]. Whatever the truth, and Croyland would seem to be the closest to it, Edward appears to have been acting autonomously when he arrived at York on 10 September. His very presence was enough to allow Warwick to muster troops and shortly afterwards Humphrey Nevill's rebellion was subdued. Humphrey and his brother Charles were executed at York in the King's presence on 29 September.

Firmly restored to kingship, Edward repaired to his castle at Pontefract. A week later, he received his brother of Gloucester accompanied by Lord Hastings, who had arrived with several lords of Edward's court and a large, heavily armed force. In October 1469, with Richard Gloucester at his side, followed by his brother-in-law Suffolk and accompanied by the Earls of Arundel and Northumberland, Essex, Lord Hastings, Mountjoy and 'many other Knyghtys and Sqwyers' King Edward made a triumphal entry into London. The royal party was greeted by 'the Meyr of London, xxij. Aldremen, in skarlett, and of the Crafftys men of the town to the number of CC., all in blewe'.[39] The King entered his capital through Cheap, although the route took him out of his way. He was determined that as many people as possible should see him, thereby removing any doubt that he was still very much their king.

It was a spectacular entrance, with King Edward supported by great magnates, the cream of English knighthood and the London authorities, all brilliantly and brightly arrayed in armour and livery. Lost in the triumph and delight of the moment, listening to the shouts of greeting and homage on either side, was the seventeen-year-old Richard, Duke of Gloucester, the loyal younger brother who had supported the King throughout.

An uneasy state of affairs now existed between the King on the one side and the Duke of Clarence and the earl of Warwick on the other. As John Paston notes:

> The kyng hymselffe hathe good langage of the Lords of Clarence, of Warwyk, and of my Lords of York [and] Oxenford, seyng they ne hys best frendys; but his howselde [household] men have other langage, so that what scahll hastely fall I cannot seye.[40]

Edward was anxious to make reconciliation. As Polydore Vergil puts it:

> he regardyd nothing more than to wyn agane the frendship of suche noble men as were now alyenated from him, to confyrme the goodwyll of them who wer hovering and unconstant, and to reduce the mynde of the multytude, being browght by these innovations into a murmooring and dowtfulnes what to do, unto ther late obedyence, affection, and goodwill towards him.[41]

Edward was keen to present a picture of openness and friendship with which he hoped to win back the goodwill of those who had turned against him in the recent crisis. Prominent among these were, of course, Clarence and Warwick themselves.

Yet what of Richard, the younger brother who had not strayed in his fidelity to Edward and had never stinted in his service to him? At last Edward began to take his younger brother seriously as a person and as an adult in his own right and he gave him an appropriate political role. Richard was made Constable of England, an office that had previously held by Richard, Earl Rivers. He was also granted the honours of Clitheroe and Halton, which belonged to the duchy of Lancaster and which had previously been held by the Stanley family. In November 1469, he was granted the castle and manor of Sudeley in Gloucestershire.[42] This estate had been removed under duress from its owner, the old lord Ralph Butler and his daughter, Eleanor, by Edward. Eleanor Butler was a former mistress of Edward IV, a seemingly unimportant relationship that would rapidly become of major consequence to Richard as the dramatic events of 1483 began to unfold.

Richard was made chief justice of North Wales, a post formerly held by Lord Hastings. Appointed to assist and advise the Duke in his new offices was Walter Devereux, Lord Ferrers of Chartley. Ferrers had been a servant to Richard's father, the Duke of York, and he would die fighting for Richard at Bosworth. Sir Roger Vaughan of Tretower Court near Brecon, and John Donne, an experienced civil servant, were also appointed.

There is no doubt that these awards were handed to Richard in gratitude for his services to the King. However, there is a stronger, political motive to be discerned behind Edward's generosity. In giving his brother grants that had formerly belonged to the Stanley family, it is clear that Edward's primary objective was to curtail the power of the Earl of Warwick. Thomas, Lord Stanley was Warwick's brother-in-law, and Edward might have been concerned as to where his loyalties lay. Needless to say, the Stanleys were less than satisfied with the arrangements the King had imposed upon them, and it would take a direct order from Edward to force them to allow Richard's men to take up their posts.[43] Even so, Richard would have a fight on his hands.

It was intended that Richard should leave immediately for Wales. Documents to that effect had been drawn up on 16 October 1469 when Richard was to be given an immediate payment of £100. He was granted full power and authority to:

> Reduce and subdue the king's castles of Carmardyh and Cardycan in South
> Wales, which Morgan ap Thomas ap Griffith, 'gentilman,' and Henry ap

Thomas ap Griffith, 'gentilman,' with other rebels have entered into and from which they raid the adjacent parts, and to put them under safe custody and governance and to promise pardon to such rebels within them as shall be willing to submit and take an oath of fealty.[44]

Richard was also granted a commission of array in the counties of Gloucester and Worcester while, on 17 November, he was appointed chief steward of the duchy of Lancaster lordships of South Wales. Two weeks later, he was granted offices in the principality of Wales and the earldom of March, a title previously held by Edward. The grants had not yet come to an end. On 7 February 1470, Richard replaced the Earl of Warwick as chief steward and chamberlain of South Wales. These grants made Richard Gloucester the principal representative of the royal authority in Wales and the Marches.[45]

Richard left for the Welsh Marches in February 1470 and, as such, would not have witnessed the removal of George, Duke of Clarence from his office as lieutenant of Ireland, which took place on 23 March 1470,[46] nor the proclamations that were issued over the next eight days in which Clarence and Richard, Earl of Warwick were attainted.[47] He was also absent from the King's side when yet another rebellion erupted.

This new rebellion began in Lincolnshire and, like others that had broken out in recent years, the presence of Duke of Clarence and the Earl of Warwick was discernable in the background. Edward called together his lords, the Earls of Arundel and Northumberland and Lord Hastings at Baynard's Castle. They then went to St Paul's where the King made an offering before they set off for Ware.[48] Edward and his forces intercepted the rebels and defeated them before they could rendezvous with Clarence and Warwick. The scene of Edward's victory was a place called 'Lose-Cote Field'. The leaders were brought to Coventry, where King Edward waited to examine them and:

Of there free willes uncompelled, not for fere of dethe ne otherwise stirred, knowleged and confessed the saide duc and Earl [Clarence and Warwick] to be partiners and chef provocars of all theire treasons. And this plainly, theire porpos was to distroie the king, and to have made the saide duc king, as they, at the tyme that thei shulde take theire dethes, openly byfore the multitude of the kinges oost affirmed to be true.[49]

News soon arrived of yet more uprisings. One, in the West Country, might have been encouraged by Clarence. Another, in Richmondshire, involved the ubiquitous Robin of Redesdale supported by kinsmen of the Earl of

Warwick. It is probably at about this time that King Edward issued orders for his brother, Richard, to join him. Richard, however, was not in Wales, where it was reasonable to expect to find him, but at Hornby Castle in Lancashire. He had become involved in a quarrel between the Stanleys and the Harrington family. The object of their dispute was the inheritance of the Harrington estate.

The Harringtons were a powerful family with extensive estates centring upon Hornby and Farleton in Lancashire and Brierley in Yorkshire.[50] They, like the House of York on whose side they fought, had lost the head of the family and a son at the battle of Wakefield. Two years prior to this Sir Thomas Harrington had made an enfeoffment of his estates, thus protecting them in the event of his attainder. In all probability, he ensured that the estates would go to his eldest son, Sir John, and his heirs. However, since John was fatally wounded at Wakefield, dying the following day, his two daughters, Anne and Elizabeth, should have inherited the estates. This did not happen. In 1463, two years after Wakefield, the estates were instead granted in their entirety to the eldest surviving son, Sir James Harrington.

James, aware of Anne's and Elizabeth's claims, held them in custody. It was at this point that the Stanley family became involved. This was occasioned by Thomas, Lord Stanley being granted custody of the lands and the daughters of late Sir John. An inquiry into the affair found that the daughters were indeed co-heiresses to their father's property and that Sir James was illegally occupying the family's lands in Hornby and its appurtenances. James and one of the feoffees were committed to Fleet prison.

Sir James and the feoff were then obliged to enter into a bond with the Stanleys, who were subsequently awarded the wardship and marriage of the two girls. They were swiftly married off: Anne to Lord Thomas's second son, Edward, and Elizabeth to John Stanley of Melling, a cousin. Sir James continued to occupy the Hornby estates.

Richard supported the Harringtons in their dispute with the Stanleys. There were two reasons. Firstly, he was aware of the sacrifice the family had made at Wakefield. He was aware, too, of how devastating it was to lose both father and brother. Secondly, Richard was still entangled with the Stanleys over the concerns arising from his recent grants and the problems caused by that family as they tried to prevent Richard's employees taking up their posts. Thomas, Lord Stanley was the former holder of the principal offices in Halton and Clitheroe, the honours of which had been granted to Richard by Edward only a few months before. As such, he had every reason to resent the Duke.

It is at this time, when Richard was staying at the Harrington seat at Hornby Castle, that King Edward found himself confronted by the latest in a series of rebellions and contacted his brother to come to his assistance. Richard, who was on his way south to join Edward, and the Stanleys, who were making their way to rendezvous with Clarence and Warwick, ran into each other.

According to an anonymous letter sent to John Paston on 27 March 1470, Clarence and Warwick decided to proceed towards Manchester, 'hopyng to have hadde helpe and socour of the Lord Stanley, butt in conclucion ther that hadde litill favor'.[51] Polydore Vergil also notes that Warwick had asked his brother-in-law to support him against the King but that Stanley 'flatly denayed to beare armes against king Edward.'[52] With no hope of assistance from Stanley, Warwick and Clarence altered their course and took the road towards Exeter instead.

The reason for Stanley's refusal might have had something to do with feelings of loyalty towards the King as Vergil suggests; however, the deciding factor surely must have been his encounter with the Duke of Gloucester. Richard's presence, in the company of a family with whom the Stanleys were in dispute, and backed up by a powerful armed force, was sufficient to persuade Stanley to retreat on this occasion. Richard was very quickly able to continue on his way, while the King took matters into his own hands:

> The king, our sovereign lord, straightly commandeth that no man of what-soever degree under colour of any wrong done unto him for any matter of variance late fallen between his brother, the Duke of Gloucester, and the lord Stanley, distress, rob or despoil any of his subjects: but that shall he find himself wronged, shall sue remedy by the course of the king's law or by none otherwise upon pain of death. Dated York 25 March.[53]

Shortly afterwards, Edward issued a general pardon to Thomas, Lord Stanley of all offences committed by him before 11 May 1470. He then sent orders to Richard to array the men of Gloucester and Hereford on 26 March. The Duke could have been at the King's side at Exeter on 17 April, where he received a further commission of array against the rebels in Devon and Cornwall.[54]

Clarence and Warwick, meanwhile, had slipped beyond the King's reach, having taken a ship from Devon. Richard returned to Wales, where he presided in the great sessions at Carmarthen on 18 June 1470, but he was back at his brother's side in July. This time, Edward and Richard made for the north to suppress a rising in Yorkshire led by another of Warwick's brothers-in-law, Lord FitzHugh of Ravensworth. A month later, on 26 August, Richard was appointed Warden of the West Marches towards Scotland.[55]

The office of Warden of the West Marches would come to define Richard's career in the north in later years. The office[56] first came into being under Edward I when a military officer was appointed as a sort of sentry, keeping an eye on the borders. The appointment then evolved to include the duties of the sheriffs of the border counties who would administer the customs and were responsible for the observance of truces between England and Scotland. The first warden to be appointed under the latter conditions took up his post following the release of King David of Scotland and the negotiation of a ten-year truce in 1357. Under Edward III the marches had developed into a buffer-zone, with southern Scotland being occupied by the English in a bid to contain Scottish attacks into English territory.

At first the wardenships were held by two groups of minor landowners. In later years, they would be held by families of magnates, the numbers of which would become smaller as time wore on. In the end, the appointment was divided between the two greatest northern magnates, the Percy family, who held the east march, while the Nevills were responsible for the western marches. It is to the western march that Richard Gloucester was appointed in 1470.

The terms of the office, which had been redefined in 1390, were that the warden would continue to be responsible for the upholding of truces between England and Scotland. The remuneration received by the respective eastern and western offices reflected the relative difficulties faced by each incumbent. Since the east of England was most vulnerable to raids from Scotland, the warden in that part of the march was paid twice as much as the western warden. As it was, each man received a fixed sum, which would be quadrupled should war break out. In that event, the warden would be responsible for the hire of as many soldiers as he considered necessary in order to defend, at their own risk, the fortresses in their charge: Carlisle in the west and Berwick in the east. In times of war, wardens were allowed to carry out raids into Scotland as long as they left behind adequate garrisons for the defence of the marcher towns. The King would undertake to relieve the wardens within a reasonable time period should they be besieged, but the warden would not be held responsible for the loss of strongholds should relief not arrive in time. In effect, the office of warden of the marches was a licence to muster, retain and command large private armies at the King's expense, and to be given free reign in the administration and defence of vulnerable border towns, which allowed for the invasion, in all but name, of a hostile sovereign state. It required a man with a sense of responsibility, who was steadfastly loyal to his king and who knew how to keep a cool head in volatile situations. Richard Gloucester, it appeared to Edward IV, was the right man for the job.

In granting this post to Richard, King Edward was apparently continuing to make amends for the earlier shabby treatment he had meted out to his brother. More to the point, however, as with the awards of the former Stanley estates of Halton, Clitheroe and others, Richard's appointment was of great political import. The office had been held in Nevill hands, passing down through the family in an almost unbroken line since 1399. For the previous nineteen years the incumbent had been the Earl of Warwick himself. As such, Richard was being awarded estates and appointed to offices that had previously been held by the Earl of Warwick. Moreover, his promotion was not without danger. If the Kingmaker should return in strength and continue his attack on the King, Richard's position would be precarious indeed; Warwick would not take kindly to his former page usurping his position.

For the moment, King Edward and Duke Richard could only play a waiting game. A sense of stillness had settled over the land, but it was an uneasy stillness in which tensions were heightened and fears, though perhaps unexpressed, nevertheless weighed heavily on the minds of the King and his youngest brother. For no one knew what would transpire from the latest sojourn in France of the Earl of Warwick and the Duke of Clarence. Warwick had cultivated very powerful friendships across the Channel, and some among his enemies who had taken refuge there were beginning to take a new, more sympathetic view of the Kingmaker.

Also at this time 'there apperede a blasynge sterre in the weste, and the flame therof lyke a spere hede, the whiche dyverse of the Kynges house sawe it, wherof thei were fulle sore adrede.'[57] Even without this celestial prophecy, it was inevitable that war would ensue.

In France, Warwick was resisting Louis's attempts to dislodge him as he entered into negotiations with the ex-queen, Marguerite d'Anjou, who had taken refuge in her native country. In supporting York, Warwick had, of course, been her enemy, but that was all in the past. What he now proposed was to invade England and restore Henry VI, who was currently languishing in the Tower. Moreover, the pact would be sealed by the marriage of Warwick's youngest daughter, Anne, to Edward of Lancaster, Prince of Wales. Marguerite agreed, and the formal betrothal took place at Angers on 25 July; the groom was seventeen years old, the bride not yet fifteen.

King Louis was won over. His share in the bargain was to receive the assistance of the re-established Henrician government in a renewed attack on Louis's arch enemy, Charles the Bold of Burgundy. The marriage of Margaret of York had lent substance to the overtures of peace between Charles and Edward. The marriage between Edward, Prince of Wales and

Anne Nevill sealed the peace between Louis and England and paved the way for hostilities between England and France on the one side and Burgundy on the other. The restoration of Henry VI to the throne of England is considered 'one of the great successes' of the Spider King.[58]

There was an area of difficulty, however. Although the young couple had been betrothed as the first stage of their marriage, Warwick was eager to press ahead with the actual wedding as soon as possible. This was because, although a betrothal was legally binding and the couple were considered to be husband and wife, such ties, when they involved royalty, were often broken as and when the political winds changed their course. Warwick was cautious. He made the wedding a condition of his invasion of England.

What Warwick had not taken into consideration was that the couple were related within four degrees of consanguinity; they were both the great-great-grandchildren of John of Gaunt, Duke of Lancaster. In other words, they were related within the prohibited degrees and their marriage would be illegal without a dispensation from the Pope. This would take time to obtain, but the restoration of King Henry VI could not wait. As such, all parties agreed that the wedding would not go ahead, nor would the betrothal be consummated until Warwick had conquered England, removed King Edward and restored King Henry. Anne was to remain with Marguerite d'Anjou while her father sought to regain the throne that, they all believed, rightly belonged to the House of Lancaster. This meant that, at this stage, Anne Nevill was not married to Edward of Lancaster in the full sense of the word. They had not consummated their union, which was a necessity if their betrothal were to be as legally binding as a marriage in church.

With all obstacles to the invasion of England removed, the happy King Louis gave 50,000 écus to Warwick and Clarence to help them on their way. Their party, which included John de Vere, Earl of Oxford, a brother-in-law to Warwick, and Jasper Tudor, half-brother to Henry VI, removed to the Channel. They sailed from La Hogue in September, landing in Devonshire four days later.

King Edward's position in the North Country meant that he was unable to resist the landing of the Lancastrian party. Warwick then issued a notice to the:

Dukes and earls, in the name and on behalf of our sovereign lord King Henry VI, charge and command all manner of men between the age of sixteen and sixty years [to] be ready, defensible and in their best array to attend and wait upon the duke and earls [and] assist them in their journey ... [59]

Edward's fortunes now looked bleak as Warwick was joined by the Earl
of Salisbury and Lord Stanley. Moreover, the restoration of Henry Percy
as Earl of Northumberland, whose oath of fealty to King Edward was witnessed by Richard on 27 October 1469,[60] led to the defection of Warwick's
brother, John Nevill, who had previously been awarded the title. Having
thus forsaken Edward, John Nevill deprived the King of his best chance to
raise troops in the north. As in 1469, Edward found himself deserted by all
except his brother-in-law, Earl Rivers, William, Lord Hastings and the ever-
constant, Richard, Duke of Gloucester.

The Earl of Warwick had already shown himself to be capable of shocking
brutality towards his enemies. Given his past record, he could be expected
to give no quarter to Edward, Gloucester, Rivers and Hastings. Moreover,
Clarence, 'false, fleeting' as he was, could not be relied upon to shield his family and their supporters from execution or lengthy imprisonment. From King
Edward's perspective, discretion was most certainly the better part of valour.
The small party, now refugees in their own country, fled to King's Lynn, where
they boarded ships secured by Earl Rivers, and set sail for the Low Countries.
It was 2 October 1470, Richard Gloucester's eighteenth birthday.

In London, Edward's queen, now heavily pregnant, sought sanctuary at
Westminster with her daughters. Meanwhile, the Bishop of Winchester, by
the assent of the Duke of Clarence and the Earl of Warwick:

> Went to the toure of Londone, where Kynge Herry was in presone by Kynge
> Edwardes commawndement, and there toke hyme from his kepers, whiche was
> nogt so worschipfully arrayed as a prince, and nogt so clenly kepte as schuld
> seme suche a Prynce; thei hade hym oute, and newe arayed hym, and dyde to
> hyme grete reverens, and brought hyme to the palys of Westmynster, and so he
> was restorede to the crowne ageyne.[61]

King Henry was dressed in royal apparel and paraded through the streets of
the city of London, once again his capital. He was accompanied by the Lord
Mayor, Richard Lee, and two sheriffs, Robert Draper and Richard Gardener.
Then, escorted by the entire city council, he made his way to St Paul's. In a
scene reminiscent of that which was played out earlier with King Edward,
the people of London thronged the streets on either side rejoicing, clapping
their hands and crying, 'God save King Henry!' For Richard of Warwick,
truly a kingmaker, the deposition of Edward and the Readeption of Henry
was the work of God, to whom he gave hearty thanks.[62]

There was not to be such a happy scene for the fugitive king. As the small
English party made its way across the North Sea, they faced foul weather,

choppy waters and a flotilla of ships from the hostile Hanseatic League from whom they barely managed to escape. Edward, still pursued by the enemy, eventually made land at the island of Texel at Marsdiep. Anthony, Earl Rivers came ashore at Weilingen in Zeeland, far to the south.

Received wisdom has it that Richard crossed in the same boat as Rivers and that, naturally, both men landed at Weilingen at the same time. However, Richard was apparently delayed in England and did not sail for the Low Countries until later.[63] A letter from Richard's brother-in-law, Charles the Bold, dated 1 November 1470, grants Edward 500 écus per month for the maintenance of his estate, but makes no mention of Richard. Almost a month after Edward's embarkation at King's Lynn, there is no sign nor reference to Richard, although other members of Edward's entourage: lords Rivers, Hastings and Say, Sir Humphrey Talbot, Sir Robert Chamberlain, Sir George Darrell, Sir John Middleton, Sir Gilbert Debenham, William Blount, son of Lord Mountjoy are all mentioned by Duke Charles. Had Richard been present, it is certain that his name would have appeared in this document.

More evidence is contained in the accounts of the city of Veere. The entry for the second week in November records: 'Item paid by order of my Lord of Boucham the bailiff of Veer which he had loaned when my Lord of Gloucester travelled in Holland 3 pounds, 2 shillings, 3 pennies.'[64] My Lord of Boucham is Wolfert van Borsele, son of Henry II van Borsele, Lord of Veere. He was Earl of Buchan by virtue of his marriage to Mary Stuart, daughter of King James II of Scotland. His brother-in-law was Louis de Gruuthuse, friend and host to King Edward IV during his exile. Richard's arrival at Veere was unexpected and, therefore, unprepared for. He was served no wine, and no lord was present to receive him.

A chronicle by Jan van Naaldwijk, knight, records Edward's arrival in Holland. It then lists several other events before noting, 'in the same year came the Duke of Gloucester to his brother King Edward at The Hague in Holland'. Richard's arrival at Edward's side is, therefore, marked out as a completely separate event.

Lastly, there is a chronicle written by Adrian de But, a Cistercian monk living at Les Dunes Abbey, situated on the road between Bruges and Calais. The doors of this monk were always open to the poor, but he also received a great many eminent and noble guests at his abbey, among them Charles the Bold, Margaret of York, Anthony of Burgundy and several Flemish nobles. Many of his visitors were in a position to enlighten him about what was going on beyond the confines of his apparently enclosed world. Writing about the Readeption of Henry VI, he notes that 'the younger brother of the now fugitive King Edward, George [sic] Duke of Gloucester, put up as much resistance as he could.' While de But has confused Richard's name with that of his rebellious brother, it is clear that he has identified the correct duke, since Clarence and Warwick were terrorising the Channel ports with acts of piracy during this time. As he continues his story, de But speaks of Edward's return to England to reclaim his throne and the assistance that had been given to him by Charles the Bold. He notes that 'Edward sailed across, together with his younger brother, the Duke of Gloucester, who had come to him from England with many men ... '

It appears that Richard had stayed behind in England as Edward and his party left King's Lynn for the Low Countries in the autumn of 1470. Such evidence as exists certainly supports such a suggestion. De But's account further indicates that Richard had been recruiting men to the King's cause, and that he had brought them over to Holland with him once he had accomplished his task. As both Visser-Fuchs and Lulofs point out, there are no English sources to corroborate this hypothesis. However, it is possible that Edward IV remained in contact with Henry Percy, the newly restored Earl of Northumberland, during his exile, and that Percy had assured Edward that King Henry had not much support in England. It is possible that Richard played some part in setting up or maintaining the lines of communication before he too set sail for the Low Countries and safety.

Edward's company had left England in such haste that they arrived penniless. Edward paid for his passage with a sumptuous gown lined with marten's fur. Richard, as we have seen, put his borrowing skills to good use to temporarily relieve Lord Buchan of £3 2s 3d. Their arrival did not go unnoticed for long. Louis de Bruges, Lord of Gruuthuse, governor of Holland under Duke Charles, came to the aid of the royal party. He took them in, gave them clothes and provided for their living expenses until they left for The Hague, which they reached on 11 October.

Louis de Bruges was a man of fine taste and great intellect. He owned a fabulous library of illuminated manuscripts, the subjects of which were mainly histories and the chivalric romances. These he made available to his guests. Still, life was not always as kind to the exiles. The Duke of Burgundy was reluctant to upset the new government in England by appearing to welcome his brothers-in-law and their company too warmly. Commines tells of how the Duke would have preferred King Edward's death to his exile in his lands, 'for he was in great apprehension of the Earl of Warwick, who was his enemy, and at that time absolute in England.'[65] At first he refused even to acknowledge their presence in his land. His stance continued until King Louis declared hostilities against Burgundy and urged England to fulfil her

26. Richard II: Richard's nomination of his Mortimer cousins as heirs to his throne was one of the foundations for Richard, Duke of York's eventual claim to the throne. Richard II is an important figure in the Yorkist interpretation of rightful kingship.

27. Henry VI: Richard, Duke of York served Henry faithfully, Henry was frequently ill and York was twice asked to act as protector during the King's incapacity. York was concerned that Henry was surrounded by men who had their own, rather than the King's or the country's best interests at heart.

28. Queen Marguerite d'Anjou: queen to Henry VI. She was beautiful, charming, proud and staunch supporter of the Lancastrian cause. She was a formidable foe to the duke of York as he sought the power he felt was his by right of his position in the succession.

29. The marriage of Henry VI and Queen Marguerite d'Anjou: Henry VI is wearing a halo. In time, he will be informally recognised as a saint by, among many others, King Richard III and King Henry VII, who will make the first attempt to secure his canonization. Today the Henry VI Society continues to press for the canonization of this saintly king.

30. George, Duke of Clarence, brother to Richard III.

31. Philip, Duke of Burgundy, provided shelter for Richard and his brother, George, when they were exiled for their own safety as their eldest brother, Edward, made his bid for the throne.

32. King Edward IV: an idealised reproduction depicting his legendary beauty.

ELIZABETH · REGINA · REGIS · EDWARDE · 4 · ANGLIE

Coll. Regin.
Fund. altera
A.D. 1465.

33. Queen Elizabeth Wydeville, queen to Edward IV. Her unsuitability as a wife for King Edward caused outrage among the Yorkists and was one of the factors that led to the rebellion by the earl of Warwick and the duke of Clarence.

34. Richard, Earl of Warwick disapproved of Edward's marriage to the unsuitable Elizabeth, but their falling out did not prevent Warwick becoming the guardian and tutor to Richard as the young duke undertook his training as a knight.

35. A late Georgian or early Victorian interpretation of King Richard III. The tradition that Richard was deformed has been accepted and incorporated into the portrait.

Above left: 36. A reproduction of the portrait held in the Royal Collection showing the tampering done during Tudor times to make Richard appear deformed; here, the right shoulder is raised in accordance with the description by John Rous.

Above right: 37. King Louis XI of France, the Spider King, assisted the rebellion led by the earl of Warwick and the duke of Clarence that saw Edward IV temporarily deposed.

38. Warwick Castle was the seat of the Earl of Warwick and the birthplace of his youngest daughter, Anne Nevill.

39. Anne Nevill, whom Richard married in 1472. Anne was the daughter of the earl of Warwick and had previously been betrothed to Edward of Lancaster, Prince of Wales. The prince was murdered following the battle of Tewkesbury.

40. Pontefract Castle was Richard's seat as seneschal of the duchy of Lancaster. It had unhappy associations for Richard: it was the scene of the death of Richard II and it was the burial place of Richard's father the duke of York and his brother, the Earl of Rutland. He may also have had a mistress who lived nearby and who gave him his illegitimate son, John.

side of the bargain and do the same. It was at this point that Duke Charles finally abandoned his pro-Lancastrian position and sided once and for all with the House of York.

King Edward and his entourage remained at The Hague until just before Christmas. The Duke of Burgundy contributed 500 écus a month for their living expenses and issued orders to some of his nobles in the north to travel to Holland with twenty-two brace of rabbits each week for Edward's table. Meanwhile, Richard took advantage of his unexpected stay in the Low Counties to visit his sister, Margaret, with whom he stayed two nights. Margaret, seeing the plight of her brothers, urged Charles to aid them financially and to supply ships for their return to England. Therefore, it was with the, admittedly grudging, backing of Duke Charles that Edward, Richard, Rivers and Hastings, together with an expedition of some 1,200 men in about thirty-six ships, set sail from Flushing on 11 March 1471. Their mission was to win England back and restore King Edward IV to the throne.

CHAPTER 12

KING EDWARD IV, 1471

The sea-journey back to England was no less turbulent than the passage into exile. Edward had intended to land in East Anglia, where the Duke of Norfolk and the former tenants of Earl Rivers and other supporters might be on hand to help him. In the event, the party was warned not to come ashore because many of their friends were being watched by the Lancastrians. At the same time, men loyal to John de Vere, Earl of Oxford were patrolling the area on the lookout for them. There was nothing for it but to put to sea once again. Edward decided to make landfall in Yorkshire, but as they sailed up the coast, the tiny flotilla was hit by storms and became dispersed. Edward eventually landed at Ravenspur. Richard, with a company of some three hundred men, made land four miles away. Earl Rivers landed farther away still, his ship having been blown fourteen miles off course.

The companies were reunited the next day, but they found that the local people, although former supporters of the late Richard of York, opposed his sons with armed resistance. *Warkworth's Chronicle* notes that they were led by a priest and a man named Sir John Westerdale. The priest asked why Edward had landed, to which Edward replied that 'he came thedere by the Erle of Northumberlondes avyse, and schewed the Erles lettere y-send to hym, &c. undere his seale.'[1]

Edward then resorted a tactic previously employed by Henry of Bolingbroke under similar circumstances some seventy-two years previously; he announced that he had come, not to reclaim his throne, but only his father's ducal inheritance. In spite of this, Hull, the nearest town, refused to admit him and the company were turned towards York. As they approached the city, they were met by a certain Martin de la Mere and the recorder Thomas Conyers, who assured the King that he would be lost should he attempt to enter within the city walls. Edward left Richard in command of the company at three bow-shots distance while he advanced on the city with fifteen armed men. The mayor met Edward and assured him that they were happy to receive him and his attendants, but they would not admit his army.

Edward decided to push ahead anyway, loud cries of 'Long live King Henry' notwithstanding. He won over the people with a speech in which he invoked the name and memory of his late father. He repeated his assertion that he did not want to depose King Henry, adding that he merely wished to settle his account with the Earl of Warwick and that 'also he came for to clayme the Duchery of Yorke, the whiche was his inherytaunce of ryght'.[2] The people greeted this with a cry of 'Long live the duke of York'. Edward and his company were then admitted into the city, where they passed the night in reasonable comfort.

The stand-off resumed the following day, however. Martin de la Mere approached Edward at ten in the morning to complain that he and his company had not yet left the city. He then told Edward that he would not be allowed to leave unless he first went to the Minster and took a solemn oath never to try to take back his crown. Edward bristled at the man's insolence and asked where were the lords of England before whom he must take such an oath. Edward informed de la Mare that he would have to wait three days until the Earl of Northumberland and other nobles arrived because it would be against all honour for him to swear an oath to anyone of lesser status.

While this conversation was going on, Richard Gloucester and Earl Rivers entered the room. Having heard a little of what was being said, Richard is said to have intimated to the Earl his belief that they would not be allowed to leave unless they killed Martin de La Mere. Earl Rivers, agreeing with Richard as to the seriousness of the situation, nevertheless signalled to Edward to keep the conversation going while he prepared the army to depart. He ordered his men to take possession of one of the city gates and to hold it open until the company had all passed through. In this way, Edward managed to leave York without a drop of blood being spilled.[3]

The non-intervention of Henry Percy, who had it in his power to summon his men to prevent Edward leaving York, allowed the fugitives to embark upon their journey southwards. Now, as he made his way unchallenged through the midlands Edward abandoned any pretence of not wanting to retake his crown. Having been joined by his supporters, among them William, Lord Hastings, who brought some 3,000 men, Edward's forces were multiplied as he advanced to face the Earl of Warwick at Coventry.

Edward stationed himself at the city of Warwick and for three consecu-
tive days he called the Earl to battle. Warwick, however, would have none of
it and remained where he was. His reluctance to be drawn out was largely
because he was waiting for Exeter, Beaumont and Oxford to join him. Also
expected were his brother, John Nevill, whom he had created Lord Montagu
during the Readeption, and George, Duke of Clarence, whom he expected to
approach from the south-west. It was Warwick's intention to attack Edward
with a combination of his own forces and those of Clarence. As it happened,
the Duke of Clarence defected and sided with his brothers instead.

According to the *Arrivall of King Edward IV*, throughout his exile,
Edward had maintained a regular correspondence with Clarence via servants and messengers. In this way, Edward had managed to convince the
Duke that his future would not be secure under Henry VI and that it would
be better for him if he were to return to his, Edward's, side.

Edward's persuasion worked well enough to plant the seeds of doubt in
Clarence's mind, common sense did the rest. Clarence must have been aware
that he had been the only person not to benefit from the agreement between
Louis XI, Queen Marguerite and the Earl of Warwick. He knew that it would
be only a matter of time before the young Prince of Wales came to England
and gathered his own favourites about him. In due course the prince would
replace his father on the throne, and it would be Warwick's daughter, Anne,
who would become queen, not Clarence's wife, Isabel. Clarence could not
even be guaranteed a position at court. Moreover, it would be remembered
that Warwick had sought to place Clarence on the throne, and that Clarence
had apparently not resisted the scheme; how would this be interpreted by
the new king and what would he do about it? The very least the Duke could
expect would be to be left out in the cold as the new king sought out his own
advisors and established his council. The children of Edward and Anne would
inherit the crown and the Duke of Clarence would fade into obscurity.

King Edward, having received news of Clarence's approach, took to horse
and rode out with Gloucester to meet him. Vergil takes up the story:

> Howbeyt because yt showld not seme soome suttle practyse concludyd betwixt
> them two, he marchid in good order of battaylle, as one that myndyd to fight.
> The duke dyd the lyke. But whan they came within view thone of thother,
> Richerd duke of Glocestre, as thowghe he had bene apoyntyd arbyter of all
> controversy, first conferryd secretly with the duke; than he returnyd to king
> Edward, and dyd the very same with him. Fynally, not warre but peace was in
> every mans mouth; than, armor and weapon layd apart uppon both sydes, the
> broothers gladly embracyd one an other.[4]

The three brothers were united once again. Edward issued a proclamation that the Duke of Clarence and his adherents 'should be frely pardonyd for ever'. His next move was to turn his back upon the Earl of Warwick, who was still immured in Coventry refusing to come out, and make his way back to London. Here, Edward went once again to St Paul's where he made an offering in thanks for his safe return. Next, he visited King Henry VI at the Bishop's Palace. The two kings shook hands and exchanged words of assurance that neither intended to hurt the other. Henry VI was then taken to the Tower for safekeeping in the company of George Nevill, who had also defected to Edward's camp, and a few other Lancastrians. Edward entered Westminster Abbey, where the Archbishop of Canterbury set the crown on his head. Next, the newly restored king enjoyed a brief reunion with Queen Elizabeth and saw for the first time the son who had been born to him on 2 November 1470 in the sanctuary of Westminster. The baby was named Edward after his father.

The family reunion was, of necessity, somewhat short. Edward and his army marched northwards on the eve of Easter Day to meet the newly re-motivated Warwick. The urgency stemmed from the need to prevent Warwick joining up with the forces of Queen Marguerite d'Anjou, whose landing on the south coast was expected imminently, although, as it happened, she would not land until 14 April.

Edward began his march in the direction of St Albans at four in the afternoon of Saturday 13 April. With him were Richard Gloucester, George of Clarence, William, Lord Hastings, Anthony, Earl Rivers and several other lords. Edward also had with him King Henry VI, his trump card and a bargaining counter should Edward not have the victory.[5]

The two sides met at Barnet, where Edward's fore-riders forced those of Warwick to retreat. Edward discovered that Warwick's men were waiting 'undre an hedge-syde', and so he refused to allow his own men the comfort of a good bed in the town, but insisted that they lie, as he did, in the field. Edward ordered his men to remain as quiet as possible. Warwick, on the other hand, ordered guns to be shot all through the night, in the hope of hitting and killing at least some of Edward's men. It literally was a shot in the dark, since Warwick had no real idea of where the King's company was. Then:

Upon the morn soo sone as the day dawid, The Capytanys enbataylyd theyre people upon eyther syde, The duke of Glowcetre ledyng the vavard of king Edward, and therle of Oxynfford the vavard of the lordys, and afftyr the Sunne was upp, eythir hoost approchid unto othir, But than it happid to be soo

excedyng a myst that nowthir hoost cowde playnly see othir, Soo that It happid therle of Oxynfford to sett upon the wyng or end of the duke of Glowcetirs
people & afftyr sharp ffyght slew a certayn of theym & put the Remenant to
flyght, and anoon as they had a whyle chacid such as ffled, soom Retournyd
& ffyll to Ryfelyng & soom of theym wenyng that all had been wonne, Rood
In alle haast to london & there told that king Edward hadd lost the ffeeld, But
ffor these tydyngys were not Renewed wyth afftir comers men gave noo grete
credence unto theym ... [6]

The Great Chronicle of London, a work attributed to the London draper
and alderman, Robert Fabyan, makes good account of the confusion that
surrounded this battle. That the victory was seen to go both ways is cor-
roborated by Warkworth. Also, Fabyan is the only contemporary chronicle
to mention the part taken by Richard in the Battle of Barnet. He shows
Richard to be in command of the vanguard opposite the Earl of Oxford.

Personal anecdotes offer an insight into both the savagery and the confusion that marked this battle. A newsletter written shortly afterwards by
Gerhard von Wesel[7] records that about 1,500 men were killed at Barnet,
and that many others were wounded, primarily on the face or the lower
half of the body. He then notes that Richard and Anthony, Earl Rivers were
slightly wounded, 'but thanks be to God, suffered no further harm'. Where
on his body Richard received his wound, von Wesel does not say:

Those who had set out with good horses and sound bodies returned home
with sorry nags and bandaged faces, some without noses etc. and preferred to
stay indoors. May God have pity at this wretched spectacle, for it is said that
there has been no fiercer battle in England for the last 10 years than happened
last Easter as I have described.

The similarity of the standards of Edward and the Earl of Oxford was said
to have led their being confused in the mist:

So the Erle of Warwikes menne schott and faughte ayens the Erle of
Oxenfordes menne, wetyng and supposynge that thei hade bene Kyne
Edwarddes menne; and anone the Erle of Oxenforde and his menne cryed
'treasoune! treasoune![8]

Edward's banner bore the rose-en-soleil; Oxford's carried the silver star.
Amid the smoke of the artillery and the heavy mist that hung over the battlefield, it is easy to imagine how such a mix-up could have occurred.

Warkworth goes on the state that Lord Montagu was slain and, seeing in this that the Yorkists were getting the upper hand, Warwick:

> Lepte one horse-backe, and fled to a wode by the felde of Barnett, where was no waye for them and one of Kynge Edwardes menne hade espyede hyme, and one came uppone hym and kylled hym, and despoiled hyme nakede.[9]

The *History of the Arrivall of Edward IV* tells a similar story:

> In this battayle was slayne the Erlr of Warwyke, somewhat fleinge, which was taken and reputed as chefe of the felde, in that he was callyd amongs them lyvetenaunt of England, so constitute by the pretensed aucthoritye of Kynge Henry.[10]

So ended the life of the Kingmaker, once the most powerful man in England after the King himself; taken as he fled the field of battle, murdered and stripped. Later in the afternoon of Easter Day, the triumphant King Edward returned to London and rode once again to St Paul's. The difference between this and the last time he had entered his capital was remarkable. Last time he was still to all intents and purposes a fugitive, trespassing on the realm of King Henry VI and very much in need of re-establishing his kingship. Now he was the victor, king in right and in deed. He was met by the Archbishop of Canterbury and the Bishops of Bath, Lincoln, Durham, Carlisle, Rochester, St David's, Dublin, Ely and Exeter. He placed his two banners on the northern rood altar as offerings and heard the 'salve festa dies' sung.

On the following day, Monday 15 April, the bodies of Lord Montagu and Richard of Warwick were brought to St Paul's and displayed in their wooden coffins, naked but for a cloth over their loins. Many thousands came to view them. The great Earl of Warwick, the Kingmaker himself, was dead. John Rous leaves the following epitaph:

> And thow froward fortne hym deceuyd at his ende yot his knyghtly acts had be so excellent that his noble and famous name cowd neuer by put owt of laudable memory. He in his testament bequathe his bodye to be buryed at Warrewik but for all that he is buryed at Byrsham up on temmys.[11]

Richard Gloucester had acquitted himself well in his first major battle. The fighting was vicious and the young Duke was in the thick of it. Although his position in the vanguard is noted by one chronicler only, Fabyan, the fact that he was wounded confirms that he did not sit on the sidelines as a mere spectator. It is, perhaps, ironic that Richard's first opportunity to try out the skills he acquired under Warwick's tutelage at Middleham should be against his former guardian and tutor.

The young Duke's bravery was commemorated in a poem celebrating the return of the Yorkist faction to London following the battle:

> The duke of Glocetter, that nobill prynce,
>
> Yonge of age, and victorius in batayle,
>
> To the honoure of Ectour that he myght comens,
>
> Grace hym folowith, fortune, and good spede
>
> I suppose hes the same that clerkis of rede,
>
> Fortune hathe hym chosyn, and forthe with hym will goo
>
> Her husband to bee, the wille of God is soo.[12]

As it happened, for the husband of Fortune there was to be no rest. On the same day that the Battle of Barnet was fought, Queen Marguerite landed at Weymouth. Accompanying her was her son, Edward, with his wife, Anne Nevill, and the now widowed countess of Warwick. The company began their march westwards, meeting up with Lancastrian survivors from Barnet. The Queen had intended to reach Wales, where she hoped to join forces with Jasper Tudor. She encountered King Edward IV instead.

Three weeks had passed since Barnet and the wound sustained by Richard was clearly not serious enough to prevent his taking part in the ensuing battle. Richard and his men had barely recovered from the gruelling thirty-six mile forced march in sweltering heat as they advanced to meet the Lancastrians. The mud thrown up by horses and wagons had rendered the water in streams undrinkable. 'When both armies had now become so extremely fatigued with the labour of marching and thirst that they could proceed no further, they joined in battle near the town of Tewkesbury'.[13]

Although the Duke of Gloucester was once again in command of the vanguard, Edward unusually placed him on the right so that he should face the duke of Somerset, the most formidable of the Lancastrian commanders. Edmund Beaufort was the son and heir to Edmund Beaufort, Duke of Somerset, who had opposed Richard's father, the Duke of York. Richard's command of the vanguard was a testament to his ability and loyalty: had the King followed the usual pattern, Somerset would have confronted Hastings, who had acquitted himself quite badly at Barnet.

Edward's strategy paid off:

> Nethles the Kyngs ordinance was so conveniently layde afore them, and his vawarde so sore oppressyd them, with shott of arrows, that they gave them a

right-a-sharpe shwre. Also they dyd agayne-ward to them, bothe with shot of arrows and gonnes, whereof netheles they ne had not so great planty as had the Kynge. In the front of theyr field were so evell lanes, and depe dykes, so many hedges, trees, and busshes, that it was right hard to approche them nere, and come to hands; but Edmund, called Duke of Somarset, having that day the vawarde, whithar it were for that he and his fellowshipe were sore annoyed in the place where they were, as well with gonnes-shott, as with shot of arrows, whiche they ne wowld nor durst abyde, or els, of great harte and corage, knyghtly and manly avaunsyd hymselfe, with his fellowshipe, somewhat asyde-hand the Kyngs vawarde, and by certayne pathes and wayes therefore afore purveyed, and to the Kyngs party unknowne, he departyd out of the field, passyd a lane, and came into a fayre place, or cloos, even afore the Kynge where he was embatteled, and, from the hill that was in that one of the closes, he set right fiercely upon th'end of the Kyngs battayle. The Kynge, full manly, set forthe even upon them, enteryd and wann the dyke, and hedge, upon them, into the cloose, and, with great vyolence, put them upe towards the hyll, and, so also, the King's vaward, being in the rule of the Duke of Gloucestar.[14]

As at Barnet, so at Tewkesbury, Duke Richard was in the midst of the fighting. He also showed himself to be a fine military strategist in this, his second major battle:

The Duke of Glocester, who lacked no policie, galled them greeviouslie with the shot of arrows: and they rewarded their adversaries home againe with like payment, both with shot of arrows and great artillerie, although they had not the like plentie of guns as the king had.[15]

However, Tewkesbury has gone down in history not so much for its feats of valour and military prowess, but for the bloody events that followed the Yorkist victory. Chroniclers and historians have ensured that there are several conflicting accounts of the incidents. The ground upon which the battle was fought very soon acquired the name of Bloody Meadow; a *Blodyforlong* is noted as early as 1498, less than thirty years after the battle,[16] and not without reason. One such incident, and the most tragic, was the death of Edward, the Lancastrian Prince of Wales.

The *Historie of the Arrivall of Edward IV* states: 'In the wynnynge of the fielde such as abode hand-stroks were slayne incontinent; Edward, called Prince, was taken, fleinge to the towne wards, and slayne, in the fielde'[17] In other words, Prince, Edward, having survived the battle, fled towards the town, was caught and slain in the field. There is no mention of who killed him.

While the cutting down of a soldier who is retreating from the scene at battle's end might be seen as a despicable act, it was, unfortunately, a feature of every battle of the Wars of the Roses. In foreign wars the ordinary soldiery would be allowed to go free, while high-ranking offices, who were always men from the highest classes of society, were captured and ransomed. In a civil war, no such concession was made. As such, this treatment of Prince Edward, which mirrors the murder of Richard's brother, Edmund of Rutland at Wakefield, was simply a necessity of war as it was understood and practised at the time.

Warkworth offers, 'And ther was slayne in the felde, Prynce Edward, whiche cryede for socoure to his brother-in-lawe the Duke of Clarence.'[18] This account is all the more pitiable because Prince Edward was really little more than a pawn in the intrigues of Clarence, Warwick and King Louis of France. As with the *Arrivall*, it shares some similarities with certain accounts of the death of the Earl of Rutland, who is said to have pleaded with his murderer to spare his life. It might, perhaps, be noted also that both Edmund of Rutland and Edward, Prince of Wales, were only seventeen years old at the time of their murder.

The Croyland Continuator writes: 'Upon this occasion, there were slain on the Queen's side, either on the field or after the battle, by the avenging hands of certain persons, prince Edward, the only son of king Henry...'[19] While Croyland mentions no one by name, Horace Walpole took it for granted that he nevertheless implicated Richard, whom he proceeds to defend.

According to Fabyan, King Edward:

Took Quene Margaret & hyr sone alyve, the which beyng browght unto his presence, afftyr the kyng hadd questionyd a ffewe wordis of the Cawse of his soo landyng within hys Realm, and he gave unto the kyng an answer contrary hys pleasure, The kyng smote hym on the face wyth the bak of his Gauntelet, Afftyr which strook soo by hym Ressayvid, The kyngys servauntys Ridd hym owth of lyffe fforthwyth.[20]

Another chronicle, also written by Fabyan, *New Chronicles of England and France*, sometimes known simply as *Fabyan's Chronicle*, attributes the murder to the King's servants. On the other hand, according to Polydore Vergil, King Edward, displeased with the young prince's reply, said nothing, 'onely thrusting the young man from him with his hand, whom furthwith, those that wer present wer George Duke of Clarence, Richerd Duke of Glocester, and William lord Hastinges, crewelly murderyd ...[21]

As can be seen, this account is a further development of the story given in the *Great Chronicle of London*, except that, now, the murders are named, not as the King's servants, but as his two brothers and his chamberlain. The story was also taken up and slightly elaborated upon by John Hardyng, although the details of the actual murder do not vary greatly. It is a tale that grows in the telling. By the 1490s, the murderer of Prince Edward was none other than Richard Gloucester. The death of the Prince of Wales has, therefore, been transformed from his being slain as he retreated from the battlefield to his being murdered by Richard Gloucester. Certainly, once the story had fallen into Tudor hands, the only acceptable account of the death of the Lancastrian prince is that he died at the hands of Gloucester.

However, that Richard was in some way involved with the murder of the prince pre-dates the Tudor period, if Walpole's assessment of Croyland's testimony is to be believed. The question must be asked, then, was Richard capable of such cruelty? A fanciful account offered by a Flemish chronicler, Joan Majeris, which was known to George Buck and also referred to by Caroline Halsted, maintains that Richard did not raise his sword to the young prince because of the presence of the Lady Anne, 'to whom the Duke was also very affectionate, though secretly, which he soon after demonstrated in marrying her.'

This version was also adopted by Agnes Strickland, who states that:

Anne [Nevill] was with her husband, Edward of Lancaster, when that unfortunate prince was hurried before Edward IV., after the battle of Tewkesbury, and that it was observed, Richard duke of Gloucester was the only person present who did not draw his sword on the royal captive, out of respect to the presence of Anne, as the near relative of his mother, and a person whose affections he had always desired to possess.[22]

Certainly Anne was present at the events that took place at Tewkesbury, although how close she was to the actual fighting is open to conjecture. She was not close enough to her betrothed to be taken alongside him. What, then, is to be made of the interesting assertion that Richard refused to draw his sword against the prince in deference to Anne? It is implied that Richard was in love with Anne, or at least very fond of her to the point that he was reluctant to obey his brother's command and assist in the slaying of the prince.

This is not the place to discuss Richard's feelings for the woman who was to become his wife. Suffice it to say that, at this point, there is nothing to allow us to assume that there was any affection between Richard and Anne other than the friendship that exists between relatives as close as were, bearing in mind that they had become acquainted during Richard's sojourn at Middleham Castle.

At the opposite end of the spectrum, Alfred Owen Legge points out that Richard was 'familiarised with scenes of anarchy' from his infancy. He goes on to note that the wars between the Houses of York and Lancaster began when Richard was only three and that Richard was only four (actually, he was eight) when his father was killed. Then, Richard 'returned from Utrecht to have his precocious intelligence ripened amid scenes of horror which unhealthily stimulated the natural firmness of his character.'[23]

Perhaps, but Legge does not take into account the lapse of time between Richard's return from Utrecht in 1461 and his going into battle with his brother, first at Barnet and then Tewkesbury, ten years later. In the intervening period, Richard had resumed his formal education in the royal household and completed it at Middleham. He had been made a Knight and the Bath, invested as a Duke and then created a Knight of the Garter. He had taken the first steps of his public life in various judicial and administrative posts on behalf of his brother the King. During this period Richard had not been exposed to the scenes of horror about which Legge speaks. It is true that Edward's accession had not brought the peace that he might have hoped it would; the spring of 1464 would see further battles at Hedgeley Moor and Hexham, but Richard, who was not yet twelve years old at the time, played no part in them.

It might be argued, however, that Richard killed Prince Edward out of revenge for the murder of his brother, Edmund of Rutland. Such an explanation would also extend to Clarence, who was also said to have been involved; the prince was no longer his ally, but his enemy. Significantly, as Walpole points out, Clarence was implicated in the murder of the prince by Edward Hall, who was writing under Henry VIII. Henry had executed Margaret Pole, countess of Salisbury, the daughter of the Duke of Clarence. As Walpole notes, Henry had no reason to:

> Load the memory of Richard the Third, who had left no offspring. Henry the Eighth had no competitor to fear but the descendants of Clarence, of whom he seems to have had sufficient apprehension, as appeared by his murder of the old countess of Salisbury, daughter of Clarence, and his endeavours to root out her posterity.[24]

As to Lord Hastings, perhaps he merely acted in response to orders from the King. However, such reasoning does not stand up when other circumstances are considered. The other Lancastrians who were captured at Tewkesbury were tried, condemned and executed very soon after the battle. Had Prince Edward been taken alive, he would have been treated in the same manner.

Secondly, that Richard Gloucester, in his capacity of Constable of England, had sat in judgement of them might have led to the mistaken belief that he had been responsible for the murder of Prince Edward.

With the victory going to the Yorkists, the Lancastrians began to disperse. Many of them fled into nearby Tewkesbury Abbey. King Edward also went to the abbey either to give thanks for his victory or, more probably, to remove Somerset's forces from their sanctuary. Again, reports are confused. Edward at first appears to have shown leniency towards his enemies. Perhaps carried away in the euphoria of his success, he generously granted pardon to all who had taken refuge within the sacred walls. According to Warkworth, Edward was acting in response to:

> A prest that turnyd oute at his messe and the sacrament in his handys, whanne
> Kynge Edwarde came with his swerde into the churche, requyrede hyme by
> the vertu of the sacrament that he shulde pardone all tho whos names here
> folowe.[25]

He then goes on to list the names of all those who were present in the abbey.

Edward quickly changed his mind, however. His soldiers began to pour through the doors where they arrested the Lancastrians within. Two days later, on Monday 6 May, they were brought before Richard Gloucester who, as Constable of England, presided over their trial. Among them was Edmund Beaufort, Duke of Somerset. Considering that 'of longe tyme [they] had provoked the great rebellyon that so long had endured in the land agaynst the Kynge, and contrye to the wele of the Realme', Richard had no option but to judge them guilty of treason and order their execution. This sentence was carried out without delay 'in the mydste of the towne, upon a scaffolde therefore made', where Somerset and his companions were 'behedyd evereche one, and without eny othar dismembringe, or settyngeup, licensyd to be buryed'.[26]

The *Arrivall* makes the point that Tewkesbury Abbey had never legally been granted the status of sanctuary: 'there ne was, ne had nat at any tyme bene grauntyd, any fraunchise to that place for any offerdars agaynst theyr prince havynge recowrse thethar.'[27] By this reckoning, Edward was acting within his rights when he arrested the enemy on this holy ground. Whether or not the *Arrivall* was correct, it was Richard's duty to condemn the men who had already been pardoned by Edward several times previously only to abuse his clemency.

Several years later, when the battles of Barnet and Tewkesbury had faded into uneasy memory, an indenture was drawn up between Richard

Gloucester and the President and fellows of Queen's College, Cambridge on the occasion of the Duke's endowment of four fellowships within the college. Among their other duties, the new priest-fellows were to pray for the good estate of the Duke, his wife, Anne and their son, Edward of Middleham, the king and queen and other members of the royal family and the souls of the various deceased members of the House of York. There was, of course, nothing unusual about this. However, they were also commended to pray for:

> The soules of Thomas Par, John Milewater, Christofre Wursley, Thomas Huddleston, John Harper and all other gentilmen and yomen *servanders and lovers of the saide duke of Gloucetr,* the wiche were slayn in his service at the batelles of Bernett, Tukysbery or at any other feldes of jorneys.

The men whose names are listed here were probably part of Richard's own household, forming part of his *meyny*, or following, at Barnet and Tewkesbury. They gathered round the person and the great banner of their captain and casualties among such men were often very high because commanders were a primary target during battle. The fact that they, and many others, fell so close to Richard is an indication that he was in the thick of the fighting at both engagements.

The request that their souls should be prayed for was more than mere gesture on Richard's part. It showed a genuine concern for the welfare of the dead, something that was of especial interest to Richard. However, Richard's commendation went far beyond that which would have been expected as due reward for services, whether rendered in the household or in the field. He respected and was grateful for their service and their sacrifice. Richard felt an affinity with the common soldier. Probably inspired by the memory of his father, he deliberately cultivated a martial bearing, seeing himself as a true knight and conducting himself in a manner appropriate to that self-image.

In the aftermath of Tewkesbury Queen Marguerite was captured as she took refuge in a religious house. Of King Edward's enemies, only Jasper Tudor and his young nephew, Henry Tudor, Earl of Richmond, remained at large. Had they been captured and treated in the same manner as the other Lancastrians, the entire course of Richard's life as king would have been altered; there would have been no Henry Tudor to take the throne as King Henry VII.

Still, King Edward could not enjoy the fruits of his victory just yet. Within a matter of days he learned of two new uprisings occurring at opposite ends of the country. To the north Lancastrian partisans were taking to arms having found out about Queen Marguerite's landing at Weymouth three weeks earlier. Edward took Richard and George and rode northwards to Worcester to meet them. Meanwhile, he despatched Rivers, Essex, Arundel and Sir John Scott to Kent to assist the authorities of London against the other outbreak of trouble under Thomas Fauconberg.

A cousin of the late Earl of Warwick and illegitimate son of William Nevill, Thomas, Lord Fauconberg, or the Bastard, as he is referred to in contemporary documents, had provided assistance during Warwick's rebellion. Following the death of the Kingmaker at Barnet, he proclaimed himself captain and leader of partisans of King Henry in Kent as well as captain of the navy of England. Some two hundred people rallied to his banner, including the mayor of Canterbury, Nicholas Faunt. As they made their way to London, they managed to do considerable damage to the new gate at the south end of London Bridge. Crossing over the river, they set fire to some beer houses, then, unable to decide which side of the river he wanted to be, the Bastard next attacked London Bridge, Aldgate and Bishopsgate. Having been beaten back, he retreated as far as Blackheath before his party broke up, probably due to the appearance of an advance guard of some 1,500 men detailed by King Edward to assist in putting down the uprising. Edward himself arrived in London on Tuesday 21 May. He was accompanied by Richard Gloucester and the Duke of Clarence. It was truly a magnificent entry by the victorious king:

> Then to the gate the kynge did ride,
> His brethir and his lordis in ordre, a good sight to see.
> iiij.m^1 harnessid men the kynge did abide,
> And worshypfully resayvid hym into the cité.
> Cryste preserve the pepull, for his grett peté!
> xx.m^1, I suppose, and many one moo,
> Welcomyd kyng Edward, the will of God was soo.[28]

This anonymous poem, written by a supporter of the House of York, describes the King surrounded by men in armour. We can imagine the scene. The bright banners of the knights flying in the breeze; the bystanders lining the route to welcome their true king back into his capital; their cheers and cries filling the air, their hands waving, hats thrown to the sky as the king waves to his loyal subjects on either side. There are trumpets and drums; horses in bright caparisons, standards and the royal arms everywhere to be seen, an ocean of colour. At Edward's side is Richard Gloucester. He is young, still only eighteen years old, and handsome; his shoulder-length brown hair catching the breeze as he rides along, his shimmering helm under his arm. Young Gloucester is the most eligible bachelor in the land, and many of the young women in the crowd that day were eager to catch his eye.

Not long after the sun had set on this most glorious of days, the dark figure of a man silently stepped out of a boat and slipped through the shadowy water gate into the Tower of London. He had come bearing orders from the King. It was not an agreeable assignment. On that night, in the silent stillness of the small chapel in the Wakefield Tower, a truly tragic event took place.

The murder of King Henry VI is one of the bloodiest and most shocking of the crimes that have been attributed to Richard III. The victim was a man of fragile health who had spent the previous ten years of his life as a prisoner or a fugitive. Either way, Henry appears to have enjoyed little control over his own fate; he was used as a figurehead for his supporters or a bargaining chip for his enemies in the battles that followed his deposition. Now, as his brief Readeption faded into the shadows of his failing mind, he took up his rosary and began to pray. What happened next is fairly well documented considering that it was an act that must, by definition, have been carried out in the utmost secrecy. The *Arrivall of King Edward IV* states that Henry, upon hearing of the disaster at Tewkesbury, 'toke it to so great dispite, ire, and indignation, that, of pure displeasure, and melencoly, he dyed the xxiij. day of the monithe of May'.[29]

This account of Henry's melancholy death reflects a similar description of the death of Richard II, who is supposed to have pined away in the castle of Pontefract. King Henry II and Humphrey, Duke of Gloucester, are also supposed to have died of sorrow.[30] Since both these men were almost certainly murdered, do we assume that deaths attributed to emotional causes, as in the case of Henry VI, are really murders? John Warkworth's account leaves no room for ambiguity:

And the same nyghte that Kynge Edward came to London, Kynge Herry, beynge inwarde in persone in the Toure of Londone, was putt to dethe, the xxj. day of Maij, on a Tyweseday nyght, betwixt xj. and xij. of the cloke, being thenne at the Toure the Duke of Gloucestre, brothere to Kynge Edwarde, and many other.[31]

Warkworth's account states categorically that Henry was murdered, or 'putt to dethe' as he states it. Although he notes the presence of Richard Gloucester, he does not actually accuse him of the murder, nor does he state the manner of death. Other writers were not so evasive. Naturally, news of the death of the former king was quickly carried abroad, where a horrified people were anxious to learn all the details. In his work, dedicated to the physician to the King of France, the Flemish historian Philippe de Commines writes:

> (If what was told me be true) after the battle was over, the Duke of Gloucester (who was King Edward's brother, and afterwards called King Richard) slew this poor King Henry with his own hand, or caused him to be carried into some private place, and stood by while he was killed.[32]

Clearly, for Commines there is only one explanation for the presence of the duke of Gloucester at the Tower that night: he is responsible for the murder of King Henry, by his own hand or at his command. Fabyan is more certain: 'the moost comon fame wente that he [Henry] was stykked with a dager, by the handes of the Duke of Glouceter … '[33]. There is now no longer any doubt that Richard's hands alone are stained with the blood of the deposed king. Fabyan also introduces the murder weapon. Richard uses a dagger, a small weapon that is easy to conceal and so can be carried undetected into the place where Henry is being held. Meanwhile, the Croyland Continuator, somewhat reluctantly, dedicates a paragraph to the murder:

> I would pass over in silence the fact that at this period king Henry was found dead in the Tower of London; may God spare and grant time for repentance to the person, whoever he was, who thus dared to lay sacrilegious hands upon the Lord's anointed! Hence it is that he who perpetrated this has justly earned the title of tyrant, while he who thus suffered has gained that of a glorious Martyr.[34]

Polydore Vergil offers:

> Henry the Sixt, being not long before depryvyd of hys dyademe, was put to death in the tour of London. The contynuall report is, that Richerd duke of Glocestrer killyd him with a sword, whereby his brother might be delyveryed from all feare of hostylytie.[35]

Once again, Richard is named as the murderer. Vergil states that Richard killed the deposed king with a sword rather than a dagger, although he later describes Richard as 'woont to be ever with his right hand pulling out of the sheath to the myddest, and putting in agane, the dagger which he did alway were.'[36]

Vergil does not mention whether Richard used the sword to stab Henry or to slice off the crown of his head. In other words, the fact that the historian omits these details deprives us of the means to determine whether or not he equated Henry's death with that of Thomas Becket, who also died by the sword while at prayer, and who had since become a martyr and saint. In a way, this is surprising. Vergil was writing his *English History* at the behest of King Henry VII, who had made an unsuccessful attempt to have his Lancastrian predecessor canonised. Long before that, Richard, too, would come to believe in the late king's sainthood. However, Vergil does suggest Richard's motive for murdering Henry: he wanted to free his brother from the fear of hostility in order, presumably, that he might be able to resume his reign in peace. In fact, this is just what happened; the restoration of King Edward IV inaugurated a period of peace that was to last until the reign of King Richard III some twelve years later.

The *Vitellius A XVI* offers '[King Henry] was slain, as it is said, by the Duke of Gloucester ... '[37] It is now common currency that Richard was responsible for the murder, although this document does not speculate regarding motive.

The death of King Henry is, of course, an essential ingredient in *The History of King Richard III* of Thomas More:

> He [Richard] slewe with his owne handes king Henry the Sixt, being prisoner in the Tower, as menne constantly saye, and that without commaundmente or knowledge of the king, whiche woulde vndoubtedly, yf he had entended that thinge, haue appointed that boocherly office to some other than his owne borne brother.[38]

According to More, Edward had taken Henry's crown in revenge for his father's death at Wakefield. By implication, if Edward were to kill Henry, he would have done so in the aftermath of the battle that took his father's life. However, Henry's death was not revenge for any wrong done to the House of York, rather, he died because he was one of the several obstacles that stood between Richard and the crown he wanted: 'Frende and foo was muche what indifferent; where his aduauntage grew, he spared no mans deathe whose life withstoode his purpose.'[39] As such, More lays the blame for Henry's murder firmly at Richard's door. By showing Richard to have acted on his own initiative, he exonerates Edward IV of any involvement in the crime. Richard Grafton similarly attributes the death of King Henry to Richard:

> Henry that was depriued not long before of his crowne, was also spoiled of his
> life, that is, was killed. And as the report & fame went, the duke of Glouceter
> was suspected to haue done that dede, which sticked him with a dagger.[40]

Grafton, whose account strongly reflects that of Fabyan, includes a speech
supposedly made by Richard as he murdered King Henry, "Nowe is there ne
heyre male of kyng Edward the thryde, but we of the house of Yorke."

This echoes Vergil's assertion that Richard killed Henry in order to remove
the focus of any future uprising against Edward. By emphasising that only
those of the House of York remain as heirs to King Edward III, it can be seen
that Richard's means to secure peace was to eliminate entirely the House of
Lancaster.

For Edward Hall, 'Richard, Duke of Gloucester (as the constant fame
ranne) which, to thintent that king Edward his brother, should be clere of
all secret suspicion of sodain inuasion, murthered the said kyng with a dagger.'[41] This account, then, draws together various points made by earlier
chroniclers and historians. It identifies Richard Gloucester as the murderer,
focuses on the wish to secure a peaceful reign for Edward, while rehearsing
the use of the dagger.

Note how each of these writers attribute their information to rumour: 'if
what I hear is true', 'as it is said', 'the contynuall report is', 'as men constantly
say', 'as the report & fame went', 'as the constant fame ranne'. In the face of
so much uncertainly, how seriously can historians take their reports of this
event? The assertion that Richard was personally responsible for the death
of King Henry VI is supported by entirely unreliable accounts. Moreover,
the authors of those accounts do not appear to believe their sources even as
they relate them for political purposes. Still, they do provide the extra gruesome detail that, as it makes its way to its final rest, the body of Henry VI
bled afresh at each stopping place. According to Warkworth:

> And one the morwe he was chestyde and brought to Paulys, and his face was
> opyne that every manne myghte see hyme; and in hys lyinge he bledde one
> the pament ther; and afterward at the Blake Fryres was broughte, and ther he
> blede new and fresche.[42]

Warkworth describes how Henry lay in state, his body displayed for all to
see. The bodies of kings were frequently treated this way in order to allay
any thought or rumour that he might be still alive; this proved that he had
died of natural causes and not under suspicious circumstances and discouraged any uprising in his name. In the case of Henry, such precautions are

misplaced. Warkworth refers to the superstitious belief that a corpse will bleed in the presence of its murderer, a phenomenon understood as a post-humous accusation. That Henry's corpse is said to have bled indicates that, despite whatever preventative measures might be in place, Henry is still able to reveal the true cause of his death from beyond the grave, thus ensuring that his murderer will be found out.

Shakespeare made graphic use of this phenomenon in *The Tragedy of King Richard III*:

> O, gentlemen, see, see! dead Henry's wounds
> Open their congeal'd mouths and bleed afresh.
> Blush, blush thou lump of foul deformity;
> For 'tis thy presence that exhales this blood
> From cold and empty veins, where no blood dwells;
> Thy deed, inhuman and unnatural,
> Provokes this deluge most unnatural.[43]

The speaker is Anne Nevill, who attends the body of her father-in-law, Henry VI, as it is being taken away for burial. The progress of the solemn group is interrupted by the appearance of Richard, Duke of Gloucester, the 'lump of foul deformity' to whom these lines are addressed.

It is interesting to note that Henry's body lay at St Paul's prior to his being taken for burial at Chertsey Abbey. Shakespeare's Richard III is the only character to use the oath 'by St Paul', which he utters several times during the course of the play. He says it in the context of the impending death of King Edward: 'Now by Saint Paul, this news is bad'. On another occasion, he makes the oath as he interrupts the funeral cortege of King Henry VI, which is part of the scene quote above:

> Villains, set down the corpse, or, by Saint Paul,
> I'll make a corpse of him that disobeys.[44]

Lady Anne attributes Richard's sudden and unwelcome appearance to the work of a black magician: 'what black magician conjures up this fiend?' Shakespeare's influence in this instance is probably the scene in Acts of the Apostles 19.11-17 where Paul is opposed by an evil spirit who gets the better of the Jewish High Priests who attempt to exorcise him. Overall, however, Shakespeare's references to St Paul are almost certainly inspired by Thomas More, in whose account of the death of Hastings Richard uses the same oath: 'for by saynt Poule (quod he) I wil not to dinner til I se thy hed of.'[45]

This scene is also taken over by the Bard, where the reference to St Paul is preserved.[46]

More appears to have been inspired by Acts 23.12, in which the Jews 'made a plot and bound themselves by an oath neither to eat nor drink till they had killed Paul'. By associating Richard with the Jews, More shows him to be both treacherous and unchristian. This is further enhanced when More describes Richard as the master of dissimulation, 'not letting to kisse whome hee thoughte to kyll.'[47] Of course, the arch-dissimulator, who nevertheless had no objection to kissing his victim, was Judas, who was for More 'worse also then ye very worst in al ye world beside'[48]. Only Richard III was on a par with him.

The precedent for the miracle of the bleeding corpse is found in the story of King Henry II, whose bleeding body drew attention to the treachery of his son, Richard, the future Lionheart.[49] However, if the purpose of the bleeding corpse is to accuse the murderer, as Warkworth and Shakespeare imply, then its efforts were wasted: the historical Richard was not present at either of the places Henry VI lay prior to burial. If the body did bleed, it was not in order to accuse the Duke of Gloucester.

If the allegation that Richard murdered Henry VI, or that Henry was murdered at Richard's command, were true, or even believed to have been true, the incident would have been reported with more certainly than it was. There were many chroniclers, letter-writers and memoirists who were hostile towards Richard and who would have leapt at the chance to spread abroad the news of such a vile act of sacrilege as the murder of an anointed king on holy ground. The crime would have been so well known that it could not have been gainsaid by any friend of Richard's who wished to retain his credibility as a witness. Instead, those who had the means to expose Richard were forced to resort to speculation, rumour and superstition, rather than hard fact. Moreover, as Legge[50] points out, the murder of King Henry would have served no purpose. The King was now childless, he was ill, and he was safely in custody in the Tower. A far more formidable threat to the Yorkists was Queen Marguerite. She, too, was imprisoned behind the Tower's walls, but she was still strong, had many supporters and was a better candidate for rescue than her feeble husband. She posed a far greater danger to Edward IV, a fact of which Richard would have been all too aware. As such, she would have been a more suitable victim for anyone with murder on his mind that night, whoever he might have been.

Are the sources at least correct in their assertion that Henry VI died a violent death? The pro-Yorkist *Arrivall of King Edward IV* states that Henry died 'of pure displeasure, and melencoly'.[51] This claim is simply propaganda and forensic evidence does not support it.

The opening of King Henry's tomb on 12 November 1910 revealed a decayed mass of human bones. These were analysed by Professor MacAlister of Cambridge University, who found them to belong to a very strong man of between forty-five to fifty-five years of age and who was at least five feet nine inches tall. The skull was broken, although the bone was found to be small and thin in proportion to the stature. One fragment still had some brown hair attached to it, part of which was apparently matted with blood.[52]

While there is little doubt that Henry suffered from some form of depressive psychosis, this could not account for the presence of blood, if that is what it was, in his hair. However, a violent death is not necessarily indicated, since it cannot be said when the skull was broken. Indeed, 'if the body had been buried in the earth for some time and then exhumed, it would account for their being in the condition in which we found them.'[53]

Yet, how to account for the matted blood found in Henry's hair? Its presence led archaeologists excavating the tomb to conjecture that Henry 'may have died a violent death'. If so, at whose hands did Henry die? The most compelling suspect is Edward IV. However, if he had wanted to quiet Henry so that he might reign in peace, he made a serious mistake in murdering him. Murder conferred the crown of martyrdom upon Henry, underpinning later claims to sainthood on his behalf.

In the end, there is nothing to substantiate Richard's alleged involvement with the death of Henry VI; at the very most, as Constable of England, it was his duty to carry the order and place it into the hands of the Constable of the Tower, Lord Dudley; the only man who could issue such an order was the King. It is clear, then, that King Edward IV must take the blame for the murder of King Henry VI. As Sforza di Bettini, Milanese ambassador to the court of France, wrote to the Duke of Milan on 17 June 1471:

> King Edward has not chosen to have custody of King Henry any longer, although he was in some sense innocent, and there was no great fear about his proceedings, the prince his son and the Earl of Warwick being dead as well as all those who were for him and had any vigour, as he caused King Henry to be secretly assassinated in the tower, where he was a prisoner. They say he has done the same to the queen, King Henry's wife ... He has, in short, chosen to crush the seed.[54]

The ambassador was incorrect about Edward's dealings with Queen Marguerite, who was captured and imprisoned after Tewkesbury. She was kept in close confinement in the Tower of London before being moved to Windsor Castle. At the end of 1471 she was transferred into the safe keeping of Alice, Duchess of Suffolk. In his assessment of Edward's motives, however, Bettini is certainly correct. King Edward had good reason, from a political point of view, to order the death of Henry VI. He would never be able to sit easily on his throne while Henry lived to provide a focus for future rebellion. It is for this reason that Henry Bolingbroke is believed to have killed Richard II and why people would later attribute the death of Edward V to Richard III.

In Edward IV's case, there is another reason why he should order Henry's death. Thomas More's assertions notwithstanding, it is conceivable that Edward killed Henry out of revenge for the death of his father and brother at the battle of Wakefield. Years before, Edward had accused 'Henry Usurper' of 'gretely and wonderfully joiyng the seid dolorous and piteous murdre of the same noble Prynce, and worthy Lordes'. He goes on to say that Henry broke the Act of Accord that had recognised Richard of York and his progeny as the rightful heirs to the throne, this Edward restored in his own *Titulus Regius* or Royal Title.[55] It is, perhaps ironic that Henry had been held in the Wakefield Tower, and it was there that he met his end.

Edward also restored Richard Gloucester's offices of Constable of England and Admiral of England, Ireland and Aquitaine, which had reverted to the Earl of Warwick during Henry VI's brief Readeption. However, Edward was not rewarding his brother for a job well done on the night on 21 May, but for his support during the rebellion that had cost him his kingdom. Richard's award is commemorated on his admiralty seal, which shows that the Duke had also been invested with the Earldoms of Dorset and Somerset.

Richard's admiralty seal seems to have enjoyed an interesting history, and for many years it appears to have been lost. Having left Richard's possession, it next appears among the belongings of a Mr Jackson, a Cumberland man who had moved to the West Country, first to Devonshire and then to St Columb in Cornwall, where he became an innkeeper. After his death, his goods were cleared and sold. A lot containing brass and iron was purchased by Mr J. Hankey, an attorney at St Columb. That the seal had been in the possession of a man from Cumberland is in keeping with Richard's whereabouts, since his wardenship of the West March towards Scotland obliged him to reside at the castles of Penrith and Carlisle, among other places in Cumberland.

Following Mr Hankey's death, in 1782, the seal passed into the hands of another attorney, Mr Dennis of Penzance. An impression of it was presented to the Society of Antiquaries by the Reverend Dr Milles, Dean of Exeter, through whom the provenance of the seal became known.

The seal itself is wrought in brass and shows a ship, the mainsail of which depicts the arms of England and France quarterly. It has a label of three points ermine, each charged with a canton gules, to which distinction Richard was entitled as a cadet of the Plantagenet family. The square-shaped forecastle is adorned with fleur-de-lys and holds a beacon, and it has an anchor suspended beneath it. The stern castle, also square, is similarly adorned with fleur-de-lys, and it holds a dragon supporting the admiral's flag bearing the same arms as the mainsail. The margin of the seal bears the inscription:

S. Ric'i Duc' Glou' Admiralli Angl' & Com Dors' & Soms'

[Sigillum Ricardi Ducis Gloucestriæ Admiralli Angliæ &
Comitis Dorset & Somerset]

That Richard is named Earl of both Dorset and Somerset suggests that the seal could have been made at any time between his appointment in 1471 and the creation of Thomas Grey, a son of Queen Elizabeth by her first marriage, as Marquis of Dorset in 1475. The reason Richard was granted the title is surely as a result of the assistance he offered to King Edward at the Battle of Tewkesbury. Here, Richard successfully aided his brother in repulsing the surprise attack launched by the Duke of Somerset, in which he drove the Duke back up the hill, thus allowing Edward the opportunity to scatter the Lancastrian divisions before going on to eventual victory. Somerset was one of the Lancastrian leaders to be tried and executed following the battle and, as such, his titles became extinct in the Beaufort family. They could well have been awarded to his vanquisher, Richard, who held them until they were granted to Thomas Grey in 1471.[56]

King Edward, having removed the last of the Lancastrian line, rode out to Kent, where the Bastard of Fauconberg was continuing to stir up trouble, having taken command of forty seven ships. The first thing Edward did upon arrival was to knight the mayor of London and some of the aldermen in reward for their services to the King; the next thing he did was to hang, draw and quarter the traitorous mayor of Canterbury.

The Bastard of Fauconberg, having been alerted to the King's approach, sued for pardon for himself and his followers. He offered to surrender his ships to the King with a promise to become his 'trwe liegeman'. After some deliberation and great consideration on the King's part, the request for pardon was granted. Once again, Richard Gloucester is seen to be standing by in support of his brother: 'Wherefore the Kynge sent thethar his brothar Richard, Duke of Gloucestar, to receyve them in his name, and all the shipps; as he dyd the xxvj. day of the same monithe; the Kynge that tyme beinge at Cantorbery'.[57]

The Bastard of Fauconberg received his pardon on 10 June and the letters of protection were issued six days later. He then went into the service of Richard Gloucester, who spent much of the summer of 1471 travelling to and fro in the North Country. According to Waurin, Fauconberg accompanied Richard to a place called Merlan, where he was allowed to go back and forth with the other servants.[58] Perhaps Edward had ordered Richard to keep an eye on him. If so, he might have formed part of Richard's entourage as the Duke journeyed south to take an oath of homage to Prince Edward as the new, Yorkist, Prince of Wales. This took place on 3 July 1471 at Westminster in the chamber of parliament. The oath, as Richard would have spoken and signed it, went, 'I Richard Gloucester:

> Knowledge, take and repute you Edward prince of Wales etc. first begotten son of our sovereign lord King Edward, etc. to be very and undoubted heir to our said lord as to the crowns and realms of England and France and lordship of Ireland, and promise and swear that in case hereafter it happen you by God's disposition to overlive our sovereign lord; I shall then take and accept you for the very true and rightwise king of England etc. and faith and truth shall to you bear: and in all things truly and faithfully behave me towards you and your heirs as a true and a faithful subject oweth to behave him to his sovereign lord etc.: So help me God and halidom and this holy Evangeliste.[59]

After this Richard returned to the north. Three months later came the mysterious demise of the Bastard of Fauconberg. What exactly happened cannot be known. The only records of the event are a few confused entries in calendars, letters and chronicles. The first inkling that something was stirring came on 11 September 1471 when Robert Cosyn and John Cole were commissioned to 'seize the goods of Thomas Fauconberg, traitor.'[60] Four days after that, John Paston wrote, 'I undrestonde that Bastarde Fauconbryge is owther hedyd or lyke to be'.[61] Almost two weeks later, on the 28 September, Paston notes, 'Item, Thomas Fauconbrydge hys hed was yesterdaye sett uppon London Brydge, lokyng into Kent warde'.[62]

Of what Fauconberg was guilty is not known. The entry in the Calendar of Patent Rolls simply refers to him as a traitor, but this cannot refer to the rebellion against King Edward in May because he had been pardoned for that. The *Yorkist Notes* say only that Fauconberg 'propter nouam offensam decapitatus est', without further elaboration.[63] Buck offers that 'after he told some tales [he was] put to death.'[64] It might be speculated that Fauconberg had raised the subject of Edward's alleged illegitimacy, but there is nothing to substantiate this.

According to Waurin, the Bastard had tried to escape from Richard, at which point he was executed. Vergil tells us that 'the Fawconbridge sped him spedyly unto his ships, but soone after arriving unadvysydly at Southampton he was taken and beheadyd.'[65] In other words, Fauconberg's escape attempt had been successful and he had managed to reach Southampton on the south coast, where he had ships and men to help him escape abroad or, perhaps, to start a new rebellion.

From these few scraps of evidence an acceptable account can be put together: Fauconberg was captured by Edward at Sandwich. He proved to be co-operative so that, when he sued for pardon, Edward granted it. Fauconberg then accompanied Richard, who had been sent into Yorkshire. The Bastard remained with Richard until he found a way to escape, or perhaps was rescued. If Buck's assertion that Fauconberg had spread tales abroad, and if they did indeed concern King Edward's legitimacy, it could be that Fauconberg was awaiting an opportunity to stage another revolt against the King. He is next seen at Southampton, where he was captured once again and, having shown himself unworthy of the King's good-will and undeserving of his pardon, received due punishment. He was executed, either at Southampton or after having been taken back to London. Either way, his head was set on London Bridge in the time-honoured manner. It might be added that, considering the circumstances, he had got off lightly in being beheaded rather than being condemned to the full horrors of a traitor's death. King Edward might have been quick to pardon, but he was just as quick to exact retribution when his generosity was not appreciated.

CHAPTER 13

WARWICK'S HEIR,
1471-1472

The leniency shown by Edward IV to his enemies following Tewkesbury meant that there were few forfeitures with which to reward those who had supported him during 'the time of his great necessity'. One of the reasons for this was that many members of the royal family were heirs to the estates concerned, and Edward was aware that they would suffer if the holders were condemned. Most of the Lancastrians were attainted, but their estates simply reverted to those who had held them previously. Some of the estates were restored to their Lancastrian owners, but at the expense of those to whom they had subsequently been granted.[1]

It was King Edward's priority to provide for his son, the infant Prince of Wales, and his younger brother, Richard Gloucester. In endowing Edward, Prince of Wales, the King was inevitably forced to deprive others of some of their holdings. One such was the Duke of Clarence.

To provide for Richard was more difficult, although a slow trickle of grants and awards did fall into the Duke's hands. On 18 May 1471 he was appointed Great Chamberlain of England 'in the same manner as Richard, late Earl of Warwick, receiving such fees as the said Earl had at the receipt of the Exchequer, with all other profits.'[2] On 4 July he was appointed chief steward of the duchy of Lancaster in the north parts, another post that had formerly been held by Warwick; he also took over from Lord Stanley as chief steward of the duchy of Lancaster within the palatine of Lancashire. On 18 August Richard resumed the office of warden of the West Marches towards Scotland, which had first been awarded to him in 1470. This present award appears to have been a second indenture to run from the period from 18 August 1475.

Since Richard was required to spend most of the summer of 1471 travelling in the North Country on a series of commissions, provision had to be made to enable him to concentrate fully on them. As such, his offices in Wales were transferred to William Herbert, second Earl of Pembroke and John Talbot, third Earl of Shrewsbury.

In a final endowment, granted on 4 December 1471, Richard received most of the estates of John de Vere, thirteenth Earl of Oxford. Edward had previously awarded these to Richard, but had withdrawn them in order to return them to de Vere. For, notwithstanding the Earl's strong Lancastrian tendencies, and the fact that he was the son of a traitor, King Edward was eager to make peace with John de Vere; he even granted the Earl's petition to reverse the attainder of an ancestor, Robert de Vere, which had been passed as long ago as 1388. Oxford's favour with the King was secure enough for him to be made a Knight of the Bath at the coronation of Queen Elizabeth Wydeville on 26 May 1465. Here, he had acted as great chamberlain of England in place of the absent Earl of Warwick, and had been appointed chamberlain to the Queen.

Oxford's method of thanking Edward for his leniency, kindness and favour was to plot with the Lancastrians against him. The angry king responded by arresting Oxford and confining him to the Tower. This was enough to make Oxford confess to the plots and he was released three months later; he received a pardon in April 1469. However, Oxford was to show Edward, once again, the folly of his ways when, early in the following June, he joined Clarence and Warwick in their rebellion against the King. At the Readeption of King Henry VI, Oxford bore the sword in the procession to St Paul's for the newly restored king's crown-wearing ceremony.

As Edward IV returned to England to reclaim his crown, it was Oxford who had prevented his landing in Norfolk. He then took part against Edward in the ensuing battles. Following Edward's victory at Barnet, Oxford fled to Scotland, from where he sailed to France. It was under these circumstances, then, that Richard Gloucester was once again granted the forfeited Oxford estates.[3] The forfeiture meant that the lands belonging to Oxford's mother, Elizabeth, would go, not to her son, John, but to Richard. To prevent this, Elizabeth enfeoffed her estates to use. Richard would have to resort to chancery and, perhaps, menaces, to get the lands that he understood to have been made over to him under the terms of this award.

In granting Richard the Oxford estates, Edward had finally given him the first substantial livelihoods that he had ever had. Moreover, it was becoming increasingly apparent that the King was making Richard the political heir to the late Earl of Warwick. Nevertheless, the income from Richard's offices, honours and seats, valuable though they were, paled into insignificance when compared with those of his brother, the Duke of Clarence. Duke Richard's income at this point was probably in the region of 2,000 marks, or £1,666 13s 4d annually. Clarence's assets were very much higher.

This does not reckon with the property of Richard of Warwick. Had Warwick died a natural death his estates would have been shared three ways. First, the Nevill patrimony, which was entailed in the male line, would have gone to Warwick's brother, John, Marquis Montagu and Montagu's son, George, Duke of Bedford. The remainder would have been shared between Warwick's daughters, Isabel, Duchess of Clarence, and Anne Nevill.

Since both Warwick and Montagu had died fighting against the King, their estates were confiscated on account of their treason. They were posthumously indicted for this in May 1472, although not formally attainted.[4] This meant that the entirety of the Warwick inheritance was forfeited to the crown; it became the property of King Edward. As a consequence, Warwick's brother, nephew and daughters were disinherited.

King Edward, fully cognisant of the help he had received from Clarence in his bid to win back his throne, was equally mindful of his obligation to reward him. He did this by granting to Clarence all the estates to which the Duchess Isabel had hereditary right. Since Isabel had no claim to the Nevill estates, the King granted these to his younger brother, Richard Gloucester. On 29 June, therefore, Richard was awarded full grant in tail male of the lordships of Middleham and Sheriff Hutton in Yorkshire and Penrith in Cumberland, 'with their members and all other lordships, manors and lands in those counties which were entailed to Richard Neville, late Earl of Warwick, and the heirs male of his body or any ancestors whose heir male he was in like manner ... '[5]

In thus disposing of the late Earl's estates in favour of his brothers, Edward deprived the Kingmaker's widow of her entitlement to a third share of the Salisbury and Nevill estates in dower. The King chose to disregard the fact that the countess's jointure and the Beauchamp and Despenser lands were her own property and had never belonged to Warwick. Only had she committed treason could the estates be forfeited; she had not.

The countess's younger daughter, Anne Nevill, the widow of the late Edward of Lancaster, Prince of Wales, could expect no better treatment. She had been taken prisoner alongside her mother-in-law, Queen Marguerite in the aftermath of Tewkesbury. 'Thes wer ther taken and presentyd to ye kynge, and pardonyd: ladye Margaret, qwene, ladye Anne, princes...'[6] Later, Anne was made a ward of the Duchess of Clarence. Due to her claims to what Duke George now considered to be his personal property, it was in his best interests if Anne did not remarry. It came as a shock to him, then, when Richard Gloucester announced his wish to make Anne Nevill his wife.

Anne Nevill was born on 11 June 1456 at Warwick, her father's principal seat as the Earl of Warwick. She was christened at St Mary's, Warwick College, which was the mausoleum of the Beauchamp family. She was only eleven months old when her father took up his post as captain of Calais in May 1457. Warwick had decided to reside in the town, administering his duties in person rather than through a deputy and, since his countess had accompanied him, it is highly probable that their two daughters did so as well.

As the Duke of York's bid for power became more aggressive, Warwick's life was taken up with diplomacy or military campaigns and he frequently lived apart from his family. There is no record of the whereabouts of the countess of Warwick and her two daughters at this stage in their lives, but it is probably safe to guess that they stayed in one or another of the countess's midlands estates. The first definite record of Anne was at the magnificent celebrations surrounding the enthronement of her uncle, George Nevill, as archbishop of York. This took place in the castle of Cawood near York, where the now nine-year-old Anne found herself in the company of the young Richard, Duke of Gloucester. It was shortly after this that Richard had gone to Middleham as a page under the tutelage of the Earl of Warwick. It can only be speculated how much contact the two children had and what opinion they held of each other.

By the time Richard left Middleham, in January 1469, Anne was not yet thirteen years of age. Once again, we can only wonder at what feelings, if any, she harboured for the young Duke, who was now a rather attractive and gallant knight. Richard, at sixteen, might have thought of Anne as no more than a child. However, it is possible that he already realised that, given her rank and status, she should not be ruled out as a possible future wife for him.

Had Richard entertained such thoughts, he had only to cast his mind back to that frightening episode some five years previously when Edward had placed him and Clarence under house arrest upon his discovery that the Earl of Warwick had suggested an alliance between his daughter, Isabel, and the Duke of Clarence. Even if Richard had not also been included in the Earl's scheme, Edward's hostility towards such a match would seem to preclude any chance that Richard would have seriously considered Anne Nevill as his future wife.

As it happened, the enmity between the Earl of Warwick and King Edward was soon to take an even more sinister turn. As the ensuing rebellion unfolded, the Lady Anne was taken to France and married to Edward of

Lancaster, Prince of Wales. At the time her husband was slain at Tewkesbury on 4 May 1471, the new princess had not yet reached fifteen years of age.

In fact, Anne might not have actually been Prince Edward's wife in the fullest sense of the word. In the original Latin version of Croyland's *Chronicle*,[7] Anne is described as *desponsata*, which means betrothed or engaged, but not yet married. After the prince's death, she is spoken of as *puella*. This is often translated as virgin, but such a translation is misleading; *puella* simply means a young woman or wife.

However, that her union with Prince Edward had not been consummated is borne out by what we know of the agreement between King Louis of France, Queen Marguerite and the Earl of Warwick to the effect that Anne would remain in the custody of Queen Marguerite until Warwick had recovered England for King Henry:

> Item that from thens forth the seyde dowghter of th'Erle of Warwick shalbe put and remayne in the hands and kepinge of Quene Margaret, and also that the seyde marriage shal not be perfyted to th'Erle of Warwick had been with an army over the Sea into England, and that he had recovered the realm of England in the moste parte therof, for the Kynge Henrye.'[8]

The marriage between Anne and Edward was not consummated, nor would it be until the princess's father won back the kingdom for Henry VI. Anne accompanied the Queen to England where, following Prince Edward's death, she was taken prisoner along with her mother-in-law.

Legge[9] notes that, in accordance with contemporary practice, Anne would have been placed in the custody of her sister. This had happened to Cecily, Duchess of York following the rout at Ludlow, when she and her children, including Lord Richard, as he was then, were sent to stay with Anne, Duchess of Buckingham at Tunbridge Castle in Kent. In Princess Anne's case she was entrusted to the care of her sister, Isabel, Duchess of Clarence, and this is how she came under the control of Duke George.

Anne, like a leaf tossed on the autumn breeze, now found her life dictated once again by chance. As she entered the household of her sister, her thoughts must have carried her back to that dreadful day when her young husband was murdered on the battlefield. We can only imagine her feelings when she replayed the tragic events in her mind knowing that they had come about as the result of her brother-in-law's treachery; that same brother-in-law in whose custody she now was. Perhaps she toyed with the idea of exacting revenge on Clarence for causing such injury to herself and her prince.

Certainly, Anne had little reason to love and respect George of Clarence. As long as she remained in her present condition, widowed and with no prospect of remarrying, she had very little chance of asserting her rights as co-heiress to her father's estate. This all worked to Clarence's benefit, of course. The Duke was all too aware of the advantages in keeping Anne single and under his control. He knew also that the biggest threat to the properties he had gained at Anne's expense was his own brother, Richard Gloucester, who, whether he had indeed realised it or not, was quite the best match for Anne.

It was necessary for Clarence to act. According to the Croyland Continuator, he 'caused the damsel to be concealed, in order that it might not be known by his brother where she was.'[10] Somehow or other, and Croyland attributes it to 'craftiness' indicating a degree of cunning or deceit, the Duke of Gloucester 'discovered the young lady in the city of London disguised in the habit of a cookmaid'.

The delightful aura of romance surrounding Richard's 'rescue' of Anne, the princess-in-rags, which is known only to Croyland, can be dismissed for the Cinderella tale that it is. However, it is possible that the basic elements are sound. Clarence might indeed have concealed Anne's whereabouts from his brother only to be thwarted by Richard's ingenuity. Richard's rescue, or perhaps more appropriately, abduction, of the young woman, against her will or otherwise, can also be believed. What can be said with certainty is that, once she was in his custody, Richard immediately placed Anne in the sanctuary of the Collegiate Church of Saint Martin-le-Grand.

That Anne had consented to and co-operated with Richard's actions in liberating her can only be a matter for speculation; it was, after all, tantamount to rape, albeit with the consent of the 'victim'.[11] For, young though she was, Anne had probably realised that the only way she could get hold of and retain her inheritance was to marry Duke Richard. The Duke was already in possession of the Nevill estates and, as such, he was her best possible hope if she were to resist Clarence's attempts to lay his hands on the remainder of her inheritance.

As a widow, Anne was technically legally free to pursue her own courtships and contract a marriage of her choice. However, she had been in Clarence's custody for several months by the time Richard carried her away. While this had given her time to conceive a plan, it had prevented her from carrying it out. Once she was out of Clarence's sight, whether disguised as a cookmaid or not, it is not impossible that she had managed to get a message out to Richard and that his chivalrous action in 'rescuing' her was actually her idea. Far from Strickland's assertion that Anne was 'compelled by violence to marry Richard',[12] there is every possibility that she viewed the

Duke's suit, when he eventually got round to pursuing it, with the practicality and level-headedness of a business woman that today might even be seen as cynical or conniving.

For his part, Richard could not have been unaware that Anne was a good catch. However, he too had been occupied since Tewkesbury, but not in a way that allowed him the leisure to contemplate his future in terms of marriage. Edward had charged him with several missions in the north, and then there had been the incident with the Bastard of Fauconberg. Richard was still awarding grants from the north as late as 11 December 1471. It had been a busy year for the Duke; when, if the initiative came from him, he arrived at his decision to marry Anne can only be guessed. It might be conjectured that, having lived in the north for some time in the past, and then returning to the area in a position of power in his brother's newly re-established régime, Richard realised for the first time that he wanted even more influence, perhaps even to be semi-autonomous, in a part of England he had come to regard almost as his home.

It has been speculated[13] that Richard must have come to any agreement with Anne on one of two occasions. The first would have been immediately after the battle of Tewkesbury when Anne was newly widowed and had been placed in the custody of the Duke and Duchess of Clarence. The second period would have been during the two months between the date of his final grant of 1471 and the council held at Sheen in the February of the following year. If it is correct that Richard came to see the north as more than just an area of operations on behalf of his brother, the latter option might seem more appropriate. If Anne had initiated events, then Richard might have seen in this the hand of Providence. Whatever the case, Richard's would have been a whirlwind 'romance'. As Shakespeare has it, 'Was ever Woman in this humour wooed? Was ever Woman in this humour won?'[14]

To woo is one thing, but in order to win Anne's hand, Richard had serious obstacles to overcome. He and Anne were close blood relatives. They were first, second and third cousins once removed, and so were related in the second, third and fourth degrees of consanguinity. Such a close blood relationship required special permission from the Pope, called a dispensation, in order for them to marry. Another obstacle existed in the fact that Richard's brother, George, was married to Anne's sister, Isabel. This meant that Richard and Anne were brother and sister-in-law and, as such, were related in the first degree of affinity. Certain degrees of affinity could be dispensed with, but not one as close as the first.

A dispensation was duly applied for, but with what hope of success? That depended upon the extent of the dispensation sought. The relationship of consanguinity within the third and fourth degrees presented no problem. However, the first degree of affinity was a major sticking point. As such, it is possible that no such dispensation was applied for; the impediment was, it seems, swept under the carpet to be dealt with if, or when, it became necessary to do so. Frankly, political necessity dictated that the marriage should take place as soon as possible. It remained only to ensure that the problems surrounding the Warwick inheritance were solved to the satisfaction of all parties.

A council meeting took place at Sheen, now Richmond on Thames, in February 1472 where the concerns of everyone involved with the proposed marriage, either directly or indirectly, were discussed. The two Dukes were summoned into the King's presence to personally put forward their respective arguments: in Gloucester's case why he should be allowed to marry Anne and thus inherit her rightful share of her late father's lands; for Clarence, it was why such a proposal should not be allowed to come to pass. The Croyland Continuator notes 'that all present, and the lawyers even, were quite surprised that these princes should find arguments in such abundance by means of which to support their respective causes'. He adds, almost with a note of regret, that 'these three brothers, the king and the two Dukes, were possessed of such surpassing talents, that if they had been able to live without dissensions, such a threefold cord could never have been broken without the utmost difficulty.'[15]

On 17 February, Sir John Paston wrote:

> Yisterdaye the Kynge, the Qween, my Lordes off Claraunce and Glowcester, wente to Sheene to pardon; men sey, nott alle in cheryte; what wyll falle men can nott seye.
>
> The Kynge entretyth my Lorde off Clarance ffor my Lorde off Glowcester; and, as itt is seyde he answerythe, that he maye weell have my Ladye hys suster in lawe, butt they schall parte no lyvelod, as he seyeth; so whatt wyll falle can I nett seye.[16]

The agenda of the meeting at Sheen seems also to have included an attempt to resolve a dispute that had arisen over Barnard Castle, a lordship to the north of the river Tees. The lordship had been part of the inheritance of Anne Beauchamp, countess of Warwick, but the right of the Beauchamp family's ownership had been challenged. Under Edward I, it had been granted to Guy Beauchamp, Earl of Warwick, but Edward IV recognised that it had been wrongly forfeited to the crown, and he upheld a reversal of the forfeiture that was written under Edward III, although never implemented.

In 1470, when Edward IV was in a desperate situation and in need of all the support he could get, he offered Laurence Booth, Bishop of Durham, the lordship of Barnard Castle. This was just what Booth wanted; he had been trying unsuccessfully for several years to recover the lordship. Edward's strategy paid off; Booth was one of the few members of the clergy to abstain from the Readeption of Henry VI. Of course, in awarding Barnard Castle to Booth, Edward had deprived Warwick of his estates and the generated income; he also disregarded the countess's right and title.

The situation had developed where the inheritance of the dowager countess of Warwick was being argued over by the Dukes of Gloucester and Clarence, while, at the same time, the lordship of Barnard Castle was being disputed by the two Dukes, the countess of Warwick and Bishop Booth.

The quarrel over Barnard Castle would simmer on for another year or so. That the dispute over the Warwick inheritance continued is evidence that Richard refused the compromise suggested by Clarence at Sheen. Richard had no interest in Anne without her inheritance. As it happened, Clarence eventually did back down and agreed to the partition of the estates; possibly, Edward had threatened to take back the lands he held by royal grant if he proved stubborn. His co-operation led to his being confirmed in possession of all the estates he already held except those previously released to Gloucester:

> Grant to the king's brother George, Duke of Clarence, to whom the king has granted all castles, honours, lordships, manors, lands and other possessions late of Richard, earl of Warwick and Salisbury, in the right of the latter or of Anne his wife, and who at the king's request has surrendered a parcel of the same to his brother Richard, Duke of Gloucester, that neither by authority of parliament nor in any other way shall any castles, honours, lordships, manors, lands, rents, services, reversions or possessions granted to him before this by the king be taken from him or his heirs, and that if any restitution should be made to anyone of any parcel of the lands late of Thomas, earl of Devon, granted to him such persons shall be recompensed by the king and not by the Duke, and no similar restitution shall be to his prejudice, provided that this grant shall not extend to any castles, lordships or lands belonging to the Duke of Gloucester by force of the said partition. By the K.[17]

At the same time, Clarence was created Earl of Warwick and Salisbury, titles that had previously been held by the Kingmaker. Meanwhile, Richard's marriage having technically been decided on, could take place whenever the couple chose, provided they had the necessary dispensations. In fact, they probably did not as yet, but since there was no reason to expect any problems, they went ahead in anticipation of the vital document.

Exactly when the nuptials were celebrated is unknown. *Hearne's Fragment*[18] suggests that the ceremony took place at Westminster in 1474. While the setting is probably correct, the timing would seem to be wrong. Two pieces of evidence suggest that it took place at some point in 1472. The first is the letter, previously referred to, written by Sir John Paston on 17 February, which shows that Duke Richard and Anne Nevill were not yet married in the late winter of 1472. The second is a petition presented by Ralph Nevill in October 1472. Here, Ralph Nevill requests the King to overturn his father's attainder and to restore his family to their inheritance as long as it does not harm the King's brothers, George, Duke of Clarence, and Richard, Duke of Gloucester, or their wives. As such, it can be accepted that the couple had married by October 1472. Since marriages were forbidden during Lent, it is possible that the marriage occurred soon after Easter 1472.[19] The most that can be said with any degree of certainty is that Richard and Anne were married between February and October 1472. It is possible that the wedding ceremony was conducted by George Nevill, Archbishop of York. Certainly he was on hand and, since he was related to both the bride and the groom, it would have been an honour and a pleasure.

Since no record exists of the wedding itself, we are left to piece together its details from contemporary accounts of other weddings. The ceremony was probably attended by the groom's family; that is, his mother, Cecily, Duchess of York; King Edward and Queen Elizabeth; perhaps the Duke and Duchess of Clarence also attended; almost certainly Richard's Wydeville in-laws were present. On the bride's side the guest list was probably more sparse, since most of her recent acquaintances were dead, exiled, or thought it prudent not to attend. Her father was dead, so it is not known who gave away the bride; perhaps it was the King, but this is mere speculation. Faithful servants and trusted friends on both sides were probably also in attendance.

Similarly, we cannot know what the bride and groom wore on their special day, but the example of a slightly later wedding, that of Princess Margaret and King James IV of Scotland gives us a reasonable idea:

The Kyng was in a Gowne of Whit Damaske, figured with Gold and lynned with Sarcenet. He had on a Jakette with Slyffs of Cramsyn Satin, the Lists [borders] of Blak Velvett, under that sam Dowblet of Cloth of Gold, and a Payre of Scarlette Hosys. His Shurt broded with Thred of Gold, hys bonnet Blak, with a ryche Balay [ruby] and hys Swerd about hym.

The Qwene was arayd in a rich Robbe like Hymselfe, borded of Cramsyn Velvett, and lyned of the self. Sche had a very riche Coller of Gold, of Pyerrery [precious stones, jewels] and Perles, round her Neck, and the Cronne apon hyr Hed: Her Hayre hangyng. Betwixt the said Cronne and the Hayres was very rich Coyfe hangyng downe behynde the whole Length of the body.[20]

Although this describes the wedding attire of a king and queen, the costumes worn by Richard and Anne would not have been so much different.[21] They would have worn their best clothes, the height of fashion and as rich as they could afford in order to add to the sumptuousness and splendour of the occasion. Their garments would have been made of the finest silk, which was usually woven with threads of gold or silver and enhanced with pearls. Indeed, we can picture Richard in his white wedding suit enhanced by crimson velvet, since crimson was one of his favourite colours. Richard would also have worn his ducal coronet, beneath which his long brown locks flowed in waves about his shoulders and framing his face.

As to Anne, of course she was not a queen, and would not be for another eleven years. She would not have worn a crown, but her hair, usually depicted as blonde and very long, would have been worn loose; for a bride, like a queen at her coronation, would allow her hair to flow loosely about her shoulders as a symbol of her virginity. Also, Anne would have worn white cloth of gold or silver, since white had become quite fashionable for brides in the late fifteenth century.

Orange blossoms were worn on the clothes and wreaths were used in the house, as were sprigs of rosemary. The wedding ring was worn on the fourth finger of the right hand, a practice that continued until the Reformation when the ring was transferred to the left hand.

A treatise on poetry attributed to the Elizabethan George Puttenham[22] gives some idea of the ceremonies surrounding the bedding of the couple on their wedding night. His narrative primarily concerns the role of musicians which, for the purpose of such ceremonies, are known as Epithalamies, to distinguish them from the musicians who played at the wedding itself or at the dinner or supper afterwards. The term 'epithalamuim' refers to the ballad or poem sung in praise of the bride and groom and which prays for their future prosperity.

Epithalamies were divided into three 'breaches' each of which served a specific purpose. The first breach was sung at the first part of the night when the bride and the groom were brought to their bed and 'at the very chamber dore'. Here, a great many ladies, kinswomen of the bride, and others who had come to honour the marriage were waiting. The tunes of the songs were 'very loude and shrill, to the intent that there might no noise be heard out of the bed cha[m]ber by the skreeking & outcry of the young damosell feeling the first forces of her stiffe and rigorous young man.' Of course, the bride was virgin, young, tender and weak, 'and unexpert in those maner of affaires.' Another ruse was to engage the bride's nurse to cast nuts about the floor of the chamber during the virgin's deflowering, so that the ladies would be so distracted as they scrambled to catch the nuts that they could not hear anything else.

The first Epithalame was meant to congratulate the first acquaintance and meeting of the couple, and the happy choice made by their parents. It was to accompany the first lovemaking of the couple and form, as it were, a soundtrack to their expectations of children to come and the increase of their love, the bride 'shewing her self in every waies well disposed and still supplying occasions of new lustes and love to her husband, by her obedience and amorous embracings and all other allurements.'

The musicians returned to the chamber door at about midnight. By this time, the ladies who had graced the couple with their company had left and gone to bed. The next part of the ballad was intended to refresh the 'faint and weried bodies and spirits, and to animate new appetites with cheerfull wordes, encouraging them to the recontinuance of the same entertainments, praising and commending (by supposall) the good conformities of them both.' It was alleged that the first embraces did not produce children 'by reason of overmuch affection and heate.' The second round, as it were, was 'lesse rigorous, but more vigorous and apt to avance the purpose of procreation.'

In the morning, upon broad daylight, the bride had to arise and dress herself, no longer as a virgin, but as a wife. She was required to show herself and be acknowledged by her parents and kinswomen 'whether she were the same woman or a changeling, or dead or alive, or maimed by any accident nocturnall.'

There then came the final part of the ceremony, the musicians greeting the couple with 'a Psalme of new applausions.' This celebrated the fact that the husband had robbed his wife 'of her maidenhead and save her life', while the bride, 'lustley' had satisfied her husband's love, while escaping with so little danger to her person. The couple were now required to refrain from such activity until nightfall, meanwhile exchanging 'twentie maner of sweet kisses'. The husband pledged to provide for them both, the bride pledged to take care of whatever her husband might bring to the home. They promised to bring up any children virtuously.

Richard and Anne then, were with great ceremony and rejoicing wedded and bedded, but questions remain as to the legality of the marriage. Considering the impediments that had to be dispensed, there were several routes the couple could have taken. They might have married for the one and only time prior to receiving their dispensation, confident that it would be granted to them. Secondly, they might have gone through with a marriage ceremony without having received their dispensation and then remarried as soon as they were in possession of it. Thirdly, they could have waited until the dispensation was safely obtained, again having only one ceremony.

As we have seen, there were several impediments to the marriage of Richard Gloucester and Anne of Warwick. Anne's marriage to Edward of Lancaster had connected her to Richard by four degrees of affinity, hence the need for a dispensation, which was required even though the marriage was probably not consummated. Moreover, Richard and Anne were related to within the third and fourth degrees of consanguinity. This required another dispensation if their marriage was to be legal. These two impediments were fairly straightforward and there would be no problems in dispensing with them. Indeed, we know that the couple had been granted a dispensation absolving them from the third and fourth degrees of affinity. It was granted to them on 22 April 1472,[23] and they would have received it a few weeks later. As such, although they probably did marry before the dispensation arrived, it has to be accepted on these grounds that Richard's marriage to Anne was lawful.

However, this does not take into account another impediment for which a dispensation was required: that of Richard and Anne being related in the first degree collateral of affinity. This came about because George of Clarence was married to Anne's sister, Isabel. Therefore, Richard and Anne were brother and sister-in-law according to natural, or divine, law. In medieval practice, this was a very close relationship indeed. In fact, Richard was considered to be Anne's brother and she his sister; any union between them was incestuous. Collateral affinity could not be dispensed except in the case of marriage with a widow of a brother who had died childless.[24] In every other circumstance, any marriage between persons of this degree of affinity would be illegal and any children born to the couple would be illegitimate.

Canon 50 of the Fourth Lateran Council of 1215 removed the need for dispensations in several cases. There were: marriages within the second and third degree of affinity; any union of offspring from second marriages to a relative of the first husband; it rendered prohibition inapplicable beyond the fourth degree of consanguinity and affinity. However, and most importantly for Richard and Anne, it did not remove the prohibition for the first degree of affinity; had it done so, King Henry VIII would not have been required to obtain a papal dispensation to allow him to marry Catherine of Aragon, widow to his late brother, Arthur. By the same token, it was necessary for

Henry to apply for a dispensation in order to marry Anne Boleyn, to whom he was also related in the first degree collateral of affinity due to his former sexual relationship with her sister, Mary.[25]

Moreover, there are no grounds, other than wishful thinking, to suppose that Richard had received no dispensation at this time because the Earl of Warwick had previously applied for and been granted one at the same time as he sought one for the marriage between his daughter, Isabel, and the Duke of Clarence. Similarly, there is no evidence whatsoever to support the theory that Warwick was granted Richard's marriage at the same time as he was given guardianship over him.[26] Certainly, Warwick appears to have attempted to corrupt Richard at the same time as he attempted, with more success, to corrupt Clarence, but it soon became obvious to him that the young Duke's steadfast loyalty to the King ensured that he could not be persuaded to come over to Warwick's side. The Earl knew Richard well; he was still at that time his guardian and his tutor, he must have been aware of Richard's resoluteness once his mind was made up on any subject. Moreover, as has been shown, as Warwick negotiated with the King of France, the lands and grants on offer were to the benefit of George of Clarence, not Richard Gloucester. As such, there would be no need to apply for a dispensation for a marriage that would not, at that time at least, take place.

This, then, is King Richard III's dark secret. It has nothing to do with the deposition of the rightful heir to the throne, or with unlimited murder, but with worldly ambition, the desire to gain estates to which he had no title and the power and wealth that went with them. His reasons may be guessed at but they are ultimately his own. It could be connected with the childhood traumas of war and exile that deprived him of his father and brother and robbed him more than once of his home and the security of a stable family life. In order to achieve his objective, Richard resorted to a marriage that was of dubious legality at best. The fact that his marriage was pursued during the property dispute with Clarence suggests that Richard's interest lay in the Warwick estates rather than in his bride, who was little more than the means to an end; a sentiment that was, almost certainly, mutual.

On 30 April 1472 Sir John Paston wrote to tell his brother than 'the Erle of Northomberlonde is hoome in to the Northe, and my Lord off Glowcester schall afftyr as to morrow, men saye.'[27] Richard and his new Duchess made their way into the North Country and a new and, hopefully, more settled life. This turning-point in Richard's life is given special treatment in Caroline Halsted's dreamy narrative, which evokes all the beauty and romance of the Brontës:

To a district endeared to them both by the unfading recollections of childhood, did Richard convey his young bride, when their destinies were at length indissolubly interwoven; and amidst the bold and wild scenery of the home of their ancestors, did the Lady Anne and her princely consort pass the early days of their married life, when, young in age, although experienced in trial, they were thus enabled to share in those halcyon days of peace that once more dawned upon the land of their birth.[28]

Naturally, Richard's efforts were in vain if he did not produce an heir to whom he could leave his estates. It was to be hoped that Anne, unlike her mother, would be able to provide her husband with the son who would carry the cadet branch of the House of York into a glowing and prosperous future. For now Anne's fertility was unproven. For Richard, there was no such uncertainty. He was already the father of a daughter, Katherine Plantagenet.

It is often considered that the illegitimate children of a bachelor were not the affront to morality that they might have been at other periods in history, but that bastards born to a married man most certainly were. As such, Richard's recognition of his daughter is taken as an indication that she was born prior to his marriage. This may be so, but it should also be taken into consideration that fifteenth-century England is not the only culture to display double standards when it came to extra-marital relationships. Behaviour that would have been considered reprehensible in a woman was often perfectly acceptable in a man. In introducing Richard's daughter at this point is to give the Duke the benefit of the doubt.

Since the first recorded appearance of Katherine occurs in 1484, there is very little that can be known about her. There are no means by which her place and time of birth can be known; the identity of her mother is equally shrouded in mystery. That she was betrothed to William Herbert in 1484 offers no indication of her age, since children could be married as young as five. There is no reason to accept that Richard had 'contracted a private Mariage with some Lady of Quality' in 1469, as speculated by the anonymous author of *The Parallel*.[29] Katherine might have been the fruit of a relationship between Richard and an unknown woman, or the result of a one-night stand. The former option would seem the more probable, given that the Duke acknowledged Katherine and gave her his name. A clue to the identity of her mother might lie in a grant of an annual payment of 100 shillings made by Richard to a Katherine Haute in 1477. Katherine was the wife of James Haute, a cousin to Queen Elizabeth Wydeville. There is no apparent reason why Richard should have made such a grant: neither Katherine nor her husband had any obvious connection with Richard beyond the fact that they are related to his sister-in-law. In favour of this supposition is the fact that Richard's daughter shares the same name as Katherine Haute: the name Katherine does not occur with any frequency in the Yorkist or Nevill families.[30]

It is possible, too, that Katherine was named after one of Richard's favourite saints, Katherine of Siena. That this saint is a patron of scholars and the clergy makes her doubly appropriate to the Duke who was himself learned and, possibly at one stage, a candidate for the church. Vivid imagery associated with Katherine's tortures and death, such as being broken on the wheel and then beheaded when the wheel broke, appealed to the medieval imagination. That her story had been brought to Europe by the Crusaders, whose spirit Richard identified with, made her all the more attractive to him. However, Saint Katherine was also the patron of young girls, and it is possible that Richard chose to call his daughter after her because he felt it to be an auspicious name for a woman.

It could hardly be surprising that Richard should have enjoyed romantic encounters. He was young, handsome: small and slender, with blue-grey eyes set in a strong, lean face. He was cultured, athletic and robust despite his diminutive stature; he may have been as idealistic in love as he was in chivalry. Richard was a duke and a prince, a brother of the King and with the prospect of a long, successful and secure future ahead of him. He would have been seen by many as a good catch.

It is not known whether Richard told Anne about his daughter. As such, we cannot guess what her reaction would have been; she might have been displeased at not being Richard's first, although it would have been unrealistic to expect Richard to be still virgin at the age of twenty. Perhaps she did not care as long as there was no scandal.

Richard Gloucester's grants of lands and offices in the north of England made him the political heir to Richard Nevill, Earl of Warwick. Upon arriving in the north the Duke carried the King's hopes that he would foster the peace and stability that had eluded the region for the past few decades. For Edward believed, not without justification, that the north of England was lawless. There were several reasons for this. First, the region bordered Scotland and this made it vulnerable to the instability that comes with close proximity to an enemy nation. Secondly, its remoteness from the capital had instilled within its people a sense of independence and self-sufficiency. This in turn meant that the region was subject to the semi-autonomous 'rule' of a handful of very powerful aristocratic families. These families enjoyed a history that stretched back over several centuries, a heritage they in fact shared with their loyal and trusted retainers, servants and tenants, and which enabled them to command at will a formidable military force.[31]

It was this latter point that proved so significant in the Wars of the Roses. The clannish nature of aristocratic northern society reached its fullest flowering during the rebellions against King Edward, and was manifested most strongly in the activities of the Nevills. Now, following the fall of that great family, with the deaths of Warwick and his brother, Montagu, Edward wanted to consolidate royal power in the region. For this he needed a man of proven ability, someone whose loyalty to the crown was beyond question. There was only one such man: Richard, Duke of Gloucester. It is under these circumstances, then, that Richard and his new bride entered their castle at Middleham, the former seat of the now ineffectual Nevill family, in the spring of 1472.

It has been said that 'Richard III is the only northerner among our late medieval kings'.[32] This is a good point. Richard is indeed often considered to be a northerner. It was the reason he was vilified even before the Tudor propaganda machine got into full swing.[33] It is a view of Richard that originated during his own lifetime and that has endured to this day. His memory is well remembered and treasured in the northern parts; to speak ill of Richard in the City of York is to invite censure, while English Heritage, the current owners of Middleham Castle, proudly promote it as the royal castle of the Dales. A picture of the King is one of the first things visitors see upon their approach to the castle.

Yet, if Richard was northern at all, it was by adoption and association; his father had northern connections, being the Duke of York and Lord of Wakefield, Sandal and Conisbrough. However, York's fatal journey to Wakefield in the midwinter of 1460 had been his first visit to the region for almost twenty years. It must be remembered too that the Duke of York was also Earl of March, with its twin seats of Wigmore and Ludlow in Shropshire; he was Earl of Ulster and Lord of Clare and, as such, had strong associations with Ireland, East Anglia and Hertfordshire. Certainly Richard Gloucester's mother was a native of the North Country; she was known as the 'Rose of Raby', born into the then mighty Nevill family at Raby Castle in County Durham. However, since she was married at a very young age, she might well have been taken away from her childhood home never to return. It is possible that she knew little of her northern home and that her only real link to it was preserved in her epithet.

Richard was born in the east midlands of England. He was brought up mainly in the castle in which he was born, Fotheringhay in Northamptonshire, as well as on the Welsh marches at Ludlow. As Hicks points out, the Duke did not speak with a northern dialect, although his sojourn at Middleham might have taught him to understand it and he might have learned to emulate one.

Rather, his speech would have betrayed his midland roots, while his stays at Ludlow might possibly have cultivated a Welsh intonation.[34]

As he took up residence at Middleham, Sheriff Hutton and his other castles, Richard settled among people who had supported Warwick in his rebellion against King Edward. When Edward landed in England following his exile in the Low Countries, Yorkshire refused to offer him any support. As he approached York he was allowed into the city only because he lied regarding his reason for returning. It was not to retake the throne, he assured the city authorities, but simply to reclaim his father's title as duke of York.

Richard, on the other hand, and in marked contrast to his brother Clarence, had supported King Edward. He had fought on the King's side and had helped him defeat the rebellion in a battle that had cost Warwick his life. Now the young Duke was stepping into Warwick's shoes. He might not have been entirely welcome in the north. At the very least, he was an outsider. At worst, he was an enemy who had to be watched and, perhaps, subdued. It was Richard's difficult task to try to gain the trust and allegiance of the great families of the north. That he had married Anne Nevill, daughter and co-heiress to the Earl of Warwick, was enormously useful in this endeavour. It was also useful that he seems to have had a knack for winning people over to his side.

Richard had already made the acquaintance of many of the most powerful people of the North Country. His friend, Francis Lovell, an 'outsider' like himself, was slightly younger than Richard, being born in about 1457. The Lovell estates lay primarily in Oxfordshire, Northamptonshire and Shropshire. In 1466 he was married to Anne FitzHugh, the Kingmaker's niece. A year later, he went as a page to Middleham, where he met the Duke of Gloucester, who was then training to be a knight. Lovell's father-in-law followed the Earl of Warwick into rebellion in 1469-70; Lovell and his wife were among those pardoned by King Edward IV. As part of his legal council, Richard employed Sir Robert Danby of Thorp Perrow.

Former retainers and associates of the Earl of Warwick now transferred their allegiance to Richard. Sir James Strangways, while remaining for the most part loyal to the Nevills rather than to the House of York, was one such man. A lawyer and administrator, he had been commissioned to suppress disorder in the North Riding of Yorkshire during the late Duke of York's first protectorate. He saw action on the Yorkist side at Wakefield and he might also have had some involvement at Towton. He was appointed speaker at parliament by King Edward and, for his loyalty and support, now taking the form of long and eloquent speeches in favour of the new régime, he was awarded 200 marks. At the rise of the Warwick rebellion,

Strangways managed to distance himself, leaving any involvement with the rebels to his son, Robert. The newly restored Edward was thus able to continue to place his trust in him. The King reappointed Strangways to the county bench and it is in this capacity that he would have had most of his dealings with Richard Gloucester.

Of the Metcalf family of Nappa, near Askrigg in Wensleydale, no fewer than nine members had been part of the Nevill affinity. The youngest brother, James, was retained by Richard on a fee of £6 13s 4d. His sons, Thomas and Miles would also enter Richard's service: Thomas as Richard's auditor of Richmondshire and, later, one of the auditors of the bishop of Durham. Miles was a member of Richard's legal council and would eventually become the Duke's chief steward of the duchy of Lancaster in the north, a position held in turn by the late Earl of Warwick and by Richard himself. They were joined by other members of this large family, including Brian and Dionisius in low-paid capacities.

Another Wensleydale family, the Conyers of Hornby Castle had, like the Metcalfs, also provided long and faithful service to the Nevills. Indeed, they were probably responsible for the series of rebellions that broke out in Yorkshire as a prelude to that of the Earl of Warwick and the Duke of Clarence. The head of the family, Sir John, had acted as steward to the Kingmaker, which post brought him an income of £13 6s 8d. Richard retained him in this capacity and increased his fee to £20. He also made Conyers constable of Middleham Castle, for which he received £16 13s 4d. It is probable that Conyers also became a member of Richard's council.

Several of Sir John's brothers also went into Richard's service. William Conyers was employed as bowbearer; Richard Conyers became receiver at Middleham, while his son, also named Richard, joined the Duke's household. Sir John's brother-in-law, William Burgh made the translation from Nevill to Gloucester; another brother-in-law, Sir Thomas Markenfield was retained by Duke Richard.

Significantly, Richard managed to attract Thomas Tunstall, the half-brother of Sir John Conyers' wife. Tunstall, with his brother, Sir Richard of Thurland Castle, near Tunstall in Lancashire, had been prominent supporters of the Readeption of Henry VI. Tunstall apparently settled in Yorkshire and, in 1473, would father an illegitimate son by one of Sir John's daughters. The boy, named Cuthbert, would one day become bishop of Durham.[35]

Equally significantly, Richard was able to retain Sir Robert Clifford. Sir Robert was the son of Thomas, Lord Clifford, who was among those who had confronted the Duke of York at Dartford in February 1452, and who died at the first battle of St Albans while fighting on the royalist side. He was not specifically anti-Yorkist, but rather was loyal to King Henry. Sir Robert was the youngest brother of Sir John Clifford, to whom the murder of Richard's brother, the Earl of Rutland, was attributed.

During his time as a page under Warwick's protection, Richard made the acquaintance of several of the large and deeply interconnected families of northern gentry and nobility. Now that his circumstances had changed, his association with the Scropes, the FitzHughs, the Greystokes and the Dacres took on a new significance.[36]

John, Lord Scrope was based in Bolton, to the north-west of Middleham. He had married twice. By his first wife, Joan, he had a daughter, Agnes. It is perhaps through this connection that Agnes's husband, Sir Richard Ratcliffe, came to enter Richard's sphere. Ratcliffe was a younger son of Thomas Ratcliffe, esquire, of the Isle of Derwentwater and his wife, Margaret, a daughter of Sir Thomas Parr of Kendal. Although a Cumberland man, Ratcliffe acquired land in Richmondshire as a result of his marriage to Agnes. Gloucester and Ratcliffe would form an attachment that would be broken only by their shared death upon Bosworth Field.

Lord Scrope's second wife was Elizabeth, the widow of William, Lord Zouche of Harringworth, Northamptonshire. Her son by her first marriage, John, Lord Zouche would also become one of Richard's strongest supporters, while his daughter, Margaret, would marry an up-and-coming lawyer by the name of William Catesby. William was the son of Sir William Catesby of Ashby St Ledgers and his first wife, Philippa Bishopestone, he was a legal adviser and estate administrator for several local landowners. His closeness to Richard in later years would earn him a place, alongside Richard Ratchliffe and Francis Lovell, in William Collingbourne's famous couplet:

The Rat, the Cat and Lovell our dog
Rule all England under the Hog.[37]

A branch of the Scrope family was based at Masham, a village to the south-east of Middleham. The Scropes of Masham were related by marriage to the FitzHughs. Henry, Lord FitzHugh was Gloucester's cousin by virtue of his marriage to Alice Nevill. Alice was the daughter of Richard Nevill, Earl of Salisbury, Cecily Nevill's elder brother; it was their daughter, Anne FitzHugh, who was married to Richard's friend, Francis Lovell.

The FitzHugh's seat was in Ravensworth, a bracing gallop from Middleham Castle. They were linked by marriage to the barons Greystoke, who held lands in Yorkshire and Cumberland, as well as the Dacres, who were based in the Cumberland town of Gilsland. The Greystokes and the

Dacres were allied by marriage, and both families had connections with the Scropes of Masham. Later, the son of Thomas and Elizabeth Scrope, Thomas, Lord Scrope of Masham, would marry Elizabeth, the daughter of Cecily Nevill's nephew, John, former Earl of Northumberland, now Marquis Montagu, thus bringing full circle the links between each of these families with the Nevills.

Richard Gloucester, of course, has his place within this tangled web, being a Nevill on his mother's side. Middleham must have seemed the natural centre of his world. However, this was mitigated by his midland birth and upbringing, an important point because, whatever charm, business acumen or sense of justice Richard might have displayed, many of these families flocked to him on little more than the strength of his being the husband of Anne Nevill.

Indeed, there were those who refused to welcome Gloucester into northern society. Prominent among these was Laurence Booth, Bishop of Durham, with whom Richard was in dispute over Barnard Castle. Another was Thomas, Lord Stanley. Richard had already incurred Stanley wrath when he was awarded various estates and honours that had previously been held by the Stanley family. He had also crossed swords with Lord Thomas when he had supported the Harringtons in their altercation with the Stanleys over Hornby Castle. Finally, there was Henry Percy, Earl of Northumberland, whose post of keeper of all the royal forests north of the Trent had been awarded to Richard. Percy and Richard would spend the next two years competing for supremacy in the North Country and, once again, King Edward would be obliged to intervene.

As Richard worked to enlarge his retinue he also assumed his duties as keeper of all the royal forests north of the Trent, which been granted to him on 18 May 1472.[38] Two days later, and just over a year after he had been awarded it, Richard surrendered his office of great chamberlain of England in favour of his brother, the Duke of Clarence. The Duke had requested this favour of his brother and Richard probably considered it worth the sacrifice if it convinced Clarence to be more reasonable regarding the partition of the Warwick estates. King Edward, as usual, was happy to indulge the selfish Clarence: 'Grant for life to the king's brother George, Duke of Clarence, of the office of great chamberlain of England… in lieu of a like grant of the office to the king's brother Richard, Duke of Gloucester, by letters patent dated 18 May, 11 Edward IV. surrendered.[39]

Richard was already familiar with the castles at Middleham and Sheriff Hutton from his time in the north as a page, although he was mainly associated with Middleham at that point. Sheriff Hutton had been built by Ralph of Raby, the first of the Nevill Earls of Westmorland. It was visited by the Tudor poet and antiquary, John Leland,[40] who described it as having been built without a ditch, which he added was not needed because of its situation on high ground. The façade of the first precinct of the castle featured three high towers and a gatehouse in the centre. The second precinct boasted five or six towers. The castle contained an imposing stairway, which led up to the hall. The whole castle was pronounced 'magnificent'; this palace, fit for a prince, was deemed by Leland to be beyond compare. Unfortunately, very little now remains of this once magnificent stronghold; a few ruins mark the spot where it once commanded the admiration and awe of the entire area roundabout.

Richard's seat as seneschal of the duchy of Lancaster in the northern parts was at Pontefract Castle. The name of Pontefract, as Richard would later inform an awestruck visitor to his court, meant 'broken bridge'. The castle, which Leland informs us was sometimes also known as Snorre Castle, was even larger and more magnificent than either of Richard's residences at Sheriff Hutton or Middleham. It consisted of eight towers and a very fine keep three storeys high. The keep was most unusual, built as it was with three large and three small round turrets, which formed a sort of flower shape. The constable's tower was built on the north-east side of the bailey. The adjoining king's tower and queen's tower, the royal apartments, were some eighteen metres in height and twelve metres square.

The castle at Pontefract had witnessed much history since its elevation in about 1080. Among its owners were members of the de Lacy family, to whom it was awarded by William the Conqueror, and their affinity, the Fitz Eustaches. In 1310, it became the property of Thomas, Earl of Lancaster, first prince of the blood and cousin to King Edward II. Thomas was one of the chief opponents of Piers Gaviston, the King's favourite. In 1322, he was captured and imprisoned in his castle of Pontefract, where Edward II presided over what amounted to a show trial. Thomas was executed, but shortly afterwards, stories were told of miracles taking place at the site of his tomb. The King's efforts to suppress the emerging cult led to popular rioting. Although the King's successor, Edward III, was urged to press for Thomas's canonization, he was not to become a saint, at least formally. Nevertheless, relics of Thomas were kept at Pontefract; his hat was believed to be a cure for headaches, while his belt was thought to protect against the dangers of childbirth.

Pontefract Castle is perhaps most famous for it having been the scene of the mysterious death of Richard II.

> Pomfret, Pomfret! O thou bloody prison,
> Fatal and ominous to noble peers!
> Within the guilty closure of thy walls,
> Richard the Second here was hacked to death,
> And, for more slander to thy dismal seat,
> We give to thee our guiltless blood to drink.[41]

This king, whose nomination of his Mortimer cousins was one of the cornerstones of the Yorkist claim to the throne, is said by some to have refused food, and so starved to death; more probable is that he had been deliberately starved under the orders of King Henry IV. Poignantly, the Duke of York, father to Richard Gloucester, who had appealed to King Richard's preference for the Mortimers as he sought power, was buried at Pontefract next to his second son, Edmund, victims of the bloody battle of Wakefield. The most probable burial place of York and Rutland was the Priory of St John the Evangelist, which was close to the castle.[42]

The castle at Pontefract, then, was of special interest to Richard. On the one hand, it was the scene of the death of a man who was later revered as a saint. Richard's piety and spiritual outlook ensured that he took a special interest in the miracles and unofficial cult of Thomas, Earl of Lancaster. Politically, it was associated with the death of the King who was regarded by the Yorkist as the last king by right before the Lancastrians usurped his throne. More personally, that both the Duke of York and the tragic Earl of Rutland were buried nearby made Richard's association with Pontefract particularly affecting. It can be imagined that, in the few quiet moments he would have to spend alone, the young Duke would silently make his way to the unhappy tombs to light a candle and say a prayer for the two souls cast too soon from their earthly life.

Although Richard was now a northern magnate of great significance, he did not 'retire' to his estates after his marriage as has sometimes been claimed. Rather, he led an itinerant lifestyle that regularly brought him back to London, both to his brother's court and to parliament. One such occasion occurred in October 1472, when Richard was summoned to Westminster to be among those who heard the petition of Ralph Nevill. Nevill requested the King to overturn the act that had convicted his father, John Nevill, for high treason during the parliament of the first year of Edward IV's reign. This was so that Ralph and his heirs might have and enjoy the inheritance that would have been theirs had the act not been passed, provided that it did not harm in any way the King's brothers, George, Duke of Clarence, and Richard, Duke of Gloucester, or their wives. Ralph Nevill's request was granted.[43]

A letter dated 13 October 1472 shows Richard to be back in the North Country and deep into the affairs of office; his use of the word 'ky', which is the plural for cows, shows him to be familiar with, and confident in, local dialect:

R. Gloucestre. Right trusty and welbeloved, we grete you well. And whereas att the freshe pursuit of our welbeloved Christopher Stansfield, one Richard of the Burgh, that had take and led away feloniously certain ky and other cattell belonging to him, was take and arested with the said manor att Spofford, whereat they yet remaine; whearfore we desire and pray you that upon sufficient surety to be found by the said Christopher to sue against the said felon, as the law will, for that offence, ye will make delivery unto him of the said cattell, as is according with right: shewing him your good aide, favour, and benevolence, the rather att the instance of this our letters. And our Lord preserve you. From Pontfrett, under our signet, the thirtenth of October.[44]

Later that month, Richard is among those awarded the grant of the manor of 'Gregories' in Theydon Boys, Essex, which had formerly been jointly owned by William Floure and John Kilpek.[45]

Meanwhile, the fighting over the Warwick estates continued apace. The main sticking point was that both Gloucester and Clarence wanted to hold the estates by right of inheritance rather than by royal grant, as the case stood at the time. This was because royal grant could easily be revoked, as Richard knew from experience and Clarence would soon find out. However, in order to achieve their aims, they had to resist the claims of the countess herself. She was still in the sanctuary at Beaulieu in Hampshire to which she had fled following the failure of the Lancastrian cause at Tewkesbury.

Anne of Warwick did all she could to hold on to her inheritance. Her petitions to the King, Gloucester and Clarence were, naturally, ignored. Pleas to Cecily Nevill, the Duchesses of Exeter and Suffolk, the King's sisters, and to Elizabeth of York, his daughter, were either not acted upon at all or not sufficiently well to produce the desired result. Even Queen Elizabeth's mother, Jacquetta, Duchess of Bedford could, it seems, do nothing for her. Alone and without counsel, the countess looked to the future with a deepening sense of unease and helplessness.

It was at some point in 1472 that Richard began to compile a cartulary, in which he would list his acquisitions. Now forming part of BL, Cotton Julius BXII, Richard painstakingly researched and catalogued every important title deed acquired between 1472 and March 1483. Once he became king, the cartulary became superfluous and it was laid aside and possibly forgotten until its rediscovery in the aftermath of Bosworth. The pages of the cartulary are of a uniform size, although it is evident that they have been trimmed. Many of them bear the same watermark, suggesting that Richard had acquired a batch of paper with the specific purpose of using it for the cartulary. The writing itself is not in Richard's own hand, but rather, a variety of hands using various inks. This has led to the suggestion that Richard had nothing to do with the compilation of the work, but that it had been done by his staff with little or no input from Richard. This is entirely possible, although the theory has recently been convincingly refuted on several grounds.[46] First, such a task would have been arduous and time-consuming and as such would require someone with a vested interest to continue it. Secondly, the complier must have known intimately Richard's mind, or else he was a prophet, because he included lands Richard intended retaining, while omitting those Richard would not retain. Lastly, Richard always insisted upon taking personal control of all his land transactions, as the case with the Warwick inheritance shows.

The cartulary reveals much about the man who put it together. His is a tidy mind; he wishes to keep records of all his transactions in one easily accessible place. He takes personal interest in his business matters. He has a firm grasp of the law as it pertains to property, inheritance and royal grants. The inclusion of titles granted to ancestors of his Duchess shows someone who is thorough and who is concerned to obtain and retain that which he believes to be rightfully his. Perhaps more importantly, it suggests a man who had intended to found a dynasty; the cartulary is a valuable archive for a great magnate, containing as it does, information that would be essential to a descendant who might want to know the extent of his titles and the means to preserve them. That Richard Gloucester was concerned about his estates and was aware of the extent and the value of them is surely beyond question.

As the year 1472 drew to a close the Duke once more travelled south to London. The ambassadors to the Duke of Milan thought that he might have been preparing to cross over to France at the head of an army: 'The King of England is sending one of his brothers, the Duke of Gloucester or the Duke of Clarence with an army to the king'.[47] In the event, neither brother went, but Richard did take it upon himself to send archers to assist Burgundy.

Instead, it is probable that Duke Richard spent Christmas and the New Year at his brother's court. However, he had more than the prospect of yuletide festivities on his mind. The primary purpose of Richard's journey was to try to resolve the dilemma caused by the enfeoffment of Countess Elizabeth of Oxford's estates.

CHAPTER 14

' ... Good in My Brother of Gloucester's Hands', 1473

As the new year of 1473 dawned, Richard Gloucester's business with Countess Elizabeth of Oxford took an unexpected turn. The course of events can be determined from a series of depositions made by six witnesses who had been called upon to present Countess Elizabeth's point of view. When these few sources are added to information contained within the Patent and Close rolls as well as the available circumstantial evidence concerning the political background to these events and placed within the context of contemporary common practice, a reasonable reconstruction can be made.

At about Christmas-time 1472-73, Richard Gloucester, who was staying with his household at a house belonging to Sir Thomas Vaughn at Stepney in London, went to Stratford to visit Elizabeth of Oxford at her abbey there. Richard informed Elizabeth that he had been granted custody of her and her possessions by King Edward. This news upset the countess so much that she wept. Sir John Pilkington, chamberlain to Richard, asked Elizabeth for the keys to her coffers, which were duly given. The coffers as well as her lodgings were then searched.

A few days after this, Elizabeth was brought to Richard's lodgings in Stepney, where she remained for some three or four days. Apparently she had been escorted to Stepney from her abbey by Sir William Tunstall, one of Richard's servants. Moved by her tears, Sir William had comforted her and assured her that she had nothing to fear from Gloucester, who was a knight and a king's brother.

While at Stepney, Elizabeth was visited, at Richard's request, 'yf he durste', by Henry Robson, one of her associates. She confided to Robson that she thanked

God 'hertely besechyng hym to haue mercy on my frendes sowles by whome I haue these londes which nowe shall save my life'. In other words, since her lands were held by her enfeoffees she could persuade them to make over their rights and titles to the lands to Richard. If she could not do so, she added, Richard had threatened to send her to Middleham. She told Robson that she feared she would not be able to endure such a journey at her great age in such harsh winter conditions and that she feared how she might be treated once she got there. Robson thought that the lady genuinely appeared to be in fear of her life. She begged him that if he and the other enfeoffees received 'eny writyng or dede vnder her seale comme to hym to be sealid that he shuld enseale hit in lyke wise as he loved her and her lyff.' When he visited her again two days later he found that Elizabeth had at last conformed to the Duke's wishes. Robson felt she had done so 'by cohercion and compulsion and fere as is aforesaid'.

From Robson's deposition it can be construed that Elizabeth's change of heart was due, at least in part, to the alleged mistreatment of her confessor, Master Piers Baxter. He was said to have been subjected to verbal abuse while at the house of the archbishop of York at Westminster, being called a 'false priest and hypocrite' by Lord Howard in the presence of Sir John Pilkington and others. Moved by the way Baxter had been treated, Elizabeth made over the requested estate to Richard. Following this she was escorted by Sir William Tunstall to Chadworth in Stepney and then on to Walbrook, another place used by Richard. Here she was led to a chamber. She gave Tunstall her thanks and a purse for his kindness.

After five or six days Richard sent a servant, Watkyn Chaundeler to conduct Henry Robson to a meeting at Saint John's, Smithfield. Here, Richard told Robson that Elizabeth had sealed a deed of enfeoffment to him of such lands as she had, as had Master Baxter, her confessor. The deeds were read out to Robson. As the names of certain enfeoffees came up, Richard asked if he knew the person and were they friends. The names were of those men who had dug in their heels and were refusing to seal their deeds as the Countess Elizabeth had asked. Richard then 'commanded' Robson to tell them that, if they did not seal their deeds, it would cost them that which they loved best.

As it appeared to those observing, although they were not all privy to everything that was going on, the Countess Elizabeth was in much distress during her stay at Stepney. Henry Robson reported that, after the deeds had been sealed and handed over to the Duke, the countess had told him that she was sorry for having saved her life by disinheriting her heirs. Robson comforted her, saying that the lands were for the most part entailed, which was a matter of record, and that whatever she had done against her will would be undone by her heirs.

The suggestion that Elizabeth was coerced into relinquishing her lands to Richard is supported by the testimony of Sir John Risley. Sir John stated that some time after the events just described, in about the year 1479, he was offered the chance to buy a place beside London Wall, called the Earl of Oxford's place. This place was the property of the Duke of Gloucester, to whom it had been released by Elizabeth of Oxford. Seeking the advice of King Edward regarding the purchase, he was told not to attempt to buy it because, 'though the titill of the ... place be goode in my broder of Gloucestres handes or in an other mannys hondes of lyke myght', it would be dangerous for Risley to have it because the Countess Elizabeth had been 'compellid and constreynyd by the seid dewke of Gloucestre to release and forsake her ryght in the seid place.'

We have, then, a series of accounts, here condensed to form a narrative, which, testify to an elderly lady being menaced by a duke, who was one third her age, into giving up her inheritance to him. At least one of her associates, her confessor, Master Baxter, was mistreated by the Duke's servants, while the lady herself was threatened with being taken Middleham, 'there to be kept'.

The account comes from six deponents, although only five have so far been mentioned. Of these six, only Sir James Tyrell and William Tunstall said that they were unaware of any coercion or compulsion, although Tunstall did confess to having heard a rumour to that effect. These two men had been in Richard's service at the time these events were alleged to have taken place, and as such it might be argued that their statements were biased in favour of the Duke. This raises important questions regarding the reliability of these depositions.

Although two of the statements came from former servants to Richard Gloucester, as has been noted, three others were made by people who were known associates of Elizabeth of Oxford. Another deponent, Sir John Risley, was bailiff of the town and lordship of Lavenham, which had belonged to the de Veres until it was forfeited to Richard. In other words, some of the deponents were biased in Richard's favour, others were against him.

More importantly, perhaps, is the reason why the case was brought in the first place. The depositions are not contemporary to the events they describe; rather, they date from 1495, some twenty-three years later. They formed part of a petition presented to King Henry VII by John de Vere, thirteenth Earl of Oxford, the son of Elizabeth of Oxford. His title to the de Vere inheritance rested on the claim that his mother had been compelled against her will to give up her lands to Richard Gloucester. If he was unable to prove this, his mother's conveyance would be deemed valid and he could be dispossessed of his estates. In that case, they would revert to King Henry, since they had been forfeited to the crown under King Edward IV. Edward had chosen to grant them to Gloucester; Henry would be free to do with them as he wished.

Under Henry VII, de Vere had witnessed the political restoration of Thomas Howard, Earl of Surrey, son of the Duke of Norfolk. Surrey had managed to recover most of his estates in a series of acts dated between 1489 and 1495. However, Surrey had not been entirely successful. An act of 1485 restored eight manors to him, but this had been reversed ten years later when the original claim that they had been released under duress was disproved. Surrey was forced to relinquish these lands. De Vere wanted to show that his mother had given up her estates under duress, thus making them invalid, and he feared that such a claim might be rejected, as in Surrey's case. However, he had taken encouragement from Surrey's earlier successes and so he decided to chance his luck with King Henry. De Vere's motive, then, is clear: he wanted his lands back and he could achieve this only if it could be shown that the conveyances were unsound. If a claim that they were made under duress could be upheld, de Vere stood a good chance of winning his petition and retaining his mother's property.

Several days after the events described in the depositions, on 9 January 1473, Elizabeth and six of her enfeoffees released their rights in her estates to Richard and his heirs and assigns in three deeds. At this point, Elizabeth seems to have returned to her abbey at Stratford. A few weeks afterwards, Richard's attorneys took physical seisin of the lands and received the attornment of the tenants.

Elizabeth's dealings with the royal family did not end there, however. On 21 March, she was ordered to a meeting before Edward IV, which she was bound to attend daily at Easter 1473 on pain of her own recognizance of £3,000 and sureties of £8,000.[1] The purpose of the order was 'to answer certain matters pending against her.' Also included in the order were Henry Bourchier, Earl of Essex, John Howard, Knight, Thomas Bourchier, Knight and James Arblaster esquire, feoffee of the countess. What the matters pending against the countess were is not known. However, it might be significant that just over three months after that, on 25 June, Elizabeth and her enfeofees acknowledged the enrolled deeds to Richard in chancery.

According to the sixth, and thus far silent, deponent, William Paston, Doctor Robert Stillington, bishop of Bath and Wells, who was also Chancellor at the time, had heard of the alleged mistreatment of Elizabeth by Richard. He called her to his Chequer Chamber at Westminster and asked her to tell him the truth, without fear, of her transactions with the Duke of Gloucester. She replied that she had been 'compellid by grette fere and drede to make the bargain which she made with the seid Duke concerning her seid maners and landes and no thyng of fre will.'

On 9 July Countess Elizabeth was discharged from the order of 21 March, having 'in nowise failed in her appearance'. Why she should have been ordered to appear before King Edward is not stated beyond the assertion that there were 'certain matters pending against her.' Put into a wider context, the matters pending might have had something to do with the activities of her son, John de Vere, the man who would later bring his petition before Henry VII. De Vere had fled England following the battle of Barnet. He spent the next two years making a nuisance of himself as he plotted with Archbishop Nevill, who had also fallen out of the King's favour, and from whom Edward had pointedly removed the Great Seal. After menacing Calais for a while, de Vere was successfully repulsed and took to piracy instead.

The reason Edward called Elizabeth to daily meetings with him was probably to persuade her to release the land he had granted to Richard. The fact that they were enfeoffed gave the king no reason to relax his guard. The feoffees were closely linked to the de Vere family or were otherwise loyal to Elizabeth. Her wish, it seemed to Edward, could well have been their command. While Elizabeth was in control of her estates, whether in person or through her loyal feofees, she was potentially in a position to finance her son or to offer him some other form of assistance. It was much better, surely, to place the estates into safe hands, and what safer hands were there than those of his brother, Richard?

This also explains Edward's reason for placing an elderly and seemingly defenceless widow into Richard's custody. It was a precautionary measure on Edward's part, and one he had used previously in the matter of the uprising by Henry ap Thomas ap Griffith and his followers. In the case of the countess of Oxford, it was designed to prevent her assisting her son in his operations against the King. With a man who had shown himself to be an enemy to the Yorkist régime and who had eagerly played his part in the Readeption of Henry VI at large in English waters, Edward could take no chances. Indeed, on 28 May, de Vere attempted to land in England, choosing St Osyth, close to the de Vere heartlands, as his landing place. His attempt was thwarted by the Earl of Essex and the Lords Dinham and Duras and he returned to piracy. In the following September, however, he would be more successful and he was able to take and hold St Michael's Mount in Cornwall.

While Oxford was little more than a nuisance, he did have significant backing. The Hansards were offering him aid and, since relations between

England and Scotland were somewhat shaky at this time, although this would turn out to be a temporary situation for now, Oxford thought it worth exploiting. More significantly, according to the not always reliable Milanese ambassador, King Louis XI of France had claimed that he had sent Oxford to England to 'stir up the enemies of King Edward against him'.[2] The ambassador notes that Oxford had sent Louis 'twenty-four original seals of cavaliers and lords and one duke.' The duke is not named, but another source suggests that Clarence was involved.[3] Moreover, Oxford was believed to have been in touch with Archbishop George Nevill, who had formed a triumvirate with the Earl of Warwick and the Duke of Clarence at the height of their rebellion.[4] Archbishop Nevill, who had apparently returned to some degree of favour with Edward following the death of his brother, suddenly and inexplicably found himself arrested and imprisoned at Hammes. Now, with Oxford menacing the Calais marches, Edward became alarmed. It is possible that the King feared a renewal of the uprising that had cost him his crown and driven him, a penniless fugitive, out of his kingdom. Oxford was poorly financed; the Milanese ambassador states that he had asked for a 'good sum of money' to begin the war. The French king was contemplating this request, but had not yet made up his mind. Should he fail to offer the requested sums, Oxford's mother, Elizabeth, was well placed to assist in his stead. As such, Edward placed her into the custody of Richard Gloucester.

This, then, explains Elizabeth's appearance before Edward and why she was confined. Unfortunately for all concerned, it would not be the end of the matter. Elizabeth changed her mind about her releases and told her feoffees that she had made them only under coercion. As such, some of her feoffees also refused to release their deeds to the Duke, one of whom was William Paston. Richard was obliged to bring the case before Chancellor Stillington. Whatever the truth of Elizabeth's feelings on the matter of her estates, she concealed them from Richard; her name appears beside that of the Duke in the case of *Richard, Duke of Gloucester, constable and admiral of England, and Elizabeth, Countess of Oxford, v. the bishop of Ely, Thomas Montgomery, William Paston, and others*. The petition was set to be heard before Chancellor Stillington on 11 February 1474.

Meanwhile, Richard was summoned to a hearing in the presence of the King at Nottingham on 12 May. Also present was Henry Percy, Earl of Northumberland. The main purpose of the hearing was to resolve the differences between Gloucester and Northumberland that had been simmering since Richard's arrival in the north. A letter addressed to Sir William Plumpton by his servant Godfrey Greene gives some idea of the Earl's dislike of people encroaching on his territory:

Also, Sir, now of late I have receaved from you diverse letters, of the which the tenure and effect is this; one, that I shold labour to Sir John Pilkington, to labor to my lord of Gloucester or to the king; they to move my lord of Northumberland that ye might occupie still Knaresborou. Sir, as to that, it is thought here by such as loves you, 'at that labour should rather hurt in that behalve then availe; for certaine it is, as long as my lord of Northumberlands patent thereof stands good, as long will he have no deputie but such as shall please him, and kan him thank for the gift thereof, and no man els, and also doe him service next the king.[5]

The rivalry between the Earl and Duke Richard had arisen over two main points. The first was Richard's appointment of justice of the forests beyond the Trent, which displaced Northumberland, who had previously held it. Secondly, since his arrival in the north Richard had worked hard to build up an affinity, while Northumberland tried to compete. Richard's greater resources ensured his success. The final straw for Northumberland appears to have been when Richard managed to attract to his side John Widdrington of Chipchase, Northumberland's master forester of Alnwick. Edward, who had sent Richard north to bring about peace, felt the need to intervene before yet another feud broke out in the region, this time between Richard and Northumberland. Despite his best efforts, no firm agreement was reached between the duke and the Earl at this meeting other than to extract a promise from Richard that he would refrain from attracting into his service any of the servants who were or who had been retained by the Earl. As a secondary item on the agenda, it is possible that some settlement was reached over the matter of Barnard Castle.

Shortly after this meeting, Richard's mother-in-law, Anne, dowager countess of Warwick, at last left her sanctuary and went to live with Richard and the Duchess Anne, probably at Middleham:

Item, how that the Cowntesse off Warwyk is now owt off Beweley Seyntwarye, and Sir James Tyrell conveyth hyr northwarde, men seye by the Kynges assent, wherto som men seye that the Duke off Clarence is not agreyd.[6]

The Sir James Tyrell mentioned in this letter is the same man who would provide a deposition for John de Vere's cause in 1495. At this time, however, he was a trusted member of Richard's household.

James was the son of William Tyrell, who had been executed, though not attainted, for his part in a conspiracy involving John de Vere, twelfth Earl of Oxford, against King Edward IV in 1462. The Tyrell estates and the custody of James were given to the care of Cecily Nevill but were purchased by William's widow and her feoffees for £50 the following year. James had fought on the Yorkist side at Tewkesbury, following which he had been knighted by King Edward. By the winter of 1471 he was active in the service of Duke Richard as a ducal councillor and feoffee. He was close enough to Richard to be in a position to witness incidents such as the alleged mistreatment of Elizabeth of Oxford. Certainly Richard employed him in delicate matters, such as upon this occasion when he was charged with the escort of Anne of Warwick. His closeness to Richard and his loyalty to him would make Tyrell the perfect candidate as the murderer of the 'Princes in the Tower' in the stories that would be circulated under the Tudor régime.[7]

Anne of Warwick's departure from sanctuary has been greeted with cynicism and disdain by many historians, who saw in it a deliberate ploy on Richard's part to bring a troublesome old lady under his watchful eye. Gairdner, for example, asserts that the one son-in-law 'she was most disposed to trust shut her up in prison'.[8]

However, there are other ways to view this. It could be that Richard wanted the lady to join him and his new Duchess in their household, perhaps as company for his wife as well as out of concern for the lady herself. Richard would be travelling throughout Yorkshire and beyond in the exercise of his various duties, but his journeys were not so far or of such duration that it warranted his wife to accompany him. Perhaps she herself asked for her mother to be brought to her, and the two ladies set up their household to resemble the way it had been in Anne's youth.

A more plausible explanation is that it was done, not so much with Edward's consent but at his insistence. Since early 1472 Edward had been seriously considering certain overtures extended to him by Duke Francis of Brittany. Duke Francis was becoming increasingly alarmed by the hostilities shown towards him by King Louis XI of France. At first Edward responded favourably to the Duke's request for English help in the form of 6,000 archers and ships equipped for service in the Channel. At the same time, the Duke of Burgundy was petitioning Edward for help with his plans for a war with France. He even proposed giving the King the county of Eu in Normandy if he would offer him the requested assistance.

Confronted on both sides by dukes eager for English aid against France, Edward opened negotiations which were intended to lead, eventually, to a joint attack on France. Such an attack would be carried out under conditions most favourable to England, which would be the bigger player in the field. The plan was that Edward would land in or near Normandy as the first stage of an invasion of France. This was planned to take place at some point in the second quarter of 1473. Therefore, as Legge suggests, Edward:

Was unwilling to leave in Hampshire one who, although he had cruelly
stripped her of all her possessions, he did not regard as powerless for mischief,
and whom he preferred to confide to the gentle custody of her daughter, as a
few months before that daughter had been committed to the custody of the
Duchess of Clarence.[9]

Edward, then, simply moved the countess out of harm's way for her safety
and his own security. It is no more than he had done with another countess,
Elizabeth of Oxford and, equally, need not be regarded as sinister.

A third explanation, which does not preclude the second, is that the countess of Warwick's release from sanctuary was the reward for her compliance
in the settlement of Barnard Castle in Richard's favour. For it is true that
by the autumn of 1473, Richard was retaining men within the lordship,
although still using revenues from the Middleham lordship. When Richard
actually took possession of Barnard Castle is unknown; he was paying his
instaurer, Matthew Metcalfe, for sheep and cattle in October 1474, suggesting that he had already established a household there.

It appears, then, that the countess was disposed to trust her son-in-law,
when the son-in-law in question was Richard Gloucester. This hypothesis is
supported by the reaction of the Duke of Clarence, who accepted the countess's move to the north with the worst possible grace. Clarence perhaps
thought that King Edward had restored the Countess Anne's estates to her
and that she in turn had granted them to Richard; certainly a rumour was
soon circulating to that effect:

...The king hath restored the countes of Warwick to all hir ineritaunce, and
she have graunted itt unto my lord of Glowceter with whom she is, and of
this foolkes merveyles greatly. I trust we shall have peas, but it is thought by
lykelehod the contry.[10]

Folks might indeed marvel; in handing over her inheritance to Richard, the
countess disinherited her nephew, George, Duke of Bedford. Moreover, any
agreement between Gloucester and Laurence Booth that would have denied
Clarence would have been greatly strengthened if the countess had given it
her full support.[11] It is, perhaps, telling that Booth made at least one visit to
Sheriff Hutton during 1473 and that, in July of that year, he was promoted
to chancery, which brought him an income worth more than twice the revenues from Barnard Castle.

The author of the above letter was right to speculate that there would
never be peace between the royal brothers. One probable impediment to

any harmonious agreement between Richard and George was the outcome of a parliament opened by Edward on 6 October 1473. In it, King Edward took back several lands that were held by various people, by royal grant, by means of an Act of Resumption. There were many exemptions, among them the lands belonging to Richard:

> [This] nor any other Acte made or to be made in this present Parlement, extend not ne be prejudiciall or hurtfull to oure dier and welbeloved Brother the Duc of Gloucestr', or to his heires, ne to, for, or of any Graunte, Yefte, Dymyfes, Releases of Confirmations, by us granted or made to oure seid Brother, by oure Letters Patentes undre any of oure Seales, by whatsoever name or names oure seid Brother be named or called in the same.'[12]

In other words, all the property granted to Clarence by royal grant was now, at a stroke, removed. Clarence was left with nothing. His estates, including those he had been granted by right of his wife, would be restored only if he co-operated in the case of the dispute with Richard over the Warwick estates; that is to say, he must share the spoils with Richard or he would receive nothing at all. This was Edward's method of ensuring Clarence's good behaviour. Clarence was presented with a choice: submit to the king's will or face ruin.

For Richard, although the situation appeared considerably more favourable, was really not much better. Certainly, Edward had exempted him from the Act of Resumption, but this was done only because the King chose to; royal will was paramount. Richard's estates, held by royal grant were safe, at least for now. However, Richard, like Clarence, would maintain a secure hold on his property only if he could do so by right of inheritance. Although he had survived the Act of Resumption with his holdings intact, it was grim warning.

As the situation between the brothers worsened, Sir John Paston wrote, on 6 November 1473, that:

> The kyng have sende hyddr ffor harneys, and it [is] seyd ffor serteyn, that the Duke off Clarance makyth hym bygge in that he kan, schewing as he wolde but dele with the Duke of Glowcester; but the Kyng ententyth, in eschyewying all inconvenyents, to be as bygge as they bothe, and to be a styffeler atweyn them; and som men thynke that undre thys ther sholde be som other thynge entendyd, and som treason conspyred; so what shall falle, can I nott seye.[13]

Two weeks later, Sir John updates his news, 'As for other tydynges, I trust to God thatt the ij. Dukes of Clarans and Glowcester shall be sette att one by the adward [award] off the Kyng.'[14] This can only refer to the Act of Resumption of 6 October in which Edward forced Clarence into submission by the removal of his estates.

In the same letter, Sir John makes mention of Archbishop George Nevill. Following his arrest and imprisonment, at first in the Tower and then at Hammes, Nevill's friends in the papal court as well as in England were campaigning for his release. One such friend was Richard Gloucester now, of course, married to Nevill's niece, Anne. Sir John Paston was optimistic about Richard's chances of securing the archbishop's freedom: 'Item, I hope by means of the Duke of Glowcester that my Lord Archebyshop shall come home.'[15] Unfortunately, it was to be another year before George would be released, for which he would be indebted to Pope Sixtus IV, not Richard Gloucester.

CHAPTER 15

'As If the Said Countess Were Now Naturally Dead', 1474

The year 1474 opened with a parliament. One of the petitions heard was that of John Darcy, esquire, concerning the inheritance and possessions that had been taken from him as a result of his being attainted for certain insurrections, rebellions, treasons, felonies, murders and other offences. Darcy's inheritance and possessions had been awarded to Richard, Duke of Gloucester. However, Darcy had since been pardoned and he had sued to Duke Richard for the return of his possessions. Richard was prepared to return them should the King agree. As such, Darcy asked the King to ordain, by authority of parliament, to annul the indictment and outlawry as well as all gifts and grants made by the King's letters patent. In this way John and his heirs might be able to have, enjoy and inherit all the lands, tenements, rents, services and other possessions, which would have been theirs had the indictment never been. He asked that this should be done immediately after the Feast of the Annunciation 1475, without his having to make further petition. This was granted by King Edward and enrolled on the parliament roll.[1]

Also in Hilary term 1474, the petition of Richard Gloucester and Elizabeth of Oxford was brought to chancery.[2] The petition had originally been addressed to Chancellor Stillington, who had previously shown concern for Elizabeth's plight. This might go some way to explaining why the countess agreed to join Richard in the petition. She hoped, perhaps, that the chancellor would find against Richard in spite of her apparent support for his case. However, before the case was due to be heard, Stillington had been removed from office. Consequently, the petition was heard by Chancellor

Laurence Booth, Bishop of Durham. Perhaps because of his earlier agreement with the Duke over Barnard Castle and his subsequent, lucrative, promotion to chancery, Booth was sympathetic to his cause. Richard and Elizabeth's case was successful, at least from Richard's point of view, and the defendants were required to make estate to the Duke. One of the conditions under which Richard's grant was upheld was that Richard should provide for the Duchess, her children, of whom one was studying for the priesthood at Cambridge, and her children's children. He also agreed to provide sufficient surety to whomever the countess might be indebted, to the sum of 240 *livres*. Shortly after this Elizabeth died; Richard attended her funeral, as did Lord Howard.

Nevertheless, her feoffees continued to hold out, repeating their claim that Elizabeth had released her deeds only under duress. Moreover, they declared that she had made a will. They were unable to say what was in the will, but for some reason they felt sure that it contained something to their benefit. Was this simply the last desperate act of a few feoffees clutching at any straw that would help them hang on to their estates? Whatever the case, even they seemed unconvinced of it; they recognised Gloucester's title on 9 February and in June the deeds were confirmed.

There is no denying that Richard had faced a long and hard battle to secure lands that he felt were his by right. However, these were not the estates that had been granted to him by the King in 1471. Rather, they were lands that should have gone to Elizabeth's son, John de Vere, had his father not been attainted. Under the terms of the grant, they were not given directly to Richard, but would automatically have gone to him after Elizabeth's death. That Elizabeth had attempted to circumvent this there is no doubt. It is this action that Richard contested.

However, what of his methods? Did he really threaten and intimidate an elderly widow in order to achieve his aims? The depositions of 1495 certainly suggest that some degree of compulsion and coercion did occur. The victim was not only Elizabeth, but also her confessor, Master Baxter. Because there is never any smoke without fire, we must believe that something occurred over the Christmas period of 1472–3. What it was we cannot now know with any certainty because the fact that the depositions were made at all, or rather, the reason why they were made, renders them immediately suspect.

We are left with evidence that can point to one or another polarising view: either Richard's petition suggests that Elizabeth had, at some stage, agreed to co-operate with him or the depositions suggest that she was pressed into doing so. Yet much of what had occurred can be explained by means other than that Richard threatened her. The fact that she was to be taken to Middleham is explained by Edward having placed her into Richard's custody with a view to preventing her from helping her son. Any pressure brought to bear can also be explained in the same way, at least in part. It need not have come from Richard at all, except that he was acting under his brother's orders. Elizabeth's weeping was possibly nothing more than the natural reaction of someone, who was a substantial heiress in her own right, being told that she and her possessions were now in the care of another; it must have been almost unbearable for Elizabeth to have been told such news. That Edward warned Risley not to buy a house held by Richard shows that he was aware that Richard's title to it was dubious, but that is all that the present evidence allows us to say. Of course Edward knew that Richard's possession of the house came about by dubious means, since he had prompted his brother's action in the first instance.

At about the same time that Richard and Elizabeth's case came up in chancery, a dispatch from the Milanese ambassador to the French court reported a rumour that:

> The Duke of Lancaster [sic: read Gloucester], who by force had taken to wife the daughter of the late earl of Warwick, who had been married to the Prince of Wales, was constantly preparing for war with the Duke of Clarence. The latter, because his brother, King Edward, had promised him the Warwick's country, did not want the former to have it, by reason of his marriage with the earl's second daughter.[3]

The argument between Richard and George continued to rumble on, and it provided a source of interesting gossip abroad. However, as was so often the case with the Milanese ambassadors, there are glaring errors in their information, or in their reporting of it.

So far it has been evident that whatever aggression existed between the two brothers originated with George of Clarence, not Richard Gloucester. Indeed, Richard had shown himself to be patient beyond the call of duty with his incorrigible elder brother. The assertion that Richard had 'abducted' Anne, thus calling into question her consent to marry, comes from no reliable source, unless such had been the intention of the Croyland Continuator, the only contemporary source to relate the story of Richard's 'rescue' of Anne from her apparent captivity. On the other hand, the rumour could have originated with Clarence, whose motive would have been to discredit his brother and call into question the validity of his marriage. Had Richard indeed forced Anne to marry him against her will, this would certainly be a serious accusation and would have led to the annulment of their union. However, immediately Richard had taken Anne from her place of concealment, he placed her in sanctuary at St Martin-le-Grand, which at the time came under the care of George Nevill. Anne was free to leave at any time she wished from that point onwards. Moreover, Richard did not seek the consent of Anne's guardian, George of Clarence, because Anne's status as a widow meant that she was free her to marry whom she chose; George's consent was not required.

If, on the other hand, Richard was indeed preparing for war, it could only have been in self-defence against his brother who, terrier-like, refused to relinquish his hold on what he saw as his property in right of his wife, Isabel.

There is little doubt that Richard treated Anne entirely honourably when he removed her from the custody of his brother. He did not rape her nor, it seems, did he take her against her will. As has already been pointed out, Anne stood to gain as much from the match as did Richard. It is for this reason also that there it is no reason to introduce an element of emotional attachment into their relationship; the fact that Richard had refused Clarence's offer of Anne's hand in marriage without her estates is evidence to that. As has already been noted, it is highly probable that, as events concerning the Warwick inheritance unfolded, both Richard and Anne realised that it was in their best interests to combine forces and enter into wedlock. Certainly they had known each other previously, although we cannot know how well. They might have become firm friends or remained emotionally distant from each other.

Whatever the truth of it, and there are no means by which to know the state of their relationship at this point, it does seem that Richard did not devote himself exclusively to Anne, that she was not his only sexual partner. What we do know is that Katherine Plantagenet was not Richard's only illegitimate child. While it is possible that she was born before Richard married Anne, this is not certain. Equally, it cannot be said for certain that another child, a boy variously referred to as John of Gloucester or John of Pontefract, was also the fruit of a liaison from Richard's bachelor days.

When John of Gloucester was conceived, then, is open to speculation. Richard might have taken a mistress while he was still under the tutelage of the Earl of Warwick. The fact that the boy is sometimes referred to as John of Pontefract would suggest that town as his place of birth. However, there is no evidence that Warwick travelled to Pontefract as he conducted business in his capacity as chief steward of the duchy of Lancaster. It is possible that Richard enjoyed a romantic encounter as he travelled back to court upon being summoned by King Edward in the January of 1469. He was seventeen at the time, hearty and just beginning to establish himself in the adult world. On the other hand, that he was aware of the child's existence, and having acknowledged him, might suggest a more meaningful relationship than a brief sexual encounter, as was probably also the case with Katherine's mother.

Richard was chief steward of the northern duchy and constable of Pontefract Castle and so had occasion to visit Pontefract several times from 1471 onwards. He was there in April 1473, although it is not known for how long. He also travelled there in October of the same year. He is next known to have visited Pontefract for a week at the beginning of March 1474. It is not impossible that Richard had a mistress who lived at Pontefract, a woman whom he had known for some time. More probable is that she had been in the service of his wife, Anne.

A clue to her identity might lie in a grant made on 1 March 1474 to Alice Burgh,[4] described as *dilecte nobis Alesie Burgh generose sibi*, 'my beloved gentlewoman'. The grant comprised an annuity of £20 for life from the issues from Middleham, and she was awarded it for 'for certain special causes and considerations'. While this form of reference is nothing out of the ordinary by the standards of the day, it would be interesting to know what were the 'certain special causes and considerations' for which Alice Burgh was being rewarded. Could it be that she had presented Richard with his first-born son? Later, Alice would be in receipt of another annuity, this award was more generous still: twenty marks from the revenues of Warwick in addition to the £20 from Middleham. This second annuity had originally been granted by Edward IV during the minority of his nephew, Edward, Earl of Warwick, the son of George of Clarence, who was born in 1475. It came from the revenues of Warwick which had been granted to the Earl. It appears that Alice had acted as the child's nurse;[5] it would be interesting to know if she had been engaged at Richard's recommendation. Richard had continued the annuity when he became king. His association with Alice, then, was a long one, and it could be that the link between them was Richard's son, John of Gloucester.

All this is, of course, purely speculation. By its very nature, any romantic liaison between Richard and a woman who was not his wife would have been clandestine. Moreover, Richard is lucky in that, being the younger brother of the King and living so far from court, his activities attracted little attention except where they had political significance. It would be nice to think, though, that having married for reasons other than love, Richard managed to find emotional fulfilment elsewhere.

In May 1474 King Edward was called upon to intervene once again in the matter of the Warwick inheritance. In an Act of Parliament the disputed estates were finally settled on Gloucester and Clarence in right of their wives:

> The same Isabell and Anne the daughters, be heires of blode to the same Countes, and so be reputed and taken from hensforth, and have, sue and take, almaner, actions, suytes, entrees, partitions, avauntages, profittes and commoditees, as heires to the said Countes, and to all other their Auncestres, in the wise and fourme, as yf the said Countes were nowe naturally dede.[6]

This last clause is particularly disconcerting. Edward had successfully solved the dispute between Gloucester and Clarence, but at the expense of the countess of Warwick, whom he declared legally dead. 'The consequence was', noted Croyland, 'that little or nothing was left at the disposal of the real lady and heiress, the countess of Warwick, to whom for the whole of her life the most noble inheritance of the Warwicks and Despencers properly belonged.'[7]

This, then, was the means and the price of the formal partitioning of the Warwick estates. The means was a royal act that took no account of the rightful holder and heirs of the estates under dispute. The price was the disinheritance of an elderly woman who, whatever Edward's suspicions to the contrary, had actually done nothing wrong, as well as innocent heirs who had every right to expect fair treatment from those in whose hands their welfare lay. Edward's motives are not too difficult to find. As the Croyland Continuator explains, the King wanted to end a dispute that had been continuing for more than two years 'in order that the discord between princes of such high rank might not cause any hindrance to the carrying out of his royal intentions in relation to the affairs of France.'[8] Edward's 'great enterprise' was uppermost in his mind and he did not want the petty squabbles of his younger siblings to jeopardise them. This, at least, accounts for Edward's ruthlessness in dealing with the countess of Warwick.

While Clarence received the lion's share of the countess's estates in the midlands, Richard Gloucester was enriched by the possession of lands, which included the Nevill estates in North Yorkshire and beyond as well as the lordship of Glamorgan, valued at over £3,000 annually. The act also finally and fully recognised Richard's service to the King: 'remembryng the grete and laudable service, that his seid right dere Brother Richard Duc of Gloucestr' hath dyvers tymes doon to his Highnes...'[9]

However, there was a catch. The claims of the son of the late John Nevill, Marquis of Montagu, had to be addressed. George Nevill, Duke of Bedford, was not, in fact, the heir to his father's estates, but he was the heir male to the Nevill portion of those of the late Earl of Warwick. In order to remove the threat of any suit on his part, it was necessary to extinguish his claim. Moreover, had Montagu and Warwick been attainted, any forfeited lands awarded to Gloucester and Clarence would have been held by royal grant, and this was not secure. In order to overcome these difficulties, Edward issued an Act of Parliament, dated 23 February 1475, in the preamble of which it was stated that the King had intended to attaint Montagu and Warwick but had been dissuaded from doing so by the appeals of Gloucester, Clarence and other lords of royal blood. This meant that Gloucester and Clarence held the Warwick estates in right of their wives and by inheritance and not by royal grant. The Act then went on explicitly to bar the claims of the heirs of the late Marquis Montagu to any part of the Earl of Warwick's Nevill estates. The estates so viciously fought over by the Dukes of Clarence and Gloucester were now safe and could not be removed by any future Act of Resumption.[10] Much later, a further parliamentary act of 1478, placed George Nevill, who at that date was about to come of age, into the vicious circle of being degraded from his dukedom on the grounds that he no longer possessed suitable estates to support him in such a dignity. Because he had been degraded, he could not make good his claim to the estates that were his rightful inheritance.

Then there was the matter of the dispensation for the marriage of Richard and Anne. Clearly, this was still a matter for concern because, should their union turn out to be invalid, they would be forced to part. It would mean, moreover, that Richard would lose his right to the Warwick inheritance because he held it only in right of his wife. Edward made provision for this also. The act of May 1474, by which Edward had granted the Warwick estates to the two daughters of the late Earl, contained two clauses that protected Richard should he ever be required to divorce the Lady Anne. The first clause allowed the couple to remarry if Richard could obtain the necessary dispensation following any declaration of his marriage to be invalid; in this event, it would be as though they had never divorced, but they would continue as man and wife as before and any children born to them would be recognised as legitimate. If, on the other hand, Richard failed to obtain a dispensation despite his best efforts to do so, and the couple were compelled to divorce, Richard would be allowed to retain for life the estates he held in right of his wife provided he did not remarry. In other words, although Anne Nevill had married Richard in order to maintain her right to her inheritance, she would do so only if their marriage were legal. If it were not, assuming she was aware of the situation, her safest option was to remain silent about it. She had so much more to lose than Richard.

Strickland[11] remarks that there were 'some illegalities' in connection with the marriage of Richard and Anne, and attributes them to reluctance on the part of the bride. Moreover, she speculates that the fact that an act of parliament was required to protect Richard's interests is proof 'that Anne meditated availing herself of some informality in her abhorred marriage'. In other words, it was Anne's intention to divorce Richard as soon as possible. This act, which allowed Richard to remain in possession of her property, prevented her from doing so. Strickland goes on:

[T]he informalities most likely arose from the want of the proper bull to dispense with the relationship; and as the free consent of both bride and bride-groom was an indispensable preliminary to such dispensation, the absence of these legal instruments negatively prove that the unfortunate Anne Neville never consented to her second marriage.

Strickland's conclusion is predicated on her belief that Anne was a helpless victim in the matter of her marriage to Richard. However, there is nothing in the historical record to allow such an assumption to be made. In fact, since Anne had as much to gain as Richard did from the match there is nothing to say that she did not initiate the events that led to her espousal to the Duke of Gloucester, whatever the difficulties or the consequences that might result.

The consequences of the marriage ending in divorce would have caused no great harm to Richard. Providing he did not remarry, he would have been free to enjoy his share of the Warwick inheritance and to live in the comfort and security it brought him. The way was open for him to take a mistress for his emotional and physical wellbeing if he so desired, perhaps one of the ladies with whom he had previously enjoyed a romance and who had given him children.

For Anne the situation would have been much different. Divorce would have resulted in her being disinherited, her properties forfeit to Richard; she would have lost the security of marriage, indeed she would have been rendered unmarriageable. The fact that she went ahead with the marriage anyway suggests an almost mercenary facet to Anne's character. She saw in Richard the only means by which she might hang on to her inheritance. It is impossible to believe that Richard, with his legal knowledge, could not have entered the marriage unaware of the impediments against it and the conse-quences of their discovery. It is possible to believe that, having contracted an illegal union, the couple were forced to continue with it, even as the events unfolded that would sweep them towards the throne.

Moreover, although it does not excuse the treatment meted out to Anne Beauchamp, countess of Warwick, many widows were forced to fight to retain their rights and properties. This accounts for her letters to the female members of the King's family. The countess evidently thought, wrongly as it turned out, that she would get sympathy and help from those who could at least identify with her plight.

Perhaps fifteenth century women were the victims of the selective reading of Ramon Lull's assertion that men were superior to women in terms of both intellect and physical strength, and that those men who had to deal with women's affairs took this to what they saw as a logical conclusion. Today we might see it as taking advantage of someone unable to defend herself. Therefore, while Richard's conduct in this entire affair might be considered unchivalrous, as indeed it was by modern standards, he was not the only participant in the incident; indeed, he was not even the driving force behind it. If Richard is to be blamed for his behaviour towards the countess, as much can be said for Edward, who ignored the countess's rights in the first place and whose political ambitions led him to a pitiless solution; then there is the grasping Duke of Clarence, who is also by no means free of guilt, but perhaps still more could be said of Isabel and Anne, the countess of Warwick's own daughters, who saw their mother disinherited for no purpose other than their own gain.

A few months after the conflict over the Warwick estates had been settled to the satisfaction of all except the rightful heirs, Richard finally came to a peaceful settlement with the Earl of Northumberland. Once again, it took the intervention of King Edward to achieve the reconciliation in an indenture made on 28 July between King Edward, Gloucester and Northumberland. The terms of the indenture were that the Earl would be a faithful servant to Richard, whom he acknowledged as his good and faithful lord. The Earl would do service to Richard at all times that were lawful and convenient whenever Richard should lawfully ask him to. This duty to the Duke was superseded only by Northumberland's allegiance and duty to the King, the Queen, Prince Edward and the other children of the King born or yet to be born.

In return, Richard agreed to be a good and faithful lord to the Earl at all times and to sustain him in his right before all persons except the King and his family as mentioned above. Also, Duke Richard agreed that he would not challenge or lay claim to any offices or fees held by Northumberland under the King's grant or by grant of any other person or persons. Richard would not interfere with the Earl or any of his servants as they carried out their duties. Perhaps even more importantly, Richard agreed that he would not accept or retain into his service any servant or servants who was or who had been retained by the Earl. This last point was a reiteration of the agreement reached at Nottingham in the May of the previous year. It appears to have referred specifically to the case of John Widdington of Chipchase, who was one of the men poached by Richard from Northumberland.[12]

The benefits to the Earl might appear to be a lot less than the benefits to Richard and the two men interpreted the terms of the indenture somewhat loosely; however, it did lead to lasting peace and co-operation between the Duke and the Earl. The Earl continued to be influential in the counties of Northumberland, north Durham and the East Riding of Yorkshire, where he had lands. Richard prevailed in the North Riding of Yorkshire where he, too, held extensive estates. One of the first instances of Gloucester and Northumberland working together came on 13 August when they were both required to pronounce judgement in the case of a certain John Penyngton of Cumberland should Penyngton refuse to obey the arbitration of a lower court.[13]

Yet Richard was, at this time, very much concerned with land acquisition. The Duke had been made further grants from the Hungerford inheritance by the King on 5 August. The agreement reached between Richard and the Lady Margaret had dissolved upon her death and now he was able to claim manors and hundreds and the reversion of several estates from the Hungerford inheritance, which belonged to the King by right of forfeiture. Certainly, there is every possibility that Richard had urged his brother to make inquisitions into the Hungerford inheritance, and this Edward had ordered in 1470 and again three years later.

In September 1474, Duke Richard exchanged his wife's lands in Derbyshire and Hertfordshire for the lucrative manor of Cottingham, near Hull, which had been worth £270 earlier in the century, as well as the castle and lordship of Scarborough in Yorkshire.

That Richard was acquisitive there is no doubt. That he was ruthless in his acquisitions is evident. What is not so clear, however, is why he should have expended so much time and energy in the pursuit of estates to some of which he had a dubious right at best. Perhaps it is because Richard had previously been deprived of grants and awards and so was anxious to acquire as much as possible in order to feel secure. He was also acutely aware that, no matter how loyal and devoted he was to the King, Edward clearly did not favour him; rather, Edward seemed all too eager to oblige Clarence at every opportunity, even at Richard's expense.

Behind all this must lie Richard's first hand experience of deprivation. He had experienced exile, not once, but twice in his life. The first time might have seemed like a great adventure to the boy, but this is only a guess and its accuracy is doubtful. Prior to being sent overseas on what must have been a difficult and frightening journey, far from his family and everything that was familiar and safe, Richard had watched as his father turned his back on him and left him to the mercy of the approaching Lancastrian forces. We can only imagine the feeling of fear, helplessness and despair that overwhelmed the seven-year-old boy as he watched his father and elder brothers disappear behind the Mortimer Tower of Ludlow Castle and into the night. His father's death just over a year later removed whatever sense of stability, security and safety remained to Richard.

Now an adult and able to exert a degree of control over his own life, it cannot be wondered that Richard would want to replace the emotional insecurities of his childhood with material things. With extensive estates comes financial gain. Rightly or wrongly, money brings with it a sense of security that the more inconsistent things in life cannot provide. Never again would Richard face losing everything he had. Never again would he be reliant upon the goodwill of others in order to have the security, however false and transitory, that material wealth can bring. Now that he had property of his own, he could feel safe in the illusion that he was dependent only upon himself.

That said, not all Richard's acquisitions were particularly lucrative. The lordship of Barnard Castle is a case in point. At best, it brought an income of £362 per annum, but this was for the period 1390-91. Since then, revenues had fallen sharply. Richard could expect to receive a net income of no more than about £325.[14] Barnard Castle's attraction for Richard was clearly not financial but geographical, lying as it did at a strategic point between Richard's lordships of Richmond and Penrith.

Barnard Castle held a further appeal for Richard Gloucester. It provided a base from which he might extend his influence farther north into the palatinate of Durham. His progress in this endeavour was stopped by Bishop Booth. Although the bishop had capitulated with regard to the lordship, he was adamant that Richard should proceed no further.

Bishop Booth appears to have been a man of integrity. This is shown most plainly during Gloucester's struggle to secure the de Vere estates. While the bishop was certainly no friend to Richard, he was not his enemy, and he was able to give an objective verdict in the case Richard and Countess Elizabeth brought to chancery. On the other hand, Booth was passionately concerned about the welfare of his bishopric. This lay behind his reluctance to allow Richard to take Barnard Castle, a lordship he had sought to protect for many years, but it was manifested in other ways as well. At the very beginning of his pontificate, Booth had alienated himself from the Nevills of Middleham by cancelling the fees that had been granted to them by his predecessor, Robert Nevill. Bishop Booth refused to use diocesan revenues for political gain. He also chose to promote the Nevills of Raby, from whose branch sprang Richard Gloucester's mother, Cecily, Duchess of York. The Middleham Nevills, however, exacted revenge on the bishop; they persuaded King Edward to seize the temporalities of the diocese and place its administration into their hands. With the demise of the Earl of Warwick the bishop perhaps hoped for a more peaceful future. His hopes were sadly misplaced.

The differences that emerged between Duke Richard and Bishop Booth could only have been compounded by the Duke's refusal to let the matter of Barnard Castle drop until he had won. However, the real difficulty between them lay in their differing approach to Scottish policy. As warden of the west march towards Scotland, Richard naturally had a keen interest in Anglo-Scottish relations. Bishop Booth did too. He fully supported the efforts of Edward IV and James III to maintain the fragile peace that currently existed between the two countries, and he was involved with the negotiations that were designed to maintain it.

Three events had brought the Kings of England and Scotland to the negotiating table. Until the 1460s, the Scottish towns of Roxburgh and Berwick were held in English hands. English armies led by the Nevills had managed to resist Scottish attempts to retake them, but as the battles that constituted the Wars of the Roses continued, the situation changed. Scotland recaptured Roxburgh in 1460, while Henry VI surrendered Berwick the following year. These two events brought to an end the Scottish Wars of Independence. The third event occurred at about the same time. This was that the French had finally defeated the English, thus bringing the Hundred Years of War to a conclusion.

During Richard's own lifetime, then, relationships between England, France and Scotland underwent a radical shift. Scotland, who had recaptured her towns, no longer had a need to continue the war with England. France's victory over England meant that the 'auld alliance', which had existed between Scotland and France since the end of the thirteenth century, was effectively suspended. Conversely, now that England was no longer engaged in fighting France, she was free to attack her northern neighbour. King James III of Scotland saw good reason to try to come to some sort of settlement with King Edward IV.

Duke Richard, however, proved difficult. As admiral he was required to settle naval disputes; he did so only with the worst possible grace. He was required to hold march-days, in which cases of infractions of the border laws were tried; again, he showed himself most reluctant to do so. The cause of Richard's behaviour probably stemmed from the tangible sense of anxiety that existed throughout the marcher lands. Moreover, such anxiety was not without reason. Whatever state of truce or otherwise that might have existed between the two countries, the Scots continued to slip across the border to carry out menaces just as much as the English did. Richard, whose position as warden put him in the front line, had to be both vigilant and diplomatic; his brother's apparent lack of support and understanding caused Richard to dig in his heels when it came to peace settlements.

Despite the Duke's petulance, the Anglo-Scottish negotiations were too important to be abandoned by King Edward. The reason for that was the same reason he had intervened to settle the quarrel between his two brothers: his plans to invade France were at last coming to fruition. The last thing he needed at such a time was a revival of the 'auld alliance'. Such a scenario was not a figment of the English king's worried imagination. In May of the previous year, King James had made overtures to King Louis of France to the effect that, if Louis were to offer James a pension of 60,000 crowns a year, he would wage war on King Edward if he should chose to invade France.[15] Had the pact succeeded, Edward would have found himself, as Henry VIII would in years to come, fighting a united enemy on two fronts: on French soil and at the Scottish border. Unlike Henry VIII, however, Edward had no Catherine of Aragon to help him meet the threat head on. Of course, Richard Gloucester was a fully capable, and certainly willing, general, but it was much better to secure peace, and so Edward and James, through their respective envoys and negotiators, among them Bishop Laurence Booth, sat down to talk.

Still, Richard's attention was not entirely taken up with matters of aggression. As we have seen, he would go on pilgrimages to holy shrines, particularly that of Our Lady of Walsingham. Now, with his life settled in the north of England, Richard enjoyed convenient access to many of the shrines that are to be found in the area. One of the most important of these was that of St Cuthbert at Durham Cathedral. This shrine was an important feature on a major pilgrim route that ran between Ripon and Jarrow. Richard and Duchess Anne were admitted into the fraternity of St Cuthbert at Durham in 1474. This was a rare privilege reserved for those who showed a strong devotion to the saint, which was usually expressed monetarily by means of gifts and donations. Still, there is no need to question the sincerity of the devotion of the Duke and Duchess of Gloucester; their pilgrimages were an almost annual event, suggesting that they were doing more than merely paying lip-service. Indeed, Richard must have felt an affinity with the saint who, in life, had also been a soldier.

Duchess Anne's presence at the shrine of St Cuthbert is interesting because it suggests that the saint had lost his reputation as a misogynist. It was believed that the saint would punish women who had the audacity to enter his church and approach his shrine.[16] Cuthbert's prejudice is usually attributed to the activities of the Nuns of Coldingham, whose feasting, drinking, conversation and other improprieties, including the making and wearing of fine garments, had offended the saint. In reality, Cuthbert had much association with women in life, especially abbesses and queens, and his first cure at Durham was of a Scottish woman. Nevertheless, it was considered prudent to keep women away from the sacred shrine. As such, a line was drawn on the floor of the nave across which women were not to step. For Richard, however, there was no such prohibition. At Durham and elsewhere, he venerated Cuthbert and listed him among his favourite saints.

Meanwhile, some important developments were taking place between England and Scotland.[17] A treaty between King Edward and King James was signed in Edinburgh in November 1474. This treaty was a confirmation of truces that had previously been signed in 1464 and 1465 by the two kings. A report by the Milanese ambassador states:

I have seen another letter from the King of Scotland to one of his ambassadors, complaining extremely about the King of France, saying that previously, only too long ago, his majesty desired to have him for a friend, and he means to make him have a greater esteem for him than he has. Accordingly I believe his majesty will send some ambassador to him, although it is considered certain that the King of England has made sure of the King of Scotland.[18]

Polydore Vergil describes the terms of the accord between Edward and James: 'James king of Scotts delt, by ambassadors, with king Edward, that he wold bestow Cecyly his dowghter upon his soone James, whom he dyd handfast to that young prince'. The treaty, therefore, was consolidated by the marriage of Edward's youngest daughter, Cecily, to James's infant son and heir, also called James.

However, while Edward and James could congratulate themselves on their achievement, the peace treaty between England and Scotland was not welcomed by everyone. Raids on both sides of the border were very lucrative, marcher society had evolved to accept a permanent state of war and this allowed the marcher lords to use their position to build up power in the region. The most powerful marcher lord, Duke Richard, demonstrated his displeasure by means of an act of piracy. His ship, the *May Flower* attacked and captured a ship belonging to King James III of Scotland, *The Yellow Carvel*. The damage to Scottish prestige and to Edward's negotiations was mitigated by diplomatic means.[19] However, such activity made it difficult to maintain peaceful relations between the two countries. As time went by, Richard visited the border at least once. He kept a close eye on his deputies and spent the king's money on defence works, including the strengthening of the fortifications at Carlisle Castle. On his side, Alexander, Duke of Albany, the youngest brother of King James, was ready to meet Richard half-way. He assembled troops at Lauder in readiness to repel a foray that was expected to be led by Richard.

Yet, war between the belligerent youngest brothers of the two kings was not to occupy the mind of Duke Richard in the coming months. Instead, it would be his brother, Edward's, 'great enterprise', the long-planned invasion of France.

CHAPTER 16

The Setting of the Sun, 1475

The year 1475 marked a turning point in Richard's life. It started well. In February he became sheriff of Cumberland for life. In June he received the castle and lordship of Skipton-in-Craven.[1] This seat in the West Yorkshire Pennines had been the principal estate of the Lancastrian Clifford family. Perhaps it gave Richard some small glow of pleasure to think of the downward spiral of that family, and that, while vengeance is more commonly exacted in heaven, evidence of its workings can also occasionally be witnessed on earth.

Also in June King Edward's long-awaited invasion of France, his 'great enterprise of France', finally got underway. It had been a long and difficult journey to reach this point. Edward had announced his wish to wage war on France as long ago as 1472. Taxes had been granted to the King by parliament to enable him to pay for 13,000 archers, but the funds had proved difficult to raise. It had been about this time that rumours had circulated among the Milanese ambassadors that Duke Richard was to go to France at the head of an army.[2] Moreover, the Bretons had become nervous at the thought that their security rested so much in English hands. Nervous of French attack, they signed a truce with King Louis which would, in the event, still be effective when Edward finally got round to staging his invasion.

A second grant of taxes to King Edward saw him no better off. A solution was reached by which Edward would impose benevolences, a polite term for enforced loans. The Milanese ambassadors had some interesting words on the subject:

You must have heard that some time ago the king here constantly said he would cross to the continent to conquer France. The last four months in particular he has been very active, and has discovered an excellent device to raise money. He has plucked out the feathers of his magpies without making them cry out.

This autumn the king went into the country from place to place, and took information of how much each place could pay. He sent for them all, one by one, and told them that he wished to cross to conquer France and deluded them with other words. Finally, he has so contrived that he obtained money from everyone who had the value of 40*l.* sterling and upwards. Everyone seemed to give willingly. I have frequently seen our neighbours here who were summoned before the king, and when they went they looked as if they were going to the gallows; when they returned they were joyful, saying that they had spoken to the king and he had spoken to them so benignly that they did not regret the money they had paid.

From what I have heard some say, the king adopted this method. When any-one went before him he gave him a welcome as if he had known him always. After some time he asked him what he could pay of his free will towards this expedition. If the man offered something proper he had his notary ready, who took down the name and the amount. If the king thought otherwise he told him, Such a one, who is poorer than you, has paid so much; you who are richer can easily pay more, and thus by fair words he brought him up to the mark and in this way it is argued that he extracted a very large amount of money.[3]

Indeed, according to the *Great Chronicle*:

It was Reportid that as he [Edward] passyd by a Town In Suffolk and called beffore hym among othir a Rych wedow and ffraynyd of hyr what hir good wyll shuld be toward his grete charge, & she lyberally hadd Grauntid to him x li., he thankid hyr & afftyr took hyr tyll hym & kyssid hyr, The which kysse she acceptid soo keyndly, that ffor that grete bounte and kyend dede, he shuld have xx li for his x li.[4]

So, the wealthy Suffolk widow increased her contributions from £10 to £20 in return for a kiss from the King.

Edward assembled his troops at Barham Downs near Canterbury. It was his intention, then, to disembark at Calais, a fact about which King Louis had been misled by Queen Elizabeth's uncle, the count of St Pol. As a result of this deception, Louis had no idea where Edward was due to land and so was unable to meet him. He was unable also to see for himself the size of the army Edward had brought with him. It was formidable. Of the sixteen barons, only three or four failed to travel to France. Of the seven earls, three were at Edward's side, two remained in England as members of the council, one sent his son in his stead, and one was too old to take part. All five Dukes were present. Clarence had brought with him 120 men-at-arms and 1,200 archers, while Gloucester had managed to muster an even greater force, and Richard's boar badge very much in evidence.

Quite why Richard had chosen the white boar as his cognizance is a matter of some dispute. The boar is a symbol of intrepidity, lust and gluttony, while as a heraldic symbol the boar is one of the four animals of venery.[5] While Richard's intrepidity cannot be doubted, it can only be wondered, did he want to protect himself from the temptations of the latter two, especially considering how Edward was affected by them? Another suggestion is that the boar was adopted by Richard because it was the symbol of St Anthony. As we have seen, Anthony featured among the favourite saints of Richard's father, the Duke of York. He is the patron of, among other things, religious houses and Christian monasticism. Richard's father took seriously his patronage of religious houses, as Richard himself would in the near future. However, there is another connection with St Anthony. He is also the patron saint of swineheards; the smallest piglet in a litter and, indeed, the smallest child of a family, is often referred to in country districts as the Tantony Pig. This epithet would apply to Richard, being the youngest member of his family, the Tantony Pig of the House of York.[6] Still another suggestion is that it was taken from Ebor, which comes from the Roman name for York, Eboracum. York was, of course, the duchy of Richard's father, and it was a city that would be much favoured by Richard in the years to come.

It truly was the flower of English nobility who landed on the sands of Calais in the summer of 1475. However, despite their magnificent show of arms and their enthusiasm for battle, the wind was very rapidly taken out of their sails when it became obvious that one important player had not turned up. Instead of being there to meet him, Duke Charles of Burgundy, who had goaded Edward into assisting him in his struggle against the King of France, was still in the Rhienland city of Neuss.

Charles had become involved in a dispute over the city of Cologne on the Rhien, and he had laid siege to Neuss, a small but strongly defended city to the south of Cologne, in July of the previous year. He was in for the long haul. The people of the neighbouring towns assisted the inhabitants of Neuss, so that the siege became merely a battle of wills. At the turn of 1475 Charles was still there, but Edward was so unconcerned at this stage that he even sent archers to reinforce Charles' army. As the time of the invasion of

France drew nearer, Edward sent envoys led by Dr John Morton to Charles, but they could report only that the siege was continuing with no sign of lifting. At last Edward began to worry. Without Charles the chances of success in France were small. Duchess Margaret was enlisted to plead the English cause, but to no avail. Anthony, Earl Rivers, the King's brother-in-law, went in person to Neuss where he tried, equally unsuccessfully, to reason with the Duke. In spite of all this, Edward had set out, and now he and his army found themselves with nothing to do.

As the English kicked their heels in frustration, their disappointment was alleviated by the divertissement afforded by the presence of the Duchess Margaret. Following her failed attempt to remind her husband of his commitments, she had ridden on to greet her brothers. It was a happy reunion for the four siblings of the House of York, who had not seen each other since Margaret left her home country to marry Duke Charles six years earlier.

The Duchess brought with her tapestries and fine Bruges cloth as gifts to King Edward although it turned out that they were actually gifts from Duke Charles who hoped that they would go some way to placating the King. Margaret was also conducting negotiations with ambassadors from Portugal on her husband's behalf as well as raising armies to defend the towns of Artois and Hainault from French assault. After spending two nights with the English court, she returned to St Omer. Shortly afterwards, the Dukes of Gloucester and Clarence rode over to visit her; they, in their turn, stayed two nights as guests of their sister.

All this activity was observed from a distance by King Louis. He had expected something to show for all the effort he had been put to in order to prepare for war, but now he could only watch as his enemy danced and celebrated at the court of the Duchess Margaret. The English soldiers would have sympathised with King Louis. From their point of view, they had followed Edward expecting to be bathed in the glory of what they anticipated to be a second Agincourt. After all, the scene of Henry V's greatest moment was but a few days' march from Calais.

The reason for the setback was, of course, Duke Charles's failure to return from the siege of Neuss. This was finally abandoned only when King Louis invaded the Duke's lands. It was a two–pronged attack during which French troops flooded into Picardy and the Somme valley before they made their way east into Burgundy itself and then on to Franche-Comté. Charles crossed country to meet his brother-in-law at Calais, where he arrived in mid July. The English were not a little bemused to see that the Duke did not ride at the head of an army as they had expected, but instead was accompanied only by a small personal retinue. In fact, the Duke was now almost penniless as a result of his activity in the Rhienland, and his army were in such a sorry state that it was said that he was ashamed to let the English see it. The party was once again joined by Margaret and the Duke and Duchess of Burgundy treated the royal entourage to a lavish entertainment in the castle of Fauquembergue on the Aa river, near St Omer.

All merriment aside, it was a tense time; Charles's absence, and then his appearance without proper backing had led some of the English nobles to suggest that the venture should be abandoned. Edward thought of the substantial taxes he had been forced to levy and the anticipated wrath of his subjects should he return to England without a shot being fired. Charles had a better proposal. He suggested that the English should make their way to Péronne. From there they would journey to St Quentin, which was the gateway to Champagne, and which the count of St Pol had agreed to give up to the English. From St Quentin, they would follow the route via Laon to Reims. Charles, meanwhile, would rejoin his troops and crush the Duke of Lorraine before he too advanced to Reims where he would witness Edward's coronation as King of France.

It was an interesting proposal to which Edward, perhaps against his better judgement, gave his assent. Having received his orders, Richard mobilised his men and rode alongside Edward and Charles at the head of the English army. They took the route through Ardres, Guines and on to St Omer, arriving at Fauquembergue on 23 July. Two days later the English forces arrived at Agincourt, where they spent two nights basking in the glory of days gone by and, no doubt, wondering when the chance would come for them to emulate them and make the name of King Edward IV shine as brightly as that of his Lancastrian predecessor. For Richard and Edward Agincourt had added poignancy, associated as it was with their great uncle, Edward, the second Duke of York, who had died in the service of Henry V and who now lay in the church at Fotheringhay. Leaving Agincourt behind, they passed through St Pol and on to Doullens. On 5 August, the English had reached as far as Péronne, where they were met, as promised, by Duke Charles.

At this point a messenger came from the count of St Pol, who reiterated his willingness to hand over St Quentin to the English. Edward sent a small detachment on ahead, but as they approached the town they suddenly found themselves under attack from great guns positioned on the city walls. The artillery was reinforced by foot soldiers and cavalry, who had sallied out to meet the English soldiers. A handful of Edward's men were killed; the rest drew back and, marching through heavy rain, made their way back to camp which was now at St Christ-sur-Somme. To make matters worse, while Duke Charles was comfortably lodged at nearby Péronne, he had done nothing to ease the plight of his English allies; they had little to protect them from the wet conditions and they had spent almost all their pay. If Edward had not become disillusioned by the behaviour of his brother-in-law by this point, then surely he became so now.

Edward was also now aware that the French had been observing his progress and had probably deduced his ultimate objective. They had devastated Artois and Picardy, towns en-route to Reims were garrisoned and fortified; Reims itself must now be out of reach. Moreover, the summer was almost at an end; it was now mid-August. Edward had to make a decision. He could venture deeper into France, but at the risk of the lives of his men for little, if any, gain. In any case, they were as disillusioned as he was; there was nothing to guarantee that they would not rebel. Alternatively, Edward could seek to find a winter camp in the cold and unwelcoming countryside, where food was scarce and shelter would be very hard to come by. It was all too obvious that he would get no assistance from Duke Charles. As Edward seethed over his brother-in-law's behaviour and anxiously sought to find the best solution, a third option sprung to mind.

For his part, King Louis of France had kept himself informed of the progress of the English army. He was aware of the route they had taken and he had for some time now pursued a course that lay virtually parallel with that which Edward was following. Yet, he was still surprised by the sudden appearance in his camp of the valet of one of his gentlemen who had been taken prisoner by the English. When the valet was examined he disclosed that he had been sent by his captors who suggested that Louis should send to Edward for a passport for his ambassadors, and that they should go to negotiate with the Lords Stanley and Howard. A man was selected to speak with Edward. He was instructed by Philip de Commines himself on what to say. He was then sent out wearing the coat of arms of a herald.

When the valet approached the English camp, he was stopped and escorted to a tent, where he requested permission to speak to the Lords Howard and Stanley. The man was treated civilly by the English and he was taken to see Edward when the King had finished his dinner. Edward was informed that King Louis had long wanted to be friends with the English and that, although he had appeared to support the Earl of Warwick in his quarrel with Edward, he had done so only because it placed him in opposition to the Duke of Burgundy, which had been his real objective. He went on to point out that the season was late and that the land would soon be in the grip of winter; adding that His Majesty of France was aware that there were those on the English side who wanted nothing but war. However, should Edward be inclined to a treaty, King Louis would not refuse to propose terms that would be acceptable to both Edward and his subjects. Edward was then asked for passports for one hundred horses so that Louis could send ambassadors to discuss these terms. Commines notes that Edward and 'part of his nobility' were pleased with the proposals. The passports were granted. The valet was given four nobles in money and sent back to his master accompanied by one of Edward's heralds.

The ambassadors met near Amiens and their instructions were carefully drawn up. These were witnessed by, among others, the Dukes of Gloucester and Clarence. The terms of the treaty, which was the outcome of their negotiations, were these: a state of truce would exist between the Kings of England and France. It would last for seven years and end at sunset on 29 August 1482. The merchants of both kingdoms would enjoy freedom of movement of goods and services, and all tolls and charges levied on the English merchants during the past twelve years would be lifted. The French merchants would enjoy similar privileges. Upon receipt of 75,000 crowns Edward would leave France peacefully, leaving behind Lord Howard and Sir John Cheyne as hostages for his speedy return. Whatever differences might exist between England and France would be referred to four arbitrators: for France, the Archbishop of Lyons and the comte de Dunois; for England, Cardinal Bourchier and George, Duke of Clarence. Neither king would enter into any league with any ally of the other without his knowledge. Moreover, the Dauphin Charles would marry Elizabeth of York as soon as they became of an age to marry. A jointure of £60,000 would be provided by King Louis. If Elizabeth were to die before she reached marriageable age, her sister Mary would marry the Dauphin. If either king found himself under threat by armed rebellion, the other would be obliged to give assistance. King Louis undertook to pay King Edward a pension of 50,000 gold crowns, with an instalment to be paid in the city of London each year at Easter and Michaelmas. A guarantee for the payment would take the form of a bond by the Medici Bank or by papal bull, which would impose an interdict on France should Louis default.[7] An additional term of the treaty was that Queen Marguerite would be ransomed by Louis XI for the sum of 50,000 crowns. She was permitted to return to France, but was forced to relinquish her claims to her Angevin inheritance. She retired from public life, living in isolation and poverty until her death in 1482 at the age of 52 years. A final term was the surrender of Henry Tudor, who had been living in exile in Brittany. Edward's persistent attempts to get hold of 'the only imp now left of Henry VI's brood' almost came to fruition under the terms of the treaty to be signed at Picquiny. Henry was duly packed off to St Malo on the first stage of his journey to England. Unfortunately for Edward, and for his brother, Richard, as it turned out, Henry realised that his ultimate destination would be the scaffold. He became ill with a fever, or pretended he had, which bought him enough time to allow the Breton chancellor, John Chenlet, to intervene on his behalf, Henry Tudor was saved and his part in the history of England was assured.

Louis was anxious to come to an understanding with Edward before Duke Charles returned. As such, he agreed at once to the English offer. He sent out letters arranging for monies to be advanced that would cover the initial instalment and serve to bribe those English nobles who were still unhappy at the outcome of the expedition. Louis also took care to win over the rank and file. He ordered the taverns of Amiens to supply drinks to the English soldiery free of charge. Commines[8] paints a picture of the consequences of the King's generosity: 'We went together into a tavern, where, though it was not nine o'clock, there were already 111 reckonings to pay that morning. The house was filled with company; some were singing, some were asleep, and all were drunk.' When King Edward found out he was ashamed of the behaviour of his men, though, surely, not surprised!

The meeting between the two kings took place on a bridge that had been especially constructed for the occasion over the Somme at Picquigny, near Amiens. King Edward was dressed magnificently in cloth of gold and wearing a black cap decorated with fleurs-dy-lys encrusted with precious stones. Commines gives an idea of the King's appearance and how he had changed in the few years since Warwick's rebellion:

> [Edward was] a prince of noble and majestic presence, but a little inclining to corpulence. I had seen him before when the Earl of Warwick drove him out of his kingdom; then I thought him handsomer, and to the best of my remembrance, my eyes had never beheld a more handsome person.[9]

Edward was accompanied by George, Duke of Clarence, the Earl of Northumberland, William, Lord Hastings, the chancellor, and other peers of the realm. Conspicuous by his absence, especially in consideration of his high rank, was Richard, Duke of Gloucester. As Commines explains, 'The Duke of Gloucester, the King of England's brother, and some other persons of quality, were not present at this interview, as being averse to the treaty.' It would have been natural if Richard, as a man most interested in military affairs, had taken the opportunity to inspect the French troops. However, protocol would surely have required his presence at such an important royal event. Certainly, his absence was interpreted as a sign of his disapproval of the treaty. Nevertheless, in the end he appears to have changed his mind and showed himself more amenable. He went afterwards to pay his respects to

King Louis, who greeted him warmly and entertained him lavishly; Richard accepted fine presents of plate and horses from the King of France.

It is easy to be cynical with regard to Richard's apparent change of heart, especially when it is considered that he had no qualms about receiving generous presents from King Louis. However, his visit to the French king might have been in response to a direct order from his brother. More important is why Richard had opposed the treaty in the first place. His reasons are not stated, but can be guessed. Holinshead, writing much later, asserts that Richard saw 'that all their traveill, paines, & expenses were to their shame lost and cast awaie, and nothing gained but a continuall mocke and daily derision of the French king and all his minions.'[10] In other words, all the taxes and benefices Edward had extracted from his people had bought nothing except the ridicule and scorn of the Spider King and his courtiers. Certainly Richard's pride was hurt, but the whole shameful event also jarred his knightly sensibilities. For a man of Richard's standing as a knight and a soldier of considerable ability, that Edward had turned his back upon someone who had asked for his help was, quite frankly, unforgivable and unchivalrous in the extreme. Richard might also have been influenced by the memory, or more importantly, the image he retained, of his father. The Duke of York had been an accomplished administrator and soldier. An honourable man, he would never have betrayed the trust of one who had sought his help.

Whatever might have been at the root of Richard's opposition, he was not alone in his thinking. Many of the common soldiery showed their displeasure by crossing over to fight alongside Charles the Bold. Commines also notes that many other men of quality were opposed to the treaty, not just Richard Gloucester. Although Commines does not name anyone, it is known that Henry, Duke of Buckingham had withdrawn even before the treaty was signed, taking his men back with him to England.

Why Richard finally accepted the treaty is equally complex. However, as would so often be the case with Richard, his motives on this occasion might well have been inspired by interests of a more spiritual nature. The meeting in which the peace was formally recognised took place on the bridge at Picquigny, which is close to Amiens in Picardy, on 29 August. This event is highly significant with regard to both the date and the locality in which it occurred. Once again, Philippe de Commines provides us with a graphic description of an incident that accompanied this controversial settlement:

> The next day, a great number of English came to Amiens, some of whom reported that the Holy Ghost had made that peace, and prophecies were produced to

confirm it; but their greatest argument to support this opinion was that, during the time of their interview, a white pigeon came and sat upon the King of England's tent, and could not be frightened away by any noise they could make in the camp.[11]

It is interesting that the English should attribute the peace to the Holy Ghost which, in this instance, descended upon King Edward's tent in the form of a white pigeon. The date upon which this took place was, as noted, 29 August. This is the day of the Feast of the Decollation of Saint John the Baptist. The Gospels relate how John saw the white dove descend upon Jesus as he came up from the water after his baptism, by which sign the Baptist knew that Jesus was the Christ. Moreover, Picquigny is only some ten miles away from Amiens. While there are at least three cathedrals in France that claim to possess the authentic head of John the Baptist, Amiens is the most insistent that its head is the genuine one. Indeed, by this time, a virtual tourist industry had been established in which pilgrims would go to view the sacred relic.

One of the holy figures to which Richard Gloucester was most devoted was the Holy Trinity. In the medieval period, it was understood that the image of the Head of John the Baptist lying in a charger corresponded with the body of Christ sacrificed on the altar; this, in turn, is represented at the Feast of Corpus Christi. Richard, whose recent settlement in the north of England had brought him into contact with many of the religious traditions that are celebrated in that region, had begun to explore and fully express his own spiritual beliefs. The Corpus Christi would provide yet another focus for Richard's devotion; indeed, he and Duchess Anne had almost certainly begun to attend the mystery plays for which the city of York was particularly famous. As such, it is not impossible that Richard, disappointed though he was with the peace, eventually came to accept it because he became convinced that it was divinely ordained. This, in turn, was indicated by the accounts of those who had seen the white pigeon which had come to rest on the tent of King Edward.

Spiritually, then, the peace was acceptable to Richard because it could be seen as having been ordained by God. Politically, however, it was a different story. It is possible that, at this time, a darker note began to creep into the relationship between Richard and his brother. Specifically, it is possible that Edward's actions forced Richard to reassess his opinion of him as the rightful heir, not only to the throne of England, but also to the House of York.[12]

During the Earl of Warwick's rebellion, the intention had been to declare Edward a bastard and replace him on the throne with his brother, George of Clarence. Now stories had once more begun to circulate in which Edward's legitimacy was called into question. Commines relates an anecdote in which Louis de Creville, servant to the Constable of France, recreates a mocking display given by the Duke of Burgundy, who:

> Stamped his foot, swore by St George, called the King of England Blancborgne, the son of an archer who bore his name, with as many invectives besides, as could possibly be used against any man. The king [Louis XI] pretended to be highly pleased at the relation, and desired him to tell it over again, and to raise his voice, for of late he had grown a little deaf; De Creville was not backward, but began again, and acted it to the life.[13]

Had Duke Charles indeed made such an allegation about his brother-in-law in front of the French? Is so, his motives for doing so are unclear. It might simply have been an unthinking expression of his anger. Certainly, he had greeted the Anglo-French treaty with understandable fury. It is his violent reaction to the news that is related here. Still, it cannot be denied that his own conduct towards Edward was a contributing factor in driving the English king into Louis's arms; the worsening weather, the uncomfortable conditions in which they were forced to live and lack of cash among the English troops did not help matters.

On the other hand, Edward was Charles's brother-in-law; he should have fulfilled his promise and supported him no matter what the cost to himself or his troops. Charles had flown into a rage at Edward's betrayal. Going before the entire English council and speaking in their own language in order to emphasise his point, he confronted Edward with the memory of all the English kings before him who had invaded France, how they had 'spared no pains, nor declined any danger, that might render them famous, and gain them immortal honour and renown abroad.'[14] Still seething with anger Charles removed himself from Edward's presence and returned to Luxemburg. Commines notes that 'the King of England and his council were extremely displeased with his language, but others who were adverse to the peace highly extolled it.' Was Richard one of those who had highly extolled the Duke's angry words? Did he now come to think that, perhaps, Warwick and Clarence had been right, that Edward was not a legitimate son of the Duke of York? Whatever his doubts on the subject, he kept them to himself.

Later, as he travelled homeward, if he had cast his mind over the events that had just taken place, Richard might just have marvelled at how the sun had lost some of its splendour. Richard had gone to France in fulfilment of a plea for assistance by his brother-in-law, Duke Charles. Edward had apparently answered this plea, but had quickly shown himself to be more inclined to comfort and ease than to the hardships of a military campaign. Richard had also wanted to answer the pleas of Sir John Fastolf, expressed in the work of his secretary, William Worcester, and restore the glory in which England had been bathed following the victory at Agincourt. For Richard personally, the importance of this battle lay in the fact that his great uncle had fallen there. However, it had a political significance that Richard could not ignore: it was the last great victory of the English on French soil. Agincourt had been a momentous occasion, and one that English kings would long use as the yardstick for valour and chivalry. However, it had been a Lancastrian victory. The current campaign would have brought glory to the House of York.

The French expedition had offered Richard the chance to achieve all this, but also to cover himself with glory while making the name of King Edward shine. Still more importantly, it offered him the chance to emulate his father's military achievements in France. For Richard the soldier, the Treaty of Picquigny was tantamount to a humiliating defeat.

His father dead, Richard had turned instead to Edward, whom he held as a paternal figure, a hero and an idol. Edward's kingship was divinely ordained. The vision Edward had seen in the sky as he went into battle at Mortimer's Cross, the sun in splendour, was like the Star of Bethlehem. Edward's epiphany was greeted with almost messianic fervour. It had been supported by prophecy. The treaty that he had signed on the bridge at Picquigny also appeared to have been supported by divine will, yet for all that, it had heralded a transformation in the way in which Richard viewed Edward. For Richard, Edward had been a bright light at the centre of his world; now he was learning that the brighter the light, the deeper the shadows. Perhaps Edward's ready acceptance of King Louis's terms had received the blessing of God the Father, but what of Edward's obligation to father the god? What of the Duke of York?

If Mortimer's Cross had been Edward's zenith, Picquigny was his nadir, not only in the hearts of his people but also, especially, in the eyes of his youngest brother. For Richard, it represented a betrayal of his father's memory and an insult to the sacrifice he had made at Wakefield. It diminished all that the Duke of York had stood for in France, all that chivalry represented. Only months before Richard was born his father had written to the city of Gloucester lamenting the loss of the English possessions in France:

> What praise, lordship, honour and manhood was ascribed by all nations to people of this realm while the king, our sovereign lord possessed the realms of France and Normandy, and what derogation, loss of merchandise and destruction and villainy reported to the English nation from the loss of the same.[15]

How poignant those words were now, when Edward had allowed himself to be bribed, bought and ridiculed by the French. Then there was the question of Edward's legitimacy. This had been raised by their own mother, Cecily, Duchess of York, as she received the news of Edward's marriage to Elizabeth Wydeville. It had arisen again on another occasion, this time by the Earl of Warwick and the Duke of Clarence at the point of their rebellion. It is not known how Richard treated such talk as this, whether or not he believed it. However, now their own brother-in-law, Charles, Duke of Burgundy, had raised the matter in the most humiliating and disrespectful way. Even Richard must have begun to have doubts; even he, loyal though he was, must have begun to wonder if there was not something in it. For Edward was not acting like the true son and heir to Richard, Duke of York. Richard knew that his father would never have turned his back on those who had requested his help. He would not have sold his integrity, his country's prestige and the pride of his men for a pension that, although generous, still mounted to nothing more than thirty pieces of silver. Edward had betrayed their father's memory and his honour. It is at this point that Richard realised the devastating truth: his idol had feet of clay. Richard's homecoming was not a happy one.

The Literature of Hate

But it was not only each epoch that found its reflection in Jesus; each individual created Him in accordance with his own character. There is no historical task which so reveals a man's true self as the writing of a Life of Jesus. No vital force comes into the figure unless a man breathes into it all the hate or all the love of which he is capable. The stronger the love, or the stronger the hate, the more life-like is the figure which is produced. For hate as well as love can write a Life of Jesus, and the greatest of them are written with hate…[1]

Albert Schweitzer wrote these words at the beginning of his exploration of scholarly research into the life of the historical Jesus. Schweitzer was pessimistic about the success of such research. He felt that each scholar's assessment of Jesus would be too heavily influenced by that which he or she brought to the study. Therefore, an interpretation of Jesus could be, and often was, affected by the social, political or religious conditions under which the scholar lived and worked.

This same phenomenon can also apply to studies of other figures, and it is found equally whether the subject falls within the province of the biblical scholar or the historian. This is all the more true when the person in question is capable of inspiring extremes of emotion in those who would study them. One such person is King Richard III. As historians divide themselves onto one side or the other, defining themselves as traditionalists, by definition the senior of the two sides, or revisionists, quite well established by now, but still with some catching up to do, it is easy to forget the one person who has become lost in the midst of battle: King Richard III.

For traditionalists, Richard was a hideous monster, a multiple murderer, a demon deformed in mind, body and soul. For revisionists, or Ricardians as they are sometimes known, he was nothing of the sort; indeed, for some, he was all but a saint. Herein lies the problem. The real Richard was neither demon nor saint; he was a man who lived out his life against the bloody backdrop of fifteenth-century England; he had to live according to the times and the place into which he was born.

In considering Richard, it is all too easy to take one view of him and put it forward as the correct one. After all, who would eulogise Richard in such glowing terms as those of Pierre Carmeliano, if it were not true?

> If we look first of all for religious devotion, which of our Princes shows a more genuine piety? If for justice, who can we reckon above him throughout the world? If we contemplate the prudence of his service, both in peace, and in waging war, who shall we judge his equal? If we look for truth of soul, for wisdom, for loftiness of mind united with modesty, who stands before our King Richard? What Emperor or Prince can be compared with him in good works or munificence?[2]

Yet, the best known, or the best remembered, attempts to sketch Richard's character were written by those who, like the scholars spoken of by Albert Schweitzer, approached their subject with hate. The traditionalist view of Richard began very early, during his own reign, in fact. Within months of his taking the throne, the view of him as a usurper, as a deeply unpopular king and the murderer of his two nephews had already appeared in print. It reached its fullest flowering under the guiding hand of William Shakespeare. In this portrait of the King, which is by far the most famous, Richard planned and plotted his way to the throne, successively and successfully removing those in his way by wicked acts of bloody murder. None were safe as Richard tore along his relentless path towards the crown: the Lancastrian king, King Henry VI; the Lancastrian successor, Edward of Lancaster; Richard's own brother, George, Duke of Clarence; his nephews, Edward, Prince of Wales and Richard, fourth Duke of York; and his wife, Anne Nevill, all fall as sacrificial lambs on the altar of Richard's vaulting ambition.

Richard's earliest historians were John Rous, Dominic Mancini and the anonymous continuator of the chronicle of the Abbey of Croyland, referred to here as the Croyland Continuator. John Rous, who was contemporary to Richard, was the 'official' chronicler of the Beauchamp and Nevill Earls of Warwick. Rous noted that the ascendant, or rising sign, in Richard's horoscope was Scorpio. This provided Rous with a useful metaphor by which he was able to say that, like the scorpion, Richard presented a smooth front but a deadly tail. This negative view of Richard continued with Dominic Mancini, who wrote the story of his accession in a work entitled *De Occupatione Regni Anglie per Riccardum Tercium*. This title is uniformly translated as *The Usurpation of Richard the Third*, although *occupatione* does not necessarily translate as 'usurpation', it can mean 'occupation', as Mancini used it, or simply 'taking', without the negative connotations. Mancini portrays Richard as a dissimulator, impenetrable. He interprets Richard's journey to the throne as having been calculated, each twist on the path carefully manipulated, every obstacle swiftly and deftly demolished. Contemporary with Rous and Mancini is the Croyland Continuator, who describes Richard as the Antichrist or at the very least his instrument. He disapproves of Richard's sensuality, his spending and his behaviour in general.

Later historians were no less unkind. The humanist scholar, Polydore Vergil, agreed with the Croyland Continuator's assessment of Richard as the Antichrist or his agent. To this he adds, in agreement with Mancini, Richard's penchant for dissimulation. Vergil's account attempts to present a character-assessment of Richard from a psychological point of view, in which he explores the motives behind the King's actions. Thomas More's unfinished *History of King Richard III* depicts the eponymous anti-hero quite simply as a pitiless villain and the personification of tyranny. Such conclusions prevail in spite of the fact that, in the opinions of Mancini, Vergil and More, Richard is inscrutable, a closed book.

Although some of these writers are contemporary to Richard, their testimony should be no more trusted simply on that basis. Like the biblical scholars who sought to present a study of Jesus, all were influenced by the times in which they lived. Their experiences, their circumstances and those with whom they associated all had a bearing on how they viewed and recorded the events of which they give account and the people who influenced them.

Dominic Mancini was resident in London during the frenetic three months between the death of King Edward IV and the accession of King Richard III. He had been sent to England by Angelo Cato, an astrologer and physician who, at the time of Mancini's writing, was court physician to King Louis XI of France. King Louis had already tried but failed to remove the Yorkist régime from power, having supplied ships, money and men to the Earl of Warwick and the Duke of Clarence in 1471. His efforts were to be better rewarded in 1485 when he helped Henry Tudor in his invasion of England. Moreover, Louis disliked Richard because, while still Duke of Gloucester,

Richard was seen to have disapproved of Edward's capitulation to French bribery in 1475. Richard, whose chivalric idealism probably extended to dreams of reliving the glories of Agincourt, was determined to regain the English territories lost to France during the Hundred Years War; this was, of course, something that King Edward IV had conspicuously failed to do. Mancini's close connection to the French court should warn us not to look upon *The Usurpation of Richard III* as an entirely unbiased account.

While Mancini was able to give detailed accounts of Edward IV and Edward V, he was unable do so in Richard's case. However, since King Edward V was at Ludlow for most of the period of his stay, Mancini could only have taken his information from those who knew him, most notably John Argentine, the physician who attended the young king in the Tower. This was also true in the case of Richard Gloucester. This course of action did not produce the best results. To take one example, Mancini, or his sources, mistakenly place Richard in Gloucester at the time of King Edward's death. In fact, Richard was in Yorkshire, probably at Middleham, when the event occurred. Mancini's mistake tells us two things. First, he thought that English princes lived on the estates from which they took their titles. This is understandable, since that is what happened in France, a country Mancini knew better than he did England. Secondly, it shows that neither he nor his informants were aware of Richard's whereabouts. This suggests that Richard was of little interest to those living in London, even though he did occasionally come to court. Mancini would have found it difficult to find any reliable information about Richard because so few people actually knew him; moreover, Mancini had probably never even had an opportunity to observe Richard first hand. This is a great misfortune since it deprived him of a chance to offer a pen-portrait of the King, which would have been of great interest to historians. Mancini left England shortly after Richard's accession. His memoir was written at Beaugency, where the young King Charles VIII and his court were staying, during November to December 1483.

The Croyland Continuator produced a fascinating document without which the content of Richard's Act of settlement, or *Titulus Regius*, might have been lost to history. It is generally, although not universally, accepted that the third continuation of the *Croyland Chronicle* was written by John Russell, an abbot at Croyland Abbey (now more usually written as Crowland Abbey), or perhaps a member of his entourage who recorded his master's version of events. Another candidate is Doctor Henry Sharp, a Protonotary of Chancery, diplomat and Doctor of Civil Law.[3] He was a close associate of John Russell, with whom he shared several diplomatic missions. Unlike

Russell, Sharp was often in the right place at the right time, one example being the period between the battle of Barnet and the defeat of the Bastard of Fauconberg, and so was in a position personally to witness these events. The fact remains, however, that unless some new evidence is discovered the third continuation should be considered anonymous and that the identity of its author will probably never be known.

The third continuation of the chronicle of Croyland Abbey covers the period from 1460 until April 1486, the point at which it was written, just nine months after the King's death. Its hostility towards Richard, which is certainly genuine in parts, nevertheless does not escape being influenced by the fact that its author was living under the fledgling Tudor régime. Also significant is the fact that the author was the near neighbour of Lady Margaret Beaufort. Lady Margaret's family owned the manor of Deeping, which bordered onto lands belonging to Croyland Abbey, at which she was a lay sister. As the mother of Henry Tudor, Margaret was a natural enemy of Richard's. John Russell, the favoured candidate as author, had been appointed Lord Chancellor in May 1483 by Edward V's council, which included Richard as protector, but he had never enjoyed Richard's confidence. As a partisan of the House of Lancaster, he disapproved of many of Richard's actions. Again, this is a less than impartial source.

John Rous, for whom Richard was the Antichrist, in fact offers two portraits of the King. In *The Rous Roll*, written prior to 1483, and therefore while Richard was still Duke of Gloucester, he is complementary. However, it is his *History of the Kings of England* in which we encounter the full force of Rous' malice towards Richard. This work was originally intended to provide King Edward IV with information about kings and prelates whom Edward might consider worthy of commemorative statues in St George's Chapel, Windsor. The work, however, was not completed until 1486, at which point both Edward IV and Richard III were dead and King Henry VII, to whom it was now dedicated, occupied the throne. Rous' attack on Richard is scathing. A reed shaken by the wind, Rous clearly wrote to gratify the expectations of whatever régime he found himself living under.

The same, incidentally, can be said of Pietro Carmeliano, a man of letters from Brescia in Lombardy, whose passionate praise of Richard is quoted above. Within a year of Richard's death, Carmeliano celebrated the birth of Henry's son, Prince Arthur, by writing another poem about Richard. Now, the last Yorkist king is depicted as a tyrant who had been responsible for the murders of Henry VI and the sons of Edward IV, the Princes in the Tower. It is not insignificant that Carmeliano was by this time Latin secretary and chaplain to King Henry VII, from whom he received a pension.

Of course it could be argued that those authors who praised Richard during his lifetime only to vilify him after his death did so out of fear. All the nice things they had said about Richard were merely the result of their belief that if Richard found out what they really thought about him he would cast them into the Tower and do them to death as he had done with others. However, this is to accept that Richard was every bit as wicked as these very historians, and others, say he was. It is to accept the misinformation that they have so successfully woven into Richard's story and which is of a genius that cannot be denied.

The next work to comment upon Richard, chronologically speaking, is that of Philippe de Commines. Written for the same man to whom Mancini's work was dedicated, Angelo Cato, we are immediately put on our guard with respect to the author's partiality. Commines was, like Rous and Carmeliano, somewhat flexible in his loyalties. He was taken into the confidence of Charles the Bold only to betray that confidence to King Louis XI. In spite of this, Commines was to remain in the service of Duke Charles until 1472, when he suddenly and finally abandoned him in favour of the French king. A confidant and diplomatic agent to Louis XI, who amply rewarded him for his services and his fidelity, Commines witnessed many of the important events of the period in which he lived, including the famous meeting between King Louis and King Edward VI on the bridge at Picquigny, near Amiens. Although he wrote about certain aspects of English affairs, it is doubtful that he ever set foot in England; indeed, the closest he came was Calais, which was English territory at the time. Much of what he had to say about King Richard III was taken from Henry Tudor, Earl of Richmond, and other Lancastrian exiles, whose partiality he simply adopted.

Polydore Vergil was a cleric from Urbino in Italy. He was a humanist scholar of some renown who travelled in the same circles as Sir Thomas More and Erasmus. He had lived in England for five years before being commissioned by King Henry VII to write a history of England, a fact that refutes the theory that he was hand-picked and imported into the country especially to write Tudor propaganda. On the other hand, he was not in a position to forget to whom he owed his livelihood and, ultimately, his freedom. In his account of Richard's reign as it appears in *Anglica Historia*, there is a strong bias in favour of the Tudor perspective, and much of the negative opinion that has clouded Ricardian scholarship can be traced to this work.

As he researched his history, Vergil probably had access to the diplomatic papers of his patron, Adriano Castelli, as well as one or more of the London chronicles, one of which was that of Robert Fabyan. Writing only slightly earlier than Vergil, Fabyan was a London draper, alderman of the City of London and, in 1493, sheriff. He is responsible for *The New Chronicles of England and France*, while another chronicle, *The Great Chronicle* has been attributed to him. These works are probably redactions of several sources, or perhaps a single source, that began contemporaneously with the events they describe only for further additions to be made as time wore on.

A strong case can also be made for Polydore Vergil's use of a version of the third continuation of the *Croyland Chronicle*. However, the most important of Vergil's sources is the eye-witness testimony of people who remembered the Yorkist period and who, perhaps, had been actively involved in events. Such people might include Bishop Richard Foxe, statesman and founder of Corpus Christi College, Oxford. Foxe, a trusted administrator to Henry VII, was responsible for, among other duties, arranging the marriage between Prince Arthur and Catherine of Aragon. Reginald Bray is another possible source. He was steward to Lady Margaret Beaufort, for whom he acted as an intermediary in the conspiracy between his mistress, the Duke of Buckingham and Bishop Morton. This culminated in the rebellion led by Buckingham against Richard in the autumn of 1483. Henry Tudor made Bray knight banneret at Bosworth, a Knight of the Bath at his coronation and, later, elected him a Knight of the Garter. Bray served King Henry mainly in financial administration, and acted as a member of parliament on several occasions.[4] A third informant could have been Christopher Urswick, a priest and an agent of Lady Margaret Beaufort. He held positions as a courtier, diplomat and almoner to King Henry, whose coronation he attended.

Second-hand testimony should also be allowed for, such as might be had from friends of the archbishop Thomas Rotherham. Significantly, the archbishop was among those present at the notorious meeting in the Tower on 13 June 1483 from which William, Lord Hastings was dragged to his impromptu execution.

Vergil, who applies the principles and methods of the historian to his work, shows an awareness of conflicting accounts and an ability to distinguish fact from fiction. Nevertheless, he is not averse to presenting some fiction as historical testimony or to inventing details where his sources fail him. One of his more interesting foibles was to destroy his sources, especially those that did not support his conclusions. Vergil's sources and the circles in which he moved ensured that his account of King Richard would follow the partial view promoted by the Tudors.

Sir Thomas More's career as lawyer, scholar, writer, MP and chancellor spanned the reigns of both Henry VII and Henry VIII. His hostility towards Richard was informed, in part, by his sources. Among these are to be counted his father, John More, as well as those men used by Vergil, such as Christopher Urswick and Bishop Foxe; Reginald Bray died in 1503, long before More began work on his book.

Perhaps the most significant of More's oral sources was Archbishop John Morton, in whose household More lived as a boy in much the same capacity as Richard had in that of the Earl of Warwick. Morton, born in 1420, was witness to many of the significant events of the fifteenth century and especially those surrounding Richard's accession and subsequent reign. However, there are certain events Morton did not witness, such as the encounter between Edward V and Richard Gloucester at Stony Stratford, Dr Ralph Shaa's sermon at Old St Paul's, Buckingham's speeches at the Guildhall and Baynard's Castle and the punishment Richard meted out to his brother's former mistress, Jane Shore.[5]

More also had access to various written sources, many of which, again, were hostile towards Richard. One such work was, of course, that of his friend and fellow-humanist Polydore Vergil, either in its completed form or perhaps in draft. Also available were Fabyan's *The New Chronicles of England and France*, and *The Great Chronicle*. Another source was Henry VII's first official historian, Bernard André, whose *Historia Regis Henrici Septimi* was written in about 1502. Prior to these works, and possibly having some bearing on their approach, were those of John Rous and Pietro Carmeliano, both of whom have been noted.

In addition to his own oral and written sources, More might have used legal documents from Richard's reign to which, as an under-sheriff, he would certainly have had access. These would include Buckingham's Guildhall speech and Richard III's Act of Settlement of 1484. However, More also exploited literary and classical models, the most important of which were the *Annals* of Tacitus and the mystery cycles performed at Corpus Christi.[6] Certainly there is more than a touch of the morality tale in the work of this saintly man.

Thomas More, then, used a variety of sources and traditions as well as providing some original input as he worked on his *History of King Richard III*. However, his association with Polydore Vergil should not be underestimated since it is a significant factor in understanding the *History*. Vergil had written a history of England, but his handling and interpretation of his sources often undermined his integrity as a historian. More's relationship with Vergil was one of fellow intellects moving within the same circles, and whose philosophy and approach both influenced and challenged those of their contemporaries. However, there was no small degree of mocking rivalry between the two men when it came to the subject of history.

Notwithstanding this, More's *History of King Richard III* is equally lacking as an historical work. Horace Walpole, whose polemic, *Historic Doubts on the Life and Reign of Richard the Third*, is intended as much to discredit Thomas More as it is to defend King Richard, said of it:

> [More] took up a paltry canvas and embroidered it with a flowing design as his imagination suggested the colours. I should deal more severely with his respected memory on any other hypothesis. He has been guilty of such palpable and material falsehoods, as, while they destroy his credit as an historian, would reproach his veracity as a man, if we could impute them to premeditated perversion of truth, and not to youthful levity and inaccuracy. Standing as they do, the sole groundwork of that reign's history, I am authorized to pronounce the work, invention and romance.[7]

Perhaps, but this is to miss Sir Thomas's point. The *History of King Richard III* is a masterpiece of sardonic wit and drama in which More satirises not only himself, particularly as he describes Richard's lop-sided appearance, but also his friend, Vergil's, treatment of recent events. As someone who had incurred the wrath of Henry VII, for which misdemeanour his father had paid with imprisonment, More might have intended to offer a show of contempt for those in authority and, it being too dangerous to direct his spectacular wit at the reigning monarch, his target was the safe and, from the Tudor perspective, more deserving, Richard III. Unfortunately, while many have been capable of writing satire, and in this More was a past master, their number is clearly not equalled by those able to recognise or comprehend it. More's work was destined to be treated as history by everyone except its author, and it continues to be so to the present day.

One of those who took More at his word, but missed his meaning, is Edward Hall. A lawyer and historian, who was occasionally elected to serve in the House of Commons, Hall was born in 1497, twelve years after the death of Richard III. His historical work, *The Union of the Two Noble and Illustre Famelies of Lancastre and Yorke* is better known today as *Hall's Chronicle*. Unfinished at his death, Hall bequeathed the work to his publisher, the historian Richard Grafton, who undertook to complete it. The part concerned with the reign of Richard III is, however, Hall's own work. His influences include Vergil's *Anglica historica* and the London chronicles. For certain sections concerning Richard III he used Thomas More as his source. Hall also had at his disposal works that are no longer available to us, as well as the oral testimony of those who still remembered the days of King Richard III. Hall set out his history in a narrative style rather than as a chronological record of events. His sources were critically evaluated and, taking a human-ist approach, he was careful to take account of political causes rather than merely adopting the methods used by many, particularly the monastic histo-rian, of searching for divine intervention in the lives of humankind.

Ralph, or Raphael Holinshead is described by Jeremy Potter as 'the next transmitter of the virus, the last link in the chain between Richard's enemies and William Shakespeare, the spell-binder who exercised his magic on the hotch-potch of rumours, gossip and anecdote which passed for history in that unscientific age'.[8] Holinshead was possibly a Cheshire man and, as such, hailed from a part of the country that had been held by the Stanley family. The Stanleys, of course, had been enemies of Richard. They had taken Henry Tudor's side when they eventually decided to join in the battle at Bosworth Field. Holinshead was educated at Cambridge and he based his history on Hall's *Chronicles*. An enlarged second edition appeared after his death, which was probably edited or, as Potter has it, 'extensively mutilated', by Queen Elizabeth I's censorious privy council. This new version was made to highlight still further the evil doings of Richard III. Moreover, it was this second edition that was owned by William Shakespeare, and which informed part of the narrative for his play, *The Tragedy of King Richard III*.

Now we have come full circle. William Shakespeare, one of England's greatest treasures, drew his ideas and inspiration from a great many sources, historical, traditional and folkloric. He drew heavily from Hall and Holinshead via More to create a delightfully comic character whose genius is comparable only to his incredibility. Every evil finds its place in the heart of the Bard's villain, who murders his way through his family and friends, smiling as he does so.

Most of Richard's early historians were, therefore, hostile towards the King. Those who were not changed their minds following Richard's death. It is important to note that a significant majority of them were writing under the upstart Tudor régime, whose kings were very sensitive to the fact that they had no true claim to the throne. This awareness manifested itself in insecurity and suspicion and led to the disparagement of the last Yorkist king, Richard III. It also ensured the continued persecution of those who had close ties or associations with the House of York, whose members were still being executed long into the reign of Henry VIII. Shakespeare lived in the Elizabethan reign, which was no less hostile towards Richard than had been the previous régime, the traditions of which had carried over and were nurtured for the same reasons.

Yet, not every chronicler and historian who showed hostility towards Richard was the subject of the Tudor monarchs. The first historian who could be considered as being truly Tudor was Polydore Vergil. Here, then, is the starting point of Tudor 'propaganda' as it is usually referred to by Ricardians. More, Hall, Holinshead and Shakespeare continued a view of Richard that had now become accepted as beyond doubt. Richard III was a tyrant, a ruthless king whose path to the throne was made slick with the blood of his victims and who abused his power once he had achieved his objective. Richard was deformed. He was hideous, sinister, evil.

Prior to Vergil, More and those who followed them were Mancini, Commines, Rous and the Croyland Continuator. The first two of these were not even English. Mancini was Italian and, although he had gathered what information he could during his stay in London, he was no longer living in England when he wrote *The Usurpation of Richard III*. Commines lived in France and had never even been to England, yet his depiction of Richard as given in the *Mémoires* is entirely uncomplimentary.

A driving force must be found to account for the hostility of historians and chroniclers of Richard III who were writing prior to the Tudor period, one that is just as strong and every bit as successful as the Tudor dogma. This second driving force is a marked regional bias of the south of England against the north.

Southern hostility towards the people of the north did not originate during Richard's reign, of course. It was apparent, for instance, in the letter by Clement Paston, to his brother, John, dated 23 January 1461. Here, he states that 'the pepill in the northe robbe and styll, and ben apoyntyd to pill all thys cwntre [country], and gyffe a way menys goods and lufflods in all the sowthe cwntry.'[9] Similarly, Queen Marguerite made an unsuccessful attempt to enter London later that same year at the head of an army made up of mainly northern men.

Most of Richard's earliest chroniclers and historians were southern English or lived in the south. John Rous, the antiquary, scholar and graduate of Oxford was a chantry priest at Guy's Cliff, just outside Warwick. Whatever loyalty Rous felt towards Richard resulted only from the King's marriage to Anne Nevill, the daughter of Richard Nevill, Earl of Warwick, whose family history he wrote. The Croyland Continuator, whose close connections with Margaret Beaufort, the mother of King Henry VII, have already been noted, showed himself to be deeply prejudiced against the people of the north: 'but immediately after Easter, a sedition was set on foot by these ingrates in the North, whence every evil takes its rise ... '[10] is but one example of many. Polydore Vergil, although born in Italy, made his home in the south of England, where he came to the notice of the court and formed friendships with Sir Thomas More and others. Vergil became a naturalised

Englishman in 1510. Sir Thomas More, was, of course, a Londoner, having been born in Milk Street in Cripplegate, close to the birthplace of his name-sake and fellow-saint, Thomas Becket. The London Chronicles of Robert Fabyan and others naturally originated in London.

Not all chroniclers and historians were southern, of course; there were exceptions. Primary among these is John Warkworth, an ecclesiastic and college head who is believed to have hailed from the Durham diocese, and who took his name from the village of Warkworth in Northumberland.[11] The chronicle attributed to him covers the years 1461-1474 and shows a pro-northern bias. Although written in about 1484, Warkworth's *Chronicle* does not include material relating to Richard's accession, which might have made an interesting appendix, nor does it speak of the crimes allegedly committed by the King in order to succeed his brother. This is somewhat surprising considering Warkworth had much reason to be hostile towards Richard. He was one of the thirteen feoffees to whom Elizabeth Howard, countess of Oxford, had entrusted her lands. Warkworth, with six others, opposed the turning over of these lands to Richard, who was then still Duke of Gloucester. Richard was forced to bring a suit against them, which was successful. Given his altercation with the King, Warkworth would have been forgiven had he taken the opportunity of endorsing the view of Richard dis-seminated by those who were most hostile towards him. That he did not is surely significant.

Then there are Mancini and Commines, neither of whom were south-ern English. Mancini, as we have seen, had relied upon people who did not know Richard for his information. His prejudice was really their prejudice. Commines wrote books one to six of his *Mémoires*, between 1488 and 1494, while books seven and eight were written between 1497 and 1501; those concerning the period of Richard's activities were books three and four. He indicates that he knew the Earl of Richmond, who had become Henry VII by that time, personally and that he got some of his information from him. This is hardly an impartial account. Other informants were Lancastrian supporters, many of whom had lived in the south of England and had left their homes when Richard came to power. Indeed, some had gone into exile in Brittany and had formed a clique surrounding Henry Tudor.

It is not difficult to understand how Richard had become caught in the crossfire of differing opinion from opposite ends of the country. Richard, although not northern by birth, had been adopted into northern society, where he was 'entireley loved and highly favoured' according to Edward Hall.[12] Polydore Vergil, speaking of Henry VII's first visit to York in the spring of 1486, notes that Henry 'did not know whence he could gather a reliable force in a town so little devoted to his interests, which hitherto had cherished the name of Richard'[13]. Certainly, Richard's kindly and effectual patronage of the city of York was a form of 'bastard' feudalism, but in which the client was a city or corporation rather than an individual. He asked for and received military assistance several times during his short reign, although this was not always gladly given.

Richard's influence, not only in York, but in the North Country as a whole, had several points of origin. First, there was his wealth, which came from estates that were his by inheritance as well as those that had come to him by royal grant. Another factor was his status as King's lieutenant and political heir to the Earl of Warwick. Finally there was the affinity he had managed to establish in the north. This resulted from his success in patching up the long-standing quarrel between the two branches of the Nevill family, as well as his coming to an agreement with Henry Percy, Earl of Northumberland. His power, however, while undoubtedly earned, came ultimately from the people of the north and he held onto it because the people allowed him to. It is true to say that Richard would not have been able to take the throne without the backing of his northern affinity and his kingship largely depended on his northern supporters as well.

This is the heart of the problem. It was less to do with the prejudice of the people of the south against those of the north. Rather, it was concerned with Richard's placing his northern followers in positions of power following the rebellion led by the Duke of Buckingham in the autumn of 1483. This had brought home to Richard just how vulnerable his position was in the south. As such, he attainted many of those who had joined in the rebellion against him. These forfeitures:

> He distributed among his northern adherents, whom he planted in every spot throughout his dominions, to the disgrace and lasting and loudly expressed sorrow of all the people in the south, who daily longed more and more for the hoped-for return of their ancient rulers, rather than the present tyranny of these people.[14]

The 'ancient rulers' of the people were those of noble blood who had been executed and attainted for their part in Buckingham's rebellion. By planting northern men into the south of England, Richard had acted as a tyrant because he had acted undemocratically. In other words, he had acted against the will and consent of the people. This was bound up with the rights of their 'ancient rulers' over which Richard had ridden rough shod; Richard had upset the natural order of things and this was unforgivable, hence the accusation of tyranny. By acting as he did, he had left himself open to the hostility of the southern people.

However, it was also Richard's misfortune that he was the last of his line. He left no heir to continue the House of York so that, when he died, the governance of his kingdom passed into the care of a new dynasty, the Tudors. Their insecurity, due to their highly tenuous claim to the throne, made it essential for them to establish themselves as the rightful holders of the crown. The vilification of King Richard III began where these two points converged.

This does not mean that we should ignore these sources, dismissing them as untrustworthy. On the contrary, they are still capable of providing much that is of use to the historian in the pursuit of Richard and, as such, are of immense value. It is necessary simply to be cautious, to apply discretion and to ask, for each source consulted, each passage used, why was it written? What purpose did the writer have as he made this statement, that assertion? How does it stand up against other sources dealing with the same topic? Approached in this way, these sources will continue to yield much.

NOTES

REFERENCES

ABBREVIATIONS

CCR – *Calendar of Close Rolls*
CPR – *Calendar of Patent Rolls*
CSP – *Calendar of State Papers*
HMC – *Historical Manuscripts Commission*
TNA – *The National Archives, Kew*

CHAPTER 1: 'RICHARD LIVES YET', 1452

1. A. Hanham, p120
2. Sasha Fenton, p, 23
3. J. Gairdner, *History of the Life and Reign of Richard the Third of England*, p.5
4. S. Turner, *History of England*, pp.443-444
5. *ibid*, p.444, note 43
6. A. Hanham, p.120
7. C. Rawcliffe, p.237
8. Thomas More, *The History of King Richard III*, p.8
9. *Richard III* Act 2, Scene 4, 27-8
10. William Cornwallis, p.3
11. Genesis 21.7; 1 Samuel 1.22
12. Livia Visser-Fuchs, 'What Niclas von Popplau really wrote about Richard III' p.529
13. C.A. Halsted, vol. 1, pp.424-5
14. T.B. Pugh, p.112
15. Agnes Strickland, vol. 3, p.317
16. C.A. Halsted, vol. 1, p.409
17. Nicholas Orme, pp.11, 14-15
18. *Calendar of Papal Letters*, vol.1, p. 263
19. William Habington, p.2.

CHAPTER 2: THE WHITE ROSE THE RED ROSE, 1453

1. *Chronicles of the White Rose of York*, pp.l-li
2. Polydore Vergil, *English History*, p.71
3. Agnes Strickland, vol. 3, p.184
4. *ibid* vol. 3, p.185
5. *Registrum Abbatiae Johannis Whethamstede*, vol. 1, pp.163, 415

6. *1 Henry VI* act 2, scene 4, 27-33
7. *Ingulph's Chronicle of the Abbey of Croyland*, p.506
8. John Ashdown-Hill, 'The Red Rose of Lancaster?', pp.406-420
9. *Letters and Papers Illustrative of the Wars of the English in France*, vol. 1, pp.79-82, 83-6, 160-3, 168-70
10. Michael Evans, p.125
11. John Watts, 'Richard of York, third Duke of York (1411-1460)', *DNB*
12. Michael K. Jones, *Somerset, York and the Wars of the Roses*, p.305
13. Colin Richmond, 'Beaufort, Edmund, first Duke of Somerset (c.1406–1455)', *DNB*
14. J. Stow, pp.666-8
15. C. Rawcliffe, p.237
16. *Rotuli Parliamentorum*, vol. V, p.24
17. *Paston Letters*, vol. 1, p.265
18. *Rotuli Parliamentorum*, vol. V, p.242
19. *CPR, 1452–61*, p.143-4

CHAPTER 3: ON THE BANKS OF THE NENE, 1454-1455

1. H. Ellis, *Original letters*, vol. 1, pp.9-10
2. H.K. Bonnay, p 22
3. *ibid*, p 27
4. *CPR, 1467-77*, p.349
5. J. Chandler, *John Leland's Itinerary*.
6. David Lloyd, *Ludlow Castle: A History and Guide*
7. Brenda Ralph Lewis, pp.74-5

CHAPTER 4: A LA GUERRE, 1455-1459

1. *Paston Letters*, vol. 1, p.315
2. 'Benet's Chronicle', p.211
3. Keith Dockray, *Henry VI, Margaret of Anjou and the Wars of the Roses: A Source Book*, p.56
4 *An English Chronicle of the Reigns of Richard II, Henry IV, Henry V and Henry VI*, pp.79-80
5. *Paston Letters* , vol. 1, p393

CHAPTER 5: AN ATTEMPT ON THE THRONE, 1459-1460

1. C.A. Halsted, vol 1, p.51
2. CPR 1467-77, p.401, 417, 592
3. Anne Sutton and Livia Visser-Fuchs, *Richard III's Books*
4. *Chronicles of the White Rose of York*, pp.5-6
5. *An English Chronicle of the Reigns of Richard II, Henry IV, Henry V and Henry VI*, p.83
6. *Rotuli Parliamentorum*, vol. V, p.349-50
7. 'Gregory's Chronicle', p.206-7
8. C.A. Halsted, vol. 1, p.75
9. D. Seward, p.30

10. *Paston Letters*, vol. 1, pp.525-6
11. Michael Bennett, p.580
12. *Rotuli Parliamentorum*, vol V, p.375
13. *ibid*, p.378
14. *ibid*, p.379
15. *Ingulph's Chronicle of the Abbey of Croyland*, p.421
16. *Three Fifteenth-Century Chronicles*, p.76
17. *CSP Milan*, p.48
18. *Henry VI* part 3; Act 1, Scene 4, 180
19. William Grainge, p.52
20. Edward Hall, *Chronicle*, pp.250-51
21. *Registrum Abbatiae Johannis Whethamstede*, vol. 1, p.382
22. Edward Hall, *Chronicle*, pp.250-51; cf. Worcester, William, *Annales*, p.775; 'Brief Latin Chronicle' (*Three Fifteenth-Century Chronicles*, Camden Society), p.172.
23. Henry Ellis, 'Enumeration and Explanation', pp.226-27

CHAPTER 6: THE SUN IN SPLENDOUR, 1460-1461

1. *Ingulph's Chronicle of the Abbey of Croyland*, p.422
2. *Brut,* vol 2, p.531
3. 'Gregory's Chronicle', p.211
4. Edward Hall, *Chronicle*, p.251
5. *Archaeologia* xxix (1842), p.344
6. *Great Chronicle of London*, p.195
7. C. Weightman, pp.19-20
8. George Buck, p.8
9. A.O. Legge, vol. 1, p.51
10. 'Annales Rerum Anglicarum', p.777
11. 'Gregory's Chronicle'. p.215
12. *Great Chronicle of London*, pp.195-6
13. *Rotuli Parliamentorum*, vol. V, pp.463-7
14. *Plumpton Correspondences*, p.1
15. *Holinshead's Chronicles*, p.277
16. http://www.bradford.ac.uk/archsci/depart/report97/towton.htm.
17. *CSP Milan*, p.67
18. *CSP Milan*, p.7.
19. *CSP Milan*, p.73
20. Jehan de Waurin, p.357
21. J.C. Cooper, *ad loc*

CHAPTER 7: RICHARD GLOUCESTER, 1461-1465

1. Anthony Tuck, 'Thomas, Duke of Gloucester (1355–1397)' *DNB*
2. *CPR 1461-67*, p.66
3. Michael Hicks, *False, Fleeting,* pp.9-10
4. *A Collection of Ordinances and Regulations for the Government of the Royal Household*, pp, 27-8
5. *CPR 1467-77*, p.295-6
6. *CPR 1461-67*, p.308

7. *Chronicle of John Stone*, p.88

8. *CPR 1461-67*, p.52

9. *Paston Letters*, vol.2, p.50

10. *CPR 1461-67*, p.197

11. *CPR 1461-67*, p.387

12. *CPR 1461-67*, p391

13. Anne Sutton and Livia Visser-Fuchs 'Richard III's Books: Ancestry and "True Nobility"', p.346

14. 'Gregory's Chronicle', p.226

15. D. Mancini, p.61

16. Thomas More, *The History of King Richard III*, p.3

17. *Three Books of Polydore Vergil's English History*, p.172

18. D. Mancini, p.65

19. *Three Books of Polydore Vergil's English History*, p.116

20. *Ingulph's Chronicle of the Abbey of Croyland*, p.439-40

21. *Holinshead's Chronicles*, p.283-84

22. D. Mancini, p.61

23. R. Fabyan, p.654

24. Jehan de Waurin, p.455

25. *British Library Harleian Manuscript 433*, vol.3, p.24

26. D. Mancini, pp.61-63.

27. Thomas More, *The History of King Richard III*, p.96

28. D. Mancini p. 63.

29. J. Warkworth, *Chronicle,* pp.3-4

Chapter 8: A Page at Middleham, 1465-1466

1. A.O. Legge, vol. 1, pp.52-53.

2. *Ingulph's Chronicle of the Abbey of Croyland*, p.483

3. John Rous, item 56

4. R. Weiss, p.155

5. John Leland, http://galenet.galegroup.com/servlet/ECCO

6. John Weaver; *Middleham Castle;* C. Peers, *Middleham Castle*

7 *The Household of Edward IV*, pp.126-27

8. *Chronicle of John Hardyng*, p.i

9. A. W. Boardman, *Medieval Soldier* ad loc; Oxford English Dictionary

10. *Holinshead's Chronicles*, p.285

11. A.W. Boardman, *Medieval Soldier* ad loc; Oxford English Dictionary

12. Ramón.Lull, p.14-15

13. *ibid*, pp17-18

14. *ibid,* pp. xli-xlii

Chapter 9: Honi Soit Qui Mal Y Pense, 1466

1. Ramón Lull, pp.57, 63-64

2. *The Tragedy of King Richard III* Act 1, scene.3.246

3. *The Tragedy of King Richard III* Act 1, scene 1, 14-15

4. Agnes Strickland, vol. 3, p.376

5. *Three Books of Polydore Vergil's English History,* pp.226-27

6. J. Gairdner, p.253

7. D. Seward, p. 85
8. Michael Hicks, *Anne Neville*, p109
9. A. Weir, p.33
10. Thomas More, *The History of King Richard III*, p.72
11. *ibid*, p.8
12. R. Davies, p. 221
13. Cecil R Humphery-Smith, (www.britishancestry.org)
14. P. Tudor-Craig, p.92
15. M. Weeks, pp. 11-15; P. Tudor-Craig, p. 80
16. *Three Books of Polydore Vergil's English History*, p.227
17. P.W. Hammond, pp. 5-10
18. P.M. Kendall, p.48
19. J. Dover-Wilson, pp. 563-4; D. Unwin, pp. 1-4
20. Thomas More, *The History of King Richard III*, pp.70-73
21. George Buck, p.79
22. H. Walpole, (1768), p.102
23. Sharon Turner, *Richard III : a Poem*, p.277
24. Jehan de Waurin, p.537
25. *Three Books of Polydore Vergil's English History*, p.226
26. A. Hanham, p.165 n.3
27. James Yonge, 'The Gouernaunce of Prynces' in *Three Prose Versions of the Secreta Secretorum*,   pp.218, 222, 223, 224, 235, 232
28. Charles Feng, www.jyi.org, 2005
29. Dr Nicholas Sanders, cited in Philip W. Sergeant, '*The Life of Anne Boleyn*, p. 27
30. George Wyatt, cited in Philip W. Sergeant, '*The Life of Anne Boleyn*, p. 28
31. B. Branston, pp. 51, 127
32. R.M. Warnicke, pp.761-78, especially p.767
33. D. Loades p.77
34. J.C. Cooper, p.167
35. Francis Sandford, p.163.
36. *ibid*, p.164
37. G. F Beltz, pp. xlii-xlvii

CHAPTER 10: THE KING, THE EARL AND A MARRIAGE, 1467-1468

1. *CSP Milan*, p.117
2. *CSP Milan*, p.131
3. *CSP Milan*, p.119
4. T. Rymer, *Foedera*, XI, p.565
5. *CPS Milan*, p.120
6. *Ingulph's Chronicle of the Abbey of Croyland*, p.444
7. *CCR, 1461-8*, p.456-57
8. Jehan de Waurin, pp.458-59
9. Edward Hall, *Chronicle*, p.271
10. D. Mancini, p.65
11. *CSP Milan* p.122
12. 'Annales rerum anglicarum', p.788
13. *York City Chamberlains' Account Rolls 1396-1500*, p.126
14. *CSP Milan* p.124
15. *CSP Milan*, pp.170-71
16. Edward Hall, *Chronicle*, p.267

17. C. Weightman, pp.43-44
18. *Chronicles of the White Rose of York*, p.20
19. *Paston Letters*, vol.2, p.316
20. J.F. Kirk, p.469
21. *Ingulph's Chronicle of the Abbey of Croyland*, p.457

CHAPTER 11: THE WARWICK REBELLION, 1469-1471

1. J. Warkworth, *Chronicle*, p.6
2. Henry Summerson, 'Robin of Redesdale *DNB*
3. *Ingulph's Chronicle of the Abbey of Croyland*, p.445
4. J. Warkworth, *Chronicle*, p.6
5. *CPR, 1467-77*, p.170
6. J. Calmette and G. Périnelle, p.108; *Pièce Justificative* no.30
7. Michael K. Jones, *Bosworth 1485*, pp.65-71
8. J. Chamberlayne, p.12
9. Augustine Vincent, p.621
10. J. Laynesmith, pp.38-44
11. P.A. Johnson, p.47
12. J. Laynesmith, p.42
13. *CSP Milan*, p.132
14. TNA - KB 9/320; *CPR 1467-1477*, p.128
15. *Rotuli Parliamentorum*, vol. VI, pp.305-7; *CPR 1485-94*, pp.149-50
16. M.A. Hicks, 'Piety and Lineage in the Wars of the Roses' pp. 174, 175
17. J. Warkworth, *Chronicle*, p.6
18. *HMC Various Collections* IV, p.206-7
19. *HMC 78: Hastings*, vol 1, pp.290-91
20. *Paston Letters*, vol.2, p.357
21. *ibid*
22. J. Ashdown-Hill, 'Walsingham in 1469', p.2
23. T. Rymer *Foedera*, XI. 641-2
24. *Chronicle of John Stone*, pp.109-10
25. Mary Dormer Harris, pp.341-42
26. S. Cunningham, pp.12-13
27. *Paston Letters*, vol. 2, p.358
28. Rosemary Horrox, *Richard III: a study of service*, p.78
29. *Collection of Ordinances and Regulations for the Government of the Royal Household*, 98
30. J. Warkworth, *Chronicle*, pp.46-51
31. *ibid*, p.7
32. *CCR*, p.115
33. Michel Hicks, *False, Fleeting,* p.39
34. J. Warkworth, *Chronicle*, p7
35. *CSP Milan*, p.133
36. Philippe de Commines, p.184
37. *Three Books of Polydore Vergil's English History*, p.124
38. *Ingulph's Chronicle of the Abbey of Croyland*, p.458
39. *Paston Letters*, vol. 2, p.389
40. *ibid*, p.390
41. *Three Books of Polydore Vergil's English History*, p.125
42. *CCR* p.102-3

43. Michael K. Jones, 'Richard III and the Stanleys', p.36
44. *CPR 1467-77*, pp.180-1
45. *CPR 1467-77*, 179-80; Charles Ross, *Richard III*, p.16
46. CCR p.138
47. CCR, pp.135-6, 137
48. *Six Town Chronicles*, p.164
49. *Chronicle of the Rebellion in Lincolnshire, 1470*, p.11
50. Michael K Jones, 'Richard III and the Stanleys', p.37
51. *Paston Letters*, vol.2, p.396
52 *Three Books of Polydore Vergil's English History*, p.128
53. CCR, vol. II, p.138
54. *CPR 1467-77*, p. 290
55. T. Rymer, *Foedera* XI, 658-60
56. R.L. Storey., pp.593-615
57. J. Warkworth, *Chronicle*, p.9
58. J. Calmette and G. Périnelle, p.120
59. *Chronicles of the White Rose of York*, p.240
60. CCR, p.100
61. J, Warkworth, *Chronicle*, p.11
62. *Three Books of Polydore Vergil's English History*, p.133
63. Livia Visser-Fuchs, 'Richard was Late', pp.616-19
64. Maaike Lulofs, p.10
65. Philippe de Commines, p.194

CHAPTER 12: KING EDWARD IV, 1471

1. J. Warkworth, *Chronicle*, p.14
2. *ibid*, p.14
3. Jehan de Waurin, pp.641-49
4. *Three Books of Polydore Vergil's English History*, p.141
5. J. Gillingham, p.196
6. *The Great Chronicle of London*, pp.216-17
7. *Society for Army Historical Research* (1968), pp.65-69 (letter pp.66-69)
8. J. Warkworth, *Chronicle*, p.16
9. *ibid*
10. *Historie of the arrivall of Edward IV*, p.20.
11. John Rous, item 57
12. T. Wright, p.280
13. *Ingulph's Chronicle of the Abbey of Croyland*, p.466
14. *Historie of the arrivall of Edward IV*, p.29
15. *Holinshead's Chronicles*, p.319
16. A.H. Smith, part 2, p.67
17. *Historie of the arrivall of Edward IV*, p.30
18. J. Warkworth, *Chronicle*, p.18
19. *Ingulph's Chronicle of the Abbey of Croyland*, p.466
20. *The Great Chronicle of London*, p.218
21. *Three Books of Polydore Vergil's English History*, p.152
22. Agnes Strickland, vol. 3, p.367
23. A.O. Legge, vol.1, p.86
24. H. Walpole, (1968), p.15
25. J. Warkworth, *Chronicle*, p18; cf. *Historie of the arrivall of Edward IV*, pp.30-31

26. *Historie of the arrivall of Edward IV*, p.31

27. *ibid*

28. T. Wright, p.281

29. *Historie of the arrivall of Edward IV*, p.38

30. M. Evans, p136; C. Brewer, p.40

31. J. Warkworth, *Chronicle*, p.21

32. Philippe de Commines, p.201

33. *New Chronicles of England and France*, p. 662

34. *Ingulph's Chronicle of the Abbey of Croyland*, p.468

35. *Three Books of Polydore Vergil's English History*, pp.155-56

36. *ibid*, p.227

37. Cited in Keith Dockray, *Richard III: a reader in history*, p.40-41

38. Thomas More, *The History of King Richard III*, pp.9-10

39. *ibid*, p.9

40. *Chronicle of John Hardyng*, p.460

41. Edward Hall, *Chronicle*, p.303

42. J. Warkworth, *Chronicle*, p.21

43. *The Tragedy of King Richard III*, Act 1, scene 2, 53-59

44. *The Tragedy of King Richard III*, Act 1, scene 2, 31-35

45. Thomas More, *The History of King Richard III*, p.73.

46. *The Tragedy of King Richard III*, Act 3, scene 4, 81

47. Thomas More, *The History of King Richard III*, p.9.

48. Thomas More, *The Workes of Sir Thomas More Knyght*, p.877

49. M. Evans, p.138

50. A.O. Legge, pp.114-15

51. *Historie of the arrivall of Edward IV*, p.38.

52. Cited in C. Brewer, pp.92-93; W.H St John Hope, pp.533-42

53. W.H. St John Hope, p. 537

54. *CSP Milan*, p.157

55. *Rotuli Parliamentorum* vol.V, 466-67

56. Rev. Dr Milles, pp.69-73

57. *Historie of the arrivall of Edward IV*, p.39

58. Jehan de Waurin, p.675

59. *CCR*, p.229-30

60. *CPR 1467-77*, p.288

61. *Paston Letters*, vol. 2, p.14

62. *ibid*, p.17

63. C.L. Kingsford, p.375

64. George Buck, (1977) p.9

65. *Three Books of Polydore Vergil's English History*, p.154

CHAPTER 13: WARWICK'S HEIR, 1471-1472

1. Michael Hicks., *False, Fleeting*, pp.97-100

2. *CPR 1467-77*, p.262

3. George Edward Cokayne, pp.167-68

4. TNA: KB 9/41/38

5. *CPR 1467-77*, p.260, 266

6. C.L. Kingsford, p.378

7. N. Pronay and J Cox, p.132

8. *MS Harl. 543*. fol. 169b in John Stow's handwriting, cited in *Original Letters illustrative*

of English History, pp.34-5

9. A.O. Legge, vol. 1, p.125

10. *Ingulph's Chronicle of the Abbey of Croyland*, p.469

11. Michael Hicks, *Anne Neville*, p.108

12. Agnes Strickland, vol. 3, p.370

13. Michael Hicks, *Anne Neville*, pp.110-11

14. *The Tragedy of King Richard III*, Act 1, Scene 2, 213-14

15. *Ingulphs Chronicle of the Abbey of Croyland*, p.470

16. *Paston Letters*, vol.3, p.38

17. CPR 1467-77, p.330

18. *Chronicles of the White Rose of York*, p.28

19. Charles Ross, *Richard III*, p.29

20. John Leland, pp.293-94

21. I am indebted to Ninya Mikhaila for her help and advice on this subject.

22. George Puttenham, pp.40-43

23. P.D. Clarke, pp.1014-29

24. J.J. Scarisbrick, p.173

25. David Starkey, pp.109, 301, 314

26. M. Barnfield, pp.55-57

27. *Paston Letters*, vol.3, p.39

28. C.A Halsted, vol. 1, pp.264-65

29. *The Parallel*, p.3

30. Hicks, *Anne Neville*, p.156

31. Charles Ross, *Edward IV*, p198

32. M.A Hicks, 'Richard, Duke of Gloucester and the North', p.11

33. See Appendix: The Literature of Hate.

34. M.A Hicks, 'Richard, Duke of Gloucester and the North', p.12

35. A.J. Pollard, *Middleham Connection*, p.5

36. Charles Ross, *Richard III*, pp.48-49

37. Rosemary Horrox, *Richard III: a study of service*, p.222

38. CPR 1467-77, p.338

39. CPR 1467-77, p.344

40. J. Chandler, p.550

41. *The Tragedy of King Richard III*, Act 3, scene 3, 8-13

42. Anne F. Sutton and Livia Visser-Fuchs, with P.W. Hammond, p.2

43. *Rotuli Parliamentorum*, vol. VI, pp.24-25

44. *Plumpton Correspondence*, p.26

45. CCR 1468-1476, pp.259-60

46. M.A. Hicks, 'Richard III's Cartulary in the British Library', p.289

47. *CSP Milan* p.163

CHAPTER 14: ' ... GOOD IN MY BROTHER OF GLOUCESTER'S HANDS', 1473

1. CCR, 1468-1476, pp.302-3

2. *CSP Milan*, p.176

3. J. Calmette and G. Périnelle, p.161

4. J. Warkworth, *Chronicle*, p.25

5. *Plumpton Correspondence*, pp.31-32

6. *Paston Letters*, vol.3, p.92-93

7. Rosemary Horrox, 'Tyrell, Sir James (c.1455–1502)', *DNB*
8. J. Gairdner, p.25
9. A.O. Legge, p.134
10. *Historical Manuscripts Commission, 11ᵗʰ Report*, App. VII, p.95
11. A.J. Pollard, 'St Cuthbert and the Hog', p.111
12. *Rotuli Parliamentorum*, vol. VI, p.71-98
13. *Paston Letters*, vol.3, p.98
14. *ibid*, p.102
15. *ibid*

CHAPTER 15: 'AS IF THE SAID COUNTESS WERE NOW NATURALLY DEAD', 1474

1. *Rotuli Parliamentorum*, vol.VI, pp.131-32
2. N.H. Nicolas, vol.1, pp.xc-xci
3. *CSP Milan* p.178
4. Michael Hicks, *Anne Neville*, pp.157-58
5. *Harl MS 433*, vol. 1.191; *Harl MS 433*, vol. 2.185-86
6. *Rotuli Parliamentorum*, vol. VI, 100
7. *Ingulph's Chronicle of the Abbey of Croyland*, p.470
8..*ibid*
9. *Rotuli Parliamentorum*, vol. VI, 124-25
10. Charles Ross, *Edward IV*, pp.189-91
11. Agnes Strickland, vol. 3, p.370
12. E.B. de Fontblanque, vol. 1, p.549
13. *CCR 1468-1476*, p.365
14. A.J. Pollard, 'St Cuthbert and the Hog', p.113
15. *CPS Milan*, p.174-75
16. Ronald C. Finucane, pp.87, 167
17. Alexander Grant, pp.117-18, 119
18. *CSP Milan*, p.192
19. A.J. Pollard, 'St Cuthbert and the Hog' p.115; Seward, D., p.74

CHAPTER 16: THE SETTING OF THE SUN, 1475

1. *CPR, 1467-77*, pp.485, 549, 556
2. *CSP Milan* p.163
3. *CSP Milan*, pp.193-94
4. *The Great Chronicle of London*, p.223
5. J.C. Cooper, p22
6. J.M. Melhuish, p.7
7. Charles Ross, *Edward IV* p.233
8. Philippe de Commines, vol 1, p.271
9. Philippe de Commines, vol 1, p.275
10. *Holinshead's Chronicles*, p.335
11. Philippe de Commines, p.279
12. Michael K Jones, *Bosworth 1485*, pp.71-72
13. Philippe de Commines, vol 1, pp.265-66

14. *ibid*, p.268
15. J. Hughes, p.271

APPENDIX: THE LITERATURE OF HATE

1. A. Schweitzer, pp.4-5
2. *Oxford Bodleian Laud. Misc. 501*, cited in P. Tudor-Craig, p.41
3. N. Pronay and J. Cox, pp.90-95
4. S.B. Chrimes, p.110
5. A. Hanham, pp.161-166
6. Retha M. Warnicke, pp.761-78
7. H, Walpole, (1986), p.26
8. J. Potter, p.147
9. *Paston Letters*, vol.1, p.541
10. *Ingulph's Chronicle of the Abbey of Croyland*, p.509
11. Edward Donald Kennedy, 'Warkworth, John', *DNB*
12. Edward Hall, *Chronicle,* pp.424-5
13. A.J. Pollard, 'Tyranny of Richard III', p.153
14. *Ingulph's Chronicle of the Abbey of Croyland*, p.496

LIST OF ILLUSTRATIONS

15. Middleham Castle, Wensleydale, North Yorkshire. The home of the Earl of Warwick and the setting for Richard's training as a knight – author's collection.

16. Middleham Castle, Richard's luxurious, palatial home, where he lived as a page and studied under the tutelage of the Earl of Warwick – author's collection.

17. Middleham Castle; the western side of the keep held the great chamber on the upper level and the kitchen beneath. The kitchen contained tanks in the floor in which fish were believed to be kept alive until needed – author's collection.

18. Middleham Castle; a chapel was attached to the eestern side of the Keep. It was entered through an ante-room at the top of the staircase. Although now much ruined, the remainder of the tracery windows can still be seen – author's collection.

19. The battle of Barnet, 14 April 1471 was the first battle in King Edward's campaign to take back his throne. It was Richard's first opportunity to use the fighting skills he had acquired under the Earl of Warwick. He was slightly wounded but acquitted himself well in the field – author's collection.

20. The 'broken sword' portrait. In this sixteenth-century portrait Richard was originally shown to be more deformed than he appears now: the left arm once ended in a stump and the left shoulder was much higher. These deformities match the description of the King by Sir Thomas More, who said that Richard's left shoulder was raised and the left arm was 'werish' – author's collection.

21. The Church of St Mary and All Saints, Fotheringhay, features the royal arms in the centre, with Richard's white boar on the right and the black bull of the Duke of Clarence on the left – author's collection.

22. The Wakefield Tower in the Tower of London. Henry VI was held here following his capture by Edward IV and murdered shortly afterwards – author's collection.

23. The chapel in the Wakefield Tower. Tradition holds that the saintly King Henry VI was murdered here while at prayer – author's collection.

24. King Edward IV is restored following his victories at Barnet and Tewkesbury. The brutal removal of his Lancastrian enemies ensured that he would reign in peace at last – author's collection.

25. Sheriff Hutton Castle, North Yorkshire. Richard acquired this castle and estates as part of his inheritance in right of his wife from the Earl of Warwick – author's collection.

26. Richard II: Richard's nomination of his Mortimer cousins as heirs to his throne was one of the foundations for Richard, Duke of York's eventual claim to the throne. Richard II is an important figure in the Yorkist interpretation of rightful kingship – author's collection.

27. Henry VI: Richard, Duke of York served Henry faithfully, but Henry was frequently ill and York was twice asked to act as protector during the King's incapacity. York was concerned that Henry was surrounded by men who had their own, rather than the King's or the country's best interests at heart – author's collection.

28. Queen Marguerite d'Anjou: queen to Henry VI. She was beautiful, charming, proud and staunch supporter of the Lancastrian cause. She was a formidable foe to the Duke of York as he sought the power he felt was his by right of his position in the succession – author's collection.

29. The marriage of Henry VI and Queen Marguerite d'Anjou: Henry VI is wearing a halo. In time, he will be informally recognised as a saint by, among many others, King Richard III and King Henry VII, who will make the first attempt to secure his canonization. Today the Henry VI Society continues to press for the canonization of this saintly king – author's collection.

30. George, Duke of Clarence, brother to Richard III–author's collection.

31. Philip, Duke of Burgundy, provided shelter for Richard and his brother, George, when they were exiled for their own safety as their eldest brother, Edward, made his bid for the throne – author's collection.

32. King Edward IV; and idealised reproduction depicting his legendary beauty – author's collection.

BIBLIOGRAPHY

A Collection of Ordinances and Regulations for the Government of the Royal Household (Society of Antiquaries, 1790)

An English Chronicle of the Reigns of Richard II, Henry IV, Henry V and Henry VI, ed. J.S. Davies (London: Camden Society, 1856)

Anglica Historia of Polydore Vergil, ed. D. Hay (London: Camden Society, 1950)

'Annales rerum anglicarum' in *Letters and Papers Illustrative of the Wars of the English in France*, ed. J. Stevenson, (Rolls Series, 1864), 2 vols.

Ashdown-Hill, J., 'Walsingham in 1469: The Pilgrimage of Edward IV and Richard, Duke of Gloucester', *The Ricardian* 11 (1997), pp.2-16

Ashdown-Hill, John, 'The Red Rose of Lancaster?' *The Ricardian*, 10 (1996), pp.406-420

Barnfield, M., 'Only if it May Stand with the Law of the Church' *Ricardian Bulletin* Autumn 2006, pp.55-57

Beltz, G. F., *Memorials of the Most Noble Order of the Garter* (London: William Pickering, 1841)

'Benet's Chronicle' in *Camden Miscellany*, ed. Michael Jones (London: Camden Society, 1972)

Bennett, Michael, 'Edward III's entail and the Succession to the Crown, 1376-1471', *English Historical Review*, vol.112, pp.580-609

Boardman, A.W., *The Medieval Soldier in the Wars of the Roses* (Stroud: Sutton Publishing, 1998)

Bonnay, H.K., *Historic Notes in reference to Fotheringhay* (Oundle: printed for T. Bell et al, 1821)

Branston, B., *The Lost Gods of England* (London: Thames & Hudson, 1974)

Brewer, C., *The Death of Kings. A Medical History of the Kings and Queens of England* (London: Abson Books, 2000)

British Library Harleian Manuscript 433 ed. Rosemary and P.W. Hammond (Gloucester: Alan Sutton Publishing Limited for the Richard III Society, 1979-1983), 4 vols.

British Library Harleian Manuscript 543

Brut, or the Chronicles of England, ed. W.D. Brie (London: published for the Early English Text Society, 1908), 2. vols.

Buck, George, *The History of the Life and Reigne of Richard the Third* (Wakefield, Yorkshire: EP Publishing, 1977)

Calendar of Close Rolls, Edward IV, 1468-1476

Calendar of Papal Letters, ed. W.H. Bliss (London: H.M.S.O., 1893), 53 vols.

Calendar of Patent Rolls, Henry VI, 1452–61; Edward IV, 1461-67; Edward IV, Henry VI, 1467-77; Henry VII, 1485-94

Calendar of State Papers and Manuscripts*: Milan vol.1*

Calmette, J. and Périnelle, G. *Louis XI et L'Angleterre* (Paris: Éditions August Picard, 1930)

Chamberlayne, J., *Cecily Neville, Duchess of York, King's Mother: the Roles of an English Medieval Noblewoman, 1415-1495 (Centre for Medieval Studies: York, 1994)*

Chandler, J. John Leland's Itinerary. Travels in Tudor England (Stroud: Alan Sutton, 1993)

Chrimes, S.B., *Henry VII* (London: Eyre Methuen, 1972)

Chronicle of John Hardyng, ed. H. Ellis (London: Printed for F.C. and J. Rivington, et al, 1812)

Chronicle of John Stone, ed. W.G. Searle (Cambridge: Cambridge Antiquarian Society, 1902)

Chronicle of the Rebellion in Lincolnshire, 1470, ed. John Gough (London: Camden Society, 1847)

Chronicles of the White Rose of York, ed. J.A. Giles (London: James Bohn, 1845)

Clarke, P.D., 'English Royal Marriages and the Papal Penitentiary in the Fifteenth Century' *English Historical Review* CXX (2005), pp.1014-29

Collection of Ordinances and Regulations for the Government of the Royal Household (Society of Antiquaries of London, 1790)

Cokayne, George Edward, *Complete Peerage of England, Scotland, Ireland, Great Britain and the United Kingdom: extant, extinct, or dormant* (London: George Bell & Sons, 1895)

Commines, P. de, *The Memoirs of Philip de Commines, Lord of Argenton* (London: Henry G. Bohn, 1855)

Cooper, J.C., *An Illustrated Encyclopaedia of Traditional Symbols* (London: Thames and Hudson, 1978).

Cornwallis, William, *The Encomium of Richard III* (London: Turner & Devereux, 1977)

Cunningham, S., *Richard III: a Royal Enigma* (Kew, Richmond: The National Archives, 2003)

Davies, R., *Extracts form the Municipal Records of the City of York* (London: J.B. Nichols and sons, 1843)

Dockray, Keith, *Henry VI, Margaret of Anjou and the Wars of the Roses: A Source Book* (Stroud: Sutton, 2000)

Dockray, Keith, 'The Battle of Wakefield and the Wars of the Roses' in *The Ricardian* 9 (1992), pp. 238-258

Dockray, K., *Richard III: a reader in history* (Gloucester: Alan Sutton, 1988)

Dover-Wilson, J, 'A Note on Richard III: the Bishop of Ely's Strawberries', *Modern Language Review* LII (1957), pp.563-64

Ellis, Henry (ed), *Original letters illustrative of English history, including numerous royal letters, from autographs in the British Museum and one or two other collections* (London: Harding, Triphook & Lepard, 1824)

Ellis, Henry, 'Enumeration and Explanation of the Devices formerly borne as badges of cognizance by the House of York, in a letter to Matthew Rapier, Esq. V.P., F.R.S. from Henry Ellis, Esq. Secretary', *Archaeologia* xvii (1814), pp.226-27

Evans, Michael, *The Death of Kings* (London and New York: Hambledon and London, 2003)

Fabyan, R., *New Chronicles of England and France* (London: Printed for F.C. & J. Rivington et al, 1811)

Feng, Charles, professor of Human Biology, Stanford University, writing on the Journal of Young Investigators web site, www.jyi.org, 2005

Fenton, Sasha, *Rising Signs. The Astrological Guide to the Image we Project* (Wellingborough, Northamptonshire: The Aquarian Press, 1989)

Finucane, Ronald C., *Miracles & Pilgrims: Popular Beliefs in Medieval England* (London: Book Club Associates, 1977)

Fontblanque, E.B.de, *Annuals of the House of Percy*, (London: Printed by Richard Clay, 1887)

Gairdner, J., *History of the Life and Reign of Richard the Third of England* (London: Longmans, Green and Co, 1879)

Gillingham, J., *The Wars of the Roses* (London: Weidenfeld and Nicolson Ltd, 1990)

Grainge, William, *Castles and Abbeys of Yorkshire* (London: Whittaker and Co, 1855)

Grant, Alexander, 'Richard III and Scotland' in A.J. Pollard (ed) *The North of England in the Age of Richard III* (Stroud: Alan Sutton Publishing; New York: St. Martin's Press, 1996), pp.115-48

Great Chronicle of London, ed. A.H. Thomas and I.D. Thornley (London: Printed by G.W. Jones at the sign of the Dolphin, 1938)

'Gregory's Chronicle' *in Historical Collections of a Citizen of London*, ed. J. Gardiner (London: Camden Society, 1876), p.206-7

Habington, William, *The Historie of Edward the Fourth, King of England* (London: Printed by Tho. Cotes, for William Cooke, 1640)

Hall, E., *Hall's Chronicle: containing the history of England during the reign of Henrythe Fourth and the succeeding monarchs to the end of the reign of Henry the Eighth* (London: Printed for J. Johnson et al, 1809)

Halsted, C.A., *Richard III as duke of Gloucester and King of England* (London: Longmans, 1844), 2 vols

Hammond, P. W., 'The Deformity of Richard III' in J. Petre (ed) *Richard III: Crown and People* (London: The Richard III Society, 1985), pp.5-10

Hanham, A., Richard III and his Early Historians 1483-1535 (Oxford: Clarendon Press, 1975)

Harris, Mary Dormer, *The Coventry Leet Book*, (London: Kegan Paul Trench Truebner, 1913)

Hicks, Michael, *Anne Neville, Queen to Richard III* (Stroud: Tempus Publishing, 2006)

Hicks, M., *False, Fleeting, Perjur'd Clarence* (Gwynedd: Headstart History, 1992)

Hicks, M.A., 'Piety and Lineage in the Wars of the Roses' *Richard III and his Rivals: Magnates and their Motives in the War of the Roses* (London: The Hambledon Press, 1991), pp.165-84

Hicks, M.A., 'Richard III's Cartulary in the British Library' in *Richard III and his Rivals: Magnates and their Motives in the Wars of the Roses* (London: The Hambledon Press, 1991), pp.284-89

Hicks, M.A., 'Richard, Duke of Gloucester and the North', *Richard III and the North* (Hull: Centre for Regional and Local History, Department of Adult and Continuing Education, University of Hull, 1986), pp.11-26

Historie of the arrivall of Edward IV. in England and the finall recouerye of his kingdomes from Henry VI. A.D. M.CCCC.LXXI, ed. J. Bruce (London: The Camden Society, 1888)

Historical Manuscripts Commission, 11th Report

Historical Manuscripts Commission 78: Hastings

Historical Manuscripts Commission Various Collections IV

Holinshead, R., *Chronicles of England, Scotland and Ireland* (London: Printed for .Johnson, et al, 1808)

Rosemary Horrox, 'Tyrell, Sir James (c.1455–1502)', *Oxford Dictionary of National Biography*, Oxford University Press, Sept 2004; online edn, Jan 2008 [http://www.oxforddnb.com/view/article/27952, accessed 14 April 2008]

Horrox, R., *Richard III: a study of service* (Cambridge: Cambridge University Press, 1992)

http://www.bradford.ac.uk/archsci/depart/report97/towton.htm.

Hughes, J., *Arthurian Myths and Alchemy: The Kingship of Edward IV* (Stroud: Sutton Publishing, 2000)

Humphery-Smith, Cecil R., *Edmund Crouchback: the Earl of Many Parts* (www.britishancestry.org).

Household of Edward IV: the black book and the ordinance of 1478, ed. A. R. Myers (Manchester: Manchester University Press, 1958)

Ingulph's Chronicle of the Abbey of Croyland ed. H.T. Riley (London: Henry G. Bohn, 1854)

Johnson, P.A., *Duke Richard of York* (Oxford: Clarendon Press, 1988.)

Jones, Michael K., *Bosworth 1485: Psychology of a Battle* (Stroud, Tempus Publishing Ltd, 2003)

Jones, Michael K., 'Somerset, York and the Wars of the Roses', *English Historical Review* (1989), pp.285-307

Jones, Michael K., 'Richard III and the Stanleys' *Richard III and the North* R. Horrox (ed) (Hull: Centre for Regional and Local history, Department of Adult and Continuing Education, 1986), pp.27-50

Kendall, P.M., *Richard III* (London: George Allen & Unwin, 1955)

Kennedy, Edward Donald, 'Warkworth, John (c.1425–1500)', *Oxford Dictionary of National Biography*, Oxford University Press, 2004: http://www.oxforddnb.com/view/article/28747

Kingsford, C.L., *English Historical Literature in the Fifteenth Century* (Oxford: Clarendon Press, 1913

Kirk, J.F., History of Charles the Bold, Duke of Burgundy (London: John Murray, 1863)

Laynesmith, J., 'The Kings' Mother' *History Today* 56 (2006), pp.38-44

Legge, A.O., *The Unpopular King* (London: Ward and Downey, 1885), 2. vols

Leland, John, *Joannis Lelandi antiquarii de rebus Britannicis collectanea. Cum Thomæ Hearnii præfatione notis et indice ad editionem primam. Editio altera. ... Accedunt de rebus Anglicanis opuscula varia è diversis Codd. MSS. descripta et nunc primum in lucem edita*. Vol. 6. Londini, 1770. 6 vols. *Eighteenth Century Collections Online*. Gale Group. http://galenet.galegroup.com/servlet/ECCO

Letters and Papers Illustrative of the Wars of the English in France, ed. J. Stevenson (Rolls Series, 1861-64)

Lloyd, David, *Ludlow Castle: A History and Guide.*

Loades, D. *Henry VIII and his Queens* (Godalming, Surrey: Bramey Books, 1997)

Lulofs, Maaike, 'King Edward in Exile', *The Ricardian* 44 (1974), pp.9-11

Lull, Ramón., *The Book of the Ordre of Chyualry*, trans. W. Caxton (London: published for the Early English Text Society, 1926)

Mancini, D., *The Usurpation of Richard III* (Oxford: Clarendon Press, 1969)

Melhuish, J.M., *The College of King Richard III, Middleham* (London: issued by permission of the Richard III Society, 1962)

Milles, Rev. Dr, the Dean of Exeter, 'Illustration of an unpublished seal of Richard Duke of Gloucester' *Archaeologicia* vii (1785), pp.69-73

More, Thomas, *The History of King Richard III* (London: for R. Triphook, Old Bond Street, 1821)

More, Thomas, *The Workes of Sir Thomas More Knyght, Sometyme Lorde Chauncellor of England, Wrytten by Him in the Englysh Tonge*, William Rastell (ed.) (London; at the costes and charges of John Cawood, John Waly and Richarde Tottell, 1557)

Mortimer, I., *The Fears of Henry IV* (London: Jonathan Cape, 2007)

Nicolas, N.H. (ed), *Proceedings in Chancery in the Reign of Queen Elizabeth I, Calendars* (Record Commission, 1827)

Orme, Nicholas, *From Childhood to Chivalry: the education of the English Kings and aristocracy 1066-1530* (London & New York: Methuen, 1984)

Oxford Bodleian Laud. Misc. 501

Oxford English Dictionary (Oxford: Clarendon Press; New York: Oxford University Press, 1989), 20 vols

Parallel: or a Collection of Extraordinary Cases Relating to Concealed Births, and Disputed Successions (London: Printed for J. Roberts, 1744)

Paston Letters, ed. J Gairdner (London: Bowes, Southgate, 1875), 3 vols.

Peers, C., *Middleham Castle* (HMSO, 1984)

Pièce Justificative no.30.

Plumpton Correspondences, ed. Thomas Stapleton (London: Camden Society, 1839)

Pollard, A.J., 'St Cuthbert and the Hog: Richard III and the County Palatine of Durham, 1471-85' *Kings and Nobles in the Later Middle Ages*, Ralph A. Griffiths and James Sherborn (eds.) (Gloucester: Alan Sutton, 1986), pp.109-29

Pollard, A.J., *The Middleham Connection* (Middleham: Old School Arts Workshop, 1983)

Pollard, A.J., 'The Tyranny of Richard III', *Journal of Medieval History* 3 (1977), pp.147-66

Potter, J., *Good King Richard?* (London: Constable and Company, 1983)

Pronay, N. and Cox, John (eds.), *The Crowland Chronicle Continuations 1459-1486* (London: Sutton for Richard III and Yorkist History Trust, 1986)

Pugh, T.B., 'Richard Plantagenet (1411-1460), Duke of York, as the King's Lieutenant in France and Ireland' *Aspects of Late Medieval Government and Society*, J.G. Rowe, (ed) (Toronto: University of Toronto Press, 1986), pp.107-41

Puttenham, George, *The Arte of English Poesie 1589* (Menston, England: The Scolar Press Limited, 1968)

Ralph Lewis, Brenda, *Life in a Medieval Castle* (Thrupp: Sutton Publishing, 2007)

Rawcliffe, C., 'Richard Duke of York, the King's "obeisant liegeman" a New Source for the rotectorate of 1454 and 1455", *Historical Research* 60 (1987), p.232-9

Registrum Abbatiae Johannis Whethamstede, (Rolls Series 28, vi,)

Rymer, Thomas, *Foedera, conventiones, literæ, et cujuscunque generis acta publica, inter reges ngliæ, et alios quosuis imperatores, reges* (Londini: per A.& J. Churchill, 1704-35)

Richmond, Colin, 'Beaufort, Edmund, first Duke of Somerset (c.1406–1455)', *Oxford Dictionary of ational Biography*, Oxford University Press, Sept 2004; online edn, May 2006 http://www.oxforddnb.com/view/article/1855, accessed 16 March 2008]

Ross, C., *Edward IV* (London: Eyre Methuen, 1974)

Ross, C., *Richard III* (London: Eyre Methuen, 1981)

Rotuli Parliamentorum, ed. J. Strachey *et al* (London: 1767-77), 6 vols

Rous, J. *The Rous Roll* (Gloucester: Alan Sutton, 1980)

Sandford, Francis. *A genealogical history of the Kings and Queens of England, and monarchs of Great Britain, &c. From the conquest, Anno 1066. to the year 1707 ... by Francis Sandford, ... and continued ... by Samuel Stebbing, ... London, 1707. Eighteenth Century Collections online. Gale Group. http://galenet.galegroup.com/servlet/ECCO*

Scarisbrick, J.J., *Henry VIII* (London: Eyre & Spottiswoode, 1968)

Schweitzer, A., *The Quest of the Historical Jesus* (London: SCM Press, 1954)

Sergeant, Philip W., '*The Life of Anne Boleyn* (London: Hutchinson & Co, 1923)

Seward, D., *Richard III: England's Black Legend* (London: Country Life Books, 1983)

Shakespeare, William, *The Complete Works* Compact Edition (Oxford, Clarendon Press, 1988)

Six Town Chronicles ed. R. Flenley (Oxford: Clarendon Press, 1911)

Smith, A.H., *Place Names of Gloucestershire* (Cambridge: at the university Press, 1964)

Society for Army Historical Research (1968), pp.65-69

St John Hope, W.H., 'The Discovery of the Remains of King Henry VI in St. George's Chapel, Windsor Castle', *Archaeologia* LXII (1903), pp.533-42

Starkey, David, *Six Wives: the Queens of Henry VIII* (London: Vintage, 2004)

Strickland, Agnes, *Lives of the Queens of England* (London: Henry Colburn Publisher, 1841)

Storey, R.L., 'The Wardens of the Marches of England Towards Scotland, 1377-1489' *English Historical Review* 72 (1957), pp.593-615

Stow, J., *The chronicles of England: from Brut unto this present yeare of Christ 1580* (Printed at London by Ralphe Newberie, at the assignement of Henrie Bynneman, 1580)

Summerson, Henry, 'Robin of Redesdale (*fl.* 1469)', *Oxford Dictionary of National Biography*, Oxford University Press, 2004. [http://www.oxforddnb.com/view/article/23822, accessed 18 Nov 2007]

Sutton, Anne and Visser-Fuchs, Livia, *Richard III's Books* (Stroud: Sutton Publishing Ltd, 1997)

Sutton, Anne, F. and Visser-Fuchs, Livia, with Hammond, P.W, *The Reburial of Richard Duke of York, 21-30 July 1476* (London: The Richard III Society, 1996)

Sutton, Anne and Visser-Fuchs, Livia, 'Richard III's Books: Ancestry and "True Nobility"', *The Ricardian* 9 (1992), pp. 343-58

Three Books of Polydore Vergil's English History, ed. H. Ellis (London: The Camden Society, 1844)

Three Fifteenth-Century Chronicles, ed. J. Gairdner (London: The Camden Society, 1880)

Three Prose Versions of the Secreta Secretorum, ed. R. Steele (London: published for the Early English Text Society, 1898)

TNA: E404/57/172

TNA: KB 9/41/38.

TNA: KB 9/320

Tudor-Craig, P., *Richard III: National Portrait Gallery Exhibition, 27 June to 7 October 1973* (London: National Portrait Gallery, 1973)

Tuck, Anthony, 'Thomas, Duke of Gloucester (1355–1397)', *Oxford Dictionary of National Biography*, Oxford University Press, Sept 2004; online edn, May 2006 [http://www.oxforddnb.com/view/article/27197, accessed 6 Nov 2007].

Turner, Sharon, *Richard III : a Poem* (London: Longman, Brown, Green and Longmans, 1845)

Turner, S., The History of England during the Middle Ages (London: Longman et al., 1830)

Unwin, D., 'A Werish, Withered Arm', *Diagnostica* 9 (1968), pp.1-4

Vincent, Augustine, *A discouerie of errours in the first edition of the catalogue of nobility* (London: printed by William Iaggard, 1622)

Visser-Fuchs, Livia, '"He hardly touched his food, but talked with me all the time": What Niclas von Popplau really wrote about Richard III' *The Ricardian* 11 (1999), pp 525-30

Visser-Fuchs, Livia, 'Richard was Late', *The Ricardian*, XI, No 147 (1999), pp.616-19

Walpole, H., *Historic Doubts on the Life and Reign of King Richard the Third*, ed. P.W. Hammond (Gloucester: Alan Sutton, 1986)

Walpole, H., *Historic Doubts on the Life and Reign of King Richard III* (London: Printed for J. Dodsley in Pall-Mall, 1768)

Watts, John. 'Richard of York, third Duke of York (1411-1460)', *Oxford Dictionary of National Biography*, Oxford University Press, 2004, [http://www.orforddnb.co,/view/article/25303, accessed 6 April 2008]

Warkworth, J., *A Chronicle of First Thirteen Years of the Reign of King Edward the Fourth*, ed. J.O. Halliwell (London: The Camden Society, 1839)

Warnicke, Retha M., 'More's Richard III and the Mystery Plays' *The Historical Journal* vol. 35 (1992), pp. 761-78

Waurin, Jehan de, *Recueil des croniques et anchiennes istories de la Grant Bretaigne, a present nomme Engleterre*, ed. by Sir William Hardy and Edward L.C.P. Hardy, Vol 5, 1447-1471 (Rolls Series, 1981)

Weaver, John, *Middleham Castle* (London: English Heritage, 1998)

Weeks, M., 'The Personality of Richard III: Some opinions of a psychiatrist based on his portraits' in J. Petre (ed), *Richard III: Crown and People* (London: The Richard III Society, 1985), pp.11-15

Weightman, C., *Margaret of York, Duchess of Burgundy 1446-1503* (Gloucester: Alan Sutton; New York: St. Martin's Press, 1989)

Weiss, R., *Humanism in England during the fifteenth century* (Basil Blackwell: Oxford, 1967)

Weir, A., *The Princes in the Tower* (London: Pimlico, 1997)

Westminster Chronicle edited and translated by L.C. Hector and Barbara F. Harvey (Oxford: Clarendon Press, 1982)

Wright, T., Political Poems and Songs relating to English History (Rolls Series 14)

York City Chamberlains' Account Rolls 1396-1500, ed. R.B. Dobson (Surtees Society, 192, 1980)

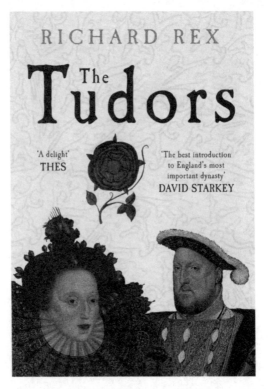

Available from September 2009 from Amberley Publishing

An accessible biography of Henry VIII by one of the country's leading Tudor experts

The future Henry VIII was born on 29 June 1491, the second son of Henry VII and Elizabeth of York. This talented, athletic and temperamental man might have proved something of a handful to his elder brother, Prince Arthur, the firstborn, had he survived to wear the crown. But Henry's life was changed forever when Arthur died in 1502 and the course of English history took a very unexpected turn...

£9.99 Paperback
60 illustrations (20 colour)
240 pages
978-1-84868-098-2

Available from September 2009 from all good bookshops or to order direct
please call **01285-760-030**
www.amberley-books.com

Also available from Amberley Publishing

The tragic love affair that changed English history forever

Anne Boleyn was the most controversial and scandalous woman ever to sit on the throne of England. From her early days at the imposing Hever Castle in Kent, to the glittering courts of Paris and London, Anne caused a stir wherever she went. Alluring but not beautiful, Anne's wit and poise won her numerous admirers at the English court, and caught the roving eye of King Henry.

Their love affair was as extreme as it was deadly, from Henry's 'mine own sweetheart' to 'cursed and poisoning whore' her fall from grace was total.

£9.99 Paperback
47 illustrations (26 colour)
264 pages
978-1-84868-514-7

Available from all good bookshops or to order direct
Please call **01285-760-030**
www.amberley-books.com

Also available from Amberley Publishing

The scandalous true story of Mary Boleyn, infamous sister of Anne, and mistress of Henry VIII

Mary Boleyn, 'the infamous other Boleyn girl', began her court career as the mistress of the king of France. François I of France would later call her 'The Great Prostitute' and the slur stuck. The bête-noir of her family, Mary was married her off to a minor courtier but it was not long before she caught the eye of Henry VIII and a new affair began.

Mary would emerge the sole survivor of a family torn apart by lust and ambition, and it is in Mary and her progeny that the Boleyn legacy rests.

£18.99 Hardback
30 colour illustrations
240 pages
978-1-84868-089-0

Available from all good bookshops or to order direct
Please call **01285-760-030**
www.amberley-books.com

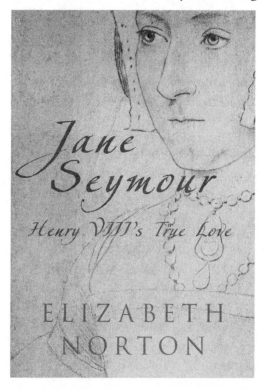

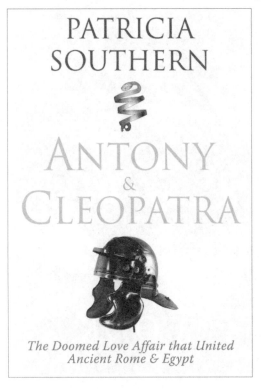

Also available from Amberley Publishing

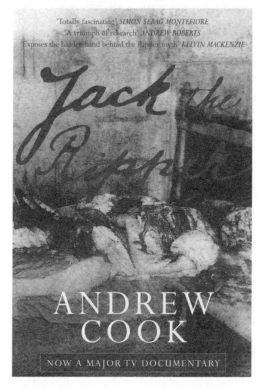

Finally lays to rest the mystery of who Jack the Ripper was

'Totally fascinating' SIMON SEBAG MONTEFIORE
'A triumph of research' ANDREW ROBERTS
'Exposes the hidden hand behind the Jack the Ripper myth' KELVIN MACKENZIE

The most famous serial killer in history. A sadistic stalker of seedy Victorian backstreets. A master criminal. The man who got away with murder – over and over again. But while literally hundreds of books have been published, trying to pin Jack's crimes on an endless list of suspects, no-one has considered the much more likely explanation for Jack's getting away with it... He never existed.

£18.99 Hardback
53 illustrations and 47 figures
256 pages
978-1-84868-327-3

Available from all good bookshops or to order direct
Please call **01285-760-030**
www.amberley-books.com

Also available from Amberley Publishing

The first new history of the Mongol Empire for over twenty years

In the space of 200 years, the Mongols built the greatest empire that the world had ever known and then lost it again. At its greatest extent, the lands they held dwarfed those under the control of Rome at its prime whilst the conquests of its founder, Genghis Khan, outshone those of even Alexander the Great. There were few parts of the known world that were not touched by the Mongols in one way or another: China, India, the Middle East, Europe, Egypt. This was truly a world empire.

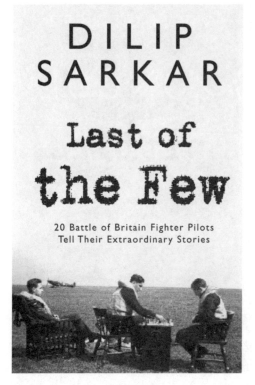

Also available from Amberley Publishing

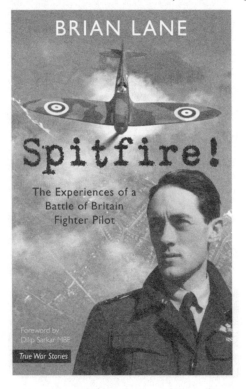

The remarkable Battle of Britain experiences of Spitfire pilot Brian Lane, DFC

Brian Lane was only 23 when he when he wrote his dramatic account of life as a Spitfire pilot during the Battle of Britain in the summer of 1940. Lane was an 'ace' with six enemy 'kills' to his credit and was awarded the DFC for bravery in combat. The text is honest and vibrant, and has the immediacy of a book written close the event, untouched, therefore, by the doubts and debates of later years. Here we can read, exactly what it was like to 'scramble', to shoot down Messerschmitts, Heinkels, Dorniers and Stukas and how it felt to lose comrades every day.

£9.99 Paperback
44 illustrations
192 pages
978-1-84868-354-9

Available from all good bookshops or to order direct
please call **01285-760-030**
www.amberley-books.com

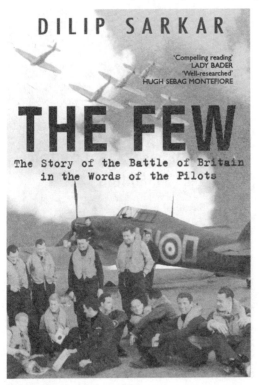

Available from October 2009 from Amberley Publishing

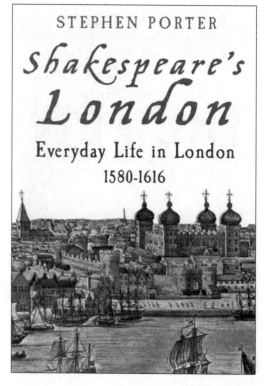

Everyday life in the teeming metropolis during William Shakespeare's time in the city (c.1580-1616), the height of Queen Elizabeth I's reign

Shakespeare's London was a bustling, teeming metropolis that was growing so rapidly that the government took repeated, and ineffectual, steps to curb its expansion. From contemporary letters, journals and diaries, a vivid picture emerges of this fascinating city, with its many opportunities and also its persistent problems.

£20 Hardback
70 illustrations (30 colour)
320 pages
978-1-84868-333-4

Available from October 2009 from all good bookshops or to order direct please call **01285-760-030**
www.amberley-books.com

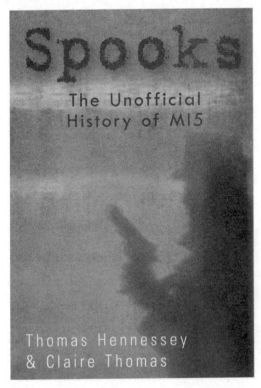

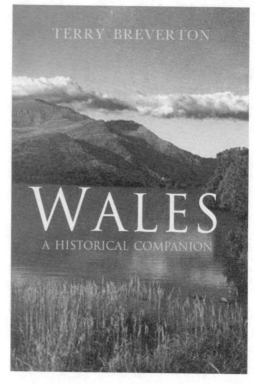

Available from September 2010 from Amberley Publishing

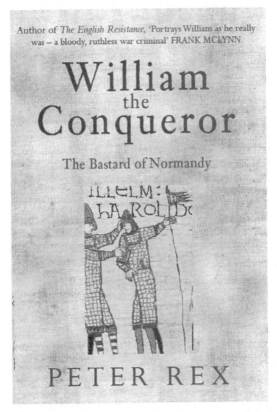

A new biography of the Norman king who conquered England in 1066, changing the course of the country forever

Of Franco-Scandinavian descent through his father, Duke Robert 'the Magnificent', William the Conqueror's life is set against his true background, the turbulent Norman Duchy which, even after the Conquest of England, remained his primary concern.

William is revealed as the brutal and violent product of his time, much given to outbursts of rage, capable of great cruelty, autocratic, avaricious and prone to a sort of grisly humour, yet, with all that he could also be a loyal friend and affectionate husband and father.

Index